The Indo-Europeans
Rediscovered

The Indo-Europeans Rediscovered

How a Scientific Revolution is Rewriting Their Story

J. P. MALLORY

Contents

Preface 7

Part 1 Setting the Scene 14

1 Discovering the World's Largest Language Family 15

2 A Brief History of Homeland Hunting and the Nature of our Prey 33

Part 2 The Fundamental Techniques of Homeland Hunting 58

3 Applying the Lessons of History 59

4 Languages, Maps and Geography 69

5 The Names of Places and Rivers: Our Earliest Linguistic Evidence? 115

6 Locating the Earliest Neighbours of the Indo-Europeans 124

7 Linguistic Palaeontology: Geographical Clues in the Indo-European Vocabulary 151

8 Cultural Anthropology: Origin Tales and Culture History 201

9 Archaeology: Evaluating Archaeological Cultures
as Linguistic Models   209

10 Hair Colour, Skulls and the Emergence of
Modern Genetics   245

Part 3   The New Way Forward   268

11 Game Change   269

12 Genetic Landscapes and Homeland Models   276

13 The Anatolian Homeland Model   295

14 The Caucasus Homeland Model   307

15 The Steppe Model   343

16 Taking Stock: Homeland Solutions and
Later Indo-European Expansions   362

Glossary   390
Notes to the Text   394
Bibliography   406
Sources of Illustrations   428
Appendix   429
Index   434

Preface

Tracking the elusive Indo-Europeans has been a favourite sport of archaeologists and philologists ever since the days of the brothers Grimm, and surely some share of their power of telling fascinating fairy stories must have descended on their philological and archaeological successors.

R. W. HUTCHINSON 1950

More than three billion people, nearly half of the Earth's population, speak languages evolved from a single source known as Proto-Indo-European, which spawned a family of hundreds of different languages. We can appreciate this better on a human level when we consider the astonishing fact that people in Iceland, Ireland, England, Spain, Norway, Germany, Lithuania, Italy, Greece, Ukraine, Iran and India converse in languages that, if we rolled them back over about five thousand years, would merge into a common language. Or we might ponder that the language reflected in the southern drawl of a Texan cowboy or a London cockney is kin to the languages we find in *Beowulf*, a Viking saga, the novels of Tolstoy, the speeches of Cicero, the dialogues of Plato, the hymns of the Iranian prophet Zarathustra, the Rig Veda of India or the sacred texts of the ancient Hittites. Already in ancient times the Indo-European language family stretched from the westernmost shores of the Atlantic to the arid frontiers of China and the Bay of Bengal. Where this family originated and how it dispersed has excited human curiosity from the Bible's Book of Genesis to the most recent issues of our foremost scientific journals and has drawn the attention of many hundreds of scholars from an array of different academic disciplines. But despite the enormous number of books and articles that have been devoted to identifying the place of origin of this language family, it has stubbornly resisted a fully satisfying and convincing solution. So how did I become embroiled in this seemingly endless controversy?

Reviewing a book on Indo-European origins penned by V. Gordon Childe (1892–1957), the leading archaeologist of his generation, the caustic head of the Harvard linguistics department, Joshua Whatmough (1897–1964), complained:

> And so, after working through 200 pages of mainly archaeological speculation and argument the reader at last wearily reaches the following inconclusive conclusion [possibly Germany?, possibly south Russia?]. Surely the reader has every right to be told all this at the beginning, in the first chapter if not in the preface, and then to be left to decide for himself whether it is worth his while to continue to read further.[1]

Fifty years ago, I shared Whatmough's frustration and determined to produce a 'conclusive' answer to the question: where in time and space can we locate the source of the world's largest language family? I had spent several years as a graduate student in Indo-European Studies at the University of California, Los Angeles, which I had initially entered with the intention of specializing in Celtic archaeology and linguistics. In the course of my graduate studies, I had only experienced one lecture on the Indo-European homeland problem and might not have given it a second thought, but when I needed an essay topic for a course on the history of archaeology I tackled the subject and much to my astonishment found my paper published in 1973.[2]

Having completed all the requisite courses and miraculously survived my PhD exams in European Archaeology, Indo-European Linguistics, Comparative Mythology and four ancient Indo-European languages (Vedic Sanskrit, Homeric Greek, Old Norse and Old Irish), I received the peculiar limbo-like degree of Candidate of Philosophy and had to finally choose a PhD dissertation topic. If I had confined my studies purely to Indo-European matters, I would probably have never tackled the homeland problem, but I had also taken courses on archaeological theory and method from Jim Hill and Jim Sackett, two 'card-carrying' New Archaeologists, at a time when the processualist school was still shining bright. Half my brain was filled with a very traditional understanding of European prehistory from the now legendary archaeologist Marija Gimbutas, while the other half was bubbling over with a host of new approaches, served up with an optimistic belief that we had not even begun to measure what archaeology could do. Whatmough had remarked that 'It still remains open, therefore, to some daring scholar to combine, if he can, the two disciplines of archaeology and linguistics in order to solve the riddle of Indo-European origins.' It came to me one evening that I would apply the critical toolkit of New Archaeology to a problem that had remained unresolved on the academic books since 1786. I would take up Whatmough's challenge and solve the Indo-European homeland problem – I was a complete idiot!

Whatmough was irked that Childe did not come down conclusively on one side or another, but if Childe had concluded that the Indo-European winner was a homeland in northern Europe, would Whatmough have been satisfied? He himself indicated in his review that he favoured a Danubian location. The problem here is that searching for the Indo-European homeland is not like looking for the source of the Nile – it is an interdisciplinary puzzle where every field of study involved has a claim on the validity of the solution but lacks the independent means to determine that solution on its own. Moreover, the different disciplines themselves are bitterly divided as to which of their own techniques should be trusted. In short, solving the homeland problem is the academic equivalent of herding cats; it has survived unresolved for at least 230 years because it has been impossible to come up with an explanation that satisfies all the different, and incredibly stubborn and irascible, scholars. Claims that it has been 'finally' resolved in international scientific journals generally refer to solutions that either ignore most of the opposing constituencies, or believe that dismissing one or two critics is sufficient to silence more than a century of raging debate.

I have used here the word 'constituencies' and you will find me frequently invoking the concept of a 'constituency problem' throughout this book. I will try to provide an admittedly rather extreme example of what I mean by 'constituency'. Let us say that two detectives have been tasked with solving the murder of Mr Black, whose lifeless body has been found in his library with a large dagger to the heart. Detective Inspector A discovers that there was a close circuit surveillance camera that filmed the entire murder and, recovering the tape and running it through facial recognition software, has a positive identification of Colonel Mustard. Detective Inspector B, however, has the room dusted and finds fingerprints all over the place, including on the handle of the dagger, which match those of Professor Plum and there is no trace of Mustard's fingerprints. What we have here are two constituencies that have not only drawn totally different conclusions but it is difficult to imagine any situation where either side is likely to ever convince the other that it is wrong. All those who have faith in facial recognition technology will flock to defend Inspector A, while those who have greater faith in the evidence of fingerprints will support Inspector B; this may continue over generations. We will time and again find similar situations in the hunt for the Indo-European homeland and this is one of the reasons why the problem has remained unresolved for several centuries.

Now, if you ask whether at the end I will pull out an envelope that reads 'The Indo-European homeland was most certainly located in...', the answer is 'no', although I will give the best answer I can.[3] Moreover, I will – if only by inevitable probability – certainly stumble over the correct homeland somewhere along the way since it can hardly be avoided: just about every conceivable patch of this planet has been suggested and argued for. And that is why the homeland problem has proved so fascinating. How could so many talented scholars come to so many totally different solutions over the course of more than two centuries? The hunt for the homeland invites us to explore a cavalcade of arguments that run from ingenious to absolutely bonkers. It also displays generations of scholars pushing their various disciplines – or the logic of them – to their limits. So, for me at least, whether the journey reaches its goal has never been as important as the scenery along the way. The title of this book refers to 'rediscovery' and I hope I can justify it by highlighting how scholars have spent their careers summoning up precisely the same arguments or rebuttals that were rehearsed generations before, apparently unaware that they are perpetuating an epistemological Groundhog Day. By the end of this book, you may not be absolutely certain where the homeland is located (although you will be pretty damn close) but I hope you will be in a position to assess for yourself the next claim that the issue has been 'finally' resolved.

In 1989, in my book *In Search of the Indo-Europeans*, I first attempted to provide an overview of the linguistic, mythological and archaeological evidence for the Indo-Europeans and the dispersals of each of its major language branches. Since then, I have resisted pressure to produce a second edition to avoid going over the same territory and wading through the mass of literature that concerned the origins and migrations of every one of the various branches: I have found engaging in the debates regarding Celtic[4] and Tocharian[5] origins more than enough to keep me busy. But the intellectual landscape regarding Indo-European origins has greatly altered over the past decade due to advances in palaeogenomics, which has come to dominate much of the current discussion. Now, I am all too aware that the publication cycle of a monograph is far longer than that of the publication of articles on genetics, which renders it nearly impossible for any author to produce a book that is truly up to date. Nevertheless, I thought it might be useful to try my hand at producing a book for general readership that examines the problem of Indo-European origins from a broad historical perspective coupled with an examination of the genetic evidence up to May 2024.

The book is organized into several broad sections. In the first, the initial discovery of the Indo-European language family is described, then both a history of the homeland problem in terms of its major trends and tropes and a sense of the incredible range of solutions is provided (Chapters 1 and 2).

The second section examines a series of fundamental approaches that have been employed by homeland hunters over the past two centuries, beginning with how historical arguments shaped some of the earliest attempts to solve the homeland problem and also how the lessons of history have been applied to evaluating homeland solutions (Chapter 3). We then venture into the variety of techniques that linguists have designed to locate a proto-language in time and space (Chapter 4). Chapter 5 takes us into attempts to locate prehistoric languages on the basis of place names, especially by way of river names, which have often been regarded as the most ancient linguistic relics on a landscape. Then follows an examination of the various ways linguists have tried to discover the Indo-European homeland by identifying its nearest linguistic neighbour (Chapter 6). The final chapter stemming primarily from the linguistic evidence examines the constituency-riddled topic of linguistic palaeontology (Chapter 7) where the cultural vocabulary of Proto-Indo-European has been employed to locate its speakers in both time and space. In Chapter 8, we next consider the contributions made by cultural anthropologists, who have sought the homeland in both origin myths and in the reconstruction of the cultural type of the Indo-Europeans, then the various homeland solutions proposed on the basis of archaeological evidence are presented in Chapter 9. At the end of this section, the application of physical anthropology from its early days of seeking the homeland on the basis of pigmentation and crude measurements of the human skull to the advent of modern genetic techniques is traced in Chapter 10.

The final section begins with an account of the game-changing publication of a series of studies in 2015 employing the evidence of ancient DNA (aDNA) to help resolve the Indo-European homeland (Chapter 11). This is followed by a general introduction describing how palaeogenomics may be a major player in the search for the homeland (Chapter 12). We then examine in some detail how the genetic evidence impinges on the various major homeland solutions: Anatolia (Chapter 13), the Caucasus (Chapter 14) and the steppelands (Chapter 15). In the final chapter I attempt to revisit the broader range of homeland solutions and provide some indication of the problems that still lie before us.

Since I have been at this game for a half-century, I have run up a fairly large social tab of acknowledgments. I will try to at least thank many of those who have both trained and helped me, although many of these are no longer with us. I blame Scott Littleton for luring me into studying the Indo-Europeans. For those who trained me in archaeology, I would thank foremost of all Marija Gimbutas, but also Lilli Kaelas, Jim Hill and

Jim Sackett and, in terms of field techniques, Gene Sterud. I have always insisted that I am not a linguist and I have the professors to prove it, among whom I number Raimo Anttila (Indo-European), J. Caerwyn Williams and Pat Ford (Celtic), Hans-Peter Schmidt (Sanskrit), Ken Chapman (Old Norse) and Evelyn Venable Mohr (Homeric Greek); and for Comparative Mythology (Jaan Puhvel and Scott Littleton). I greatly benefited from having spent a week each under the generous tutelage of Nikolai Merpert (Moscow), Igor Vasiliev (Samara) and my friend Dmytro Telehin (Kiev), with whom, along with Alexander Häusler (Halle), I enjoyed many years of crucial book exchanges. Special thanks also to Doug Adams, Martin Huld, John Koch, Victor Mair, Vaclav Blažek, Malcolm Lillie and David Anthony for all their generosity throughout my career, and also the late Colin Renfrew, who was stuck serving as my sparring partner for the past half-century. In addition to my former professors and colleagues I need to thank my former student John Day, who acquainted me with many of the more 'daring' solutions to the homeland problem, and Tibor Fehér for advice on some of the genetics tables. I must also thank both Martyn Jope and Mike Baillie, who helped ensure that an archaeologist with a somewhat unusual set of academic skills managed to finally escape the unemployment queue and find a post at Queen's University Belfast.

An earlier draft of this book was read by Peter Schrijver (Utrecht), Lara Cassidy (Trinity, Dublin) and Fintan Mallory (Durham). They are in no way responsible if any howlers have still managed to slip through. Finally, I would like to thank the eternally patient Libby Mulqueeny (Belfast) for preparing the illustrations, and Colin Ridler and Joanne Murray for enduring the massive editing of the manuscript.

Cargacreevy, County Down

Part 1
Setting the Scene

CHAPTER 1

Discovering the World's Largest Language Family

An event, which the German philosopher Georg Wilhelm Friedrich Hegel (1770–1831) likened to the 'discovery of a new world',[1] was buried in a lecture delivered in Kolkata, India, on 2 February 1786. In his 'Third Anniversary Discourse' to the Royal Asiatic Society of Bengal, a society that he had founded, Sir William Jones (1746–1794) set out to survey the five nations (Indians, Chinese, Tartars, Arabs and Persians) that he believed constituted the peoples of Asia. Beginning with India, he briefly discussed its geography and some of the earliest references to the land and then reviewed the main sources for retrieving information about India's past. After introducing the subject of Sanskrit, the ancient language of the Hindus, he dropped what has been dubbed 'the most momentous soundbite of yore'.[2] To the assembled civic leaders, soldiers and merchants who constituted the Society, Jones claimed:

> The *Sanscrit* language, whatever be its antiquity, is of wonderful structure; more perfect than the *Greek*, more copious than the *Latin*, and more exquisitely refined than either; yet bearing to both of them a stronger affinity, both in the roots of verbs, and in the forms of grammar, than could possibly have been produced by accident; so strong, indeed, that no philologer could examine them all three without believing them to have sprung from some common source, which, perhaps, no longer exists. There is a similar reason, though not quite so forcible, for supposing that both the *Gothick* and the *Celtick*, though blended with a very

different idiom, had the same origin with the *Sanscrit*; and the old *Persian* might be added to the same family…[3]

The crux of Jones's pronouncement was that the ancient languages of India, Greece and Rome were so similar that they must have derived from a single common language, and further, this common language was not only the ancestor of the Classical languages but also of the Gothic (Germanic languages, which include English, German, Dutch and the Scandinavian languages) and Celtic (Irish, Welsh, etc.) languages and the ancient language of Persia (modern Iran). Classical scholar Gerald Henry Rendall (1851–1945) captured the original impact of this statement in 1889 when he wrote that 'it seemed for a moment as though the primitive, perhaps the universal, language of mankind had been unearthed, and India was its home'.[4] Today, we call this common language Proto-Indo-European or Proto-Indo-Anatolian.

Sir William Jones based his conclusion on the similarity of verbal roots between Sanskrit and the Classical languages, but he did not cite any forms in this or any of his later annual discourses. Nevertheless, I am reasonably certain that if Sir William had had access to PowerPoint, he would have included a slide that looked something like 1.1.

Sanskrit		Greek		Latin	
ádmi	'eat'	édō	'eat'	edō	'eat'
dádami	'give'	didōmi	'give'	dō	'give'
émi	'go'	eîmi	'go'	eō	'go'
pátami	'fly'	pétomai	'fly'	petō	'fly'
pūyami	'stink'	púthō	'become rotten'	pūteō	'stink'
sárpami	'crawl'	hérpō	'crawl'	serpō	'crawl'
tanómi	'stretch'	tanúō	'stretch'	tendō	'stretch'

1.1 Some correspondences between Sanskrit, Greek and Latin verbs.

Up to this point, Jones's conclusions are correct and, from a modern perspective, he only slipped up when he came to identifying this common source, suggesting that it 'perhaps, no longer exists'. The 'perhaps' can be explained by the historical context of linguistic science in the

18th century where others, such as the physician and natural scientist James Parsons (1705–1770), who also 'discovered' the Indo-European language family, believed that some Indo-European populations, after they originally dispersed, 'kept their original language uncorrupted to this day, in their ultimate residence in Britain and Ireland'.[5]

So Sir William's pronouncement has both the virtues and vices of a great historical soundbite. Its speaker was a man of extraordinary accomplishment, especially in the study of the languages of Asia; some of his conclusions are correct and reveal sound reasoning. On the other hand, his lecture was also riddled with some pretty profound errors.[6] Moreover, those observations that were correct hardly originated with him. But, as we will see later, Jones does provide us with a convenient introduction to one of the most fascinating and divisive problems of prehistoric research.

Before Sir William Jones

Although the semi-official discovery of the Indo-European language family is set to 1786, the genetic relationship between Indo-European languages had been noted multiple times before that date. The ancient Romans were hardly blind to the obvious similarities between Latin and Greek seen in 1.1. They traditionally explained these resemblances by assuming that Latin had derived from Greek and was, in essence, a debased form of Greek. The priority of Greek literary history and the prestige of its learning ensured that no one entertained the reverse – that Greek had derived from Latin. This provided an academic pecking order, with Greek at the pinnacle, followed by Latin and then any of the other languages of Europe that appeared to share some affinity with Latin. For example, when Michalo Lituanus (Michael the Lithuanian; 1490–1560) listed seventy-four words in Latin and Lithuanian that resembled each other, he explained their similarity by arguing that the Lithuanians had originated in Italy.[7]

While one could approach the linguistic diversity of Europe from this 'Classical' model, the impact of biblical tradition established an alternative hypothesis with a different source language than Greek. At the very start of the Book of Genesis, God employed language to effect the creation of light (Hebrew *yehi 'ohr*: Latin *fiat lux*), and by the fifth verse he was giving names to 'day' and 'night'. Once Adam had been created, he too set about naming all the creatures in the Garden of Eden. Given the source it is little wonder then that both Jewish tradition and early Christian theologians such as St Augustine had little difficulty identifying the original language of humankind as Hebrew.[8] Some argued that Hebrew remained the sole language until the events described in Genesis chapter 11, when the attempt to build the Tower of Babel resulted in the scattering of nations and languages across the world. Although this explained why languages were different, it still left the source language as Hebrew, and scholars throughout Europe sought the remnants of Adam's language in their own. Lists of words in Hebrew were poured over by advocates of this theory, who searched through their own languages for any similarities that might indicate that a bit of Adam's language had survived in their own. Self-delusion ran so high that in 1690, for example, the French theologian Louis Thomassin (1619–1695) claimed that Hebrew and French were 'one and the same language'.[9]

Of course, not everyone identified the original language as Hebrew. The Dutch linguist Marcus van Boxhorn (1612–1653) rightly saw little similarity between Hebrew and the European languages and was an early, if not the earliest, discoverer of what we would later regard as the Indo-European language family when he derived Greek, German, Latin and Persian from a common extinct language. On the other hand, not all critics of the Hebrew theory were on the right track. A good example is Dutch linguist and physician Jan Gerartsen van Gorp (1519–1572), more commonly known under his Latin name Johannes Goropius Becanus, who argued that as the earliest language should have also been the most primitive, this source language should be the one with the shortest words. He found the best candidate for the original language of humankind in (surprise!) his own language, Flemish, and thought the Garden of Eden was likely to have been located near modern Antwerp in Belgium. He bolstered his bizarre theory with imaginative etymologies that traced words in other languages 'back' to Dutch.[10] Described by one 17th-century critic as 'uselessly subtle and laboriously inept',[11] his legacy is the pejorative 'Goropianism' that early linguists applied to anyone who engaged in similarly far-fetched attempts to recover an original language. He was hardly the only practitioner, however, and by the 17th century there was on offer an array of equally bizarre alternatives. For example, one scholar suggested that God used Spanish to forbid Adam and Eve to eat of the forbidden fruit, but they were lured into eating it by an Italian-speaking serpent and then went on to apologize to God in French. The Swedish philosopher Andreas Kempe (1622–1689) found the whole thing laughable and published a satirical pamphlet in 1688 indicating that Adam actually spoke Danish but God spoke Swedish (of course) while, certainly playing to the gallery of Anglo-Saxon prejudices, the silver-tongued Devil spoke French.[12]

Any source that began with Hebrew, a member of an entirely different language family from the languages of Europe,[13] was unlikely to advance the study of linguistic relationships. But the Bible also offered another potential model earlier than Babel: the division of peoples following the Deluge when Noah's sons (Shem, Ham and Japheth) set out to colonize the world. Shem was recognized as the founder of the Semitic peoples (including the speakers of Hebrew and, according to some, the only ones engaged in building the Tower of Babel) and Ham was seen as the forefather of the Hamitic peoples of northern Africa. The Europeans were then derived from the offspring of Japheth. During the 17th and 18th centuries the term 'Japhetic' could be used as a cover label for the languages of Europe. Alternatively, since the time of the early Church fathers, the offspring of Japheth had been especially associated with the Scythians, an Iron Age people who occupied the area north of the Black Sea. In due course the term 'Scythian' acquired an increasingly broad remit as Scythia was identified as the font of the peoples of Europe.

So the languages of Europe, whatever their internal relationship, could be labelled as Japhetic or as Scythian (or sometimes as Thracian). As long as one made comparisons between specifically Japhetic or Scythian languages there was hope of real progress, since most of the languages spoken in Europe during the historical period were clearly related. Although the great polymath Joseph Scaliger (1540–1609) thought that these languages could be divided into eleven different unrelated groups, he did find grounds for grouping many of them into four major 'matrices' on the basis of how they expressed the word for 'god'. The four groups consisted of Greek (*theos*); Latin (*deus*) and the Romance languages; Dutch (*god*) and the other Germanic languages; and Russian (*bog*) and the other Slavic languages. Further comparisons – for example, by the great German *Über-polymath* Gottfried Wilhelm Leibniz (1646–1716) – found grounds to unite Scaliger's disparate groups such that Greek, Latin, Germanic and Celtic could all be derived from a single language carried by the Scythians as they moved westwards across Europe.[14]

The real breakthrough came when the European languages were compared with related languages of Asia. Recall that Jones emphasized that the correspondences were not only confined to a similarity in vocabulary but also seen in their morphology (that is, their grammatical systems). If we turn to 1.2, it would hardly take anyone more than a glance to see that the two languages most similar to one another are Sanskrit (the ancient language of India) and Avestan (the ancient liturgical language of Iran), and that the other languages, although less similar, are still obviously related in a systematic manner.

	Sanskrit	Avestan	Greek	Latin	Gothic	Old Irish
Sg. 1.	bhárāmi	barāmi	phérō	férō	baíra	biru
2.	bhárasi	barahi	phéreis	fers	baíris	biri
3.	bhárati	baraiti	phérei	fert	baíriþ	berid
Pl. 1.	bhárāmas	barāmahi	phéromen	férimus	baírim	bermae
2.	bháratha	baraþa	phérete	fértis	baíriþ	beirthe
3.	bháranti	barǝnti	phérousi	férunt	baírand	berait

1.2 Comparison between the verbal endings of *bher-* 'carry'. Note that Sanskrit *s* corresponds to Avestan *h*; *þ* denotes a 'th' sound.

Some limited comparisons were made between European languages such as German and Persian (an Iranian language) in the late 16th century, first perhaps by Frans van Ravelingen (1539–1597), otherwise known as Franciscus Raphelengius, and Bonaventure de Smet (1538–1614), aka Bonaventura Vulcanis, who was also the first to publish the evidence of the Gothic language. But the real impact of Asian languages was stimulated by Europe's discovery of the vast corpus of Sanskrit documents. Almost from their first encounter with Sanskrit, Westerners remarked on its similarity with the Classical languages.[15] Once the enormity and complexity of Indic culture was appreciated, the Sanskrit language came to challenge the fundamental role that Hebrew and Scythian had previously occupied. Sanskrit's relationship to the other languages of Europe, as Hegel suggested, showed that 'India ... was the centre of emigration for all the western world'. The whole concept of Indo-European would come to challenge the biblical accounts and force Europeans to abandon nearly two thousand years of their beliefs and reconsider their own origins.

So, the precursors of Sir William Jones were many [1.3].[16] In some cases – for example, the Swedish priest Andreas Jäger (1660–1730) – the

Author	Date	European languages					Indo-Iranian languages	
		Celtic	Latin	Germanic	Slavic	Greek	Iranian	Indo-Aryan
T. Stephens	1583	0	X	0	0	X	0	X
F. Sassetti	1586	0	X	0	0	0	0	X
B. De Smet	1597	0	?	X	0	0	X	0
A. Van der Mijl	1612	0	X	X	0	X	X	0
M. Boxhorn	1640	X	X	X	X	X	X	X
C. Salmasius	1643	0	X	X	0	X	X	X
G. Stiernhielm	1671	X	X	X	X	X	X	?
A. Jäger	1686	X	X	X	X	X	X	0
G. Leibniz	1704	X	X	X	X	X	X	0
B. Schulze	1725	0	X	X	0	0	0	X
G.-L. Coeurdoux	1767	0	X	0	0	X	0	X
J. Parsons	1767	X	X	X	X	X	X	X
J. Burnett, Lord Monboddo	1773	X	X	X	0	X	X	0
N. Brassey	1778	0	X	0	0	X	0	X
W. Jones	1779	X	X	?	?	X	X	0
W. Jones	1786	X	X	X	0	X	X	X

1.3 The identification of related languages by Sir William Jones and some of his precursors. X denotes those branches each scholar regarded as related to the others in the row.

grasp of the relationship between the connected languages was better imagined. In 1686, Jäger was not looking for some language that might still have existed, but quite definitely 'an ancient language' that had 'ceased to be spoken and left no linguistic monuments behind' other than a series of daughter languages.[17] Of the precursors, a significant number recorded their statements in either letters or posthumously published works; even Jones had noticed the connection between European and Iranian in a letter seven years before his celebrated lecture.[18] Indeed, the official birthday of Indo-European studies is a later construct, since Jones's initial pronouncement took some time to arrive in Europe and percolate among those fascinated by the new discoveries emerging out of India.[19] The real work of establishing the foundations of the Indo-European language family from sound philological principles was left to Danish linguist Rasmus Rask (1787–1832)[20] and German linguist Franz Bopp (1791–1867),[21] who prepared comparative grammars of the various languages.

The Indo-European language family

Although some of the early names such as Japhetic, Scythian or Thracian persisted for a while, various scholars began suggesting new terms for the family of related languages. There were essentially two approaches: geographic and ethnic. In 1810 the geographer Conrad Malte-Brun (1755–1826) observed that as the languages in question extended from the Ganges to Iceland he would employ 'Indo-Germanic'.[22] While Icelandic was certainly a Germanic language it was questionable whether this should be employed to define the western border of the ancient Indo-Europeans since Iceland was not settled until the Middle Ages. Moreover, 'Indo-Germanic' appeared to many to privilege German over the other European languages (despite the fact that the Germans employ 'Deutsch' to label their own language).[23] And if one confined the definition to ancient Europe, one could argue that Celtic should have been the westernmost group, and 'Indo-Celtic' was indeed at least proposed as a name for the family although it never really 'took' (James Joyce's *Finnegans Wake*, originally published in 1939, did give us 'Iro-European', however[24]).

One of the reasons for this is that initially Celtic was regarded by some to lie outside the newly established family.

Today, 'Indo-Germanic' is still the standard designation employed in German-language publications, but it is rarely used elsewhere – the commonest term is 'Indo-European'. There are good reasons to attribute its coinage to the remarkable English scientist Thomas Young (1773–1829), who introduced it in 1813 in an extensive review of one of the major compendia of the world's languages. It might be noted that some have always regarded 'Indo-European' as defective because it appears to privilege Indo-Aryan (or Indic) at the expense of the other Asian language groups such as Iranian.

The elephant in the linguistic closet, however, was another widely employed term, one moreover with the oldest claim to use. Rather than forging a name from the geographical extremes of the language family, Abraham Hyacinthe Anquetil-Duperron (1731–1805) – the leading French scholar in the early study of both Indic culture and the Iranian Avesta (the sacred book of the prophet Zarathustra) – employed the common self-designation of both the Indians and the Iranians, namely 'Aryan'. This too was recognized as a misnomer, since the term was more properly confined to Indo-Iranians but, as critics remarked, it did have the advantage of being shorter than all the other alternatives[25] and so it enjoyed increasing popularity. Almost from the start, however, it began acquiring increasingly racist baggage, which culminated in the rise of Nazi ideology in Germany and White-supremacist ideology elsewhere.

Over the course of the 19th century and into the first decades of the 20th century, the languages assigned to the Indo-European family grew so that they now constitute twelve well-attested branches [**1.4**] and a series of extinct and usually very poorly known languages. Reading from west to east, we can start in Atlantic Europe with the Celtic languages, which in ancient times comprised Gaulish (mainly in France but also Belgium, Germany, Austria, Switzerland and Italy), Hispano-Celtic (in Iberia) and Lepontic (in northern Italy), while the main modern survivors are Gaelic (Irish and Scots Gaelic), Welsh and Breton [**1.5**].

1.4 Distribution of the major ancient branches of the Indo-European languages at around 500 BCE.

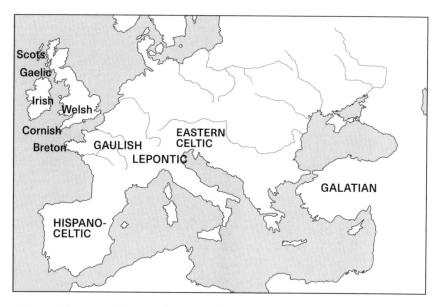

1.5 The distribution of the Celtic languages. The major ancient Celtic branches are indicated in upper case and the surviving (or resurrected) modern Celtic languages in lower case. The latter would also include Manx. Migrations of Celtic speakers as far east as Anatolia (Galatian) can also be traced.

1.6 The complicated linguistic landscape of ancient Italy comprised the Italic languages (Latin, Faliscan, Volscian, Oscan, Umbrian and South Picene). Sicel may also have been an Italic language. Venetic is sometimes classified as an Italic language; others argue that it is an independent branch that shares characteristics with Italic and Germanic. Messapic is an intrusive Indo-European language carried across the sea from the Balkans. In Tuscany and further north were the non-Indo-European Etruscan and related Raetic languages (in upper case). The poorly known North Picene is also suspected of being non-Indo-European. Lepontic was an intrusive Celtic language, while Ligurian defies linguistic classification.

Much of the Celtic area of Atlantic Europe has been replaced by members of the Italic branch, essentially Latin and its daughter Romance languages of Italian, Spanish, Portuguese, French and, in the east, Romanian. Latin was not the only Italic language and the remains of long extinct Italic languages such as Oscan and Umbrian are known from the Classical period [**1.6**].

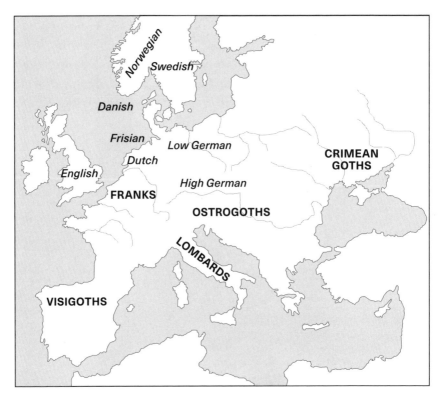

1.7 The distribution of the Germanic languages. Some of the locations of the major ancient Germanic groups are indicated in upper case; modern Germanic languages are indicated in *italics*.

In northern Europe we find the earlier seat of the Germanic languages [1.7], which included the ancient Gothic group and the languages of Scandinavia (Icelandic, Norwegian, Swedish and Danish), as well as German, Dutch and English.

Further east lie the Baltic languages, once occupying a substantial area of northeastern Europe but now confined to Lithuanian and Latvian; the extinct Old Prussian language also belongs to the Baltic group. Further east and to the south lay the Slavic languages (Polish, Czech, Russian, Belarusian, Ukrainian, Slovakian, Slovenian, Serbian, Croatian, Bosnian and Montenegrin, Macedonian and Bulgarian) [1.8].

The Slavic languages had expanded both east and south, replacing earlier now extinct languages such as Illyrian (in former Yugoslavia) and

1.8 The distribution of the Baltic (Latvian, Lithuanian and extinct Old Prussian in *italics*) and Slavic languages (in roman). BCMS comprises Bosnian, Croatian, Montenegrin and Serbian, which replaces the earlier designation 'Serbo-Croatian'.

Thracian (in Bulgaria), while Romanian replaced the Dacian language. Of the ancient Balkan languages only Albanian survives.

We then descend geographically towards Greek and then east to a series of ancient languages known from Anatolia, especially Hittite and Luvian and, later, the intrusive Phrygian. Of the early Indo-European languages of this region, only Armenian survives in the southern Caucasus.

Iran and the neighbouring areas of Central Asia, as well as the great grasslands of much of the Eurasian steppe, were home to speakers of Iranian languages. Closely related were the Indo-Aryans of the northern two-thirds of India who provide us with the truly vast corpus of Sanskrit literature and its numerous modern daughter languages such as Hindi, Gujarati, etc. Finally, in eastern Turkestan, the modern Chinese province of Xinjiang, we have relics of two extinct Tocharian languages [1.9].

CHAPTER 1

1.9 The distribution of Tocharian and the Indo-Iranian languages. The main Iranian languages (in roman) occupy the north and northwest and include the ancient languages of the Scythians and Saka. Indo-Aryan languages (in *italics*) occupy the northern two-thirds of India, while most of the lower third of India is inhabited by non-Indo-European speakers of the Dravidian languages. The earliest evidence for Indo-Aryan is found as personal names and loanwords in the language of the non-Indo-European Mitanni. The Nuristani languages are situated between the Iranian and Indo-Aryan branches. The Tocharian branch occupied the Tarim Basin in the far west of modern China.

The Anatolian languages occupy a disputed branch of the Indo-European tree. The grammars of the earliest reconstructable Indo-European language had already been devised before the Anatolian languages were known. As linguists came to understand the Anatolian languages better they came to regard them as the earliest Indo-European branch to separate from the proto-language (in which case they could still be covered by the term 'Indo-European'), but others argued that Anatolian was not a 'daughter' but a 'sister' branch to Proto-Indo-European because all the other Indo-European branches (nuclear Indo-European) had shared a series of common innovations that evolved *after* Proto-Anatolian had separated. They argued that the differences were so significant that a new name was required for the ancestor of the Anatolian and (later) Indo-European branches and this common stock is referred to as Indo-Hittite or, now preferably, Indo-Anatolian. This leads to the type of horrible linguistic ambiguity or imprecision that one endures when someone from the United States claims to be American (at the expense of everyone else living in the 'Americas'), or the linguo-geographical injustice that the Dutch have long endured from Anglophone foreigners who reduce their country to Holland instead of the Netherlands. Throughout this work I will use the more familiar term 'Indo-European' to cover all the branches *including Anatolian*, but where the occasion demands I will distinguish between Proto-Indo-Anatolian, for all the Indo-European branches including Anatolian, and Core-Indo-European, for all the branches except Anatolian.

Today, the number of native speakers of Indo-European languages is reckoned at over three billion or about 45 per cent of the Earth's population (the next largest family, which comprises Chinese and its neighbours, accounts for about 21 per cent). The Indo-Europeans share Europe with several other language families or groups, most notably members of the Uralic family (Finnish, Saami, Estonian and Hungarian), the Semitic (Maltese) and Basque, which is generally recognized as a language isolate without close relatives.

CHAPTER 1

In the pursuit of interesting truths

At the start of Sir William Jones's third discourse, he revealed his larger agenda: 'in the pursuit of interesting truths', he would examine the origins of each of the different peoples of Asia, who might at first appear to be unconnected but that would eventually lead to a common source. At the end of his lecture, he provided a preview of his future discourses in which he indicated that not only all the peoples of Asia but also the Greeks Egyptians, Phoenicians and others had 'proceeded from some central country, to investigate which will be the object of my future Discourses'. He then devoted the succeeding annual discourses to exploring from whence they had come, concluding his search with his ninth lecture in 1792 ('On the Origin and Foundation of Nations'). Let us recall that his predecessors in the discovery of the Indo-European language family had also suggested a place of origin, although these were normally required to fit into the Japhetic or Scythian model. Jäger, for example, had what we would now call the Indo-Europeans living originally in the Caucasus mountains and then migrating from there in waves through Europe and Asia.[26]

In his later discourses, Jones outlined his reasons for locating the Indo-European homeland – most of his arguments are anchored entirely in what we might call the 'historical paradigm': the belief that all that can be known about the past derives from historical sources and, as the Bible relates history all the way back to the creation of the world, it provides us with our earliest historical record. In addition, Jones was not simply intent on tracking what we might regard as the Indo-Europeans to their home but, in effect, all the peoples of the world.

By his sixth discourse, Jones offered several lines of evidence to locate the original homeland of the Indo-Europeans and other peoples. He argued on historical evidence that the oldest monarchy in the world was to be found in Iran and, hence, this is where we might find the world's oldest society.[27] If history begins in Iran (which it does not; the totally unrelated Sumerians can claim to be the first literate civilization), which of Jones's various populations (Hindu, Arab or Tartar) were associated with the earliest rulers? An examination of the earliest liturgical language of Iran (Avestan) suggested that it was closely related to Sanskrit as there were hundreds of Iranian words that could be regarded as pure Sanskrit and there were clear examples of grammatical similarities (see **1.2**). He quite rightly emphasized that the words in question were not obvious loanwords pertaining to culturally exotic items but basic vocabulary, such as the names of parts of the body and natural features, which were unlikely to have been borrowed. He concluded (alas, erroneously) that the ancient Persian language was a 'dialect' of Sanskrit (rather than an 'independent' branch that derived from the same source as Sanskrit).

As to the critical question of whether the Iranians had moved from India or Indians from Iran, Jones (a jurist who was an authority on the ancient law code of India) introduced as evidence the ancient Indian law that forbade Hindu priests (brahmins) from leaving their country. This presented a logical conundrum that, depending on your point of view, reveals either a subtle logic or sleight of hand. For Jones it made better sense to assume that the Indians (and their priests) originated in Iran from whence they were forbidden to return (why?); otherwise, had they originated in India itself presumably their law code would have confined them to the subcontinent and the Indo-Europeans would still be stuck, bound by the Laws of Manu, in India.

Jones also noted that the medieval *Anglo-Saxon Chronicle* derived the British from Armenia, and other sources traced the Goths or Scythians from Iran; Irish tradition sought their own origins on the shores of the Caspian Sea. All of these sources hence traced different peoples (the 'Gothick' and 'Celtick' of his 'Third Anniversary Discourse') back to the Scythians or somewhere near Iran. Jones took these medieval speculations at face value since he regarded them as 'a coincidence of conclusions from different media by persons wholly unconnected, which could scarce have happened if they were not grounded on solid principles'. Of course, the various origin myths were not based on 'solid principles' but were merely local variants of the same grand Judaeo-Christian template that traced Europeans back to Japheth and the Scythians. He concluded that 'the language of the first Persian empire was the mother' of Sanskrit, Iranian, Greek, Latin and Gothic.

This accounts for the origins of whom we would regard as Indo-Europeans, but Jones continued his quest to locate the origins of all his races and languages. Here he proposed a historico-geographical argument. He observed that Iran was occupied by three races or languages: Assyrians (Semites), the descendants of the biblical Shem; the Tartars (Turks), whom he assigned to the offspring of Japheth; and what we would call the Indo-Europeans, whom he (somewhat unexpectedly) derived from Ham (and that meant including the Egyptians as well).[28] As Iran was central and situated contiguous to both the main regions of Semites (Arabia) to the south and Turks to the north and contained elements of all three groups within its borders, it was clear that, by what we might recognize as the principle of least moves, the starting point for the three main races of Eurasia was also in the middle, i.e. Iran. So for Jones, all peoples and languages 'proceeded from Iran, where they migrated at first in their great colonies'.[29]

We have seen that the observation of the genetic relationship between most of the languages of Europe and some of the major languages of western Asia led to the discovery of the Indo-European language family and initiated the search for their common linguistic homeland. Sir William Jones believed he had solved the riddle of the origins of the Proto-Indo-Europeans (and several other ancient peoples). In fact, the hunt for the homeland had only just begun.

CHAPTER 2

A Brief History of Homeland Hunting and the Nature of our Prey

From the end of the 18th century, scholars and many not so scholarly have sought the original location of the Indo-Europeans – what in German is called the *Urheimat* ('original homeland'). The significance of finding this homeland was far greater than the scratching of some academic itch to position an extinct language in space and time. After all, the Urheimat had in effect replaced Noah's Ark or the Tower of Babel, and more than a few imagined the Indo-European homeland as an Aryan Garden of Eden. Moreover, as the study of the Indo-European languages had been increasingly hijacked by those who had other agendas, particularly national or racial, locating their origins in one's own country not only was a matter of national pride but could also be employed to emphasize one's linguistic, cultural or racial purity and superiority (assuming, as some did, that the Indo-Europeans were 'the chosen ones'). It should also be emphasized that the quest for the Indo-European homeland was not unique; from the 19th century onwards linguists and archaeologists attempted to trace just about every other major language family to its source location. While the Indo-European homeland has attracted the most research and debate, scholars have shed more than enough academic gore trying to determine the homelands of the Afro-Asiatic (Semitic) languages, Uralic, Altaic, Bantu, Japanese and all of the various major language groups of the Americas.

But let us cut to the chase: where precisely was the Indo-European homeland? After well over two centuries of speculation and debate, the arguments have run from ingenious to ingenuous to outright weird. Before we proceed, therefore, be reassured on three critical points. The first – the good news, if you will – is that the Indo-European homeland has been definitely located.

But hold your applause.

The second point – the bad news – is that the first statement does not rest on any conclusive argument but rather on an enormous range of solutions. For who could imagine the Urheimat further north than the North Pole or further south than Antarctica? It has been found across Eurasia from the Atlantic Ocean to the shores of the Pacific and, according to the 'esoteric Hitlerism' expounded by Chilean diplomat and fascist Miguel Serrano (1917–2009), the Indo-Europeans came from outside our galaxy. That pretty well covers all the options, at least in our own dimension, and I leave it to others to search for it in the multiverse. To illustrate the point, cast your eyes over **2.1**, **2.2** and **2.3** (and see the Appendix for details) for an extensive but admittedly still partial mapping of the various 'mainstream' homelands through time.

The third point – and the really bad news – is that after more than two centuries of debate, there is still no totally convincing solution to the homeland question that fully explains the origins and expansions of all the Indo-European languages. Nevertheless, before completely losing heart at this early stage of the game, the revolution brought about by the application of ancient DNA (aDNA) to the quest has brought us tantalizing close to an agreed solution as we will ultimately discover (although note I only said 'close').

There follows an extremely brief history of the various homeland solutions and the names of some of the most influential homeland hunters connected with them, covering both what we might regard as the canonical account and a sampling from the vaults of the apocryphal material.

Homeland hunting: the standard account

The standard account [**2.4**] goes as follows. In the beginning (1805), mesmerized by the antiquity and abundance of Sanskrit, the Indo-European homeland was placed either within India itself (Fredrich von Schlegel;

see Chapter 3) or at least not too distant from India, generally somewhere around ancient Bactria, between Afghanistan and the Hindu Kush mountains (Adolphe Pictet; see Chapter 7) and here it generally remained up until the 1880s. Much of this was driven by a firm belief articulated by German editor and publisher Baron Hans Paul von Wolzogen (1848–1938): 'Times change. People change. But the belief in the Asiatic cradle has never changed.'[1] From these emerge two of the standard homeland theories that we will label the **Indian model** (today, often called the 'Out of India' model) and the **Bactrian model**.

In the 1850s, English ethnologist Robert Gordon Latham (1812–1888) suggested a European homeland, but this was dismissed as the ravings of an eccentric (see page 41 and Chapter 4). Several other linguists, such as Theodor Benfey[2] (1809–1881), also made a case for a European homeland in the European steppe but their arguments also fell on deaf ears. In 1878, Theodor Poesche (1825–1899), a German anthropologist who had fled to America, published an influential book[3] that argued – primarily on the evidence of the physical descriptions of early Indo-Europeans in Classical and Indic literature – that the homeland lay where we would find the highest concentration of blue-eyed blonds. Confusing albinism with light skin pigmentation, he set the homeland in the Pripyat Marshes, between southern Belarus and northern Ukraine (the gift shop could have been in the Chernobyl power plant), which adumbrated the first real inflexion point. In addition to arguments from physical anthropology, Poesche also pressed a second argument: Lithuanian appeared to be the least changed Indo-European language, and so the homeland should have been situated near Lithuania, which signals one of the main arguments supporting the **Baltic model**.

At this time, however, most attention quickly turned towards the works of Karl Penka (1847–1912), a teacher in a Vienna boy's high school who (despite some critics who had dismissed him as a rank amateur) had previously published a monograph on the case endings of Indo-European nouns. Penka rejected Poesche's attempt to plunge his noble Aryan race into a swamp, issuing instead several extremely influential publications[4] that associated Indo-European origins with a Nordic physical type. This helped popularize the trope that the Indo-Europeans were tall, blond,

CHAPTER 2

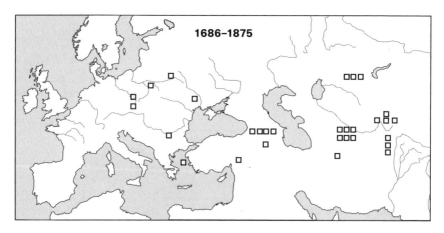

2.1 The earliest proposed homelands were usually situated in Asia, either between northern India and Afghanistan on the basis of the supposed antiquity of Sanskrit, or near the Caucasus, the final resting place of Noah's Ark. As the Asian homeland was the default explanation, it is still grossly under-represented in this map. The few European candidates tend to be the more recent, and were largely ignored or rudely dismissed.

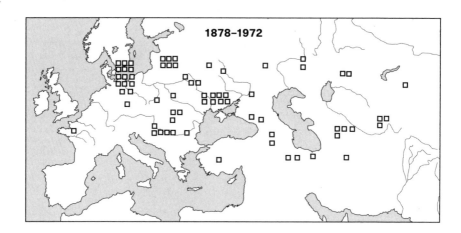

2.2 A middle period of homeland hunting saw a major shift away from Asia to Europe, where homelands were proposed primarily in Scandinavia on the basis of racial arguments, the Baltic on the basis of the conservatism of the Lithuanian language, the Danube on the centrality of the Linear Ware culture, and the Pontic-Caspian steppe on the basis of geographical centrality and reconstructions of the earliest Indo-European culture. Nevertheless, there still remained some who supported some form of Asian homeland.

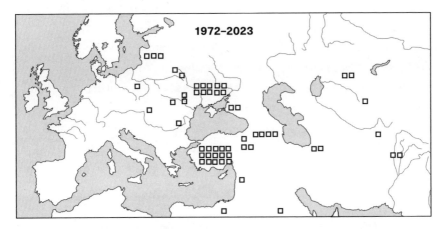

2.3 The latest phase of suggested homelands saw the domination of the Steppe theory as the European solution, while an Asian Urheimat once again became popular, now focused on agricultural origins in Anatolia or more recent genetic evidence involving populations situated around the Caucasus.

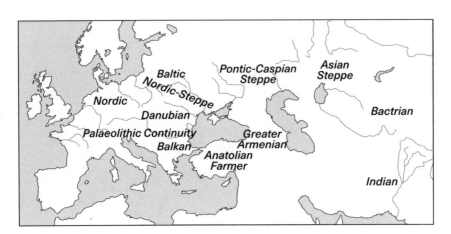

2.4 The major historical candidates for the Indo-European homeland. Some have proposed homelands embracing several zones, e.g. Palaeolithic Continuity and Nordic-Steppe.

blue-eyed Nordics with a homeland in south Scandinavia or northern Germany, which, of course, became the **Nordic model**, a vigorously supported doctrine up to 1945 (and which, among white racists, still persists). To be fair, it occasionally had some adherents for reasons other than political. The growing support for some form of Nordic theory was augmented by the influential archaeological arguments of Gustav Kossinna (1858–1931)[5] in the early 1900s, which found both anthropological and archaeological evidence locked in step. Kossinna, trained both as a linguist and archaeologist, was a major player in the European archaeology of the early 20th century (as we shall see in Chapter 9).

During the 1890s the German linguist and cultural historian Otto Schrader (1855–1919) began to press for a homeland north of the Black Sea.[6] Although others had earlier suggested a somewhat similar location, it is with Schrader that one traditionally associates the beginnings of the **Steppe model**. Schrader is also one of the monumental scholars of research into the origins and cultural institutions of the Indo-Europeans. Nevertheless, his work on the homeland enjoyed only limited traction among the homeland hunters of his day.[7] At the same time as both the Nordic model and the Steppe model were entering the scene, English biologist Thomas Huxley (1825–1895) ventured into the debate and resolved the issue by positing a homeland that stretched from the Baltic to the Urals.[8] Such a solution, which I will call the **Nordic-Steppe model**, has resurfaced from time to time and is currently being argued by the Ukrainian archaeologist Leonid Zaliznyak.

Over the first half of the 20th century a series of different homeland models competed with the Nordic camp. In addition to a location sited in or around the North Sea, the Baltic model was still being promoted by linguists such as American philologist Harold Bender (1882–1951)[9] based on the perceived antiquity or conservatism of the Lithuanian language. There was also a **Danubian model**, intermittently supported in 1922 by the Scottish linguist Peter Giles (1860–1935),[10] much later by the noted Italian linguist Giacomo Devoto (1897–1974),[11] and then extended by the Hungarian archaeologist János Makkay (1933–2023).[12] This model was very much focused on the Linear Ware culture of the Neolithic, which spanned Europe from the Atlantic to Ukraine.

It was also in the 1920s that the Steppe camp gained some support from the archaeologist V. Gordon Childe[13] as well as other archaeologists and geographers such as Harold Peake (1867–1946) and Herbert Fleure (1877–1969). In the 1930s an alternative steppe solution also arose, based primarily on cultural anthropology and linguistics. This sought the homeland on the Asian rather than European steppe (Wilhelm Koppers, see Chapter 8;[14] and Wilhelm Brandenstein[15] and Alfons Nehring, see Chapter 7[16]), hence we have here an **Asian Steppe model**. Likewise, in the 1930s the great German archaeologist Herbert Kühn (1895–1980) tackled the Urheimat problem. Working backwards, he found that there was no uniform culture plausibly ancestral to the Indo-Europeans later than the Palaeolithic and suspected that the homeland might lie in the Aurignacian, a cultural phase of the Upper Palaeolithic. This provides us with a good example of what has come to be known as the **Palaeolithic Continuity model**,[17] which still (barely) survives today.

During the second half of the 20th century the Lithuanian-born archaeologist Marija Gimbutas (1921–1994) greatly invigorated the case for the Steppe model, which secured a broad consensus for it.[18] The Steppe theory, modified and updated, continued to receive monograph-level support from archaeologists[19] where the most detailed version is currently found in the works of David Anthony.[20] Although many linguists appeared to be content with Gimbutas's Steppe solution, two major challenges arose in the 1980s. The first of these, originally floated in 1972, came in the form of a mammoth monograph published in 1984 and a series of subsequent articles from the linguists Tamaz Gamkrelidze (1929–2021) and Russian Vyacheslav Ivanov (1929–2017). They argued for a homeland in the south Caucasus (Greater Armenia), emphasizing the influence of Afro-Asiatic and Kartvelian (for example, Georgian) languages on the formation of Indo-European.[21] This theory, which we will label the **Greater Armenian model**, was dismissed by British philologist Peter Kitson as 'one eccentric hypothesis which puts the Urheimat in the Caucasus'[22] (shades of the dismissals of Latham's 'European homeland'). It must be admitted that this solution had much greater currency in Russian language publications than in the West. Kitson also claimed that the hypothesis 'involves movements of peoples which all archaeologists I know of regard as impossible'[23] and other than being employed to support a Near Eastern origin for the Indo-Iranians,[24] it lacked serious fighter cover from archaeologists until it was given support by Stanislav Grigoriev.[25] It also prompted major criticism from the renowned Russian linguist and ancient historian Igor Diakonov (1915–1999), who countered it with arguments for an admittedly rare **Balkan model.**

Only a few years after the Russian publication, British archaeologist Colin Renfrew launched his monograph on Indo-European origins, *Archaeology and Language* (1987), bringing it into the framework of a larger thesis wherein many of the world's largest language families were associated with the various local centres of agricultural origins and dispersals. In this way the spread of early farming societies from Anatolia (the **Anatolian Farmer model**) to the rest of Europe was seen as the origin and vector for the spread of Indo-European languages.[26] In the early 21st century much of the homeland discussion focused on various attempts to 'test' the Anatolian Farmer and Steppe models against each other, employing quantitative approaches to try to estimate the time and place of Indo-European dispersals on the basis of lexical evidence.[27]

This standard account attempts to present the trajectory of those theories that have been supported by well-recognized scholars whose research was widely accepted within the mainspring of Indo-European research at the time of their publication. I should probably emphasize that a perfectly competent scholar might have produced a homeland solution that for one reason or another simply did not catch on; failure to win an academic popularity contest does not necessarily reflect on the quality or validity of the research. In summary, for most of the 18th and 19th centuries, the major default position was an Asian homeland. After 1870 there was a growing acceptance of a homeland in northern Europe, which flourished until about 1945. From about 1900 onwards the Pontic-Caspian steppe began to rise in popularity and remained so after the fall of the Nordic model; it rose to major prominence from *c.* 1960 onwards, although it received multiple challenges from the Baltic and Danubian models. By about 1980 there were two new challengers, the Greater Armenian model of Gamkrelidze and Ivanov and, more popularly, the Anatolian Farmer model. By the 21st century most homeland debate concerned the comparative merits of the Steppe and the Anatolian Farmer models. Then, in 2015, came the revolution that transformed the whole discussion. This step change in our understanding of approaches to the homeland issue will form the focus of the later part of this book, when we assess the current status of each homeland solution.

Homeland hunting: some selections from the apocrypha

Here I offer an alternative history of homeland hunting, emphasizing some of the more 'daring' theories that have decorated our path. This section is to be enjoyed rather than studied; it will not be on the test!

In a world of scholarship absolutely certain that the Indo-European homeland lay in (Central) Asia, anyone who contested this, no matter how distinguished, could be dismissed and this was certainly the case with Robert Gordon Latham, who, from the 1850s onwards argued for a European homeland on grounds that might not be totally conclusive but were at least academically very defensible. Latham was both a distinguished ethnologist and linguist. Already by 1851 he promoted a theory that he admitted 'will, probably, find more favour with the naturalist than with the scholar' (an interesting distinction!), where he proposed a homeland in Europe because the common logic of the natural sciences dictated that a single relatively uniform Asian branch (Indo-Iranian, a language 'species') was far more likely to be the offshoot of the substantially more differentiated European languages (a language 'genus') than the reverse.[28] He maintained this stance (and belief in a homeland somewhere on the eastern border of Lithuania),[29] which got him labelled as an eccentric British crackpot, 'to the lifelong detriment of his reputation'.[30]

The Reverend Dunbar Isidore Heath (1816–1888) did have something of a background in disputation as he had been a member of the Cambridge Apostles, a student discussion group that had later included Bertrand Russell, John Maynard Keynes and Ludwig Wittgenstein. Heath was a competent Egyptologist and edited the *Journal of Anthropology*; he was also successfully prosecuted in 1861 as a heretic (I'm not sure whether that counts for or against him). Five years later he gave an entertaining address to the Anthropological Society[31] maintaining that the Indo-Europeans had arrived in Europe from the East (Asia or Atlantis was of no consequence), not just spreading the five hundred known roots then attributed to the Indo-European proto-language but language itself since the previous Palaeolithic and Mesolithic populations of Europe had evolved locally from earlier apes and were mutes, an inferior race that was going to be enslaved to the superior Indo-Europeans and learn their language.

In 1888, American Charles Morris (1833–1922), former 'professor' at Philadelphia's Academy of Ancient and Modern Languages as well as a dime novelist and popular science and history author, published what he claimed was the first full monograph on the Indo-Europeans, who were 'the apex of human development, and the culminating point in the long-continued evolution of man'.[32] He asserted that the ancestors of the Indo-Europeans were originally members of the Mongoloid race who first moved west onto the Pontic-Caspian steppe and then into the Caucasus where they learned agriculture, perfected their language and gained their white pigmentation augmented by an infusion of enthusiasm and imagination from more southerly races before dispersing across Eurasia. In the same year Canon (of York) Isaac Taylor (1829–1901), antiquarian and philologist, also appeared to agree with Morris that 'The Aryans must have had ancestors who were not Aryans', but did not seek these ancestors among the Mongolians but rather in the Baltic region among the Uralic peoples, describing the Indo-Europeans as 'an improved race of Finns'.[33]

But these scholars were looking in the wrong place, at least according to Daniel Garrison Brinton (1837–1899), the distinguished Professor of Anthropology at Harvard University who had published widely on the native literature and languages of the Americas, including his *Rig Veda Americana*, a collection of Nahuatl (Aztec) poems. He believed that the origins of the Indo-European proto-language must have required a coalescence between an agglutinative (then thought as a structurally more primitive language like, sigh, Finnish) and a semi-incorporative language. So he looked to a linguistic and cultural marriage between Berbers and Basques (for him the ancient Indo-Europeans were certainly not blond Nordics but brunettes), and is one of the very few who placed the homeland in Atlantic Europe.[34] He is one of the earliest representatives of what we might also call the *Mischsprache* (mixed-language) school (see page 53).

In 1897 the noted Austrian physician and anthropologist Franz Tappeiner (1816–1902) asserted with certainty that skulls of pre-Pleistocene Europeans must have been those of Indo-Europeans (here: Aryans) as the perfection of the Indo-European language family was such that it required the Aryan brain to have 'the greatest capacity and finest construction';[35] Tappeiner left his collection of these superior Aryan skulls to the Vienna Museum of Natural History and Tyrolean State Museum.

The distinguished historian of the Roman legal system Rudolf von Ihering (1818–1892) died before completing his monograph on Indo-European origins, but his friends and colleagues did his reputation no favours when they posthumously published what he had written in 1897. Here we find a number of arguments that the earliest Indo-Europeans originated in a hot climate (Ihering was thinking of Central Asia). One of the critical arguments was derived from a Roman legal practice whereby a Roman, accusing a neighbour of theft, could only conduct a house search of the suspect's premise wearing an apron. After dismissing almost any logical explanation for such a practice, Ihering concluded that the apron was a relic of the 'usual dress of the ancient Aryans' and this would only make sense if they lived in a warm climate.[36] Another interesting contribution to the Indo-European homeland problem was that although the author could not indicate in what century the dispersals began, he could be certain that they began on 1 March, the day when the Romans would begin to celebrate the *ver sacrum*, a festival that in part involved the expulsion or sacrifice of a segment of the younger population, which has been interpreted as a memory of past migrations.[37]

But not everyone associated the earliest Indo-Europeans with a hot climate, especially when one considers the research of Bal Gangadhar Tilak (1856–1920), 'the father of Modern India' (according to Mahatma Gandhi). In 1903 one of the main leaders of the Indian independence movement[38] published his monograph, which merged the evidence of geology (that before the end of the last Ice Age there was an interstadial period providing a warm climate in the far north of Eurasia) and astronomical evidence gleaned from the Vedas and the Avesta. From these texts Tilak suggested that they were composed in a location where the sun rose in the south, the stars revolved around the pole rather than rose and set, and that a year consisted of a single long day followed by a single long night, and so concluded that the Indo-European homeland was in the polar regions. At the end of the interstadial, the freezing temperatures drove the Indo-Europeans south into their historical seats. Once a theory like this starts (and variations on a polar Atlantis had been around for a long time), it tends to build traction in some circles and so in 1906 German author Georg Biedenkapp (1868–1924) produced another monograph supporting the polar homeland, adding that the dragon/serpent myths found in various Indo-European traditions (Vṛtra in ancient India, the Midgard serpent in Norse mythology) had been inspired by the wavy bands one sees in the Northern Lights.[39] And later the noted Indian linguist Irach Taraporewala (1884–1956) added another block to the igloo by interpreting the Zoroastrian rule against burying the dead 'until the birds should fly' as a reference to the frozen conditions of the homeland where the graves could not be excavated until the spring.[40]

To these arguments could be added some early misguided attempts to derive the Proto-Indo-European word for the 'bear' – $*h_2ṛtḱos$ – from $*h_2rǵ$ 'white', which would populate the homeland with polar bears. The **Polar model** continued and, to paraphrase Conan Doyle, 'enjoyed a certain Soviet vogue' in Russia as well as in Germany,[41] and variations of this model survived at least to the late 20th century. To all of these we should add the controversial and overtly racist Polish-Austrian art historian Josef Strzygowski (1862–1941), who in 1936 published his perspective on the homeland problem, emphasizing how Nordic art lay at the foundations of the art of the Classical world, and concluded that what we call Indo-European was an artistic stream that came from the north, around Greenland, during an interglacial period.[42] Finally, bothered by the great age imputed to Indo-European culture in Tilak's account and the fact that according to geological evidence, Tilak's earliest Indo-Europeans must have been treading water for millennia, the American Charles Hapgood (1904–1982) suggested a far more 'logical' solution by relocating the homeland to the South Pole, arguing in a series of popular books that a great world civilization had existed until Antarctica was glaciated somewhere between 10,000 and 15,000 years ago.[43]

Another route to a northern homeland came by way of Alexander Jóhannesson (1888–1965), who produced a mammoth etymological dictionary of Icelandic and also served as the Rector of the University of Iceland. Very much a believer that language originated in imitating the sounds of nature, the author turned his attention to Indo-European origins and published a short monograph in 1943.[44] Here he examined the various Indo-European roots such as *ker-, which he found to have underlain the greatest number of words in Old Norse and that he regarded as a word originating as imitative of the call of a raven. Similarly, other roots all beginning with a velar or guttural sound, such as *kel-, *gel- or *gher-, signified the harsh noise and commotion of the hard natural world of northern Europe, although, at the finish, Jóhannesson opted for a Baltic (Lithuanian) rather than a Scandinavian homeland.

While we will have to deal with some challenging theories regarding the relationship between physical anthropology and the Indo-Europeans in a later chapter, this is probably the appropriate place to dispense with Horst Maurus's 1913 study *Die 'natürlichen' Grundstämme der Menschen*, which at least provides our deepest ancestry for the Indo-Europeans.[45] He divided the main 'tribes' of modern humans into three: Syroids, Sinoids and Euroids, with their associated languages (Euroids include Hamites, West Africans and Inuit along with Indo-Europeans). The Syroids traced their ancestry back through gorillas to armadillos, while the ancestors of the Chinese were once orangutans and earlier porcupines. As for Euroids, which included the Indo-Europeans, their family tree goes back to chimpanzees who evolved from lemurs who could be traced back to (I bet you won't see this one coming) anteaters. And before you ask, yes, we can reconstruct a word for 'ant' in Proto-Indo-European (*morwi- ~ *morm- ~ *mouro-) but, alas, the reconstructed lexicon lacks any evidence for our ant-eating ancestors.

As for our chimpanzee ancestors, another 'savant' handled their linguistic abilities and relationship to Indo-European in 1932. Georg Schwidetzky (1875–1952) published his main contribution to

Indo-European studies (banned by the Nazis) in his *Schimpansisch, Urmongolisch, Indogermanisch* ('Chimpanzee, Proto-Mongolian, Indo-European') where we learn first the range of the chimpanzee vocabulary – for example, the joy at eating an apple (*kha kha*), rye-bread (*khak khak*) or when tucking into a banana (*m m ngahk m m*), and then we have word lists comparing Proto-Chimpanzee (PC) with a variety of other languages, including Indo-European – for example, PC *ka ka, mgak, ngak* 'disgust, evacuation of bowels' can be compared with Greek *kakkáō* and Latin *caccō*, both 'defecate'.[46] His daughter was Ilse Schwidetzky (1907–1997), a very well-known physical anthropologist whose work on Indo-European migrations we will encounter later (see page 256).

In 1981 a Near Eastern or North African origin was proposed by the specialist in Afro-Asiatic languages Carleton Hodge (1917–1998), on the basis of what he regarded were cognates (words related because they share a common ancestor and are not just borrowed) in Indo-European and ancient Egyptian, which pointed to a common homeland for both on the Nile. The Indo-Europeans apparently migrated north no later than 13,000 BCE and moved through Palestine and Syria to Anatolia, by which time they could be adopted into the Anatolian Farmer model or make their way north to participate in the Steppe model.[47] Many of these elements have been unwittingly resurrected by the Ukrainian linguists Valentin Taranets and Inna Stupak. They have traced the origin of Indo-European back to Africa (where it has deep roots with Bantu and other African languages) and was then carried northwards into Anatolia by 7000 BCE. There it left the Anatolian, Greek, Armenian and Albanian branches, while the rest worked their way around the Caspian to spread west where, after experiencing the effects of a Cucuteni-Trypillia (a Neolithic culture northwest of the Black Sea) substrate, spread through the rest of Europe.[48]

An eastern, and I mean far eastern, homeland appears to emerge in an attempt by the historian and archaeologist A. K. Narain (1925–2013) to determine the origins of the Tocharians, who, he argued, had a fairly local origin in the Gansu region of western China, which dragged the entire Indo-European homeland towards the Yellow River.[49] If you don't want to go east, you can also head south. Following an old, but hardly venerable tradition of sifting through modern languages, in this case

Old English and Latin, to discover their roots in Classical Arabic (long live Goropianism!), T. A. Ismail in 1989 concluded that it provided the ancestor of the Indo-European language family and that the Indo-Europeans were driven out of their homeland on the Arabian peninsula due to drought; invoking one of the analytical tools that we will later examine, he argued that as Arabic was the least changed, its population had remained in or close to the homeland.[50]

Finally, I will confess to having omitted a number of mystic Nazi theories linking the Aryan homeland to Atlantis (which lay in the Azores)[51] or a lost race from the Himalayas,[52] but still we might as well finish with the theories of Miguel Serrano, who had served as Chilean Ambassador to India, Yugoslavia, Bulgaria, Romania and Austria. He is reputed to have included among his friends both Carl Jung and the Nobel-prize-winning novelist Hermann Hesse. He was also a major anti-Semite and believed that Hitler was an avatar of one of the Indic gods (Vishnu or Siva) or the Germanic god Wotan, had escaped his bunker and made his way by submarine to live out his life in a secret underground base in Antarctica. He proposed that the true gods had originated in the rays of a Black Sun (not our own and invisible to us), but in order to quash a rebellion by an upstart junior god who had populated the Earth with debased creatures, they took advantage of an astral doorway through the planet Venus (Hitler had taken this route back home to the Black Sun) to settle in the polar region and maintain their pure blood. These, according to Serrano, are the ancestors of the Aryans who, due to a cosmic collision that flipped the poles, were forced to seek refuge at the South Pole, so one could argue for a homeland at either pole as well as whatever galaxy housed the Aryans' Black Sun.[53]

Homeland tropes

Returning to the more standard history of Indo-European homeland hunting, a series of recurrent themes or issues is revealed that renders a simple geographical answer such as 'the homeland was located in Afghanistan' an inadequate solution. Here I will give a brief introduction to some of the major themes or academic tropes that impact on the assessment of any homeland solution, which we will explore in more detail in later chapters.

Urheimat versus Ausgangsland

Homeland hunters have frequently made a distinction between the territory in which a language family formed (Otto Schrader identified this as the *Urheimat*, the 'original home', Austrian linguist Wolfgang Dressler used the term *Keimzelle*, or 'germ cell',[54] and German army doctor and archaeologist Georg Wilke employed *Geburtsland*, or 'birth-land'[55]) and the area that marked the final region in which the proto-language was spoken before it disintegrated (Schrader called this the *Ausgangsland*, while the noted American linguist Isidore Dyen, who had a penchant for making up descriptive cover names and acronyms for linguistic phenomena, called it a DPL – a Disintegrant Proto-Language, or the last stage of a proto-language before its breakup[56]). One then imagines a proto-language forming in a restricted territory and then, over the centuries, sees its borders expand as former dialects evolve into distinct languages. The beginning and end of this process are both problematic.

Let's start with 'a proto-language forming' and remind ourselves that there is absolutely no intrinsic linguistic difference between a proto-language and any other language. Common Latin is a proto-language because it produced a number of sufficiently different daughter languages, the Romance languages; Armenian is not a proto-language because it is not ancestral to more than one language. The difference is historical not linguistic: Latin speakers had armies that enabled its speakers to build an empire whose population spawned a variety of different languages; the Armenians have spent most of their existence defending themselves from larger neighbours and have not given birth to different daughter languages. In short, any language that manages to produce daughters can be a proto-language.

Once we acknowledge that a proto-language is nothing intrinsically special, then we must realize that proto-languages do not have starting points but are merely a continuum of linguistic evolution. No one ever knew they were speaking what future linguists would define as a proto-language. The medieval Irish claimed that their language had been assembled from the very best elements of the seventy-two different languages spoken at the Tower of Babel. Some 19th-century scholars seem to have believed that Proto-Indo-European was assembled in a remote location, such as the Caucasus or Himalayas, and only after it was 'perfected' was the product launched into the greater world. Even well into the 20th century a distinguished linguist such as James Marchand (1926–2021) could imagine that Proto-Indo-European was originally a homogeneous language, without dialects, and like Latin, probably confined to a small area.[57]

But real languages do not usually work that way, and often have related neighbouring languages, or if their neighbours are unrelated, their language may be permeable to loans from their neighbours. So, unless they have a social mechanism that prescribes a standard language, they are probably going to have dialects or some other form of variation between their speakers. The bottom line here is that there was a real language, as fuzzy on its geographical and temporal borders as any real language known today, which once was spoken somewhere. That language eventually expanded to form the different Indo-European languages.

We now have to tackle the far messier concept of 'the final area in which the proto-language was spoken before it disintegrated'. As this is not an event but a process – and, as we will see in the following chapters, the nature of that process often governs our ability or inability to locate a homeland – we are faced with a brain-frying problem that we cannot completely cover here. I will merely provide a single illustration of the difficulty using a familiar example. We know that the modern Romance languages (Italian, French, Spanish, Portuguese, Romanian, etc.) all derive from Latin. We also know that they do not derive from Classical Latin but rather the Common Latin that was spoken by the general populace from about 200 BCE onwards. As for the emergence of the actual differentiated Romance languages, we generally look to *c.* 800 CE when the Church, recognizing that the general masses could no longer understand sermons preached in Latin, urged priests to use the rustic common tongues (the earliest forms of French, Spanish, etc.) of their respective regions. In 200 BCE Common Latin was basically confined to Italy. By 200 CE it spanned the territory from Britain to the Black Sea and the

Near East. So where is the Romance homeland: does it comprise only a small portion of Italy, all of Italy or the entire Roman Empire, or somewhere in between? We will return to this issue.

Time depth

English is not a proto-language but it could have been, and there is always the possibility that it might become one. A combination of near universal literacy and global communications has retarded the level of differentiation among the variety of Englishes spoken in Britain, Ireland, North America, India, South Africa, Australia, New Zealand and elsewhere from becoming as different from one another as they might have been, although I have always wondered how well a Mumbai fruit seller could converse with a Cork taxi-driver. But even if we treat all of these as merely dialects of English it is clear that they do not derive from the language found in *Beowulf* or Chaucer, even though these too are forms of English. Similarly, linguistic evidence makes it clear that India was not invaded by Alfred the Great nor did the troops of Richard the Lionheart manage to colonize North America. All of the current Englishes derive from Modern English from about 1600 onwards – if English speakers from around the world wished to make a pilgrimage back to where their language began and found themselves in a Homeland Interpretative Centre at Stonehenge, which offered tourists an authentic English homeland experience, there would be real reason to complain. Even if the place is right, if the time is wrong it is not the homeland.

Similarly, the Indo-European homeland is not simply a space problem but a space-time problem, but unlike the situation of English, where we have a written record of its different stages before its expansions as a colonial power, we lack such evidence for Proto-Indo-European other than some disputed attempts at reconstructing past states of the proto-language through internal reconstruction. Any attempt to assign reliable absolute chronologies to the early period of dispersals involves methodologies that are at best problematic, as we will see in Chapter 7. Although the majority of homeland hunters have sought their quarry sometime between the late Neolithic and the Early Bronze Age (*c.* 4500–3000 BCE), there are major schools of thought that prefer the early Neolithic (7000–6000 BCE) and an admittedly much smaller school that seeks the homeland in the Palaeolithic or Mesolithic.

Migration phylogeny

Many of the earliest attempts to locate the homeland of Indo-European imagined that it was within that initial area itself that all the branches first emerged, each walking or riding out in their already formed state. For example, Charles Morris[58] argued that the Indo-Europeans queued up according to the distance that they had to travel so that the Celts, who had to travel furthest, naturally left first, followed by the Germans, then the Italics and Greeks, and finally the Balts and then Slavs. On the other hand, Scottish linguist Alexander Murray (1775–1813)[59] had argued in a book published in 1823 that the language branches queued according to the complexity of their grammatical systems, so that the simplest (for him that meant Germanic) got the deckchairs first, and then the slightly more complex Celtic followed, until finally the Indo-Aryans departed bearing the most perfect inflexional system. To some extent this foreshadows current approaches that are based on phylogeny (the family tree of the Indo-European languages), arranged in terms of evolution: Anatolian separates first, then, more precariously argued, follows Tocharian, then (perhaps) Celtic and Italic, and so on. The departure 'windows' are still a matter of considerable disagreement and can seriously affect one's solution to the homeland problem, especially the dispersals.

Secondary homelands

Ever since the 19th century, homeland hunters have not been content to propose just a single homeland from which all the branches departed, reminiscent of early maps depicting Noah's Ark with arrows indicating the paths of his three sons and their progeny. For example, Rudolf von Ihering (the one who set the migrations to 1 March) argued that the homeland lay in Bactria, but there was a *zweite Heimat* ('second homeland') that lay between the Danube and the Don.[60] Secondary homelands deal with the problem of migration phylogeny by assigning space-time locations to the ancestors of multiple branches downstream from the initial homeland. Their creation was a result of several different issues that have dogged homeland hunting since the 19th century.

The first of those arose from the reconstruction of the proto-language. All Indo-Europeans were deemed to have had a widely shared common vocabulary for domestic livestock, and yet while there was at least a network of common items for both domesticated plants and trees among the European languages there was very little evidence for common agricultural terms in the Indo-Iranian languages.[61] So homelands were proposed where either the European or Indo-Iranian branches were seen to reflect the culture and environment of the primary homeland, and the other was relegated to a more recent secondary homeland. Either the Proto-Indo-Europeans lived in a purely pastoral region where their economic vocabulary was preserved by the Indo-Iranian languages while the future Europeans moved west and adopted agriculture in a secondary European homeland, or the Proto-Indo-Europeans were settled farmers in Europe whose Asian brethren wandered east across the Eurasian steppe and through Central Asia where they forgot both their agricultural ways and the vocabulary associated with it. With the discovery of Tocharian and Anatolian, the issues became even murkier, especially as the residue of agricultural terms in both Anatolian and Tocharian[62] is quite limited.

The second and probably more obvious driving force is that if one divides the Indo-European languages into different branches such as Celtic, Germanic, Slavic and so on, then there is an almost uncontrollable urge to provide each branch with its own homeland, which effectively spawns multiple homelands or staging areas for the various branches. We will later deal with whether this urge needs to be cultivated or suppressed.

Ur-urheimaten and *Mischsprachen*

Although Canon Isaac Taylor had race in mind when he wrote: 'The Aryans must have had ancestors who were not Aryans', many realize that this makes far better sense if taken linguistically. As we have seen, many imagined that Proto-Indo-European was the finest linguistic creation gifted to the people of planet Earth and must have been almost divinely engineered in some remote location before being launched, meaning that the Urheimat itself required a still earlier homeland. As Taylor observed, there had to be something prior out of which Indo-European evolved. There have been at least two approaches to this. One is to presume that Indo-European is itself a branch of a still earlier proto-language that has left relicts of its existence not only in Indo-European but also in other language families. So Indo-European has been seen as a daughter language of, for example, Indo-Uralic (a common mother language for both Indo-European and Uralic), Eurasiatic (Indo-European, Uralic, Altaic and other languages of northern Asia) or the still larger Nostratic family that embraces not only the Eurasiatic languages but also more southerly languages such as Afro-Asiatic, Elamite and Dravidian.[63]

A second approach had already emerged by the end of the 19th century when Daniel Brinton suggested that Indo-European was the product of the fusion of two linguistic types, and from the 1930s onwards there were linguists arguing that Indo-European was a *Mischsprache* – a 'mixed language' – produced by the collision of a 'northern' and a 'southern' language. Many linguists deplored the whole notion of a mixed language (as early as 1871, Max Müller declared *es gibt keine Mischsprache*, 'there is no mixed language',[64] while Sigmund Feist argued that there was an obvious *Mischsprache*[65]). Although English retains the vestiges of its Germanic origins in its grammar and basic vocabulary, its overall inheritance of a Germanic vocabulary is often estimated at about only 20–30 per cent and 80 per cent of its vocabulary is largely derived from loanwords from French (*c.* 30 per cent), Latin (*c.* 30 per cent), Greek and Old Norse. This, however, is employing the concept of a mixed language too broadly since there is hardly a language that has not borrowed in some way from other languages. In fact, the number of real mixed languages (where so much of its grammar, not vocabulary, has been spliced together from two languages that it doesn't have a single clear genetic ancestor) is extremely rare. The idea that Proto-Indo-European was itself such a mixed language of some sort has historically been very much a minority enterprise. We will see, however, that the idea has once again found a place at the table of current homeland discussions.

CHAPTER 2

Granular homeland

Before the rise of archaeology, a language homeland proposal could be described employing the environmental and cultural evidence gleaned solely from linguistic sources. A circle on a map could be filled with imaginary Proto-Indo-Europeans whose world may have only been constrained with some evidence of the natural environment, such as the distribution of a species of tree or animal believed to have been known to the population. But as archaeology began to provide evidence for closely dated prehistoric cultures, it revealed the inadequacy of simply taking a marker pen to a map, defining an area and labelling it 'the homeland'. Obviously, setting your homeland at the North Pole, where there has never been evidence of human settlement, was going to be a hard sell. But almost any other region was going to offer far more granular and, often, contradictory evidence. When Rudolf von Ihering located his secondary homeland between the Danube and the Don – a popular area for many homeland hunters – he was placing it in a territory occupied at the same time both by the largest farming villages in Europe (west of the Dnipro river) and by mobile pastoralists who left barely any evidence of their campsites, much less revealed any knowledge of domesticated cereals. And with the evidence of both physical anthropology and now palaeogenomics (aDNA evidence), human populations and their marriage and cultural networks have added another dimension to homeland solutions. Moreover, no putative Urheimat is likely to gain traction if it cannot offer convincing evidence (linguistic, archaeological *and* genetic) that a language had expanded from the proposed homeland and dispersed to all of the regions where we find the daughter languages. Satisfying only one or even two of these constituencies will never be quite enough to put the homeland problem to bed.

Language dispersals and language shift

By now we can see that a possible homeland only works if it is situated in a convincing location at a convincing time, and with clear evidence that a language spread from this centre to form the various Indo-European languages. Unlike tracing the expansion of a written language where we follow the spread of documentary evidence (inscriptions and written documents), chasing after a language before it has been set to writing is, to say the least, a bit challenging. From the perspective of a homeland hunter, for most of the last two centuries of the hunt scholars have attempted to employ proxy evidence for language – archaeology and physical anthropology (often served up as 'racial history') – to track the Indo-Europeans back to their homeland. Except for some academic zealots, anyone using such evidence realized that they were dealing with circumstantial evidence. They understood that there need be no exact equation between the decoration on the pot one ate out of or the width of one's skull and the language one spoke. Rather, it was conjectured that when we found people using a particular style of hand-made ceramics (here presumed to have been made by women – yup, gender stereotyping – who passed on the art to their daughters), that if over time the pottery – admittedly with some evolution in style – appeared to spread to the next territory, then whatever language was spoken by the earlier mothers was, again with some evolution, passed on down the line to their daughters, granddaughters and so on. The archaeologist could then produce a chart of the cultural prehistory of a vast area, defined by a series of cultures (identified primarily by their ceramics) from which one could attempt to read trajectories of cultural expansion or migration.

Similar arguments might be made regarding the apparent dispersal of human physical traits (usually defined in terms of skull shape), which were regarded as primarily inherited. Thus, one could follow a chain of genetically related descendants presumably speaking genetically related languages. There has always been much debate between those who dispute that there could be any acceptable physical proxy for identifying a prehistoric language,[66] versus those who argue that a long-term cultural or genetic border between two very different populations is also likely to reflect a 'persistent identity', and may have also been a linguistic border. But even if we set aside this part of an almost interminable dispute, the exercise in tracing dispersals ultimately raises the question that even if we can discern the movement of prehistoric communities, who wins when two languages come into contact with one another?

Historical evidence suggests that populations in Eurasia have a very strong track record of language shift, whereby earlier communities adopted the language of later inhabitants. Neither Iberian nor Celtic has survived in Spain; the language of the Gauls has disappeared from France; that of the ancient Britons in England is no more (but does survive in Wales); while the language of Bohemia is now Czech and not Celtic. We may then move eastwards across Europe to the land of the Thracians, a people Herodotus claimed as the most populous in the world, who now speak a Slavic language (named after a Turkic tribe that had once attempted to master the territory), and from there go east across Ukraine and southern Russia where the major rivers (the Dnipro, Dnister and Don) still carry their earlier Iranian names but where the population now speaks Slavic even though much of the territory once hosted Turkic speakers. To imagine that language shift did not happen at earlier times simply because we can't look at it through historical documents seems perverse. Yet how can we pick winners and losers in the prehistoric record?

The traditional approach to language shift is to invoke one of two mechanisms: either the invaders greatly altered the population balance by depopulating the territory (at least of the males) or outbreeding the locals; or they engaged in elite dominance where the general populace adopted the language of the privileged elite. This last was the default explanation of many if not most of the homeland solutions of the 19th and 20th centuries. Critics countered with empirical evidence of elites adopting the language of the local conquered population – for example, the Turkic Bulgars who adopted Slavic, or the Germanic Franks and Norse-speaking Vikings who adopted French. The arguments involved archaeologists and historical linguists, but the nexus of the debate were issues that were really the purview of a different type of linguist: the social linguist. It is the social or anthropological linguists who engage with the cultural processes involved in language shift. Alas, I think most would agree with Susan Gal, that 'a straightforward search for the social correlates of language shift and maintenance has been unsuccessful'.[67] We can make an attempt to break down the variables and processes that might lead a population to abandon its own language and, after a period of bilingualism, adopt another,[68] but in the absence of truly predictive rules, drawn from those who have studied these issues among living populations, our conclusions will always remain debatable.

The Indo-European homeland has been sought as far north as the polar regions and as far south as Antarctica, from the Atlantic to the Pacific and beyond the solar system. Whatever the proposed solution, in this chapter I have listed just some of the issues that make the search one dogged by 'constituency problems', which have attracted various academic camps who vigorously defend conclusions that are diametrically opposed by other camps. We will encounter them frequently in the following chapters. In order, therefore, to find a homeland location that satisfies (nearly) everyone we will have to navigate a sea of tropes that raise so far unresolved problems and have often left the academic world bitterly divided.

Part 2
The Fundamental Techniques of Homeland Hunting

CHAPTER 3

Applying the Lessons of History

Before we begin, we should note that the earliest evidence for writing is from Mesopotamia from *c.* 3000 BCE. Furthermore, the earliest records pertinent to the existence of the Indo-Europeans concern Anatolian personal names, which are usually dated to *c.* 2000 BCE, although it has recently been suggested that there may be some evidence as early as 2300 BCE.[1] There is subsequent evidence for Indo-Aryan *c.* 1500 BCE and Mycenaean Greek *c.* 1400 BCE. The latest terminal date for Indo-European dispersals is usually set to *c.* 2500 BCE, although such a recent date would be opposed by the overwhelming majority of homeland hunters, who would look to a date before 3000 BCE. In short, the Indo-European homeland is positioned temporally *before* the existence of relevant written records – it is a prehistorical and not a historical problem. However, the earliest attempts to locate the Urheimat emerged at a time when knowledge of the past was confined to what could only be gleaned from historical sources. As it was believed that the Bible carried 'history' all the way back to the creation of the world, it provided a convenient chronology for all historical discourse. Whether you took the date of Creation from Jewish tradition (3924 BCE), the slightly older date calculated by Archbishop Ussher of Armagh that became enshrined in the King James version of the Bible (4004 BCE) or the still deeper chronology of Saint Jerome (5199 BCE), all terrestrial existence could be compressed into the last six or seven thousand years. The West's encounter with the literature of Eastern religions was not initially seen as a challenge to such a chronology but, in fact, an opportunity to find additional support for the biblical tradition.[2]

CHAPTER 3

The biblical chronology was defended by, among others, Sir William Jones, who could find no evidence that could be seen to oppose it. Like a lawyer verbally bludgeoning a jury, he wrote: 'We find no certain monument, or even probable tradition of nations planted, empires and states raised, laws enacted, cities built, navigation improved, commerce encouraged, arts invented, or letters contrived, above or at most fifteen or sixteen centuries before the birth of Christ.'[3] This helps explain how Jones could tie Indo-European origins to the foundation of the Persian monarchy and, also, helped him reconcile the Indic account with the Bible. As an aside, Jones was also a victim of a canny Indian researcher-translator who, after being informed of the basic narratives of Western culture, was tasked with searching Indic literature for comparable events and produced supposedly ancient Sanskrit verses depicting a major flood that was survived by the Indian patriarch Satyavarman (who Jones identified with Noah) and his three sons: Śarma (Shem), Kharma (Ham) and Jyāpati (Japheth), the latter who took his people north.[4] This was only one incident of a host of forged Sanskrit documents produced by local pandits to feed a growing market of Western collectors who naively purchased their knock-off Upa-vedas.[5]

As the Indo-Europeans still survive today, their expansion must have occurred (according to the biblical tradition) after the Deluge. Thus, employing the reckoning of Archbishop Ussher, we hardly need to look for them earlier than c. 2348 BCE (1,656 years after the creation of the world), a date that today would generally reflect the floruit of major civilizations in Mesopotamia and India, and the Bronze Age for European populations. In fact, the Ussher chronology would have the Europeans, the sons of Japheth, setting out from the plains of Shinar in 2247 BCE.[6]

The idea that there was something earlier than the historical or written record began to emerge over the course of the 19th century, although initially it was a problematic concept for those interested in tracking the Indo-Europeans to their home. Major-General Vans Kennedy (1784–1846), who was posted to India and became both a Sanskrit scholar and professional translator, was troubled by the fact that 'the first dawning of profane tradition and history is scarcely discernible earlier than 1,200 or 1,300 years B.C. It is impossible, therefore, to determine what may have been the previous state of the world, or to ascertain, the origin of the languages which then prevailed.'[7] But this was the same century in which Christian Thomsen (1788–1865) devised a chronological framework for the antiquities in the National Museum of Denmark, which he organized according to a three-age system: Stone, Bronze and Iron Ages. At this time there was a growing realization that not every object found in a field or museum must be attributed to a historically named people, such as Roman, Dane, Gaul or Hun. At about the same time, advances in geology demonstrated a vastly greater antiquity of the Earth and, coupled with the remains of early human stone industries in France, indicated that the biblical chronology was wrong by many orders of magnitude. By 1851 the Scottish-Canadian archaeologist Daniel Wilson (1816–1892) had coined the term 'prehistory'.

Yet if a new paradigm had been created by the emerging disciplines of geology and archaeology, the lessons of history still played a significant role in early attempts to locate the Indo-European homeland.

Ex oriente lux

The easiest and one of the most persistent solutions to Indo-European origins through the 19th century was the application of the concept *ex oriente lux* ('from the East – light'). This expression is rooted in the observation that history begins in western Asia where we find the earliest written documents.[8] This was not only the setting of the events of the Book of Genesis but also the area of the earliest civilizations in Mesopotamia (and, nearby, Egypt). The great Swedish archaeologist Oscar Montelius (1843–1921) wrote in 1899 that: 'At a time when the peoples of Europe were, so to speak, without any civilisation whatsoever, the Orient and particularly the Euphrates region and the Nile were already in enjoyment of a flourishing culture. The civilisation which gradually dawned on our continent was for long only a pale reflection of Oriental culture.'[9]

In addition to that elusively defined 'civilization', western Asia was also seen to be the birthplace of humans. In the absence of a concept of deep prehistory, it was always going to be a relatively short chronological hop from Adam and Eve to the earliest civilizations. A short chronology could not help but conflate the origins of humans and civilizations, so that there was little expectation that they could have occupied different places geographically. From this point of view, if humankind and civilization had both first emerged in western Asia, then it was logical that the Indo-Europeans along with all other ancient peoples should also have begun their spread from Asia. Jacob Grimm (1785–1863), the older of the Brothers Grimm and a leading linguist of his day, believed that all of European prehistory could be compressed between 10,000 and 2000 BCE, and that all the peoples of Europe and their ancestors had wandered from Asia into Europe at some time in the past.[10] After all, there was a clear trajectory from the earliest high civilizations in Mesopotamia and the Nile, then a somewhat later civilization that spread to Greece, then Italy, and finally, perhaps, to the rest of Europe.

However, with the discovery of Sanskrit the homeland of the Indo-Europeans shifted eastwards from the largely Semitic civilizations known from Mesopotamia.[11] In 1805 German poet and philosopher Friedrich von Schlegel (1772–1829), who regarded Sanskrit itself as the primal language of the Indo-Europeans, set the homeland in northwest India, with its capital in Hastinapur, about 100 km (60 miles) from Delhi.[12] Similarly, in 1813 when Thomas Young wanted to conjecture as to the location of his newly coined 'Indo-Europeans' (see page 23), he decided to 'place it to the south and west of the supposed origin of the human race'.[13] For Young, this pointed to Kashmir. Particularly important was the fact that this argument was also shared by such respected linguists as August Friedrich Pott (1802–1887), who located the homeland in Central Asia, and Max Müller (1823–1900), who famously placed it vaguely 'somewhere in Asia'.[14] Such arguments were already the targets of sarcasm by the end of the century when William Ripley (1867–1941), American economist and author of *The Races of Europe*, wrote that 'in our school days most of us were brought up to regard Asia as the mother of the European peoples.... We were told then an ideal race of men swarmed forth from the Himalayan highlands, disseminating culture right and left as they spread through the barbarous West....'[15]

Over the course of the 19th century the original paradigm – that history began as laid out in the Book of Genesis or in Mesopotamia – had been supplanted by a realization that there had been a long period of prehistory unaccounted for in the biblical narrative; its antiquity was continually being announced with new archaeological and geological discoveries. We could regard this as an example of paradigm shift but, perhaps, it might be better to employ psychologist-economist Daniel Kahneman's term of 'theory-induced blindness'.[16] This reminds us that even the opponents of *ex oriente lux* were capable of locking their own logic into some fairly flawed models. One of the critics of the Asian homeland theory, Canon Isaac Taylor, dismissed it, noting that 'There is no more curious chapter in the whole history of scientific delusion.'[17] But his arguments, based on the most recent archaeological research, reveal his own blindness. They rested on the discoveries, especially in France, of Palaeolithic people, which indicated that the earliest evidence for humankind was now to be found not in Asia but in Europe, where one could trace the same physical types from the most ancient periods to the present. These discoveries had revealed that 'The geographical centre of human history has now been shifted from the East to the West. The earliest existing documents from the history of mankind come not from Asia, but from Western Europe.'[18]

The problems with such reasoning are obvious enough. To begin with, a comparison of the European Palaeolithic with the remains of Near Eastern civilizations is hardly appropriate; it should have been fairly evident that either the civilizations of the Near East must have had prehistoric antecedents as well, or European scholars were going to have to explain how one went from French caves to Iraqi ziggurats. More importantly, the antiquity of *Homo sapiens* in western Europe, which we now know to be long after their first presence in the Near East, has no logical connection with Indo-European origins, a phenomenon that occurred tens of thousands of years later, even according to the chronological scales employed in the late 19th century.[19]

Asian Hordes

Not everyone believed that the Indo-Europeans were the great civilizers of Europe. Instead, some believed they were its barbarian conquerors.

Review the history of Europe, especially from the perspective of the location of Hungary: we find a settled population during the Iron Age that soon encountered the westward migration of the Scythians, Sarmatians, Alans, Huns, Avars and, finally, the Magyars (Hungarians) themselves. All of these people were on an east-to-west trajectory emerging out of Asia as they poured into Europe. It was all too easy to imagine that the Asian steppe was a major cradle of population that periodically spewed out hordes of barbarians into Europe. Such a model readily suited the requirement of explaining how populations in Asia and in Europe all spoke related languages.

It was adopted with respect to the Indo-Europeans at least as early as German linguist Johann Christoph Adelung's *Mithridates* (1806),[20] which pondered how to explain the linguistic relationship between the German and Persian languages. Adelung (1732–1806) saw no reason why the explanation might not lie in a common home in Central Asia, somewhere between Iran and Tibet, 'a country whose unstable hordes have sometimes populated, and more than once shaken Europe'.[21] Cultural historian and librarian Victor Hehn (1813–1890) provided a modern example in the migration of 150,000 Kalmucks from China to the Junggar Basin of eastern Turkestan (now Xinjiang Uyghur Autonomous Region, China), a distance of some 3,200 km (2,000 miles), undertaken in 1771.[22] This model continued throughout the century and well into the 20th century. German linguist Sigmund Feist (1865–1943), for example, noted that we could accept for the prehistoric period the same type of patterns that we find in early history: the movement of populations out of Central Asia into Europe.[23]

The logic of these arguments was, of course, challengeable. Canon Taylor could rattle off a counter-example for each migration from east to west. While Genghis Khan might march from Bactria to Europe, Alexander the Great could lead his troops from Europe to Bactria and so on.[24] Harold Bender could argue that we might just as easily reverse the historical analogy and cited the eastward expansion of the Germans into Slavic territory, or even the Crusades, to demonstrate a west-to-east movement. Both, Bender reasonably argued, were irrelevant to the discussion of Indo-European prehistory.[25]

Immigrants from the North[26]

Migration from or to the east was not the only 'natural' direction envisaged by those who perused historical records. For example, the American historian Willis Boughton (1854–1942) observed that historical evidence (or historical presumptions) indicated that the Celts had invaded Italy from the north, the Goths had spread southwards to conquer and settle in both central and southern Europe, the Indo-Aryans had presumably invaded India from the north and the Dorians – bearers of the most recent of the Greek dialects – had entered Greece from the north.[27] Such evidence suggested that there were three thousand years of evidence that Indo-Europeans had expanded from the Baltic region, thus making it likely that this was the direction from whence they originated. The arguments could be repeated (they almost always were) as late as the 1960s, when Ram Chandra Jain observed that 'No nomadic migrations in Asia have been noticed in history from South to North' hence any attempt to explain Lithuanians, for example, as immigrants from a south Russian homeland was '*prima facie* improbable'.[28] Starting in the north or, at least, dismissing any attempt to explain northern peoples as the result of a migration from the south, goes back to at least Tacitus in his *Germania*, where he asks 'who would leave Asia, or Africa, or Italy for Germany, with its wild country, its inclement skies, its sullen manners and aspect, unless it indeed were their home?'[29]

In all of these cases, it was argued the path of migration had been from north to south, which could be explained by climate. Those occupying a more northerly land would naturally be inclined to migrate to a sunnier south, while no one in their right mind would suppose people had migrated in the opposite direction. This indicated that the Indo-European homeland should lie in a northern region. Of course, and with apologies to the Scandinavians and Balts, this leaves unanswered why anyone in their right mind would ever have migrated northwards to settle in the north in the first place. The logic of this argument presupposes that the Indo-Europeans were a group of masochists whose ancestors had settled in a later homeland that no rational person would have settled to begin with. It is perhaps a bit ironic that the countries occupying the same territory dismissed as absolutely miserable consistently tend to be numbered among the happiest countries in the world.[30]

Past performance principle

Does history always pick winners? The famed Scottish constitutional lawyer and Indologist Arthur Berriedale Keith (1879–1944) attempted to counter German claims of a north European Urheimat by observing the track record of the Germans in expanding their own language. He noted that Germanic-speaking peoples such as the Franks (who settled France), Lombards (Hungary, Italy), Burgundians and Vandals had all failed to extend their Germanic languages outside of Germany. This prompted him to ask rhetorically: 'Is it then likely that the Indo-European speeches were carried as far as India and established by the ancestors of races who later could not maintain outside German borders their own speech?'[31]

This demonstrated that wherever the homeland was, it was not likely to have been in Germany. Of course, no one seemed to envisage applying the counter-argument that the great success in expanding their languages enjoyed by the English and Spanish, for example, indicated an Urheimat in London or Madrid, or that Keith himself was expressing himself in a Germanic language, and that India possessed the second largest number of people speaking a language derived from the early medieval (and decidedly Germanic) Anglo-Saxons.

Another target of the argument by failure would be the steppelands north of the Black and Caspian seas. Shortly after it was proposed as a homeland, German linguist Herman Hirt (1865–1936) argued that it must be dismissed because no one from this area had ever succeeded in incorporating a significant part of Europe within its language sphere.[32] In the 1990s, Peter Kitson reminded us that Arabic is not the language of Iran, Hunnish the language of Europe or Mongolian the language of China, and that 'in all these cases and most vaguely comparable cases of intrusions of pastoral conquerors, the linguistic matrix is that of the preceding settled population'.[33] And still more recently, the British linguist Paul Heggarty offered precisely the same objection: 'History offers precious few instances of the languages of Steppe pastoralists replacing those of farmers, and far more counter-examples.'³⁴ Indeed, this argument emerged as one of the major lines of rebuttal against the Asiatic Hordes model: Scythians, Alans, Huns, Avars and Turks may all have charged into Europe on horseback, but none of them had ever managed to spread a language that actually 'took' among European populations; only one eastern migrant did so, the Magyars, who settled Hungary in the Middle Ages.

The problem with such arguments (both ways) is that they very much resemble appeals to ethnographic analogy, a major topic of debate for archaeologists since my graduate student days.³⁵ Such analogies, to use the language of Lewis Binford, the pioneer of the New Archaeology, may indeed 'provoke questions' that encourage a much closer analysis of all the variables that one might associate with the possibility of a language shift induced by pastoralists, but such historical analogies do not provide answers in themselves. This is especially so as the Asiatic Hordes model derives from a period of widespread horse-mounted pastoralism and not the incipient mobile communities envisaged in the current Steppe model. A possible indication of how vulnerable Heggarty's earlier rebuttal is can be seen in a more recent article, where he and his colleagues have now accepted the spread of a significant number of the European Indo-European branches from an expansion from the steppe by the same people who only a decade earlier were dismissed as linguistically inconsequential.³⁶

In summary, although the Indo-European homeland is positioned temporally before the existence of relevant written records, historical evidence may play a major role in the location of the later expansions of the individual branches of Indo-European. Today, appeals to historical precedents are often limited to providing convenient metaphors for trivializing some of the major current models. For example, the notion that the Indo-Europeans brought agriculture to Europe from Anatolia can be dismissed as just another application of *ex oriente lux*,³⁷ or the theory that brings the Indo-Europeans from the steppelands becomes Asian Hordes reloaded. But these amount to nothing more than cheap shots and the failure of appeals to historical precedent to convince rests primarily with how the results are arrived at and how appropriate the analogies. We have well over a century of conjecture and sniping, but very little thorough analysis that might translate historical examples into useful elements of reasoning (the elusive 'laws' that the New Archaeology always dreamed of recovering). They also largely involve issues of language shift and, as we saw in the previous chapter, the pessimism of anthropological linguists to predict the conditions that would guarantee language shift remains a major obstacle.

CHAPTER 4

Languages, Maps and Geography

Unlike a purely historical approach, attempts to resolve the Indo-European homeland problem by means of examining the geography of languages have demanded much more attention and still remain one of the major techniques of homeland hunting. Behind all of these is the assumption that the spatial distribution of the different Indo-European groups provides a useful clue as to their place of origin. In short, the hope is to determine the point of impact from the splatter pattern.

Robert Gordon Latham

We have already seen in Chapter 2 that Robert Gordon Latham, one of those original sparks that eccentric England was wont to produce,[1] was not only credited with being one of the first scholars to argue for a European homeland, but also did so on the basis of geographical arguments that still retain considerable currency. He came to the study of language only after having served as a doctor and lecturer in forensic medicine, which he abandoned to pursue a career in ethnology and philology. It was a cruel irony that a scholar who had spent a life in the study of language should have ultimately suffered from aphasia before his death.

In the mid-19th century the Indo-European family could be divided into two major groupings, depending on how sounds in Proto-Indo-European (PIE) originally beginning with a velar – the guttural sound we represent today as $\acute{k}, \acute{g}, k, g, k^w$ or g^w – were preserved and altered (or merged) in the daughter languages. To take the most iconic example, the Indo-European branches could be divided into how they reflected the initial $\acute{k}$ sound of PIE *$\acute{k}mtom$ 'hundred'. One group retained the initial velar sound (as either a hard *k* or *b*), while the other palatalized it (like an *s*, except in Albanian where it became a *th*). We can see the palatalization of a velar in the different pronunciations one finds in English of 'Celts' (kelts), an ancient people of Europe, versus the name of the basketball team, the Boston Celtics (seltiks). The first group, the one that retained the velar sound, was labelled with the Latin word for 'hundred', *centum*, while the Iranian word for 'hundred', *satem*, provided the name of the palatalizing group [**4.1**]. The obvious pattern here is that western languages tended to be centum, while east European and Asian languages tended to be satem, so early linguists often dealt with this apparent split in the Indo-European world by imagining some geographical barrier that divided the Indo-European homeland into centum and satem languages:

Centum languages
Celtic (Old Irish *cét*)
Italic (Latin *centum*)
Germanic (Gothic *hunda*)
Greek (*hekatón*)

Satem languages
Baltic (*Lithuanian šimtas*)
Slavic (*Old Church Slavonic sŭto*)
Iranian (*Avestan satəm*)
Indo-Aryan (*Sanskrit śatám*)
Armenian (*sirt* 'heart' versus centum Old Irish *cride*, Greek *kêr*, etc.)
Albanian (*athët* 'sour' versus centum Latin *acer* 'sharp')

4.1 The centum and satem languages recognized in the 19th century. By the early 20th century both Anatolian and Tocharian were added to the centum group, which undermined the notion that it was purely an east–west phenomenon.

Reviewing the distribution of the Indo-European branches, Latham observed that we have two main geographical groups: a variety of different Indo-European languages (both centum and satem) in Europe and two quite similar satem languages (Indo-Aryan and Iranian) in Asia [**4.2**]. Indo-Iranian's nearest linguistic relations appeared to be the satem languages of Baltic and Slavic. In determining whether the original home of all these languages was in Europe or Asia, Latham argued that we should apply the same logic employed by biologists in determining the centre of dispersal of the various species of a single genus: the geographical origin should be located where we find the greatest degree of variation

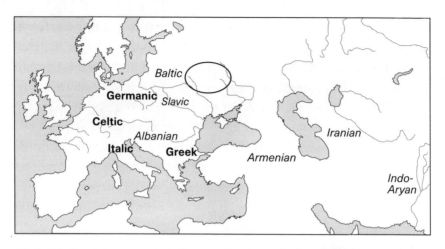

4.2 R. G. Latham's argument: Indo-Aryan and Iranian are both very similar to one another and their nearest linguistic relations are their sister satem languages of Baltic and Slavic. There is far greater linguistic diversity in Europe, where one finds both centum languages (in **bold** on the map) and satem languages (in *italics* on the map). This suggests that it was in Europe that diversity runs deepest and therefore the Indo-Iranian languages should be derived from Europe rather than deriving all the European languages from Asia. The circled area represents the approximate location of Latham's homeland solution, who advanced his arguments before Armenian, another satem language, was recognized as a separate branch of Indo-European.

(or speciation). The logical conclusion, therefore, was that the narrow range of a single Indo-Iranian branch had dispersed from somewhere adjacent to Balto-Slavic rather than have all the different languages of Europe (both centum and satem) proceed from Asia. He argued that to reverse the derivation (as all his contemporaries were arguing) was comparable to deriving the reptiles of Britain from Ireland or the Uralic languages from Hungary.[2]

Latham's reasoning incorporates several models of linguistic spatial analysis borrowed from other disciplines. As to why Indo-Iranian should be derived from Europe, we see the implicit argument that a relatively homogeneous chain of languages suggests they have dispersed comparatively recently because, had they been in place for a long time, one might expect that they should have differentiated more. English, for example, is the common language of populations in Europe, North America, Australia and New Zealand, but excepting extreme dialectical confrontations, these Englishes are all mutually intelligible because they have not had more than a few centuries to develop their own way. The Slavic and Romance languages, on the other hand, began diverging between one and two millennia ago. The degree of similarity between them has evolved significantly enough from their common ancestors to form different languages, although still with some degree of mutual intelligibility. And the Germanic languages, which spread some centuries earlier, are different enough that the narrow English Channel renders English and its closest linguistic relatives (Frisian and Dutch) mutually unintelligible.

Conversely, the heterogeneity of the European languages suggested that they had probably been in place longer than Indo-Iranian, and hence had had a longer time to diverge. Since a fellow satem language, Indo-Iranian, appeared more closely related to Balto-Slavic (there are a few other similarities as well), which is on the eastern periphery of the European chain, it was more logical to view Indo-Iranian as the more recent offshoot of the European chain rather than the reverse. Latham's principle was that the homeland should lie in the area of greatest diversity, and this principle has been employed to identify the homelands of many other language families across the Americas, Asia and Africa.[3] His approach has emerged as the Centre of Gravity technique of homeland hunting, but it has some very serious flaws – which are revealed when we consider the state of homeland hunting at the end of the 19th century.

Anchor bias

Two of the major protagonists of Urheimat research about 1900 employed the geography of Indo-European dispersals to derive two different homelands that would spar with one another over the following decades. Otto Schrader was one of the giants of homeland research who attempted to bring together the evidence of linguistics, ethnology and archaeology to reconstruct as much as possible of the world (both natural and cultural) of the Indo-Europeans. In trying to determine

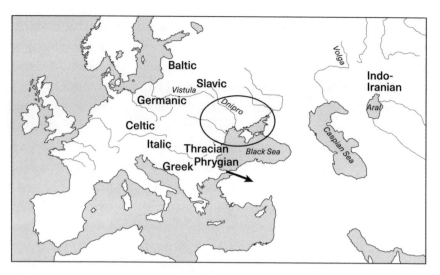

4.3 Otto Schrader's positioning of the earliest locations of the different Indo-European branches supported setting the homeland of Indo-European in the Pontic-Caspian region (represented by the oval line).

the origins of the language family, he began by examining the earliest position of the different Indo-European branches before they showed evidence of later expansions [**4.3**]. For example, the Slavs were positioned between the Vistula and the upper reaches of the Dnipro, with the Balts situated to their north, extending to the Baltic Sea. The Celts occupied both central and Atlantic Europe and the Germans held northern Europe. The Balkans not only were the area of residence of the historically attested Thracians, but ancient testimony also suggested that this region served as the staging area for the migrations of the Phrygians to central Anatolia and the Armenians still further east. It is also from this region that the Greeks might have migrated to the south. Mirroring the north-to-south movements of the Greeks were the Italic peoples, who should have entered Italy via the northeast (Venice) and hence might also have been settled earlier in or near the Balkans. All of these European branches might then be rolled back to an area northwest of the Black Sea among the fertile black soils (chernozems) between the Carpathians and the Dnipro. It is from this area that one could most easily envisage the dispersal of the European branches, along riverways such as the Danube, to the north, west and south. As for the Indo-Iranians, their staging area should have been Central Asia from whence they descended into both the Indus and Iran. This provided a second fixed point. Both of these staging areas were about equidistant from the Volga, and the most economical geographical solution (along with a series of other arguments that we will explore later) suggested that the homeland might be located in the Pontic-Caspian steppe from whence Indo-Europeans migrated to the east (the Indo-Iranians) and to the west (the Europeans).[4]

Herman Hirt's reputation rests primarily on his works on Indo-European phonology and a seven-volume grammar of Indo-European. However, like Schrader, he attempted to produce a major synthetic account of all the Indo-European groups as well as the Proto-Indo-Europeans. Hirt examined precisely the same evidence as Schrader but drew a different conclusion as to the location of the homeland [**4.4**].[5] He believed that the homeland must be located in the area where we find the 'greatest associated mass' of Indo-Europeans, which, for him, meant the area of the Celts, Germans, Balts and Slavs between northern France and western Russia.[6] Like Schrader he attempted to pull each group back into their most likely staging area. The Celts were placed east of the Rhine before their expansion and the closely related Italics were immediately to their south on the Danube, while the staging area of the Greeks was set in Hungary. The Germans were set in northern Germany and southern Scandinavia, the Balts and Slavs essentially in northeast Poland and Belarus, the Thracians immediately to their south. The Indo-Iranians were located immediately east of the Balts and Slavs, east of the Dnipro. Schrader's appeal to major rivers as conduits for Indo-European expansion was rejected by Hirt, who saw them rather as barriers that frequently coincided with political or linguistic borders. So, when he ultimately placed the Urheimat more or less between eastern Germany and Poland, he had the Vistula forming a natural barrier that accounted for the split between western centum speakers and eastern satem groups.

These two geographical models were constructed before Anatolian and Tocharian were recognized as Indo-European branches, and their incorporation into the Indo-European family caused havoc with

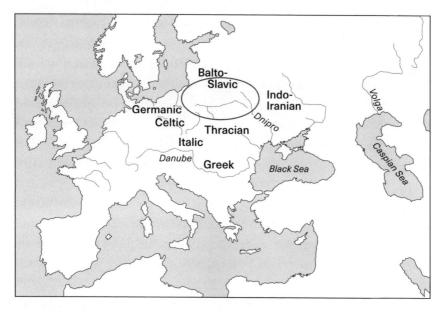

4.4 Herman Hirt's emphasis on the positioning of the major north and west Indo-European branches supported an Indo-European homeland in northeast Europe (represented by the oval line).

these earlier frameworks. To some extent, Anatolian was less problematic as both models already accounted for later immigrants to Anatolia (Phrygians) from a secondary homeland in the east Balkans. The Anatolians could, therefore, simply be regarded as earlier immigrants from the same region. But Tocharians were a real nuisance, not so much because it required explaining the presence of Indo-Europeans in what is now a part of western China (both the Indic settlement of the Ganges and the Tocharian occupation of the Tarim Basin are at about the same longitude), but rather because the Tocharian phonological system was centum and not satem, so any homeland had to explain how a 'western' language such as Tocharian could manage to find itself to the east of the 'easternmost' satem languages (which, according to Gordon Childe, gave a boost to the supposedly defunct Asian homeland solution).[7]

Both models of Indo-European origins can hardly avoid charges of anchoring bias, since they are constructed around establishing a single fixed point that predetermines the location of their respective homelands. Schrader, for example, begins his survey of branch homelands with the Slavs and, after excluding their historically attested migrations, we have a Slavic Urheimat stretching from the Carpathians east to the middle Dnipro, and then each Indo-European group can be positioned with respect to that of the Slavs or the growing assembly of homelands clustered around the Slavs. Only the Indo-Iranians lay out of contact and hence Schrader split the difference to produce his steppe homeland. Hirt, on the other hand, subtly employed the Germanic territory as a fixed anchor, which draws the staging areas of the other languages further to the north and west. And, as Hirt argued, just as one seeks the homeland of each group towards the centre of their expansion, so too should the homeland of the entire family be located towards the centre of the various homelands of the different branches.[8]

It should be emphasized here that once a homeland, any homeland, is selected, the branches will fall into place and although they may be argued about at length, often the dispersals require no more thought than what end of the Sharpie one should hold. I offer an example prepared by the noted Italian linguist Giacomo Devoto from his massive and impressively illustrated monograph[9] on the Indo-Europeans, where we view the dispersal of the Indo-European branches from a Danubian (Linear Ware) homeland [4.5]. Be aware, though, that it only takes a little judicious tweaking of the direction of your arrows to make just about any homeland look plausible (excepting perhaps Serrano's Black Sun).

But a more serious problem, and one that has perpetually dogged homeland hunters, is that both Schrader and Hirt built their homelands on a cartographical mirage. We have already seen in Chapter 2 Latham's early application of the Centre of Gravity approach to identifying the homeland, which he borrowed from the natural sciences (the great Russian geneticist Nikolaj Vavilov (1887–1943) employed it in determining the homelands of domesticated plants and Edward Sapir applied it to linguistics). Adopting a similar but statistically reinforced approach to the *current* distribution of the Indo-European languages finds that the Indo-European homeland should actually lie in northern Pakistan.[10] That was easy, wasn't it? Of course, it is entirely a product of

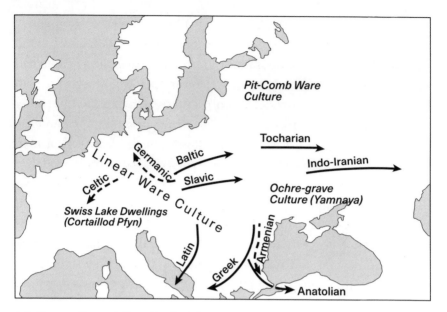

4.5 Giacomo Devoto's Danubian Indo-European homeland and proposed expansions of its branches.

the proliferation of modern Indo-Aryan languages (70 per cent of the modern Indo-European languages belong to the Indo-Iranian branch, so inevitably the Centre of Gravity is going to lie in South Asia), although the insertion of earlier extinct languages suggested secondary and tertiary homelands in Anatolia and the Balkans. The obvious problem with such exercises is the census date of your map of the Indo-European world.

Fig. 1.4 on page 24 provides us with a standard image of the different Indo-European groups *c.* 500 BCE, which is about as recent as one can make a map without causing too much of a temporal distortion of the various branches by placing contemporary languages on the same map as extinct ones. It situates all the groups in their general (often later) historical positions, but it is questionable that each branch represents a comparable position in their evolution. Some of the branches may have only recently crystallized from Late Indo-European (e.g. Germanic), while others may be well into their fragmentation or even extinction (Anatolian). For example, if the map had been drawn at 500 CE, Italic

CHAPTER 4

would have ranged from the Atlantic to the Black Sea (Proto-Romance), while Celtic would have been largely confined to Britain and Ireland (the good cartographer would have been aware that the Bretons had only begun migrating to Armorica a century before). Moreover, even if we stick to 500 BCE, the borders of all these branches are incredibly vague: is Celtic (at this time) rooted in central Europe or on the Atlantic coast? Where precisely was Tocharian located at this time, as our map dates to about a thousand years before we have documentary evidence of its existence?

What happens if we only employ the earliest historically verified evidence to draw our map? This would be a map representing the situation *c.* 1500 BCE [**4.6**], where we would find several Anatolian languages occupying central and western Anatolia, a 'hint' (names recorded in non-Indo-European documents) of the existence of Indo-Aryan in

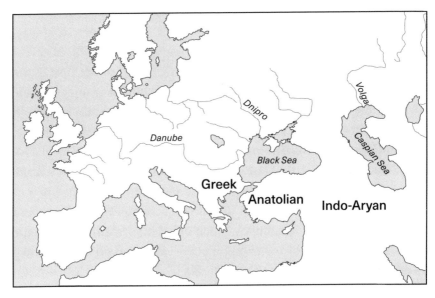

4.6 A map of the documented Indo-European world *c.* 1500 BCE, which was confined to Anatolian, (Mycenean) Greek and traces of Indo-Aryans in the Near East in northern Syria. The temptation of placing the homeland in the middle (Anatolia) is countered by the fact that Greek and Indo-Aryan are much more closely related to one another than either is to Anatolian.

northern Syria, and our earliest attestation of Greek in the Linear B tablets of Mycenaean Greece. What does this tell us about where these languages came from? About the only clue we have is that, as writing had spread to these areas from southwest Asia, their homeland was not likely to have been south of a chain that ran from Greece through Anatolia to northern Syria, since we do not find any written testimony of their presence there. Beyond that, the geographical evidence is not particularly informative because we do not know where the ancestors of all the other Indo-European languages were hiding at this time; we are only getting a biased glimpse of the Indo-European world as it entered the periphery of the earliest literate world. And, as we will later see, even if the entire Indo-European family consisted only of a chain of Greek, Anatolian and Indo-Aryan, and we were tempted to set their homeland in the middle of the chain (Anatolia), we would run into another problem, namely we know that Greek and Indo-Aryan are far more closely related to one another than either is to Anatolian, so how did they wind up on either side of Anatolian? Our different Indo-European branches do not simply occupy places across Eurasia; they also live in family trees.

Phylogeny

The phylogeny of Indo-European is one of those disputed territories that every homeland solution must somehow satisfy. Armed with a family tree of the linguistic relationships of all the Indo-European branches to one another, it might be possible to translate the relative age of each branch and its relationship with the other Indo-European languages into plausible spatial and temporal relationships. Almost every history of Indo-European studies attributes the initiation of the concept of producing a family tree of the language family with German linguist August Schleicher (1821–1868); there were, however, some earlier simpler (and admittedly less well-informed) attempts, such as one produced by the Scottish military officer and translator Vans Kennedy who, in 1828, produced his own (somewhat peculiar) sketch of the Indo-European languages [4.7].

CHAPTER 4

```
              BABYLONIAN, OR SANSKRIT
               Language of Asia Minor
      ┌───────────────┬───────────────┐
    Latin           Greek       Thracian, extinct
  ┌───┼───┐                  ┌─────────┼─────────┐
French Italian Spanish, etc.  Anglo-Saxon German Swedish, etc.
```

4.7 The relationship of the Indo-European languages according to Vans Kennedy in 1828. Kennedy believed that the 'proto-language' was Sanskrit, whose original home was located in Mesopotamia (hence 'Babylonian'). He deliberately excluded Celtic from the family tree.

But we must turn to Schleicher, whose life was tragically cut short by tuberculosis. His impact on Indo-European studies is fundamental, for it was with Schleicher that we find the earliest attempts to reconstruct the actual form of the proto-language as well as the application of the model of a biological tree to language relationships. Schleicher's first published tree of the Indo-European languages came in 1853 when there were only eight branches to be arranged [**4.8**]. Already at this time the phylogeny could be employed to help establish the homeland. First, as often noted, the position of each branch on the tree roughly correlated with their relative geographical location.[11] However, Schleicher himself observed that the tree not only indicated the different relationships between the branches, but also the more western the location of the language (or people), the earlier their separation from the original language, meaning the exit roster from the homeland would read Celts first, then Balto-Slavic-Germanic, then Latin and Greek, with the Indo-Iranians remaining behind (in their Asiatic homeland) before they migrated southeastwards.[12]

Schleicher later revised his tree and settled down to the more familiar abstract representation of 1861 [**4.9**]. In this he plotted the internal relationship of all the different Indo-European branches from the single stocks (Celtic, Italic, etc.) down the tree to the earlier and thicker branches, with glorious Germanic compound names such as

LANGUAGES, MAPS AND GEOGRAPHY

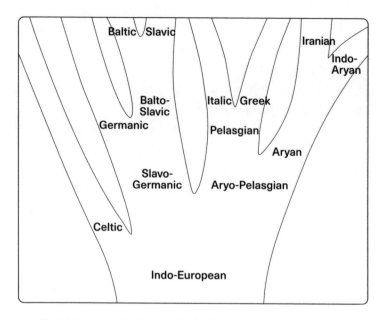

4.8 August Schleicher's first family tree of Indo-European languages (1853). Pelasgian was the ancient Greek name for the people who supposedly occupied Greece before the Greeks.

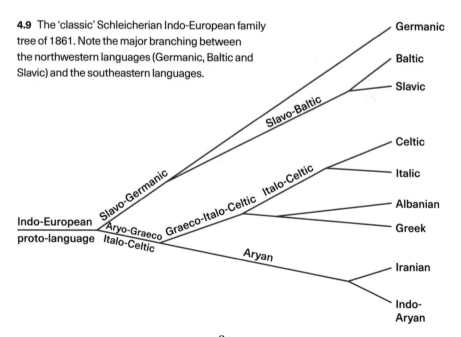

4.9 The 'classic' Schleicherian Indo-European family tree of 1861. Note the major branching between the northwestern languages (Germanic, Baltic and Slavic) and the southeastern languages.

ariograecoitalokeltische (Aryo-Graeco-Italo-Celtic).[13] This marked the beginning of the pursuit of the perfect tree, which has moved from the dusty philological shelves of libraries to the premier scientific journals in the world, involving sophisticated computer programs and monumentally unimpressed linguists.

It is useful to consider how far (or not) we have come since Schleicher's time on the problem of the phylogeny of Indo-European. Schleicher recognized a division of Indo-European into two major branches: a northwestern group (Germanic, Baltic and Slavic) and a southeastern group that comprised all the other languages. He also recognized a series of joint branches: Indo-Iranian, Balto-Slavic, Italo-Celtic and perhaps Albanian and Greek.

A half-century later in a classic study of the relationship between the Indo-European dialects, the great French linguist Antoine Meillet (1866–1936) divided the (known) Indo-European branches into two natural groups: eastern (Indo-Iranian, Balto-Slavic, Armenian and Albanian) and western (Italo-Celtic, Germanic), but here Greek was placed intermediate, sharing some forms with Italic in the west but also with the eastern languages, while Germanic behaved like an aberrant planet whose orbit takes it all over the place from one phylogeny to the next.[14] The divisions were based on examining a large series of isoglosses (features shared by some but not all the languages). For example, verbs expressing a past tense might not only change their endings but also prefix an *e*- to the verbal root: hence the root **bher-* 'carry' becomes 'he carried' in Greek *e-phere*, Armenian *e-ber* and Sanskrit *a-bharat* (Sanskrit changed both PIE **e* and **o* to *a*), but this *e*-augment is only found in these languages (and Phrygian). It should be emphasized that the two groups showed no evidence of hard and fast borders, and there were also isoglosses that linked individual languages of each group with the other, as could be seen in the case not only of Greek but also Germanic. From the evidence, however, Meillet believed that the languages had dispersed outwards radially with the relative geographical positions in place from the earliest expansions. Although Meillet presented an exhaustive list of all the shared points, or isoglosses, both phonological and grammatical, his ultimate conclusions were not explicitly quantitative.

In 1928, the Polish anthropologist and founder of computational linguistics Jan Czekanowski (1882–1965) attempted to examine twenty-two isoglosses statistically, measuring the presence or absence of such isoglosses in each language to determine a coefficient of similarity, allowing him to express statistically to what extent the various branches resembled or differed from one another. Then ten years later a much larger attempt to statistically classify the Indo-European languages was undertaken by a somewhat unlikely source, Alfred Kroeber (1876–1960), one of the world's greatest anthropologists whose expertise lay primarily with Native American peoples and languages. Kroeber and his collaborator C. D. Chrétien (1904–1969) examined seventy-four of Meillet's phonological and grammatical elements.[15] The results confirmed the principal ones suggested by Schleicher nearly a century before – Indo-Iranian, Balto-Slavic and Italo-Celtic – after which the coefficients fell dramatically to yield Germanic-Baltic and Iranian-Slavic. These results also supported Meillet's view that the spatial arrangement of the languages correlated with their linguistic relationships.

Several years later Kroeber and Chrétien obtained sufficient data from Hittite, the primary representative of the Anatolian branch, to add it to their computations and were rather surprised by the results. They believed, nevertheless, that they correlated with the recent assertion that, in the strict sense, Hittite (and the other Anatolian languages) was not derived from the same proto-language as the other Indo-European languages but rather was a sister (rather than a daughter) language, and both Anatolian and Proto-Indo-European were daughters of an Indo-Hittite (now more frequently known as 'Indo-Anatolian') language family.[16] Finally, in the year of his death (1960), the 84-year-old Kroeber returned to the subject, admitting that his earlier work looked like 'a dead limb of effort' as it had hardly been followed up. He revisited his earlier work in which he had withdrawn his attempt to provide a diagrammatic representation of the relationships, and now explained and offered just such a diagram [**4.10**].[17] Although Kroeber had lamented the dearth of statistical approaches to language diversity, during the last decade of his life another scholar of Native American languages was developing a new statistical approach that claimed not only to be able to subgroup the

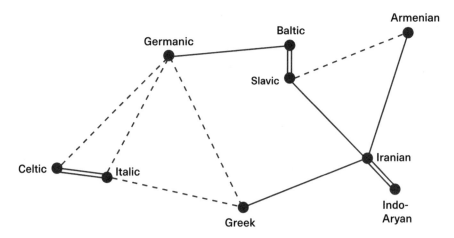

4.10 A simplified version of Alfred Kroeber's diagram of the relationship between the major Indo-European branches. Double lines indicate similarities close enough to support joint branches, e.g. Italo-Celtic, Balto-Slavic and Indo-Iranian.

Indo-European (or Indo-Anatolian) languages, but also to provide absolute dates to the language branches and ultimately evaluate the validity of any homeland solution.

Lexicostatistics and glottochronology

Like Kroeber, Morris Swadesh (1909–1967) specialized in the indigenous languages of the Americas, ultimately settling in Mexico both for intellectual and political (the 'Red Scare') reasons. Swadesh developed two statistical approaches to historical linguistics that employed as its database the vocabulary of languages rather than the evidence of phonology or grammar. He was not the first to do so since a century earlier the German polymath Ernst Förstemann (1822–1906) – mathematician, linguist and librarian who made some early contributions to Mayan decipherment – had wondered whether it was possible to establish the linguistic and chronological relationships of the Indo-European languages by examining statistically the patterns of their shared vocabulary.[18] Förstemann's data was drawn from four language branches (Sanskrit, Greek, Latin and

Germanic), and in each he compared the presence or absence of cognate names of Indo-European mammals and birds. The results were several tables indicating the number of pairwise correspondences [4.11]. He indicated that his list was likely to be quickly supplanted because cognates between Indo-Iranian and the European languages were being discovered at an enormous pace. He also noted how pairwise comparisons might not correlate with the overall chronology of language separations thanks to unequal rates of language change or later re-establishment of contacts involving borrowing. It is almost as if he knows that something numerically useful can be done with such data but he can't quite see the way forward.

Sanskrit and Latin	33
Sanskrit and Germanic	38
Sanskrit and Greek	42
Greek and Latin	56
Greek and Germanic	63
Latin and Germanic	65

4.11 Ernst Förstemann's 1854 list of pairwise correspondences across 119 words for mammals and birds in four Indo-European language branches.

Förstemann's concentration entirely on a narrow semantic field (animals) was not likely to lead very far. Swadesh realized that the linguistic data to be crunched must be drawn from the basic vocabulary of a language (sun, moon, ear, eye, see, hear, etc.), which he thought (in some cases erroneously) were universal concepts marked in any language and the least likely to be replaced by borrowing. A comparison of cognate forms between daughter languages indicated how close or far any two languages were from each other, and permitted one to arrange the languages into their appropriate subgroups (lexicostatistics). But Swadesh also argued that while the overall vocabulary of a language was liable to massive replacement (for example, about 30–40 per cent of the English vocabulary is, very roughly, estimated to derive from French), the basic vocabulary (defined by a 100-word list) was far more robust and tended to decay (like radiocarbon) at a stable rate, from which one could predict how long two related languages had been separated (glottochronology). For example, after a thousand years a single language would be expected to lose 14 basic words out of the 100-word list

– i.e. retain 86 per cent of its basic vocabulary – and if compared with a related language we would expect that they would both share 66 per cent of their basic vocabulary after 1,000 years of separation. In 1953, a century after Förstemann,[19] Swadesh entered the world of the Urheimat hunters when he commented on Marija Gimbutas's first foray into the Indo-European problem where on archaeological grounds she had suggested that Germanic had separated from Slavic c. 2000–1800 BCE. Employing English, French and Russian as proxies for the Germanic, Italic and Slavic branches, Swadesh claimed that the lexicostatistic date indicated a separation of 3,700 years (1700 BCE), which provided support for Gimbutas's theory.[20]

Swadesh's paper, although usually ignored, represents one of those 'small steps' in an 'enormous leap' scenario. As mentioned earlier, the search for the homeland is both a geographical and a space-time problem. One of the absolute prerequisites of a valid homeland solution is that it not only locates the source of the Indo-European languages in the right place at the right time, but also is able to trace from this place the paths of all the branches to their historical seats, again at the right time, and this is what Swadesh was hoping to deliver.

His next major contribution (perhaps more to the debate than the solution) was an appendix to a monograph on the Indo-European homeland by another political refugee in Mexico, the Spanish archaeologist Pedro Bosch-Gimpera (1891–1974).[21] Here Swadesh provided a series of separation dates between the Indo-European branches where the average date of separation between nine of the languages and Hittite was c. 3900 BCE. One might then gain the impression that the proto-language could be set in very general terms between 4500 and 3500 BCE, which has been the ballpark figure for most, although by no means all, scholars in pursuit of the homeland. For example, in 1950 American linguists George Trager (1906–1992) – who dismissed glottochronology and preferred to draw his conclusion from the well-honed 'hunch' of linguistic experience – and Henry Lee Smith (1913–1972) settled on a date of c. 3500 BCE for the separation of Hittite,[22] while the Canadian linguist Henri Wittmann employed glottochronology to date it first to c. 3900 BCE and then 3600 BCE.[23]

But before we become comfortable about the reasonably close correspondence between linguistic estimates and glottochronology, note that in 1973 the Austrian Hittologist Johann Tischler (1946–2019) applied Swadesh's 200- and 100-word lists to dating the break-up of the Indo-European languages, which revealed that the word lists hardly gave consistent evaluations: Hittite separated at 6400 BCE according to the 200-word list but 8800 BCE on the 100-word list, and generally there was an 800–1,000-year discrepancy between the lists.[24]

Since it was first proposed, glottochronology has had a bumpy ride, facing a series of objections – for example, some of the test items (harder to test than one might imagine) are not as 'basic' as others; determining which word most appropriately fills the semantic slot from a range of synonyms – but foremost of all being the contention that there is, in reality, an average rate of lexical decay. The technique has nevertheless managed to survive by practitioners constantly tweaking the algorithm and improving the screening of the input data. The literature and issues on the subject are far too great to be addressed here,[25] and we can cut to the chase by jumping to the 1990s when computational approaches to phylogeny began to be taken more seriously – that is, we begin to see computationally generated trees that often agree in general with traditional evaluations. The first of these began to appear in the 1990s from a team around the American linguist Don Ringe, based primarily on the evidence of phonology and morphology rather than lexical items, which is far more in concert with the traditional approach to assembling language phylogenies. The version published in 2002[26] [**4.12**] has been influential in assessing solutions to the homeland problem; we will regard it as a sort of standard model (not necessarily the correct one) against which we can compare more recent attempts.

Next came a series of publications centred on the work of the University of Auckland team of Russell Gray and Quentin Atkinson,[27] evolutionary biologists and psychologists, based on purely or primarily lexical evidence but employing a different analytical approach that not only presented somewhat different phylogenies but also absolute dates. Particularly influential was their major publication in 2012 in the international journal *Science*, which came down solidly in favour of associating the origin

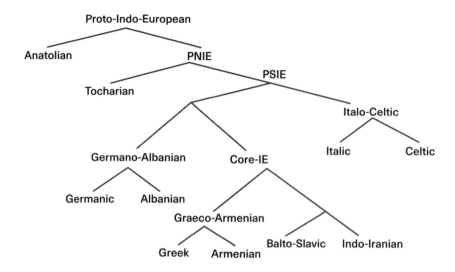

4.12 The 2002 phylogeny proposed by the team led by Don Ringe. The first split involves Anatolian, while the second split reflects all of the other Indo-European languages, referred to here as Proto-North-Indo-European (PNIE), splitting between Tocharian and Proto-South-Indo-European (PSIE). Note: In this book, PNIE equates with Core-Indo-European (rather than the more limited designation indicated in this tree).

of the Indo-Europeans with the expansion of the Neolithic economy and farmers from Anatolia. Three years later a somewhat similar exercise emanating from the University of California, Berkeley under the leadership of linguist Andrew Garrett presented a competing phylogeny and set of dates that supported the steppe homeland [**4.13 A**].[28] And by 2015 linguist Asya Pereltsvaig and historical geographer Martin Lewis launched an entire monograph largely devoted to refuting the earlier Gray and Atkinson paper.[29] Then, in 2021, linguists in Moscow – a well-known centre of computational linguistics – produced their own phylogeny whose dates again favoured a steppe origin for the Indo-Europeans [**4.13 B**].[30] By 2023, however, the Auckland team (now based in Leipzig but let's leave it as 'Auckland') had updated their tree and again threw the date of Proto-Indo-Anatolian back into the Neolithic [**4.13 C**].[31]

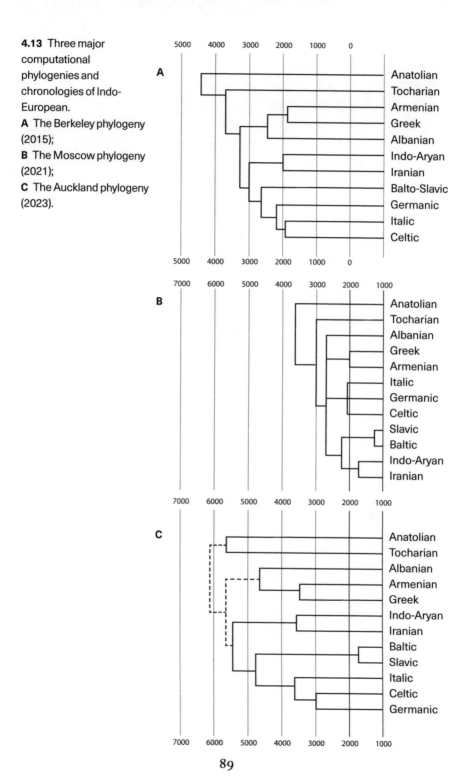

4.13 Three major computational phylogenies and chronologies of Indo-European.
A The Berkeley phylogeny (2015);
B The Moscow phylogeny (2021);
C The Auckland phylogeny (2023).

How does the homeland hunter deal with a constant stream of ever-changing phylogenies and dates? Any acceptable solution must explain how the various Indo-European languages ultimately achieved their historical positions and that at least must not be contradicted by the evidence of the phylogeny – the internal relationship – between the Indo-European branches. If we take the last twenty years of computative analysis, we can at least discern areas of broad agreement that provide a convenient checklist of constituency gates that any viable homeland solution must pass through.

First, all the solutions acknowledge that the first split was between Anatolian and the rest of the Indo-European languages, some regarding the split so deep that Anatolian should be regarded as a sister branch of Indo-European, while others would still adhere to its traditional position as a daughter branch of Proto-Indo-European that simply left home very early. However one decides to view the split, it does have important geographical and chronological ramifications. Either Anatolian left the area of the ancestors of the other Indo-European languages, who together developed a series of common innovations (twenty-three semantic, morphological, phonological and syntactic innovations have been claimed as strongly attested[32]), or it was the last common ancestor of the other Indo-European languages that left first to evolve into Core-Indo-European before it split into its daughter languages. And, to complicate matters, it is always possible that both Proto-Anatolian and Proto-Indo-European left their original home. These different scenarios will become critically important when we examine the impact of palaeogenomics on the homeland problem.

The second split is somewhat more contentious, but majority opinion regards the next separation to be associated with Tocharian.[33] This means that the earliest two Indo-Anatolian languages achieved their historical seats about 4,000 km (2,500 miles) apart from one another (or, if an early Hittite speaker in Anatolia with exceedingly strong lungs had shouted, a proto-Tocharian with exceedingly good hearing would have had to wait nearly three and a half hours before he heard the shout).

There is, of course, another issue beyond the phylogenetic relationship between Anatolian, Tocharian and the other Indo-European languages

– the date of the splits. Here matters are more problematic as we can see if we survey the split dates of Anatolian and Tocharian from a series of studies published this century [**4.14**].

	Auckland 2003	Auckland 2012	Berkeley 2015	Moscow 2021	Auckland 2023
Anatolian	6700	6000	4500–4000	3700	4932
Tocharian	5900	4900	3800–3300	3000	4932

4.14 Split dates for the earliest two Indo-European branches in approximate years BCE from five major computational studies (note the Auckland 2023 date is the median of 6613–3403).

While there is some agreement that Anatolian followed by Tocharian represent the first splits, the date of those splits descends into a constituency problem where the Auckland team suggests dates consistently about 1,300–1,500 years earlier than those of Berkeley and Moscow, and the team sets Tocharian at least a millennium earlier than the other papers. We will return to these issues in Chapter 7.

After Tocharian, there is far more disparity in positioning the various branches except for the recognition of Schleicher's paired branches, which still appear to stand. Few if any would dispute Indo-Iranian as a single branch, and even sceptics of Balto-Slavic and Italo-Celtic branches in the strict sense (i.e. that they shared a common intermediate proto-language that we can reconstruct) still tend to admit that they must have had close contact relations before separating/evolving. Since all of these pairings comprise geographically adjacent language groups, they are not particularly problematic nor necessarily very instructive. You do not have to be excessively creative to find a common homeland for Baltic and Slavic somewhere between the Baltic and the Carpathians, or situate the ancestors of the Celts and the Italics somewhere north of the Alps. If we advance further up Schleicher's tree, Balto-Slavic connects with Germanic in a 'North European' group. You will find the same constellation in the traditionally assembled (non-computational) tree of Gamkrelidze and Ivanov [**4.15**].[34] But while many trees combine Balto-Slavic and Germanic with Italo-Celtic into a bundle of western or northwestern branches,[35] Ringe's trees link Balto-Slavic much closer to

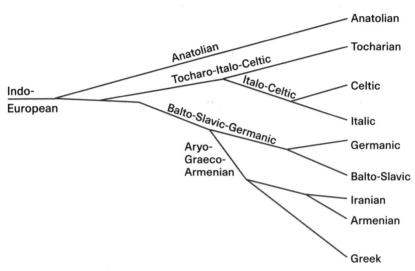

4.15 A traditional (non-computational) Indo-European family tree from Tamaz Gamkrelidze and Vyacheslav Ivanov (1984).

Indo-Iranian than the other European languages. Moreover, there is a tradition of regarding Italo-Celtic as an archaic peripheral language to be linked with the same centrifugal expansion credited to Tocharian, while others have placed Italo-Celtic much further downstream. Unravelling all of these conflicting relationships is again a major issue of satisfying different constituencies. So long as geographically proximate languages are being grouped together this does not have a major impact on sorting out the various homeland theories, but there are a few other generally agreed relationships that do impinge on at least some of them.

It is difficult to find anyone who groups Europe's two Classical languages, Greek and Latin (Italic), closely together. Thus, any attempt to associate the spread of Indo-European across the Mediterranean with the spread of farming receives no support from a phylogeny that does not accommodate a chain of migrations: Anatolia > Greece > Italy.

Another potentially interesting relationship is found in both traditional and computed phylogenies that support a Graeco-Armenian pairing, since these two languages are not only not adjacent to one another but are also separated by a totally different branch – Anatolian. As we saw earlier, the way around this problem was the presumption that the Armenians along with the Phrygians derived from the Balkans, which was the same presumed staging area as the Greeks. The position of Armenian, however, has long been a contentious area. Some support the idea of a Proto-Graeco-Armenian, where the two languages once shared an immediate common ancestor; others believe that at best one could say their ancestors were in mutual contact with one another, but that Armenian also had contacts with not only Phrygian but also Indo-Iranian and possibly Balto-Slavic. We are now in a territory where we must distinguish between the purely linguistic arguments and geographical implications. It is one thing for linguists to assert that there is insufficient evidence to accept the existence of Proto-Graeco-Armenian because, by employing the comparative method, a distinct Graeco-Armenian proto-language or stage between Proto-Indo-European and the two historical branches cannot be reconstructed, yet on the other hand, when it comes to the geographical relationship between Greek and Armenian, conclude that, while there was no common proto-language, 'the dialects ancestral to Greek and Armenian were in proximity in prehistoric times, say up to the late 3rd millennium BC',[36] or as the Armenian scholar Hrach Martirosyan concluded:

> that Armenian, Greek, (Phrygian) and Indo-Iranian were dialectally close to each other. Within this hypothetical dialect group, Proto-Armenian was situated between Proto-Greek (to the west) and Proto-Indo-Iranian (to the east). The Indo-Iranians then moved eastwards, while the Proto-Armenians and Proto-Greeks remained in a common geographical region for a long period and developed numerous shared innovations.[37]

So, although one can deny a relationship as close as a shared proto-language, the geographical relations that place Greek and Armenian at some time close to one another are still very much on the table. And it is problems such as this, where the position of a language in the family tree seems to share connections with multiple branches, that long ago led some linguists to be very sceptical of relying so heavily on a tree-like phylogeny to describe the dispersal of the Indo-European languages. Exit August Schleicher and enter his rebellious student, Johannes Schmidt.

The wave model

As long ago as 1872, Johannes Schmidt (1843–1901) recognized the difficulties caused by the tree model and proposed his famous alternative approach to understanding the interrelationship of the Indo-European languages – his Wellentheorie ('wave theory'). In a short 68-page book,[38] Schmidt presented evidence that while the individual branches could often lead us back to a single consistent reconstruction, all too often we were left with different reconstructions that suggested we were working from dialect forms. Moreover, we also have abundant evidence that supposedly distinct branches of Schleicher's trees were sharing isoglosses – similar sound changes, grammatical forms or unique lexical items – that suggested that the branches could not have been evolving on their own entirely separate from one another but were often in contact, influencing each other [4.16].

One of the problems of employing a wave model to triangulate the location of the homeland is that many of the early projections were based

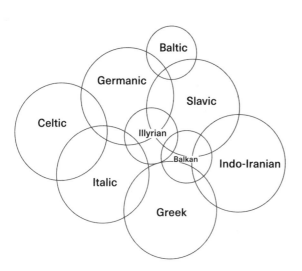

4.16 An example of Johannes Schmidt's wave model.[39] The 'Balkan' designation covers Thraco-Phrygian, Albanian and Armenian. Since such wave models tended to reflect the relative geographical position of the historically known Indo-European branches, it was often assumed that the branches had formed during the final stage of Indo-European unity and had experienced a gradual centrifugal dispersal.

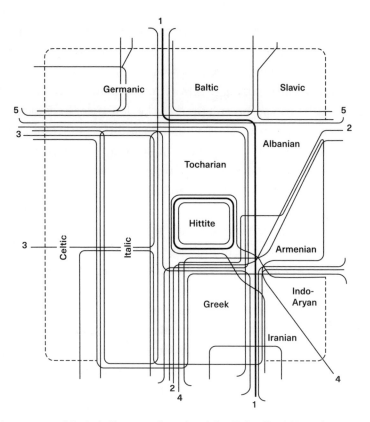

4.17 A wave map of the Indo-European branches (after R. Anttila 1989, 305).

on a minimum of evidence. To get a more recent visualization of this we can jump a century ahead to look at a frequently reproduced wave model of Indo-European by my own former professor, Raimo Anttila (1935–2023) [4.17].

The various lines indicate isoglosses, marking out branches that share a common feature. For example, the dark line (1) indicates the division between the centum (left) and satem (right) languages. This division is obviously crossed by other isoglosses such as (2), which indicates how the satem languages of Indo-Iranian and Armenian share the same genitive ending *-osyo with the centum language Greek. Note how this challenges the earlier notion that the division between centum and satem was regarded as so fundamental that homelands were often positioned to straddle different sides of a major river to account for such a split but, as you can see, that particular genitive ending managed to swim across. In some cases, isoglosses affect only part of a branch – for example (3), where the PIE *k^w sound was retained in some Celtic and Italic languages but changed to *p* in other languages of the same two branches. From the perspective of borders, one might read the density of lines bordering a language as an indicator of its similarity or difference from its neighbour. Only one isogloss (4) separates Indo-Aryan from Iranian as might be expected from two branches that share a shallow common Proto-Indo-Iranian ancestry, while Baltic and Slavic only have two lines. On the other hand, the nine lines between Greek and Italic indicate that the two Classical languages had very different histories and we can understand why linguists tended to be unimpressed with models of Indo-European dispersals where one imagines Indo-European travelling from Anatolia to Greece and then to Italy.

Regarding his map of Indo-European, Anttila noted two important problems: one, any dialect map like this requires value judgments as to which isoglosses are the most critical for assessing relationships (recall here that Kroeber and Chrétien employed seventy-four diagnostic dialect features in their earlier studies drawn from even more listed in Antoine Meillet's classic survey of the Indo-European dialects); and, two, it is difficult to turn such a map into one that indicates *when* the isoglosses formed. For example, while many if not most of the isoglosses were presumably formed after the initial spread of Indo-European, Anttila believed that (5), the replacement of the case marker *-*bh* by *-*m* in Germanic, Baltic and Slavic, was already established in the proto-language itself;[40] in 2021, American linguist Douglas Adams reinforced this idea by projecting both endings to PIE (but both only surviving together in Tocharian).[41] If one were to accept this, it suggests that the (northwest?) corner of the homeland was occupied by the ancestors of Germanic and Balto-Slavic (see **4.15** and **4.16**), yet others (see **4.12**) have not regarded Germanic as particularly close to Balto-Slavic. This leaves the homeland hunter playing whack-a-mole with isoglosses.

In any event, Schmidt argued that the idea of an Indo-European tree sprouting distinct language branches should be abandoned for a far more realistic and empirically supported model. Schmidt's image of the black box period (Indo-European after Anatolian and Tocharian – both of which were in any case unknown in Schmidt's time) was of an inclined plane stretching from the territories where we later find Sanskrit in the east to Celtic in the west. Across this was a common Indo-European language lacking distinct language boundaries but rather a chain of dialects (A, B, C, D ... X). Innovations occurred across this chain, welled up in one area but spread only so far. Due to a variety of potential causes – political, religious, social – one dialect might swallow its neighbour(s) and this would transform the smooth plane of a chain of mutually intelligible dialects into a staircase structure of increasingly differentiated dialects and then languages, as more distant (and different) neighbours eventually pushed their borders against one another.

This model, or something very much like it, still survives in theory. Andrew Garrett, 136 years after Schmidt, also proposed that the tree model made a poor fit with the linguistic evidence and that what we regard as branches were really the result of converging dialects in a continuum.[42] Garrett suggested that:

> we cannot regard IE 'subgroups' as subgroups in a classical sense. Rather, the loss or 'pruning' of intermediate dialects, together with convergence *in situ* among the dialects that were to become Greek, Italic, Celtic, and so on, have in tandem created the appearance of a tree with discrete branches. But the true historical filiation of the IE family is unknown, and it may be unknowable.[43]

Employing a wave model instead of a tree model is not simply a different way of looking at the phylogeny of Indo-European; it also affects both our image of what the process of Indo-European expansions looked like[44] and our ability to employ the phylogeny of the languages as a tool for locating the homeland. In terms of expansion, some argue that the tree model tends to constrain migrations to separate movements of the higher-order branches – for example, Balto-Slavic, Italo-Celtic – which should have evolved largely independent of one another as they journeyed towards their historical seats. From an archaeological perspective we might expect distinct trails of migration from a homeland to the historical seats of the different language branches. A wave model, however, would best be imagined as an ever-expanding envelope of Indo-European speakers only gradually crystallizing through a variety of processes into distinct Indo-European branches, something like matter from the Big Bang eventually coalescing into galaxies that, over time, may have swallowed each other up. The process of the various adjacent languages being coalesced into greater wholes (linguistic branches) accords with some models of linguistic prehistory, which suspect that from the late Neolithic onwards 'language extinctions outstripped replacement'.[45] Recent simulations on how well one might be able to recover linguistic homelands from their phylogeny have concluded they are valid for expansions that involve small-scale movements that gradually increase the linguistic territory of a language family, but they fail in the cases where there was directional migration (where populations leave their homeland and migrate to another place carrying their language).[46]

In any event, we have a problem of how we model the expansion and differentiation of the Indo-European languages and, for the time being, we will tuck this problem to the back of our minds, knowing that we will have to face it again later.

Migration Theory

Modern lexicostatistical research into Indo-European often relies on a database originally constructed by the American linguist Isidore Dyen (1913–2008). Although Dyen's regional specialism was primarily the languages of Austronesia, he was also a pioneer in promoting lexicostatistics. That brought his research methods into the study of Indo-European, where he worked from the modern languages to see how well the technique grouped the language family.[47] While most of his results were in accord with traditional techniques there were some deviations. For example, the modern Indic and Iranian languages have evolved to a degree where their mutual Indo-Iranian identity is no longer apparent; and there is no evidence for Italo-Celtic. In addition to this foray into lexicostatistics, Dyen made a much earlier (and generally ignored) attempt to design with logical precision a technique to determine homelands utilizing phylogenies and the geographical location of daughter languages.[48] When I initially encountered his paper (working on my PhD and still mesmerized by the New Archaeology's application of a scientific approach to the past) I had optimistically thought that it might be the key to determining homelands. Yet the only major follow-ups to his work that I have ever been able to discover are by linguist Richard Diebold (1934–2014) – who attempted to reintroduce Migration Theory and provide examples of how it could be employed to determine the homelands of two native American languages: Mayan and Salish[49] – and anthropologist William Elmendorf (1912–1997), who attempted to track Salish origins utilizing a somewhat similar approach based on employing shared cognate lists and the contact intervals between related languages.[50] The historian Patrick Manning also employed a rather simpler version of this approach, which we will see below.[51]

To summarize Migration Theory very briefly with respect to the Indo-European homeland, we would start with an agreed phylogeny of all its languages (cue laughter and rolling of eyes) and their geographical locations and begin our analyses with the smallest minimal group – for example, Eastern Slavic, which consists of Russian, Ukrainian and Belarusian – from which we would attempt to determine its homeland. Each language area would be tested to determine the most likely 'propriate' (Dyen not only liked to create new acronyms but also resurrected dead words) homeland, under the principle that 'if two reconstructed migrations differ in the number of necessary language movements, the one with the fewer movements has the greater possibility'.[52] Law-like statements of this type invoking the parsimony rule (the simplest solution is probably the right one) were catnip to a naive New Archaeologist. If this homeland can be determined, one moves up the family tree to, in our example, the Slavic homeland and so forth, all the way back to Proto-Indo-European. To take a familiar example (where we know the answer), consider the homeland of the Romance languages. Our first step is to chart the position of the different (here to keep things simple) major Romance languages [4.18]. What we observe is a chain of languages (Portuguese–Spanish–French–Italian) and two separate

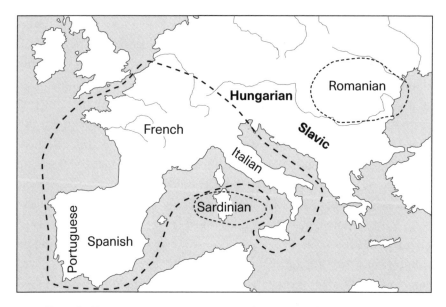

4.18 The major Romance languages form a chain (Portuguese, Spanish, French, Italian) and two separates (Sardinian, Romanian). Romanian is separated from the chain by Slavic and Hungarian, a language of the Uralic family.

languages (Sardinian and Romanian). As we have seen, the homeland according to Migration Theory involves an Occam's razor-like probabilistic approach that selects among a range of 'propriate' homelands by assessing which one demands the least number of moves.[53] When viewing our map of the chain and the separates (Sardinian, Romanian), one can propose four possible models to explain the location of Romanian:

- *Model 1.* The homeland is the chain, thus the separate (Romanian) involves two moves from the chain/homeland.
- *Model 2.* The homeland is the area of the separate (Romania). This involves more moves (all the languages of the chain each count for a move) and is less probable, and here we see Latham's arguments resurrected in that there is a greater probability of a separate leaving a chain than a chain deriving from the area of a separate (we are going to see this again where it really counts, see page 317).

- *Model 3*. The homeland is the area of both the chain and the separate. This is regarded as possible when the original chain is believed to have been broken by an intrusive language (here Slavic and Hungarian) that has produced a chain and the separate.
- *Model 4*. The homeland is neither within the area of the chain nor the separate. This is also unlikely because any homeland located outside the area of the daughter languages introduces still more moves and so Dyen suggests that 'the homeland of any minimal group is probably that of at least one of its units'.[54]

In terms of the overall evaluation, Models 1 and 3 are regarded as most probable and between them, Model 3 has the edge because there are clearly intrusive languages (Hungarian, Slavic) between the chain and the separate.[55] This leaves us with a Romance homeland stretching from the Atlantic to the Black Sea – the homeland occupied by Common (formerly 'Vulgar') Latin during the Roman Empire. If you are disappointed that it did not give us a homeland in central Italy you will have to wait for Chapter 7 for the reveal. On the other hand, Manning employed his version of Migration Theory with respect to the Romance languages by plotting out the centres of each language branch (French, Portuguese and so on) and then located 'the point that minimizes the total distance from it to each of these points', which gives northern Italy as the Romance homeland.[56] He then briefly (in less than a paragraph) resolves the Indo-European homeland problem by observing that employing the same 'least moves' approach indicates that the Urheimat was 'near the shores of the Black Sea';[57] unfortunately, this does not tell us whether it is north or south and still leaves all the major competing homelands very much in play.

While Migration Theory might have looked promising on paper, it runs into so many practical problems that it was never going to be a game-changer in terms of the hunt for the Indo-European homeland. To begin with, it requires synchronous linguistic evidence, otherwise we are buying into a cartographical mirage that is impossible: many of the branches of the Indo-European tree sprouted into the historical record at markedly divergent times. If we tried to follow the Romance trail any earlier, we would find all the candidates for the Italic homeland gathered together in central to southern Italy and so the homeland of Italic would be placed within Italy itself. In addition, as Wolfgang Dressler observed, the entire theory relies on a primitive family tree model of the Indo-European languages,[58] and that leaves us with two problems: the efficacy of employing a tree, and whose tree? Moreover, from what we know of the linguistic history of Eurasia there have been widespread language shifts not only involving intrusive non-Indo-European languages but also between competing Indo-European languages (for example, the Celtic and Germanic, Celtic and Italic, and Slavic and Balkan languages) that complicate any cartographical exercise.

One of the interesting aspects of Migration Theory is that it has thrown up several principles of evaluating language dispersals that at least have the appearance of testable hypotheses. For example, we have:

1. The homeland of any minimal group is probably that of at least one of its units. But can we seriously imagine that any homeland is impervious to language shift?
2. The homeland of any minimal group is probably the same as the areas of all of its chains.
3. Migrations tend to move from complex areas to uniform areas (Latham's rule).

These are testable, i.e. falsifiable, hypotheses, but not principles of evaluation.

Conservatism

We have by no means exhausted the linguistic-based techniques of homeland hunting: one has been around at least since 1686, when Andreas Jäger asked which 'Scythian' language was the most ancient and argued that it would be the language that had least deviated from its mother language.[59] As we have already discussed, Goropius's quest to discover the most ancient Japhetic language in Flemish may have been as bizarre as the attempts to recover elements of Hebrew in the modern European languages, but variations of this approach continued in the 18th century

(James Parsons found that the most 'original', i.e. unchanged, Japhetic branch was Celtic), while somewhat more sophisticated arguments of a similar nature emerged in the 19th and have continued to the current century. The appeals were not to the recovery of relic Proto-Indo-European forms in particular languages, but rather they served up the old saying – the 'apple doesn't fall far from the tree'. Of course, this was dressed in scientific garb, such as German-American anthropologist Theodor Poesche's description of languages derived from a 'Motherstone' (the closer in time and space, the more similar the language; the further – the more changed),[60] or Harold Bender's appeal to the biological principle of adaptive radiation: 'we expect to find the origin of a genus near the geographical centre of its various species, with the greatest conservatism of type near the center and the greatest variation at the end of the radii.'[61] The principle is perhaps best summed up in the caustic description of the Latin scholar Robert Seymour Conway (1864–1933) who, at a time when only nine Indo-European branches were reckoned, mocked: 'there they stood, all nine of them, in all the beauty of newly-printed grammars; only begging you to choose one from the nine as being the likest of all to the lost mother, and likely to have been reared longest in the old home'.[62]

We have already seen that after its discovery, scholars were mesmerized by the antiquity of Sanskrit – even the distinguished philologist, the Reverend Archibald Sayce (1845–1933), invoked the 'apple-rule' ('the nearer a dialect is to its primary centre, the less alteration we are likely to find in it') to place the homeland in Bactria[63] (he would go on to change his mind, first to northern Europe and later to Anatolia). Moreover, this argument became a core element of the Out of India school itself, where it was employed to support a homeland not near but actually within India (Vans Kennedy produced thirty-five pages of Sanskrit 'words' in other Indo-European languages).[64] Against the obvious temporal objection that comparing a Bronze Age language such as Vedic Sanskrit with more recently attested European languages was hardly a level playing field, Sanskrit scholar L. Kalla retorted that it was impossible to compare the other branches of Indo-European with Indo-Aryan because they had not even come into existence when Vedic hymns were being recited. In any case, Kalla pointed out, it was going to take some time for the bearers of Indo-European languages to make it to Europe from India.[65] This argument, of course, won't float since the Anatolian branch is attested earlier than Vedic and is far more archaic, and the rebuttal involves the *a priori* assumption that the homeland was in India in the first place.

Other than providing fighter cover for the Bactrian or Indian homeland camp, the arguments regarding Sanskrit antiquity have long since been dismissed. Besides, since the 19th century there emerged a far more impressive candidate – Lithuanian.

We have already encountered the hints of a Baltic homeland in the works of Latham when he anchored the Indo-Iranian languages in the area just south of the Baltic languages. And by 1870, when Poesche argued for a homeland in the Pripyat Marshes of Belarus and Ukraine (see Chapter 10), he based his case not just on phenotypic racial grounds (a blond, blue-eyed population) but also on the apparent antiquity or conservatism of the Lithuanian language.[66] The argument for Lithuanian as the most conservative language was acknowledged and employed by many other homeland hunters. Hirt, for example, nudged his Urheimat from a Nordic homeland eastwards because of Lithuanian.[67] The attraction of this argument can be best illustrated by comparing part of the declension of the Proto-Indo-European word for 'son' in Sanskrit and Lithuanian [**4.19**] and a list of cognate words in the two languages [**4.20**].

The crux of the argument is that Lithuanian is comparable to Sanskrit in retaining the phonetic distinctions, the grammar and the vocabulary of Proto-Indo-European, despite the fact that Vedic Sanskrit was a Late Bronze Age language while Lithuanian is a modern language, some three thousand years more recent. Consequently, in the Baltic region we have the closest thing to a pristine Indo-European language, leading supporters of Lithuanian archaism to embrace a Baltic homeland. But not everyone was convinced and we therefore need to explore why many others agreed with the Swedish Indologist Jarl Charpentier (1884–1935), who argued that 'the sooner a theory like this disappears from the handbooks of comparative philology the better'.[68]

Max Müller led the way by observing that employing the same logic to the Scandinavian languages, we would have to locate their homeland

Singular	Sanskrit	Lithuanian	PIE
Nominative	sūnus	sūnus	*suHnus
Vocative	sūno	sūnau	*suHneu
Accusative	sūnum	sūnų	*suHnum
Genitive-Ablative	sūnos	sūnaus	*suHnous
Dative	sūnave	sūnui	*suHneui
Locative	sūnā(u)	sūnuje	*suHnēu

4.19 A comparison of grammatical forms of the Proto-Indo-European (PIE) word 'son' in Sanskrit and Lithuanian (after O. Poljakov, 2015).

English meaning	Sanskrit	Lithuanian
god	devá-	diẽvas
goddess	devī́	diẽvė
man	vīra-	výras
husband, lord	pati-	patìs
mother	mātár-	mótė
son	sūrù-	sūnùs
daughter	duhitár	duktė̃
foot(step)	pád-	pãdas
horse/mare	áśvā-	ašvà
dog	śvā	šuõ
sheep	ávi-	avìs
fire	agní-	ugnìs
day	dína-	dienà
sleep	svápna-	sãpnas
grain(s)	yáva-	yavaĩ
branch	sákhā-	šakà
then	tadā́	tadà

4.20 A comparison of some basic vocabulary between Sanskrit and Lithuanian (after O. Poljakov, 2015).[69]

in Iceland because Icelandic was the most conservative (although only settled in the Middle Ages).[70] Sigmund Feist was unimpressed with the argument because he believed (wrongly) that the Lithuanians had only achieved their historical seats about fourteen hundred years ago.[71] Hirt added that the Lithuanians may have not only arrived late in their territory but also found the territory poorly inhabited, so neither the

Lithuanians nor the Indo-European homeland need have been located in the Baltic region.[72] Similarly, Swiss Assyriologist Emil Forrer (1894–1986) dismissed the argument because he believed the Lithuanians had migrated from the black earth lands in the south to settle in an unoccupied forest.[73] Finally, we have the argument of the Belgian linguist Joseph Mansion (1877–1937) that because the Baltic region housed two branches – Baltic and Germanic – then a Lithuanian homeland is hardly consistent with the fact that Germanic had strayed so far from the proto-language yet was geographically so close to the alleged Baltic homeland.[74] (Gustav Kossinna took care of that double-edged sword, which threatened his precious Nordic homeland, by suggesting that Germanic had changed so much because its speakers were culturally progressive while the Balts were culturally stagnant.[75])

The arguments for and against locating the homeland in the Baltic because of Lithuanian conservatism have bought into the impressive lists of similarities that are provided in **4.19** and **4.20**, but these are very much surface similarities. The problem remains that we have not devised a convincing system of analysis that can determine which languages are most conservative. The Hungarian linguist István Fodor (1920–2012) tackled this very problem to reveal how difficult it actually is. In examining the Slavic languages, he found Russian to be better at retaining the noun endings compared with the south Slavic languages such as Macedonian and Bulgarian, but the other two were better at retaining the verbal system.[76] On the other hand, the Polish linguist Witold Mańczak (1924–2016) concluded that the most archaic retention of vocabulary among all the modern Indo-European languages was Polish, and that the Indo-European homeland was between the Oder and Vistula (to which we might add a recent claim that the Poles 'are genetically the closest to the Proto-Indo-Europeans').[77] In any attempt to rate languages empirically we need to determine which elements (phonology, morphology) are the most important and how best to weigh each variable in the calculation. As we will soon see, Germanic has greatly changed the Proto-Indo-European consonantal system but, unlike many other phonological systems, the changes have retained many of the distinctions better. In sum, although there have been some useful explorations in quantifying, for example, the phonological differences between related languages,[78] we still lack any convincing method of determining the conservatism of the various Indo-European languages and whether it would actually help us to locate their homeland.

At this point, it is perhaps time to stand back and consider the entire logic of the 'apple approach', which presumes that the Indo-European homeland is geographically closest to the location of the language or branch that has changed the least. The basic logic is that one should expect that the further a language moves from the homeland, the more likely it will experience change. This simple principle can lead to brain freeze. For example, the principle was challenged by Gerald Rendall, who took time out from writing about the disputes of the early Christian church and the authorship of Shakespeare's plays to produce a small well-written book on the Urheimat in 1889. He claimed that: 'There is nothing to show that a tribe upon the move modifies its language faster or slower than a tribe at rest. There is no fixed equation between language-change and place-change.'[79] But then he weakens his argument in acknowledging that 'there is a probability that the race which remains in undisturbed possession of its first home will deviate least from the archetypal sounds and forms of speech'. It is, however, not so much a matter of distance as the probability that the longer and further a daughter population spreads, the greater opportunity that it will encounter other populations of non-Indo-European speakers who will impact on its evolution and lead to linguistic change. So the flip side of seeking the homeland on the basis of conservatism is excluding the territories of all those languages exhibiting the greatest amount of linguistic interference.

Interference

For homeland hunters, linguistic evidence for interference is employed within the context of the *Ausschliessungsmethode* ('exclusion method') or, if you prefer one of the most oft-quoted lines from the philosopher of 10 Baker Street: 'When you have excluded the impossible, whatever is left, no matter how improbable, must be true.' In short, tell me where

CHAPTER 4

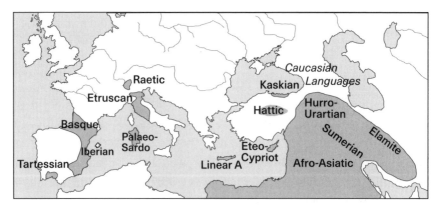

4.21 Areas traditionally excluded as potential Indo-European homelands because of the evidence of very early non-Indo-European languages.

the earliest Indo-Europeans *could not be* and I will tell you where they must have been.

The starting point for such an approach has usually been the location of the earliest attested non-Indo-European populations across the early Indo-European world [4.21]. Hence the presence of ancient non-Indo-European Iberians in eastern and southern Spain and the distribution of the Basque language across southern France and northern Iberia have usually rendered the Iberian peninsula off-limits for any discussion of the homeland, for the existence of such languages appears to precede our evidence for the arrival of Indo-Europeans (Celtic and Lepontic) in Iberia. Likewise, the existence of Etruscan in central Italy and Raetic in northern Italy, Switzerland and southern Germany in the five centuries before the Common Era have usually rendered Italy as a non-starter for a homeland. In Anatolia, the presence of Hattic in central Anatolia and a series of Bronze Age languages across eastern Anatolia and the Zagros mountains (Hurrian, Kassite, Elamite), as well as Sumerian and Akkadian in Mesopotamia, have all tended to reduce the attractiveness of these areas as homeland territories. Given the fact that other than Armenian, all other languages in the Caucasus are non-Indo-European (with the exception of later language intrusions from already well-established branches such as Ossetic, an Iranian language),

Charles Morris's Caucasian homeland looked pretty unlikely. Finally, the Dravidian languages of the southern third of India along with the Munda languages of central India have rendered these territories usually outside of homeland discussion.

Just one problem: the homeland predates the evidence of writing or the historical attestation of ancient populations, so there is an underlying premise that all these peoples whose lands have been excluded were themselves resident in their respective territories during the time of the formation and dispersal of the earliest Indo-Europeans.[80] In some cases, such as the Basques or Dravidian speakers, it would be exceedingly difficult to deny them temporal priority in their regions with respect to Indo-European dispersals. But the Etruscans (and by extension the Raetians) were frequently derived from the eastern Mediterranean, while the Hatti of central Anatolia and the Hurrians of eastern Anatolia and Syria have been dismissed as Bronze Age intruders from the north. Thus, in certain areas such as eastern Anatolia (or central and northern Italy), there is some wiggle room for avoiding the exclusion method. In short, we have another constituency issue.

There is another admittedly highly contested approach: the evidence for the impact of non-Indo-European substrate languages on the various Indo-European branches. The implicit assumption in the arguments for conservatism is that a language such as Lithuanian better retains its Indo-European past because it has not been affected by a non-Indo-European substrate. Most models of Indo-European expansions imagined massive language shift – the adoption of Indo-European by non-Indo-European speakers, who would have imperfectly learned Indo-European and affected its phonology, grammar and probably introduced loanwords from their own languages. So a search for the most conservative language was in effect also a search for areas where there was little or no non-Indo-European substrate to disturb the natural evolution of Indo-European through time.

The problem here is that there is no 'pure' Indo-European language that does not show the impact of what are believed to be non-Indo-European influences. A vague rule of thumb is that any language will exhibit a substrate vocabulary at least in the order of 2–4 per cent.[81] It would be pointless to run through every branch, but some mention should be made of those cases that directly impact on the more popular homeland models. For example, in the phonological system of Sanskrit there are sounds known as retroflexes that are not inherited from Proto-Indo-European but are found in Dravidian, and so it has been concluded that Indo-Aryan spread over a population of Dravidian speakers.[82] Dravidian, however, is not the only local source and it is claimed that there are some three hundred words in the Rig Veda deriving from a local non-Indo-European language of the Punjab, which may bear some resemblance to the Munda languages of central India.[83] There are also reasonable arguments that the Munda languages once occupied a significantly larger area of India that formed the substrate over which Indo-Aryan spread across eastern India.[84]

Another favoured homeland dogged by substrate claims is northern Europe, where the principal branch of the Nordic homeland theory, Germanic, found itself under frequent attack by the substrate brigade. This began as early as Sir William Jones, who in his famous soundbite, suspected that 'both the *Gothick* and the *Celtick*' had been 'blended with a very different idiom'. Sigmund Feist, the author of the standard Gothic etymological dictionary, for example, credited the principal feature of Germanic phonology – the Germanic sound shift (Grimm's law; [**4.22**]) – to the impact of a non-Indo-European substrate[85] (Celtic scholar Julius Pokorny later argued that it was not the impact of a foreign substrate but rather a change in climate that affected the means of articulation among the ancestors of the Germans – they had chronic colds?[86]). Feist also famously claimed that 30 per cent of the Germanic vocabulary derived from a pre-Indo-European substrate. The substrate theory was widely accepted among many linguists, including the American Robert Hall (1911–1997), who regarded the deviant features found in Germanic as just the 'kind of brusque restructuring that we find in pidgin and creole languages'.[87] Here he was suggesting that Germanic (the purest Indo-European for supporters of the Nordic model) was actually a pidgin, a grammatically simplified trade language (e.g. 'you wannum shiny beads?') serving the prehistoric amber trade between the Baltic and the Mediterranean that ultimately replaced the local language. To add to the arsenal of substrate claims is the fact that German shifted the free accent of Indo-European to the first syllable and, allegedly, lacked Indo-European etymologies for a third of its vocabulary. Substrates have also been blamed for the shift in accent in Celtic and Italic.[88]

Stage 1		Stage 2		Stage 3	
PIE	PG	PIE	PG	PIE	PG
*p >	*f	*b >	*p	*bh >	*b
*t >	*th	*d >	*t	*dh >	*d
*k >	*h	*g >	*k	*gh >	*g
*kʷ >	*hʷ	*gʷ >	*kʷ	*gʷh >	*gʷ

4.22 Grimm's law: the Germanic sound shift involved a three-stage alteration of the Proto-Indo-European (PIE) sound system in Proto-Germanic (PG).

Needless to say, critics of the substrate theory have been unimpressed, not so much with the concept that substrates may impact on the evolution of a language but how it is actually being demonstrated. The most obvious aspect of languages is that they change through time, and we do not require the imperfect learning of languages by substrates as the only explanation. Every branch of the Indo-European family deviates from Proto-Indo-European: one could appeal to substrates for every one of them and there could be an element of truth. But in the case of Germanic, critics argue that you cannot simply pin all changes on, for example, the phonology of an unknown substrate: you need to present either a historical example of how this has happened elsewhere in the world, or at least devise the appropriate phonological system of your non-Indo-European substrate to explain the sound changes. Since those supporting a substrate-induced sound change have not presented such evidence, Alfred Schmitt (1888–1976) concluded that the Germanic sound shift had a value of ±0 for resolving the homeland problem.[89] And as for the non-Indo-European vocabulary, this has been whittled down (the Indo-Europeanist Günther Neumann (1920–2005) claimed it was only about a hundred words),[90] and once again there is no branch that is not exempt from elements of their lexicon for which we do not have (yet?) an Indo-European etymology. In a recent review of the subject, German linguist Harald Bichlmeier reveals how the estimates of the enormous quantity of substrate words in Germanic derived primarily from a misreading of an 1899 study, and that despite claims of enormous numbers of substrate loanwords, no study has listed more than fifty or sixty words.[91]

The concept of a Greek substrate is another major area of dispute that here has implications for the Anatolian Farmer model. If there is substantial evidence for a non-Indo-European vocabulary associated with the local environment of Greece and its agricultural economy, it becomes difficult to argue that its Neolithic colonists introduced an Indo-European language. In Dutch linguist Robert Beekes's (1937–2017) *Etymological Dictionary of Greek*, very roughly 14 per cent (1,106 words) of the approximately 8,000 entries are attributed to a Pre-Greek language where the words are 'often the names of plants or animals, or part of viticulture'.[92] How secure these non-Indo-European words are in terms of a Neolithic substrate is arguable, since Greece, Anatolia and the Levant were in constant communication from the Neolithic onwards. Thus, some loanwords may date to a much later period. Greece also imported both objects and words from elsewhere across the eastern Mediterranean.

This leads to arguments for repurposing the Anatolian Farmer model into a more recent theory of the Agricultural Substrate hypothesis. Here some linguists agree that, while agriculture was introduced and spread across Europe by the incursion of early farmers from Anatolia, these early farmers bore a non-Indo-European language that formed the substrate to later Indo-European expansions. They argue that traces of the Anatolian Farmer vocabulary are recoverable in the agricultural lexicon of the Indo-European languages of Europe.[93] Supporters of this thesis claim to have found evidence of substrate words deriving from the Neolithic from Greek in the southeast to Germanic in the northwest, which, as we will later see, is mirrored in both the archaeological and palaeogenomic evidence.

We are once again clearly dealing with a constituency problem. That the expansion of Indo-European saw the absorption of non-Indo-European speakers at different stages of its spread is an absolute certainty. That these substrates may have had an impact on the formation of the different Indo-European branches is at least eminently plausible, although assessing the importance of that impact is nearly impossible.

Moreover, even if one accepts that substrates made an impact, it is difficult to locate precisely where that impact may have occurred. The substrate effect would have taken place in a situation where a native population had become bilingual in their own language and that of the intrusive Indo-Europeans. After some time, the population eventually abandoned their native language. This could have happened anywhere along the expanding envelope of Indo-European dispersals and, once introduced into the continuum, travelled far from its original source of formation. In other words, some of what might be suspected as representing a north or west European substrate may have actually been picked up as Indo-European spread through central or eastern Europe.

To sum up this review of the mapping of language dispersal, we can see that it is difficult if not impossible to generate a geographically useful map that depicts the location and state of the different Indo-European branches at a suitably early date to triangulate the location of their homeland and that any solution must be in accord with the phylogeny of the branches. It is almost generally agreed that the Anatolian branch separated first and that the other Indo-European languages experienced a period of common evolution. While it is usually accepted that Tocharian was the second branch to separate, after that, the remaining phylogeny has tended to be a constituency problem. That most sub-branches or groups (Indo-Iranian, Balto-Slavic, Italo-Celtic) involve geographically proximate branches mitigates this problem for the ultimate location of most but not all of them. The phylogenetic position of Armenian remains a major constituency issue, as it requires either a secondary homeland in the Balkans (to explain Greek and Phrygian) or a secondary homeland that might also associate Armenian with Indo-Iranian.

Attempts to address the homeland problem by applying a set of logical procedures such as Migration Theory have not found much traction among Indo-Europeanists because they rely on the Indo-European phylogeny and the rigid application of theoretical procedures to data that are far too fluid, while endeavours to calculate the time depth of Proto-Indo-European and the various separation dates of the branches are a major constituency problem, especially between what may be termed traditionalists and those employing computational means. In essence, traditionalists tend only to accept computational dates if they approximate their own: traditional dates for Proto-Indo-Anatolian tend to fall broadly between 4500 and 2500 BCE, which accords with most but not all (e.g. Auckland) computational dates.

Locating the homeland on the basis of which language is closest to Proto-Indo-European have traditionally focused on Lithuanian. This argument rests largely on the assumption that language change is primarily dependent on the distance a language has travelled from the homeland and does not take into account all of the social and demographic factors that might influence the evolution of a language. Moreover, no one has yet designed a method that satisfactorily determines the degree of conservatism in the evolution of the Indo-European languages nor its underlying reasons. And finally, attempts to locate the homeland from evidence for interference suffer from an inability to distinguish between natural evolution of a language and the specific effects on a language-contact situation where one of the languages is completely unknown.

CHAPTER 5

The Names of Places and Rivers: Our Earliest Linguistic Evidence?

Onomastics is the study of place names and has long been employed as a key to unlocking the past. While the languages of previous occupants of a land may disappear or be replaced by new settlers, they often leave a linguistic legacy on the landscape. In Britain generations of scholars have poured through lists of Celtic, Anglo-Saxon and Viking place names on which they could structure their local histories. It is also known that there are many place names, although altered by later populations, that were established long before there were written records and these can also be used for recovering the existence of prehistoric languages. It is little wonder, then, that in the search for the Indo-European homeland, onomastics would also be regarded as an appropriate tool.

Ancient place names

Observing the presence of a place name built on a root *morg-*, believed to lie in central Anatolia, the Polish-American Hittologist-Assyriologist and specialist in early writing systems Ignace Gelb (1907–1985) argued that it reflected an Indo-European root that was also found (forty instances in his survey of a gazetteer) across the Indo-European world from Wales to Baluchistan and hardly outside of this area (obviously ignoring the plethora of Morgans and Morgantowns across the US). For Gelb, therefore, *morg-* was clearly 'at home in the Indo-European area and nowhere else'. As he believed there was evidence (suffixes) indicating an Indo-European presence in the Near East in the 3rd and early 2nd millennium BCE, he suggested that the homeland lay north of the Fertile

Crescent, from where, apparently, Indo-Europeans dispersed across the Mediterranean, presumably founding settlements that occasionally bore names built on *morg-.[1] The assortment of names would include personal names (Morges, a king), Morgetes (the people King Morges led) and Morgantina (the town that Morges and his people settled, which, according to archaeological evidence, dates from about 1000 BCE onwards). I have never found anyone who was impressed with this argument.

Perhaps the name of a river might tell us where the homeland was located? Swiss Sanskrit scholar Hermann Brunnhofer (1841–1916) felt confident that the Indic Rasā- and the Avestan Raṇha rivers were cognate with the Greek Araxes (Armenian Aras) river, and that it was the Araxes that provided the template for all other similar-sounding names. Consequently, he suggested that the Araxes along with its sister the Kura were the prototypes of all similarly named rivers and that the Indo-Europeans had departed from a homeland between the Kura and Araxes – that is, Armenia.[2] Not so, argued the Indologist and archaeologist Friedrich Knauer (Feodor Ivanovitch; 1849–1917), who managed to publish his paper on Indo-European origins several years before being exiled to Siberia. Knauer rightly observed that the river tracked by Brunnhofer was also cognate with the Rahā, the Scythian name of the Volga, but further argued that it was also cognate with a frequent Russian river name 'Ross' and even the Russian national name 'Rus', although the latter is generally regarded as originally an Old Norse name that has gone through several language filters before being associated with the Norse foundation of Kievan Rus. From Knauer's perspective, once he had settled the Indo-Iranians and Slavs on the Volga, this made a suitable home for the satem branch of Indo-European and by extension also helped locate the homeland as a whole.[3] There is no doubt that there was a Proto-Indo-European word *ros, which in most Indo-European languages returns a meaning like 'moisture' or 'dew' (including in Russian) and also provides river names in Indo-Iranian, including a mythic river in both Indic and Iranian religious texts. But hunting mythic rivers is not likely to tell us where the Indo-European homeland was located. Nevertheless, there have been many who argue that the best route to the homeland is 'more rivers'.

Hydronyms

The few attempts to locate the homeland on the basis of a single river name have had little if any impact on the overall quest, but whole systems of river names, at least for a period, did play a significant part in Urheimat discourse. The reason for this is that of all the linguistic relics that one might uncover, river names have been widely regarded as the most conservative and least likely to be replaced over time. English-speaking populations in the New World are settled along the Mississippi, Saskatchewan and Wabash, but the names of these rivers derive from their previous occupants as do the Thames, Avon and Wear in Britain. And although Slavic languages are spoken from the Danube eastwards, it is an East Iranian word for 'river' (*dan*) that provides the names of most of the major rivers of the steppelands – Danube, Dnister, Dnipro, Don, Donets – while the Dnipro Basin alone is fed by more than thirty rivers with Iranian names.[4] The Bulgarian linguist Vladimir Georgiev (1908–1986) surveyed the origins of the river names of Bulgaria and argued that there was a correlation between the length of the river and the antiquity of its name, the longer rivers bearing earlier Thracian names and the shorter rivers carrying more recent Bulgarian (Slavic) names.[5] Demonstrating that the overwhelming majority of the longest rivers (over 500 km/300 miles) in Europe bore Indo-European names, he concluded that an early Indo-European hydronymy (river-name system) stretched from the Rhine to the Don and south Scandinavia to the Alps, including the Balkans, and that this area could therefore be regarded as the Urheimat.[6]

Although German linguist Hans Krahe (1898–1965) was not the first to determine a major system of early Indo-European river names in Europe – the Polish linguist Jan Rozwadowski (1867–1935) had proposed the existence of an early Indo-European river-name region ranging from north of the Caucasus to northern and eastern Europe – his system has proved durable, although not without widespread scepticism. He accepted that river names were the earliest hard evidence we had for the languages of Europe, and that there was a network of recurring river names whose roots and various suffixes could be regarded as Indo-European and predated the division of Indo-European into the major branches (Celtic, Italic, Germanic, etc.).[7] Evidence for the antiquity of the system could be seen, for example, by interpreting the difference in suffixes between river names, such as Ala*ra* and Ala*nt*ia – here, *-r* versus *-nt* – as forms of well-known Indo-European suffixes known as heteroclitics. Heteroclitic suffixes were used to form different grammatical cases in Anatolian, but are usually attested only as relics in the other branches where they had already settled on one or the other form – for example, *-r* in Lithuanian *vasarà* 'summer' but *-nt* in Sanskrit *vasantah* 'spring'. So at a time when Anatolian, Indo-Aryan, Iranian and Greek had already formed as separate branches, notionally *c.* 1500 BCE, the area from Britain east to the Baltic and south to the Alps was occupied by a block of not yet differentiated Indo-European languages that would later emerge as Celtic, Germanic, Italic, Venetic (a language of northern Italy) and Messapic (a language of southeast Italy). Krahe called this hydronymic system *Alteuropäisch* (Old European), which is still employed to refer to Krahe's (and earlier Rozwadowski's) river-name area and should not be confused with the 'Old European' of Marija Gimbutas (see page 228), which for her referred to the decidedly *non*-Indo-European Neolithic population of southeast Europe that preceded the expansion of Krahe's Indo-European river names. It should also be emphasized that Krahe himself did not regard the area of Old Europe as the homeland; he basically followed the Steppe model.[8]

Krahe's Old European provided a basis for a different homeland theory by his former student Wolfgang P. Schmid (1929–2010),[9] who believed that Krahe's geographical limits were too confined – the system could be extended as far east as the Dnipro river – and, far more importantly, too confined temporally: for Schmid, the river names were not some late form of undifferentiated European but actually Proto-Indo-European itself. Schmid argued that in order to explain some of the *Alteuropäisch* names – for example, Baltic river names such as *Indus*, *Indura* and *Indra* – one had to go outside the Old European world and draw on Indo-Iranian (here, Sanskrit *indu* 'drops') or employ more archaic Indo-Aryan grammatical formations to explain the river names. He asserted that the geographical centre of the names is the Baltic and that it was here that the names scattered over Europe would most often find a parallel, which

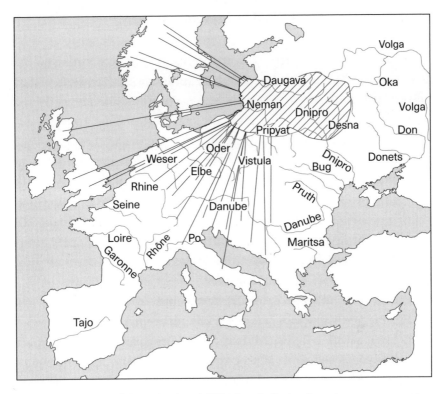

5.1 Wolfgang Schmid's homeland model. The lines indicate where river names across Europe find a corresponding name in the Baltic region. Supporters of this approach argue that as the greatest number of common names cluster in the Baltic it indicates that this was their point of origin and, therefore, also the Indo-European homeland.

might be seen as further support for the Lithuanian homeland model [**5.1**]. Schmid's model has been continued to the present by the next in the chain of scholars, Jürgen Udolph, who has further argued for the antiquity of the Old European river system and that the lack of a similar system of river names in south Russia, the Caucasus and Anatolia is a good reason to eliminate them as potential homelands (the exclusion principle, see page 107). Rather, all of this evidence suggests that the homeland was in the Baltic region.[10]

CHAPTER 5

Homeland hunter assessment

The hydronymic evidence poses an interesting problem for the homeland hunter. Onomastics, including the study of river names, is widely recognized as offering arguably the earliest retrievable evidence for the dispersal of a language of a preliterate society. Moreover, it plays a significant role in discussing the distribution of languages throughout the world, including Indo-European languages, with major studies (and debates) ranging from Celtic in the west and Iranian and Indo-Aryan in the east. A problem, however, arises when dealing with *Alteuropäisch* and related proposals, which has seen them develop into a body of evidence that has been largely marginalized in Indo-European homeland hunting. The reasons for this involve straight linguistic issues, chronological issues and, I suspect, human mortality.

Critics of ascribing an extensive system of European river names to a stage of Indo-European before the emergence of the local European branches have often noted that many of the proposed roots are so short that they could belong to almost any language. Deriving their names from roots as simple as **el/ol*, **er/or*, **ab-*, **ap-* and so on is seen as highly suspect.[11] When other linguists explain many of these same roots as clear evidence that the occupants of Europe spoke a Dravidian language,[12] or another voluminously argues for a linguistic landscape shaped by Basque or Semitic, one begins to lose confidence. The Dutch historian and scholar of place name studies, D. P. Blok (1925–2019), dismissed the whole enterprise as 'linguistic Kabbalistik'.[13]

Moreover, as argued by Harald Bichlmeier, those proposing the Old European system tend to operate in a linguistic framework that is pre-Second World War, so obsolete that he suggests their approach to the data has been abandoned by 80–90 per cent of current Indo-Europeanists and 99 per cent of those under the age of fifty.[14] Often the technique seems to be to isolate the root of the name and then sift through the reconstructed lexicon of Indo-European to establish if there is any potential fit – in this case, a root with a meaning that one might have employed to name a river. A linguist exploring the cognates for the word 'cow' in a language will generally be pouring through dictionaries in related languages for

120

their word or a word that is semantically close (e.g. heifer, calf, beast, buffalo). Not so for identifying the root word and meaning for a river name in an unknown language where there is an enormous number of potential sources: the roots employed might be any word denoting size, shape, colour, verb of motion (running, falling) or vegetation (trees, species of trees), any word remotely associated with moisture and, at least in Ireland, even 'cow' will do (the Boyne river derives from a Celtic 'white-cow'). When a much-investigated river name such as *Druantia*, which is traditionally derived from **dreu-* 'run', could just as easily be derived from **dru-went-* 'rich in trees',[15] one wonders how much house cleaning is needed to demonstrate that the river names have been convincingly etymologized as Indo-European. To this we can add the suspicion that many of the river names could be non-Indo-European in origin and simply passed through a later Indo-European filter.[16] Many of the frequently cited Indo-European roots have also been employed to define areas of non-Indo-European languages in ancient Iberia.[17]

The second major problem is the chronology of the river names. As we have seen, Krahe assigned them to a period prior to the emergence of the various European branches (Celtic, Italic, Germanic, etc.), which he felt dated to *c.* 1500 BCE; Udolph sets the emergence of the various different branches to *c.* 1000 BCE.[18] Udolph's most consistent critic argues simply that the earliest putative dates should fall before the emergence of the different branches, but it remains very unclear how far back we can set the names.[19] Further, a variety of linguists have been unimpressed with the arguments for great antiquity because of the frequency of the *a*-vowel, which has traditionally signalled either that the names were in fact non-Indo-European or that they dated to the Late Bronze Age.[20]

In short, the river names *may be* set to a period by which we already have evidence of independent Anatolian, Indo-Aryan, Iranian and Greek, and Krahe's dating is not far off the tendency of both computational and traditional phylogenies to set the split dates of the different branches to the period *c.* 2000–1000 BCE.[21] Even if we notionally accept that there was a fairly uniform system of Indo-European river names – not as ancient as the initial dispersal of the Indo-European languages but earlier than the emergence of some of the European branches – what bearing does that have on the location of the homeland, which may be millennia earlier? And even if Indo-Europeans dispersed from the North Pole, two or three thousand years would have been ample time for their Bronze Age descendants to thaw out in the rivers of Old Europe. Udolph has tried to assert a critical role for the Old European river names, arguing that 'The homeland of the Indo-European languages can only be sought within the Old European hydronymy.'[22] He puts forward a narrative where the Old European hydronymy is associated with the best agricultural soils and that these farmers replaced the earlier Mesolithic (?) populations, and it is their names that were fixed on the landscape with the centre of expansion being set to the Baltic. We will see later that this scenario won't fly, however, because it is opposed by both archaeological and genetic evidence that places the earliest farmers of the Baltic region as relatively late immigrants.

On the other hand, Udolph does raise an interesting argument that we do not encounter an early Indo-European system of river names outside of this area in, for example, Anatolia, the Caucasus or the steppelands,[23] so he consequently excludes these three putative homelands from discussion. And we must admit that while we have an entire series of good Iranian names for the major and many minor rivers of the European steppe, we find no evidence for still earlier Indo-European names in a number of the most popular homelands that have been proposed.

Or do we? This takes us to my third (admittedly conjectural) point that finds the discussion of river names and the Indo-European homeland a peculiar victim of the frequently recited aphorism, originally credited to Max Planck, that science advances by funerals, intended to indicate that new ideas only triumph when its opponents eventually die out. But here we have a situation where both the proponents and the critics have been reduced to such a small number that the debate seems to have fallen below the intellectual carrying capacity to maintain the argument either way.

So, although the study of river names has long been regarded as a source of evidence for early if not the earliest linguistic landscapes of a region and is reasonably well regarded in areas where one is working from a language clearly identifiable in a territory – for example, the Indo-European branches such as Celtic, Germanic and Slavic – attempts to identify linguistic landscapes before the formation of the major Indo-European branches have led to far greater scepticism because of the weakened criteria for identification. Thus, endeavours to recover an actual Proto-Indo-European hydronymic landscape have enjoyed very little credibility and have been largely, although not entirely, marginalized as part of the toolkit of Urheimat hunters.

CHAPTER 6

Locating the Earliest Neighbours of the Indo-Europeans

One popular approach to locating the homeland of the Indo-Europeans is to determine who its neighbours were. When we follow the linguistic genealogy of a language back in time to Proto-Indo-European there is no reason to imagine that we have come to the earliest advent of speech. Just as the biblical narrative found Japheth setting off to eventually spread Indo-European and other languages, his brother Shem was departing to found the Semitic languages, while Ham would be the progenitor of the Hamitic languages of North Africa. So, in modern terms, a fair number of linguists have argued that the location of Proto-Indo-European could be determined by establishing its closest relatives.

Before we begin to explore some of the ways homeland hunters have exploited the external relations of a language to determine a homeland, we need to make some distinctions about the different types of linguistic relations. Our first type is between genetically related languages that share an immediate common ancestor, which presupposes that they shared a common homeland deeper in time. Another type involves proto-languages that are not genetically related, at least in a discernible way, but have borrowed some elements from a neighbour because they have come into contact with one another. This distinction is not an either/or situation, because a language may be a product of both processes. English shares a common ancestor with Dutch, German and the Scandinavian languages that takes us back to a common Germanic homeland in northwest Europe, but English has also borrowed many words from its Germanic neighbours such as Norse (e.g. skill, kill, knife, die), Dutch (bluff, booze, cookie, etc.) and German (hamster, kindergarten, etc.).

In fact, the percentage of 'native' Germanic words inherited from Old English is estimated by some at no more than a third of its vocabulary and the majority of the English lexicon derives from either French or directly from Latin. Moreover, to add a further dose of complexity, even the Anglo-Saxons who settled Britain arrived carrying a smattering of Latin words that had earlier penetrated the ancient Germanic world. As we sift through the major arguments regarding the external relationships of Proto-Indo-European, we will need to keep in mind how these relationships bear on homeland hunting.

A close genetic relationship between Proto-Indo-European and one other language family could have an obvious bearing on our search presuming we knew where the other language family was located at the relevant time. A more distant genetic relationship where Proto-Indo-European is merely one child of a much larger linguistic macro-family will not be so useful, because it plunges any common homeland so far back in time that the earlier homeland may no longer be geographically relevant to that of the Indo-Europeans. We will also have to deal with those cases where Proto-Indo-European has either borrowed or loaned elements of its language to another language family and how they might be made geographically relevant. And, finally, we will briefly survey some of the models that support the idea that Proto-Indo-European came into existence through a marriage (cordial or shotgun) of two different language families, an idea that emerged in the 19th century and appeared intermittently afterwards and has now found a renewed lease on life. Such models are not looking for some incestuous relationship between two sister languages, but rather the mixing of two wholly unrelated language families.

The main players

The logic of using a different language family as an anchor for locating the Indo-European homeland is obvious enough. Take, for example, the German Semiticist Fritz Hommel (1854–1936) who in 1879 laid out the evidence that Indo-European and Semitic were related, which, for him, rendered the Indo-European Urheimat problem 'half-solved'. He concluded that, because the ancient Semitic languages (such as Akkadian) occupied essentially modern Syria and Iraq, the only logical homeland for the Indo-Europeans must lie somewhere immediately to the north between the Caspian and Bactria.[1] Similarly, the great Danish linguist Hermann Möller (1850–1923), who published a comparative dictionary of Indo-European and Semitic, suggested a homeland in Anatolia or north of Iran.[2]

Although the current languages of Europe are overwhelmingly Indo-European, they also share the continent with another language family, Uralic (along with a Semitic language, Maltese, and a language isolate, Basque). Finnish, Saami, Estonian and Hungarian are the best known, but there are clusters of other Uralic languages on the Volga and western flanks of the Urals, as well as over a large area of northern Russia to the east of the Urals. In the late 18th century, the different Uralic languages were recognized as belonging to a single language family, and then by 1853 the remarkable (albeit controversial) Finnish linguist and folklorist Daniel Europaeus (1820–1884) published his comparison of some Uralic languages with Indo-European and suggested that they were genetically related.[3] In 1869 this idea was further promulgated by Danish linguist Vilhelm Thomsen (1842–1927), followed by Nicolai Anderson (1845–1905), a German-Estonian school teacher in Tartu.[4] Less than a decade later, the Russian scholar Theodor Koeppen (1833–1908) also argued that Indo-European was genetically related to the Uralic family and that the Indo-Uralic (in his terms 'Aryo-Finnic') homeland lay in the Middle Volga region in Russia where the two language families split, possibly as a result of being pushed onwards by intruders from Asia or perhaps because of climatic change.[5] To remind us of the persistence of some arguments, one of the most recent attempts to locate the Uralic homeland has also employed climatic change as the driving force.[6]

There have also been attempts to associate Indo-European with the Kartvelian family, a small language family of the southern Caucasus, of which Georgian is by far the most famous member. One of the major founders of Indo-European linguistics, Franz Bopp (see page 22), believed that Kartvelian[7] was related to Indo-European, but this idea then lay largely dormant until a new burst of activity from the 1960s onwards. It was about this time that the Swiss Celticist (and my fellow colleague at Queen's University Belfast) Heinrich Wagner (1923–1988) argued that the relationship between Indo-European and Kartvelian could be best explained if the Indo-European homeland lay north of the Caucasus between the Balkans and the Aral Sea (or at least what little is left of it).[8] The Romanian-born Robert Austerlitz (1923–1994), an expert on both Uralic and Altaic languages, employed broad typological features to position Proto-Indo-European west of a chain of Eurasian agglutinating languages such as Uralic and north of the Caucasian languages.[9] The Russian linguist Georgy Klimov (1928–1997), a leading scholar in Kartvelian linguistics, was unimpressed with the meagre evidence for Kartvelian–Indo-European relations.[10] But Tamaz Gamkrelidze and Vyacheslav Ivanov argued that the Indo-European homeland should be positioned between Kartvelian and Semitic – that is, between the south Caucasus and northern Iran, the location of their Greater Armenian model (see Chapter 14).[11]

These are the primary potential relatives or potential neighbours of Proto-Indo-European, although several other language families have also played a part in the search for the homeland, such as Altaic and the families of the north Caucasus. We will now take a closer look at how these various theories might serve the goals of a homeland hunter.

The Indo-Uralic gambit

Daniel Europaeus argued that Indo-European and Uralic were closer to each other than either was to any other language or language family and, although this claim remains controversial, the theory certainly has far more supporters than any other language family has to be genetically associated with Indo-European. The evidence has rested on a spectrum of grammatical (see **6.1** and **6.3**) and lexical evidence (see **6.5**), which has been abundantly promoted as well as vigorously challenged.[12] Support or scepticism is to some extent regional, with a significant body of Indo-Europeanists at Leiden University in the Netherlands – one of the major centres of Indo-European research in Europe – in support of Indo-Uralic,[13] along with a well-known group of linguists based in Moscow,[14] while it is claimed that most Uralicists, at least Finnish Uralicists, are either agnostic or sceptical.[15] The problem lies in what constitutes convincing evidence of a genetic connection between two language families that, as Finnish linguist Juha Janhunen reminds us, 'are in many respects fundamentally different'.[16] In such a case we are not in the position of Sir William Jones to remark on the (frankly rather obvious) correspondences between Sanskrit, Greek and Latin but rather the meagre relics of commonality that allegedly survived thousands of years of language change. Dutch linguist Frederik Kortlandt, a supporter of the Indo-Uralic hypothesis, argues that the expected evidence would likely consist of some grammatical correlations and 'a few common items of basic vocabulary', which, he argues, has already been convincingly demonstrated.[17] Likewise, Alexei Kassian and his Moscow colleagues, employing a fifty-word basic vocabulary list, recovered seven matches that they argue were 'left over from the original Indo-Uralic protolanguage'.[18]

On the other hand, Johanna Nichols suggests that the dozen or so carefully reconstructed words upon which arguments for either a genetic or contact relationship have been built are 'not enough to exceed chance, given the size of the total wordstock surveyed and the semantic and formal latitude allowed in the search'.[19] Admittedly, she does acknowledge that some of the proposed lexical and grammatical correspondences 'are striking and raise questions', which are conceivably 'genuine sharings and very ancient', but it is unclear how they might impinge on the homeland question. Similarly, Lyle Campbell and William Poser classify Indo-Uralic as one of the 'plausible but inconclusive proposals'[20] of family relationships. Zsolt Simon is even more sceptical and, after reducing twenty-one of the thirty frequently cited examples to the *nicht haltbar* ('untenable') category and seven to problematic status, suggests that even those that might be possible could be explained as loanwords borrowed from the linguistic ancestors of the Tocharians as they migrated eastwards.[21] Why is all this so inconclusive?

The problem with establishing distant genetic relations between languages and, here, different language families, is the amount of evidence required to prove a relationship. One of the most influential Indo-Europeanists, Antoine Meillet (see Chapter 4), laid down the generally accepted rule that you needed three lines of evidence: in the area of grammar, in phonology (sound correspondences) and in the vocabulary deemed least likely to have been borrowed. Supporters of the Indo-Uralic theory can point to what they regard as a remarkable similarity in personal pronouns, which has been repeatedly acknowledged as a part of the grammar particularly resistant to borrowing (although there is certainly evidence of pronouns being borrowed, including English where *they*, *their* and *them* were pinched from Norse). So a supporter of Indo-Uralic presents some personal pronoun endings of Proto-Uralic and Proto-Indo-European [6.1] that show striking resemblances, suggesting that they both derive from an earlier common ancestor.

	Singular		
	1st person	2nd person	3rd person
PU	*m- ~ -n-	*t ~ -nt-	*s-
PIE	*m-, *n-	*t-	*s-

6.1 A comparison of some Proto-Uralic (PU) and Proto-Indo-European (PIE) personal pronoun endings.

A sceptic, however, counters with an equally striking list of correspondences shown below [6.2].

	Singular			Plural	
	1st person	2nd person	3rd person	1st person	2nd person
PI	*-m	*-s	*-t <** Ø	*-me(s)/-mo(s)*-m	*-te
PEM	*-m	*-s	*Ø	*-mas	*-to-k

6.2 A comparison of some Proto-Indo-European (PIE) and Proto-Eastern Miwok (PEM) personal pronoun endings.

This comparison also seems to appear impressive, but here the similarities are supporting a genetic relationship between Proto-Indo-European and Eastern Miwok, the language of a Native American tribe in northern California.

Or take the similarities between the main Indo-European and Uralic interrogative (who? what? etc.) forms [6.3].

PU	*ku/ko-	*mi-
PIE	*ku-, kʷi/e	*mo

6.3 A comparison between interrogatives in Proto-Uralic (PU) and Proto-Indo-European (PIE).

Against this the sceptic can throw the interrogative form *ču*, which is in easy phonetic striking distance of PIE **ku* and shows that Proto-Indo-European was not only genetically related to the language of a northern Californian tribe but also Quechua, a language of Peru (I think we're going to need a bigger map!).

Similar correspondences for other small words and endings can be cited but the sceptic can generally continue to throw up counter-examples, arguing that pronouns and pronoun endings across the world by their very nature tend to be small words with endings that tend to exploit a narrow range of the least distinctive consonants, which frequently include *m*, *n*, *t*, *k* and *s*, and so their occurrence may often (as in some of the examples shown here) be merely a matter of chance rather than an indication of shared ancestry.[22] In short, you are going to have to come up with a grammatical comparison that knocks the socks off the critics.

Meillet wrote that examples of a 'shared aberrancy' needed to be found – an example that made any chance similarity infinitesimally small. A textbook case would be comparing the irregular forms of the comparatives of adjectives in German and English to prove that they were derived from a common source. Let's say you choose to compare German *gut* 'good' with English *good* to demonstrate that German and English are related. Your crafty critic responds that you could have just as well compared English *bad* with Persian *bad* 'bad', but these words are in no way related to one another. You then present the case for a 'shared aberrancy' by reminding your critic that in English, comparatives and superlatives are usually formed by simply adding suffixes – *small – smaller – smallest*; *slow – slower – slowest* and so on – but in English we do not say *good – gooder – goodest* (at least after the age of three) rather *good – better – best*. When we find that Germans also say *gut – besser – best*, that's a clincher. The sceptics of Indo-Uralic are still waiting for the clincher.

The other evidence, usually regarded as inferior to the grammatical, is drawn from the lexicon and whether the proposed cognates are systematically related by their phonology (sounds). At first glance one might imagine (and a number of people still do) that you can assess this evidence by simply perusing the dictionaries of any two modern languages, looking for words of a vaguely similar phonetic shape and meaning, e.g. Basque *amu* 'fish-hook': Scots Gaelic *cam* 'bent'.[23] This is commonly dismissed as 'reaching down': you are employing lower-order single languages to compare two family trees that are probably radically different in appearance and possibly in meaning from their form in their own proto-languages, when presumably they were much more closely related. To give a flavour of the scale of the problem, let's perform a somewhat random and, for me, personal thought experiment. My maternal grandparents arrived in Philadelphia from two very different parts of the Indo-European world, both, so far as I know, speaking their own native languages, Irish and Armenian. Let us compare a part of the vocabulary that tends to be more resistant to borrowing such as the basic numerals [**6.4**]. The comparisons are far from obvious, especially with the Armenian outcomes of Proto-Indo-European.

English meaning	PIE	Irish	Armenian
one	*h_1oi-no	aon	**mek**
two	*$dwoh_3(u)$	dó	erku
three	*treyes	trí	erek'
four	*$k^w etwores$	ceathair	ch'vors
five	*$penk^w e$	cúig	hing
six	*$ksweḱs$	sé	vets'
seven	*$septm̥$	seacht	you'
eight	*(H)oḱtoH	ocht	ut'
nine	*h_1neun	naoi	iny
ten	*deḱm̥	deich	tasy
hundred	*ḱm̥tom	céad	**hazar**

6.4 A comparison of Proto-Indo-European (PIE), Irish and Armenian numerals. Despite the lack of surface similarity, all of the Armenian numerals except for one and one hundred are cognate with the Irish names and derive from Proto-Indo-European.

That was the easy part. Now imagine that both Irish and Armenian developed into proto-languages, experienced major diasporas and after another 3,000–5,000 years each left a string of daughter languages, what are the chances of recovering their original relationship?

So from this we can see that it is the proto-languages that need to be compared, not the individual languages, and that has a major impact on the size of the project. Depending on the sources, the number of Proto-Indo-European items (roots, words) appearing in the major etymological dictionaries tends to run to around fifteen hundred and Proto-Uralic has somewhere between two hundred and seven hundred items.[24] The number of proposed cognate pairs between the two families varies in both number and quality. The great Swedish Uralicist Bjorn Collinder (1894–1983) numbered fifty of what he thought were the best in 1965,[25] while more recently Rasmus Bjørn has narrowed the 'stars' down to less than twenty [6.5].

English meaning	PIE	PU
drill	*bherH-	*pura-
give	*deh₃-	*toye
ten	*dek̑m̥	FV *tVksVn
mountain	*gʷorH-	FU *wẹre
gold	**h₂eusom	*vaśke
exchange	*h₂mei-gw-	*miɣ(w)e
orphan	*h₃or-(bh-)	FU *orpa
ice	*ieg-	FU *jäŋe
dry	*k̑seh₁-ro-	*kośke
dog	*k̑(u)wōn	*kVn-
to gather	*leǵ-	FU *lẹŋẹ
mead, sweet	*médhu-	*mete
to submerge	*mesg-	*mośke
to swing, shudder	*pelh₁-	*pele
seven	*septm̥	U *säptä
water	*wed-r	*wetä
to lead	*wedh-	FU *weta
price	*wos-no-	FU *wosa

6.5 The most probable Proto-Indo-European–Uralic cognates listed by Rasmus Bjørn in 2017. In the Proto-Uralic (PU) – i.e. Finno-Ugric and Samoyedic language – column, FU denotes where there is no cognate in the Samoyedic languages, FV denotes Finno-Volgaic and U denotes Ugric.

Some of these forms – for example, 'water' – have been regarded as persistently strong and found outside of Indo-European and Uralic, while many others will probably always remain problematic and that is because of the nature of the beast. It is estimated that pure chance resemblances will emerge in the order of 5–7 per cent of the time,[26] which means that if your Proto-Uralic lexicon is limited to between two hundred and seven hundred items, anywhere from ten to thirty-five 'matches' may have been the result of chance. Moreover, even among those listed as the most probable, Bjørn still leaves open the possibility of loanwords.

If one abandons a close genetic connection between Indo-European and Uralic, there are still many who support some form of contact relation where loanwords are believed to have passed from Indo-European to Uralic at different periods in the evolution of both families. For example, Finnish linguist Jorma Koivulehto (1934–2014) employed a number of the words often cited as evidence for Indo-Uralic as loans between Proto-Indo-European and Proto-Uralic that occurred so early they cannot be regarded as later borrowings from or to the different branches of both families.[27] Obviously, from the perspective of a homeland hunter, this interpretation would also geographically associate the ancestors of the proto-languages of both families.

The earliest unequivocal evidence that Indo-European was in contact relationship with Uralic is seen in the presence of Indo-Iranian loanwords. For example, Finnish *porsas* 'pig' was borrowed from Indo-Iranian **parsa-* 'pig', which is a textbook example of the earlier PIE form **pórḱos* (Latin *porcus*) after it evolved into its satem (Indo-Iranian) guise. If one opts for the existence of Indo-Uralic, a contact relationship between Indo-European and Uralic or simply loanwords passing from already formed Indo-European branches and Uralic, what does this tell us about the Indo-European homeland?

Setting aside the historical, archaeological and genetic evidence that the Magyars (Hungarians) were 10th-century CE immigrants, the distribution of Uralic languages is basically across the northern tier of Europe and western Asia, extending as far south as the upper reaches of the Volga [6.6]. The quest for the Uralic homeland has been running about as long as the Indo-European search but, fortunately, putative homelands have not usually been projected quite so wide (excepting, of course, assertions that Hungarian theoretical physicists come from Mars). The overriding question regarding the Indo-European homeland in the late 19th century was whether it was located in Europe or Asia; for the Uralic homeland, that has also been the main question and remains so today. Most Uralic homeland solutions tend to place it between the Volga and the Ob or Yenisei river on the east, essentially in the northern forest or taiga (and between the southern steppe and northern tundra) zone of Eurasia, where the population practised a hunting-fishing-gathering economy.[28] The most recent thorough attempt to locate Late Proto-Uralic, the language just before dissolution, situates it in the central Ural region between the Middle Kama and Middle Tobol rivers.[29]

As to the date of its existence, estimates have generally run from *c.* 4000 to 2000 BCE, which, as we will see, falls in the late or post-Proto-Indo-European period. As the evidence for relationships between Uralic and Indo-European are – compared with the relationships within the Indo-European family – rather distant, it is presumed that any common proto-language should be sunk at least several millennia earlier than Proto-Indo-Anatolian (the earliest tier of Indo-European), around 7000–6000 BCE.[30] This is generally assumed to point to a Proto-Indo-Uralic homeland somewhere between the Middle Volga and territories perhaps immediately east of the Urals, which would embrace at least a fair number of solutions to the Uralic homeland problem as well as the Steppe solution to the Indo-European. On the other hand, one proponent of Indo-Uralic has recently set its homeland in the southeast Caspian region where Indo-European emerges out of the local Neolithic culture (Jeitun), while Uralic is associated with the primarily hunting-gathering Kelteminar culture that roamed south of the Aral Sea.[31]

Of course, the (hopefully) sceptical reader will already recognize a problem here: if you don't know *for certain* where the Uralic homeland is [6.6], how can that help you locate the Indo-European one: isn't this a case of the blind leading the blind? Is it really that bad? No, it's worse. Let's take two quotes from the same conference on the relationship between Uralic and Indo-European. Here we find Hungarian archaeologist János Makkay asserting that 'the early Uralic homeland surely lay close to the

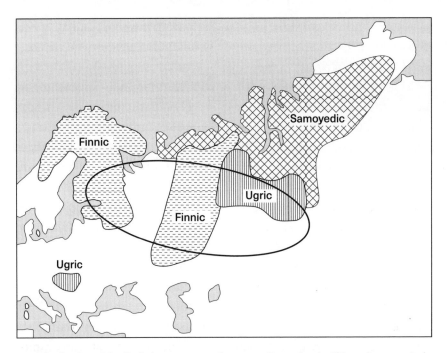

6.6 Distribution of the Uralic languages and proposed homelands. Although suggested homelands have run from as far west as Denmark and as far east as the Yenisei river, most theories situate the homeland somewhere within the ellipse indicated.

Proto-Indo-Europeans',[32] while Juha Janhunen argued that 'there is little reason to assume that the homelands of Uralic and Indo-European were anywhere close to each other'.[33] Recently, supporters of the eastern origin of Uralic have warned Uralicists not to be mesmerized by dubious genetic or contact relationships between Proto-Indo-European and Uralic and so be lured into locating their homeland to fit with an Indo-European Urheimat in Europe.[34] This hasn't prevented one recent attempt to repurpose the Steppe model to explain Uralic rather than Indo-European origins.[35] With each side positioning their homelands on the basis of the other, confidence in this route to resolving the Urheimat (either one?) can't run very high. And again, this is one of those constituency problems that are often ignored in the international science journals when authors boast how their computational models or genetic evidence have proved one homeland theory or another and dismiss contradictory evidence with a footnote from whatever sympathetic authority serves their song sheet.

This is not the only proposed relationship for Indo-European and Uralic. Both of these families have also been gathered under a single umbrella along with Altaic (an even more controversial mega-family consisting of Turkic, Mongolian and possibly Korean and Japanese), Chukchi-Kamchatkan and Eskimo-Aleut to form the Eurasiatic family promoted by the late American linguist Joseph Greenberg (1915–2001) [6.7].[36] A recent attempt to locate Proto-Indo-European within the context of a Eurasiatic homeland has suggested a location between Lake Balkhash and the Altai.[37] How such a model could run archaeologically or genetically remains to be seen.

Finally, we have the whopper family with fries, Nostratic, first proposed in 1905 by the Danish linguist Holger Pedersen (1867–1953), which incorporates Eurasiatic, possibly as one branch of a family that also includes languages to the south of the Caucasus such as Kartvelian, Afro-Asiatic, Dravidian and possibly the ancient Elamite language and several others [6.7, 6.8]. The problem with employing these linguistic constructs as a geographic anchor is that as they increase in size they also increase in terms of time depth, so that they become increasingly irrelevant to the problem at hand. Imagine for the moment that you are seeking the homeland of the English language: being told that the Indo-European homeland lies in Armenia or Bactria doesn't really help you much because such earlier homelands are too far removed in both space and time to provide an insight into the location of the ancient Germans, much less those who sailed to Britain. About the only potentially useful geographical information that might be mined from these larger constructs with respect to locating the Proto-Indo-Europeans is that, if you are a supporter of any model from Indo-Uralic up to Eurasiatic, you are going to expect a homeland somewhere north of a line running from the Caucasus eastwards over the Pamirs and Hindu Kush since all the constituent linguistic groups are in northern Eurasia. If, on the other hand, you go whole hog for Nostratic, then all bets are off, with the edge for an ultimate homeland south of the Caucasus as a more

LOCATING THE EARLIEST NEIGHBOURS

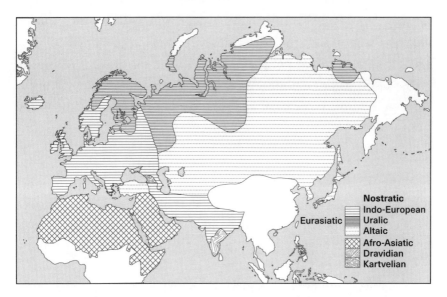

6.7 The distribution of the proposed Eurasiatic and Nostratic macro-families. The major Eurasiatic branches consist of Indo-European, Uralic and Altaic (whose scattered Turkic and Mongolian tribes provide an exaggerated image of the eastern area of their distribution). To these, Nostratic adds Kartvelian, Afro-Asiatic and Dravidian. There are additional branches located to the extreme east or that have been long extinct.

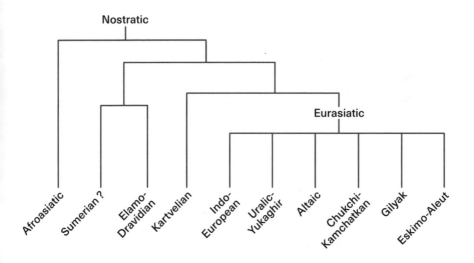

6.8 One of the family trees proposed for the Nostratic languages (after Allan Bomhard, 1996).

137

likely source of human migrations into northern Eurasia. This would, however, still leave you with a secondary homeland for Indo-European and a number of other Eurasiatic languages to the north. And can we go back any further in time? Yes, there are linguists who are willing to take some words back as far as Proto-World, which is as close to the Ark as you can get.

The Afro-Asiatic gambit

Although the case for a common origin for Indo-European and Semitic has been occasionally advanced,[38] and Indo-European or Afro-Asiatic have found themselves together (perhaps reluctantly) in the Nostratic macro-family (see **6.7** and **6.8**), publications have rarely led to a discussion of a common Indo-Semitic homeland, although Carleton Hodge's proposal for a common source on the Nile for the ancestor of Indo-European and Egyptian runs pretty close (see page 47).[39] Most discussion concerning Indo-European and Semitic has focused on a contact relationship or their parts in larger macro-families. The first major example of this is associated with Johannes Schmidt, a real heavyweight in the Indo-European world who, as we have already seen in Chapter 4, is most noted for introducing the Wellentheorie ('wave theory') of language relationships. Schmidt's attempt to locate the Urheimat was based primarily on evidence that although the Indo-European numeral system is clearly decimal, there is also evidence of it having crossed with a duodecimal (or hexadecimal) system. Evidence comes from Germanic (note how we say 'eleven' and 'twelve' and not 'one-teen' and 'two-teen', or that German recognizes a 'large hundred', i.e. 120) and there are also some traces in other European languages. As the Babylonians (and their Sumerian predecessors) also employed a duodecimal system, Schmidt believed that the Indo-European homeland should be located near Mesopotamia to account for the impact of the 12-based system, locating the homeland on or near the Pamirs in Central Asia.[40]

This hypothesis did not have much staying power, especially as another heavy hitter, Herman Hirt, attempted to dismantle it in detail by pointing out that Schmidt's evidence was limited to some European languages and that Indo-Iranian, which was geographically situated closest to Mesopotamia, lacked evidence for such a system. Moreover, Hirt argued, Mesopotamian influence could have travelled far and wide (as far as Germany) without requiring the Europeans to come from Mesopotamia, and systems based on 6 or 12 appeared to have sprung up independently throughout the world.[41]

While Schmidt's arguments in general did not convince, he was not far off in terms of compelling evidence for some relationship between Semitic and Indo-European. While most of the numerals in Indo-European can be provided with some form of internal etymology, usually referencing a part of the body, PIE *septm̥* 'seven' is frequently presumed to derive from Semitic *sab?atum* 'seven'.[42] The number of potential loanwords varies greatly from one source to another, as well as the vector by which the loans entered Indo-European. For example, Albert Schott (1901–1945), Professor of Assyriology in Bonn, presented 175 potential Indo-European–Semitic cognates,[43] and Ants-Michael Uesson (1926–2009), a supporter of Indo-Uralic, estimated that a quarter of them were associated with agriculture and, therefore, were probably introduced to Europe by the spread of farming from the Near East.[44] In the mammoth study of the Indo-Europeans by Gamkrelidze and Ivanov, they list seventeen Semitic loanwords in Indo-European, largely concerned with agriculture, and six loans from Sumerian.[45] Then in 1985 another noted Soviet-era linguist, Igor Diakonov, virtually shredded twenty-three items of evidence for Semitic–Indo-European loans,[46] while a much more recent sifting of the evidence by Rasmus Bjørn has reduced the number of truly favourable suspects to about ten, leaving thirteen others in the 'do not look promising but could use further investigation' category (see **6.11**).

Bjørn has more recently assigned twenty-one lexical items to various periods of potential borrowing and proposed the existence of Old Balkanic, the Neolithic language of the early farmers of the Balkans, which is identified as an extinct branch of Afro-Asiatic that provided the cultural and linguistic vector for various domestic livestock (cow, sheep, goat) and some of the numerals (six, seven, eight) and related concepts to the Pontic-Caspian steppe [**6.9**].[47] And, as for Sumerian loanwords, only one is left and it is presumed that any potential Sumerian loans were probably not made directly by Sumerians but via other languages of the area (Semitic).[48]

Old Balkanic		PIE	
*okk-t-ō	'eight'	*(H)oḱtoH	'eight'
*š(w)iki-t-	'six'	*ksweḱs	'six'
*šap-tam	'seven'	*sept$m̥$	'seven'
*kwri-	'to trade, pay'	*k^{w}rei(h$_2$)-	'to pay'
*gow	'cow'	*g^{w}ōus	'cow'
*Howi	'sheep'	*h$_{2/3}$ówis	'sheep'
*duχn	'grain'	*dhoHn-	'grain, bread'
*g(l)rnu-	'millstone'	*g^{w}rH-n-	'millstone'
*medu-	'sweet, honey'	*médhu-	'sweet, mead'

6.9 Some representative loanwords from Old Balkanic borrowed into Proto-Indo-European (PIE) according to Rasmus Bjørn, 2023.

The Kartvelian gambit

The Caucasus is home to a series of different languages that are traditionally divided, admittedly with some problems, into three different groups or families. The least questionable is the southernmost group, the Kartvelian family, which is regarded as a language isolate – a language family with no known relatives (although it has been grouped by some into the Nostratic macro-family; see **6.8**). More interestingly, it does not appear to be related to the other two groups of Caucasian languages found in the north Caucasus. There are about five million speakers of Kartvelian languages, of which, as we have seen, the largest by far is Georgian, a language attested in written form since the 5th century CE. Georgian was the native language of Tamaz Gamkrelidze, the co-author (with Vyacheslav Ivanov) of one of the monumental studies of Indo-European culture and origins. These authors referenced certain structural similarities between Kartvelian and Indo-European, and listed twenty-one lexical borrowings that they argued occurred when Proto-Indo-European was in a contact relationship with Semitic and Kartvelian in the 4th–3rd millennia BCE.[49] Bjørn [**6.10**] has winnowed the number down to ten items, seven of which represent loans from Proto-Indo-European into Kartvelian and another three that appear to have moved in the other direction.⁵⁰

PIE		PK		
*dheĝh-om	'earth'	*diywam-	'fertile soil'	
*h₁webh	'weave'	*yweb-	'trough; beehive'	
*yugóm	'yoke'	*uy-el	'yoke'	
*k̂ērd	'heart'	*m̥k̂-k'erd-	'chest'	
*mat-	'wug'	*maṭl-	'worm'	
*(H)ok̂toH	'eight'	*otχo	'four'	
*tek(?)-(s)-	'to craft'	Georgian-Zan *txaz-	'to plait'	
*ĝemH-	'son-in-law'	*kmar-	'husband'	
*tep-	'hot'	*tep-	'hot'	
*woinom	'wine'	*ywin-	'wine'	

6.10 The most probable loanwords between Indo-European and Kartvelian according to Rasmus Bjørn, 2017. The first seven are Proto-Indo-European (PIE) loans into Proto-Kartvelian (PK), while the last three are perceived as PK loans to PIE.

The Pontic gambit

Kartvelian is one of the three local language families of the Caucasus. To its north lie two other unrelated language families, Northwest and Northeast Caucasian. Of these, the Northwest family consists of a series of languages with ever-decreasing numbers of speakers, of which Kabardian (c. 1,700,000 speakers) is the largest, while Ubykh became extinct on 7 October 1992 with the death of 88-year-old Tevfik Esenç. Esenç had passed on to linguists (one of whom was the famous authority on Indo-European mythology, Georges Dumézil) everything he knew of his native tongue. Already by the 1960s some linguists had begun to write about their suspicions that the Northwest Caucasian languages had some relationship with Indo-European. This relationship, however, had only been hinted at until the 1990s when John Colarusso, a Caucasian language specialist, introduced his concept of Proto-Pontic, a proto-language that harboured two families – Proto-Indo-European and Proto-Northwest Caucasian.⁵¹ Arguing on the basis of phonetic, grammatical and twenty lexical items, Colarusso suggested the existence of a Proto-Pontic language family that dated back to about 8000 BCE and was situated in the northwest Caucasus, extending into southern Ukraine, including Crimea. It was here that Colarusso believed that Northwest Caucasian and Proto-Indo-European eventually separated into two language families.

In 2012, Croatian linguist Ranko Matasović revisited the subject. While he did not find convincing evidence for many lexical loans, he did make a tentative case for contacts seen in a variety of phonological and especially grammatical features that are found in Indo-European but are generally absent elsewhere except in the Caucasus.[52] The proposed relationship between Northwest Caucasian and Indo-European has been, to put it mildly, at best controversial and at worst simply ignored, but it emerged again when one of the leading authorities of the Nostratic theory, American linguist and Buddhist scholar Allan Bomhard, presented it in 2015 (with 150 lexical items);[53] then in an extensive review article in 2019 he expanded the potential number of lexical cognates between Northwest Caucasian and Indo-European to nearly two hundred items.[54]

It is with Northwest Caucasian that the most fully developed case for genetic relationships has been attempted, but the Northeast Caucasian language, which continues the chain of North Caucasian languages to the Caspian Sea, has also been very much part of the narrative concerning relationships, usually contact, between the Caucasus and the Indo-European family. Relevant examples have been examined in Bjørn's study of the foreign elements in Indo-European.

The languages of the Caucasus may not be particularly numerous in terms of number of speakers and, with the exception of Kartvelian, are only really attested in written form in modern times, yet it takes little imagination to appreciate their potential importance in the quest for the homeland. Not only has the Caucasus been seen as the actual location of the homeland, but also the great majority of the most energetically supported theories situate the homeland adjacent to the Caucasus, either to its north or south. And this naturally leads us to the problem of deriving Proto-Indo-European from the collision of two very different language families.

The mixed language gambit

It must be acknowledged that all languages borrow elements from their neighbours and so there is no truly 'pure' language; in some cases, however, the level of mixing is so extreme, especially with respect to the grammatical elements, that it is difficult to determine a single ancestral language. We have already seen that as early as 1890 scholars such as Daniel Brinton believed that Proto-Indo-European could not have simply evolved from an earlier version of itself, but had been the result of the 'coalescing of two or more uninflected agglutinative or semi-incorporative tongues'.[55] Here he was playing into the then (misguided) idea that the languages of the world stood in an evolutionary scale of complexity (and cultural superiority). The most primitive (isolating) had a grammar expressed through word order, as there were no endings on words, such as we find today in Chinese. Such grammars were (delusionally) associated with the 'Savagery' level of human social development. Then came agglutinative languages, where grammar is expressed by appending a series of suffixes to the ends of words, each one expressing a different grammatical element, as one finds in Uralic and Caucasian languages. Those who had 'progressed' to an agglutinative language could pat themselves on the back as they had managed to achieve 'Barbarism'. Finally, at the top, came inflexional languages, where the word may change in a variety of ways, usually with endings that are loaded with multiple functions. Indo-European was clearly an inflexional language (which meant that in evolutionary terms it was 'Civilized'). Brinton imagined that an inflexional language like Indo-European could only have come into being when two agglutinative languages crossed with one another. This was not a theory that seemed to have any legs until the 1930s when a series of linguists, each of whom had reputations for thinking outside of the box, began suggesting that Indo-European was a mixed language consisting of two very different elements.

In 1934, Swiss Assyriologist Emil Orgetorix (named after the famous leader of the Helvetians in the time of Julius Caesar) Forrer argued that Indo-European formed through the movement of a father language (*Vatersprache*) from the Baltic region into the Black Sea region, where it mated with a mother language (*Muttersprache*) that had formed somewhere between the Alps and the Altai, a sort of forerunner of Eurasiatic.[56] A year later we had the theory of the Dutch linguist C. C. Uhlenbeck (1866–1951), whose linguistic expertise ranged from Indo-European to the Blackfoot language. Uhlenbeck also suggested two components: 'A', which paralleled Uralic and Altaic and provided Indo-European with its pronouns (the similarity of Uralic and Indo-European pronouns had long been observed), verbal roots and some nouns derived from verbs, and a component 'B', perhaps derived from the Caucasus, providing numerals, kinship terms and words relating to fauna and flora.[57] And before the decade ended the famous Russian linguist Nikolai Trubetzkoy (1890–1938) had left a posthumously published and influential paper on Indo-European languages, which he saw as a bridge between Uralic and Altaic in the north and Caucasian and Semitic in the south, these providing the two components to the formation of Indo-European.[58] These ideas were further elaborated in the 1960s by the Russian linguist Boris Gornung (1899–1976), who saw Indo-European as the product of two components: local Mesolithic tribes resembling Forrer's *Muttersprache* and Uhlenbeck's 'A' component and farmers from the Balkans.[59] From a somewhat different social perspective the Italian linguist Vittore Pisani (1899–1990) saw the two components of Indo-European in terms of a warlike aristocracy from western or Central Asia (horse-riding nomads) who superimposed themselves on a priest class from the Caucasus.[60]

The evidence for a major input of the Caucasian languages into the formation of Indo-European helped convince Kortlandt to suggest that Indo-European was 'a branch of Indo-Uralic which was transformed under the influence of a Caucasian substratum'.[61] This model provides the background for Bomhard's broad discussion of the concept of Indo-European as a combination of Indo-Uralic (or more broadly Eurasiatic) and a Northwest Caucasian language.[62] It must be emphasized that both the proposed cognates as well as the entire model occupy a very narrow and extremely controversial niche of current Indo-European discourse but, as we will see in a later chapter, it may offer an attractive bridge between some of our current homeland solutions.

The homeland hunter's dilemma

So what can be said? First, there is agreement that the Uralic languages did absorb a substantial series of loanwords from various periods of the Indo-Iranian languages, probably at various stages of the evolution of Indo-Iranian as it evolved on both the European and Asiatic steppe.[63] Some of the attested loanwords are, on the one hand, unproblematic and, on the other, labelled 'pre-Indo-Iranian' because they do not reflect all the sound changes associated with the Indo-Iranian branch (e.g. satem forms). This places some form of early Indo-European at least in contact with the Uralic languages notionally before *c.* 2000 BCE. Beyond this, linguists are wildly divided and for the homeland hunter it results in a massive constituency issue. If your constituency does not accept any relationship earlier than one between Indo-Iranian and Uralic, the only requirement of your homeland solution is to get Indo-Iranians from your homeland onto the Eurasian steppe by *c.* 2000 BCE. Theoretically, you can bring them there from the Eurasian steppe itself or a Black Sun in a different galaxy, but there will be a plausibility issue: the Indo-Iranians are a substantial component of the Indo-European world and the further you have to drag them to come into contact with Proto-Uralic or a chain of early Uralic branches between the Volga-Ob region, the less plausible your model. If, on the other hand, you are trying to satisfy supporters of some relationship between Proto-Indo-European and Uralic, then you are likely to have your Proto-Indo-Europeans occupying the Eurasian steppe a millennium or more earlier. If you adhere to the concept of Indo-Uralic, unless you can confidently anchor the Uralic homeland within this region you have no idea whether your homeland is in Europe or Asia. If you prefer loanwords spreading from Indo-European to Uralic, there is an alternative option.

The Steppe model, as we will later see, envisages a dispersal eastwards from the Volga-Ural region as far east as the Yenisei river in the late 4th millennium BCE, which is supported by both archaeological and genetic evidence and is plausibly associated with one of the earliest Indo-European language dispersals (earlier than Indo-Iranian). Bjørn has argued that the Indo-Europeans were the vector for the spread of a series of Indo-European loanwords (*$septm$ 'seven', *$h_3neh_3mn\text{-}kleu\text{-}wos$ 'name-fame', *$g_lh_3\text{-}wos$ 'sister-in-law', **$(H)oktoH\text{-}$ 'honey', *h_2eusom 'gold') eastwards across Central Asia, which were borrowed into various early stages of Uralic, Turkic and Chinese.[64] In short, there is a model of Indo-European origins that proposes a highly mobile element in the eastward expansion of what might otherwise be regarded as 'late' Proto-Indo-European. If you imagine the Uralic languages moving west from a homeland near the Yenisei, then it is obviously possible that Proto-Uralic could interact with a late form of Indo-European.

Links between Indo-European and both Semitic and Kartvelian tend to be expressed primarily in terms of loanwords rather than a specific genetic relationship (outside of the mega-families such as Nostratic). Some of this evidence appears to be widely accepted (e.g. the numeral 'seven') and so any homeland location will need to accommodate the presence of some Semitic (or earlier Afro-Asiatic) and, possibly, Kartvelian loanwords, although the latter may require the loans to move in the other direction. The problem with loanwords in homeland research is that, as Hirt observed over a century ago, they can travel long distances. Within Indo-European studies there has long been research into loanwords between different Indo-European branches such as Celtic and Germanic[65] or Germanic and Slavic,[66] and between Indo-European branches and Uralic (e.g. very early Germanic loanwords in Finnish[67]). Here the evidence is often so massive that it is best explained by a contact relationship – if the two branches are in direct contact with one another, this means there is a presumption that their linguistic relationship indicates geographical proximity. On the other hand, there are also words that travel widely between languages – *Wanderwörter* ('wandering words') – and can tell us very little about specific geographic relationships. For example, by 1200 CE the Arabic *za faran* had not only been adopted into Old French *safran* but also been passed from French into English as *saffron*, illustrating that the possibility of intermediary languages – and wider distances – between the source of a loanword and its occurrence in Indo-European (or the reverse) is fairly large. This prompts the question: from which direction are most loans into Proto-Indo-European coming?

In his survey of foreign lexical loanwords in Indo-European, Bjørn made an attempt to arrange the most probable candidates chronologically. By this I mean that he employed the temporal constraints of a particular Indo-European phylogeny to calibrate at what stages of the devolution of Proto-Indo-Anatolian the loans were most likely made. The earliest comprised two loanwords that could be traced as early as Proto-Indo-Anatolian, and these were ultimately derived from Afro-Asiatic (*$g^w\bar{o}us$* - 'cow' and *$sept\m$* 'seven'), while most of the other items were correlated with most of the Indo-European branches other than Indo-Iranian, Greek, Armenian and Albanian (the latter two being pretty infertile sources of inherited vocabulary due to very heavy borrowing from other languages). If we arrange the information by geographical source (north versus south of the Caucasus), we find 38 per cent derived from northern sources and 62 per cent from southern sources [6.11]. His more recent proposal that the Afro-Asiatic or Semitic sources derive from Old Balkanic significantly reduces the geographical valence of 'southern' as he suggests that these words passed northwards via the Neolithic cultures of the Balkans to the local hunter-gatherers of western Ukraine (the Bug-Dniester/Ukrainian Boh-Dnister culture) and then eastwards. This is an interesting approach but, as we will see in a later chapter, a quite problematic hypothesis. Moreover, the status of a number of the words (e.g. wool, wine, axe, field) as loanwords into Indo-European is quite controversial. All of these can probably be accommodated in most of the prevalent homeland hypotheses that locate the homeland both immediately north or south of the Caucasus.

Finally, we have the arguments for a *Mischsprache* – a marriage of Uralic and possibly Northwest or Northeast Caucasian. This whole concept of a mixed language, which has existed since at least the Middle Ages, may well be merely a dead end in our quest for the homeland but if so, it is a diverting cul de sac. Usually, the mixing was regarded as a process of the debasement of 'pure' languages such as ancient Latin, although the crafty Irish argued that that their own language had been cobbled together from the best elements of the seventy-two languages spoken at Babel. The idea of a mixed language did not fare so well in the late 19th century when, in 1871, Max Müller, Queen Victoria's favourite

Northern loanwords into PIE

Uralic	*g̑l̥h₃-wos	'sister-in-law'
Uralic	*(h₂s)kwal-	'catfish'
North Caucasian	*h₂eg̑-	'to lead'
Northeast Caucasian	*wl̥h₂neh₂	'wool'
Northeast Caucasian	*dig-	'goat'
Northeast Caucasian	*kʷer-	'kettle'
North Caucasian	*h₂e(i)g-	'goat'
North Caucasian	*twer-	'curdled milk'

Southern loanwords into PIE

Kartvelian	*g̑emH-	'son-in-law'
Kartvelian	*tep-	'to heat'
Kartvelian	*woinom	'wine'
Afro-Asiatic	*gʷōus	'cow'
Semitic	*septm̥	'seven'
Semitic	*ksweḱs	'six'
Semitic	*kʷrei(h₂)-	'to pay'
Semitic	*de₂p-	'sacrifice'
Semitic	*médhu	'mead; sweet'
Afro-Asiatic	*(s)teuros	'bull'
Semitic	*h₁sh₂-	'arrow'
Semitic	*pelekus	'axe'
Sumerian	*h₂eg̑ros	'field'

6.11 The distribution of early loanwords in other language families into Proto-Indo-European (PIE) according to Rasmus Bjørn, 2017. North Caucasian denotes a debatable proto-language from which both Northwest and Northeast Caucasian evolved.

linguist, dismissed the entire idea of the concept.[68] But in the next decade Hugo Schuchardt (1842–1927), a specialist in the Romance languages as well as Basque and the original lingua franca of the Mediterranean, argued that there was no such thing as an unmixed language.[69] The case of English certainly supports Schuchardt, where we are dealing with a language whose grammar is essentially Germanic but the majority of its lexicon is Romance. We may also recall that Armenian was initially presumed to be an Iranian language because Persian loanwords had swamped the original Armenian vocabulary of its speakers. But these are all cases involving massive lexical borrowing where we still have clear evidence of the genetic origins of the 'host' language.

A *Mischsprache* involves a far more extreme situation, and there are only a handful of languages known today that are so thoroughly mixed that establishing a single ancestor seems impossible and, therefore, they can be truly regarded as *Mischsprachen*. For example, Ecuador boasts about two thousand speakers of Media Lengua, a language whose vocabulary is Spanish but whose grammar and pronunciation is native Quechua. Similarly, Canada is home to less than a thousand speakers of Michif, where French contributes many of the nouns but Plains Cree is the primary source of the verbs. Here we have a true mother-father language, to match the suggestion of Forrer, where the fathers were French trappers and the mothers were from the First Nations. We have seen that there are modern proponents who view the formation of Indo-European as straddling two language families. Kortlandt, for example, regards Indo-European to be have evolved from Indo-Uralic after it was subjected to the influence of a language from the north Caucasus.[70] This does not describe a *Mischsprache* in the strict sense, but it does involve two very different source languages. And, unlike some of the other models, pinning Indo-European origins between two language families does have at least some geographical valence where it has been used to support the Steppe model.

The problems here are several: first, one has to accept the concept of Indo-Uralic, which as we have already seen is a 'hard sell'; second, one has to accept the arguments for a major linguistic impact of Northwest Caucasian on the formation of Indo-European, which is not a particularly well-explored or tested hypothesis; and, third, one has to accept a model that, at least in the wild, has so far only been seen to emerge in a handful of cases involving extremely small populations. The other examples are the approximately seven thousand people who still speak the Mbugu language of a mountainous region of north Tanzania, and Medny Aleut, the (now) extinct language of a small island in the Aleutians that combined the Russian grammar of male fur trappers and the vocabulary of local Aleutian women. In short, scaling these processes up to the ancestor of the world's largest language family could certainly seem a tall order unless we play the 'Wakanda' card and assume that the earliest Indo-Europeans were gifted with something so extraordinary that a small group might have a global impact.

The general approach of locating the Indo-European homeland by determining its closest linguistic neighbours has a long tradition, but, as we have seen, it has not achieved a major consensus except for the probable presence of a limited number of loanwords that can be attributed to Proto-Indo-European. Attempts to link Proto-Indo-European with Proto-Uralic, either as sisters derived from a common Proto-Indo-Uralic or as neighbours in a contact relationship, probably has the widest currency among Indo-Europeanists, but still remains essentially a constituency issue with many critics. That there were contact links between Indo-Iranian and the Uralic languages, however, does have very wide acceptance and is supported by convincing evidence.

Efforts to link Indo-European with Afro-Asiatic or Semitic at a common genetic level have been made in the past, but does not appear to have many if any current supporters. Lexical loans from Afro-Asiatic or Semitic into Proto-Indo-European are widely supported, however, and an Indo-European homeland is usually expected to accommodate such loans.

Current attempts to link Indo-European with Kartvelian also tend to focus on a contact relationship indicated by loanwords that may go from Indo-European into Kartvelian.

The concept of explaining Proto-Indo-European as a *Mischsprache* remains a minor constituency enterprise that came and went in the past and has re-emerged now, still as a minority viewpoint but, as we will see later in Chapter 15, is a possible solution to one of the current issues in homeland hunting.

CHAPTER 7

Linguistic Palaeontology: Geographical Clues in the Indo-European Vocabulary

Sir William Jones had noted that there were 'some hundreds of words' that one might recover from his languages of Ham (i.e. Indo-European) but he did not list them.[1] This was remedied by Jones's successor, Henry Thomas Colebrooke (1765–1837), another jurist and the 'father of true Sanskrit scholarship in Europe',[2] who also came to lead the Royal Asiatic Society. In about 1801 or 1802 he prepared a list of the type of comparisons that Sir William Jones had alluded to earlier.[3] The list contained numerals, parts of the body, animal names, natural phenomena and physical features, kinship terms, pronouns, prepositions, articles, some verbs and other items. The structure of each entry was the English meaning followed by Sanskrit and then related words in Greek, Latin, Germanic and Celtic and, when possible, other Indo-European languages. To take one of the more obvious cognates, we can present his entry for sheep, which he listed under 'ewe':

Sanskrit *avi*, Greek *ois*, Latin *ovis*, Saxon *eowe*

Colebrooke's list was not published in his lifetime, but Rasmus Rask undertook a similar exercise in 1818 at the end of his famous prize-winning essay on the origins of Icelandic, where he provided 352 sets of cognates, arranged semantically, beginning with nouns subdivided into natural objects, next plants and animals, anatomy and kinship terms and technology, and then moving through the major parts of speech, such as adjectives, verbs and numerals. Rask's label 'Thracian' covered what we call Indo-European and his list for 'sheep' was:[4]

Greek *ois*, Latin *ovis*, Lithuanian *awi-is* [*avis*], Icelandic *á*

Rask admitted that he could not provide an entire dictionary, but by 1836 French linguist Frédéric Eichhoff (1799–1875) was able to publish his study of the parallels among the Indo-European languages. The main strength of his dictionary was his extensive list of comparisons across all parts of speech, with nouns again arranged into major semantic fields – for example, parts of the body, nature and animals. At nearly five hundred pages of comparisons, it provided the first major attempt to list all of the words that we might attribute to the original Indo-European language. For example, among animals, we find his listing for words for 'sheep':

Greek *ois*, Latin *ovis*, Gothic *awi'*, German *euwe*, English *ewe*, Lithuanian *awis* [*avis*], Russian *owen* [*ovec*], Irish *uan*, Welsh *oen*.[5]

Where Eichhoff is of less use are those cases where he merely recites loanwords among various languages – for example, Greek *kamēlos*, Latin *camelus*, Old Norse *kamel*,[6] which reflected borrowing among different languages rather than indicating the Indo-European's acquaintance with the 'camel'.

It was in 1845 that Adalbert Kuhn (1812–1881), founder of an Indo-European linguistics journal that has survived 172 years, provided a brief survey that actually analysed the cultural vocabulary of the Indo-European languages to determine what we might say about their ancient society.[7] After examining the evidence for kinship terms, Kuhn reconstructed the Indo-European economy. He first listed the shared names for livestock – cattle, cow, horse, sheep, pig, goat and dog (he noted that there was no word for 'cat' and so the mouse 'must have had a marvellous life in the homeland of our fathers').[8] As to the question of whether the Indo-Europeans were pastoral nomads or settled farmers, he confirmed the presence of the quern stone and common names for grain, wheat and barley along with words for 'house' and 'village' to conclude that the ancient Indo-Europeans were a 'settled people'.[9] He also confronted a recurring problem related to the Indo-European economy: while he could recover a word for 'plough' from the European languages, he could find no trace of it in Indo-Iranian. Like all of his contemporaries, Kuhn presumed that the homeland of these feline-deprived Indo-Europeans was probably in Asia. But it wasn't until 1859 that the technique of retrieving a past culture from the relicts of languages was given a name.

Adolphe Pictet (1799–1875) was a multi-talented Swiss savant whose interests ranged from history, philosophy and literature (he wrote a fantasy novel featuring his friends Franz Liszt and Georges Sand), ballistics (he obtained the rank of colonel in the artillery) and linguistics, where his first book was on a comparison of Celtic with Sanskrit. Pictet had a major influence on the incomparably more significant Swiss linguist Ferdinand de Saussure (1857–1913). Pictet's magnum opus is his two-volume (1859–63) attempt to reconstruct as fully as possible the culture and origins of the Indo-Europeans by means of 'linguistic palaeontology'.[10] A Romantic heart runs through much of his other work and here, in his attempt to ferret out etymologies, his imagination often ran on steroids. For example, in order to secure a Sanskrit cognate for a chain of European words cognate with Latin *hordeum* 'barley', Pictet went for the vaguely similar-sounding Sanskrit *hṛdya* 'loved, desired', because the ancient Indians were passionate about barley, which is seen again in his comparison of Welsh *haidd* 'barley' and Sanskrit *sadhu* 'excellent, beautiful'. As Pictet had already accepted the commonly held homeland to lie in Bactria, his interpretations were guided towards painting the reconstructed landscape into Bactria or at least adjacent areas. In terms of the history of Indo-European studies, Pictet managed to both create a term to cover the use of comparative linguistics in reconstructing past cultures and give 'linguistic palaeontology' a bad name, so much so that later linguists have sought (in vain) to replace it.[11] Sigmund Feist tried 'linguistic archaeology' but this never took.[12] The one acceptable alternative is the workmanlike German expression *Wörter und Sachen* ('words and things').

Whatever its name, linguistic palaeontology (or 'lexical-cultural reconstruction' if you are not sufficiently passionate about the name) has been widely utilized around the world to help locate the homelands of many language families in both space and time: in the *Glossary of Historical Linguistics* it is listed as the first of the two techniques employed in locating the homeland of a language family,[13] and, for most Indo-Europeanists, it provides a litmus test for any potential homeland. As long ago as 1869, Theodor Benfey employed the *absence* of re-constructable words for 'lion', 'tiger' and 'camel' to exclude an Indo-European homeland in Asia and, against common opinion, place it in Europe.[14]

In the 19th century linguistic palaeontology became the go-to linguistic tool for describing the culture and environment of the ancient Indo-Europeans and locating their homeland. A measure of its success is that its application seemed to prove 'absolutely conclusively' that the Proto-Indo-Europeans were both pastoral nomads as well as settled farmers whose home lay in Scandinavia, Germany, Lithuania, Hungary, the Ukrainian-Russian steppe, the Kirghiz steppe of Asia, of course Bactria, and even the Himalayas. So we should not be too surprised that there have always been some linguists who have vigorously objected to its utility and rejected its ability to assist us in determining the time or place of the homeland. This is a point that cannot be overemphasized, since the acceptance or rejection of the evidence of linguistic palaeontology often remains a central issue in determining the merits of competing homeland solutions. And although it has been an absolutely critical issue since the 19th century, there has seldom been an extended analysis of the legitimacy of the method[15] – instead, supporters or sceptics have sniped at each other for years, often unknowingly repeating the same jibes as previous generations, with no resolution. This problem is too large a topic to be resolved here, but we at least need to understand some of the major difficulties inherent in the method.

Reconstruction: votes and vetoes

Let's briefly consider in 7.1 the reconstruction of the 'sheep' word, already encountered above.

In this list every major branch other than Albanian and Iranian (whose immediate ancestor Indo-Iranian is covered by Sanskrit and there is a derivative in a modern Iranian language[16]) provides a cognate that means

Old Irish	*oí*	'sheep'
Latin	*ovis*	'sheep'
English	*ewe*	
Lithuanian	*avìs*	'sheep'
Old Church Slavonic	*ovĭnŭ*	'sheep'
Greek	*óis*	'sheep'
Armenian	*hoviw*	'shepherd'
Luvian	*hāwa/i-*	'sheep'
Sanskrit	*ávi-*	'sheep'
Tocharian B	*āu*	'ewe'

7.1 Cognate words for 'sheep' in Indo-European languages.

either 'sheep' or something very close to it and, consequently, linguists reconstruct a meaning 'sheep' for PIE *$h_2ówis$ (or *$h_3ówis$). Unfortunately, this is not a wholly typical reconstruction for two reasons.

The first is that we have managed to reconstruct the entire word while many of the reconstructions, especially verbs, only recover the root and whatever suitably vague meaning might be assigned to a proto-form that could serve to underlie an often myriad potential meanings (for, example, in the standard etymological dictionary of Indo-European, over twenty words are derived from the concept of 'swell'). Thankfully, most of the reconstructed forms that have been advanced to elucidate Indo-European proto-culture are nouns, and their reconstructed meanings have not disappeared into a cloud of vagueness as often. On the other hand, we frequently can only reconstruct the root shape and not the 'original' word. From alterations in the root vowel (consider English *sing, sang, sung, song*), to a variety of suffixes (*singer*), and a variety of final endings, we are often uncertain about the actual appearance of the word in the proto-language.

The second aspect that is untypical of our reconstruction of a PIE (or in this case Proto-Anatolian) 'sheep' is with reference to the large number of the different Indo-European language branches supporting the reconstruction. The number of reconstructions with total (all the branches) support is about 1 per cent of the entries in our etymological dictionaries, and these largely consist of numerals and pronouns. In fact, only about a quarter of all reconstructions have the support of seven or more branches and about 45 per cent of the reconstructions are supported by four or less branches.

The issue here, and it is a serious one for any homeland hunter, is how much evidence from the various branches do we require to claim that our reconstruction goes back to the proto-language and is not merely the later creation of a few languages long after they had dispersed from the homeland? Imagine for a moment that our list of 'sheep' words consisted solely of two cognates, one from Baltic and another from Slavic. In this case it would be presumed that the reconstructed word was a Balto-Slavic isogloss (Balto-Slavic *owis) that was created when their linguistic ancestors had been introduced to sheep. But what if the two cognates were Celtic and Baltic, two branches reasonably well separated from one another but still confined to Europe? Would that be enough to secure a reconstruction to Proto-Indo-European or is it evidence of a word floating around in Europe long after the Indo-Europeans had dispersed but before Celtic and Baltic had evolved as separate branches? The problem, then, is how to distinguish between a word that would go all the way back to Proto-Indo-Anatolian (and therefore derive from the language spoken before the individual branches had differentiated) and a word that is only as old as the parent of a single branch or circulated in a specific geographical area after the Indo-European languages had dispersed?

Linguists have proposed various criteria to deal with this problem. In 1907, Otto Schrader, the author of the first encyclopaedia of Indo-European culture, set out what he regarded as the appropriate criteria to determine whether the reconstruction could be regarded of 'high antiquity'. He required that the cognates be drawn from Indo-Iranian and a European branch, or a northern and a southern branch, or from both Greek and Latin.[17] Various other linguists have, in their practice, indicated their own criteria – for example, Antoine Meillet argued that a Proto-Indo-European reconstruction should come from at least three branches that were not in geographical contact.[18] When Douglas Adams and I compiled our encyclopaedia (1997) and handbook (2006) of Indo-European culture,[19] we required a cognate from Anatolian and one other branch (on the grounds that the separation of Anatolian from the rest of the Indo-European languages was commonly regarded as the first split); so a cognate from Anatolian and any other branch should go back to Proto-Indo-Anatolian, the earliest tier associated with the Indo-European language family. Alternatively, we accepted as Proto-Indo-European a cognate set that involved a European and an Asian (Indo-Iranian, Tocharian) language in that such a geographical separation should guarantee its Core-Indo-European antiquity, although not Proto-Indo-Anatolian. This was not an ideal solution (a Slavic-Iranian cognate set would have met this criterion, but we know that speakers of these two groups did come into contact with one another, certainly during the Iron Age and possibly considerably earlier), so we attempted to add some further nuance (both spatial and possibly temporal) between a northwest group (Celtic, Italic, Germanic, Baltic and Slavic), a central group (Albanian, Armenian, Phrygian and Greek) and also a Graeco-Aryan one because there have always been a troublesome set of Greek-Sanskrit cognates that resisted easy explanation. Thus, our criteria were still far from perfect.

In 2015 I was invited to Copenhagen to give several lectures on Indo-European origins. During my discussion of this very issue of cognates I showed a slide of the family tree generated by Don Ringe and his team (see **4.12**) and posed the hypothetical question: 'Do you really need any more than cognates from two distantly separated language groups?' If, for example, you had a Tocharian and Latin cognate set, their position in the family tree should guarantee that the word had existed in the proto-language before all the other languages had diverged (and apparently lost it), because it had been present before Tocharian and Proto-South-Indo-European (PSIE) had separated. I had simply extended the logic of the Anatolian and one-other-branch test to the whole Indo-European family. It was one of those throwaway 'food for thought' suggestions and I have no idea whether anyone was still listening (I note with horror that it was slide number 59 in my talk, by which time most of my audience should have been well into REM sleep).

But my rhetorical question has now been more than answered. Danish linguist Thomas Olander has been leading a major effort to

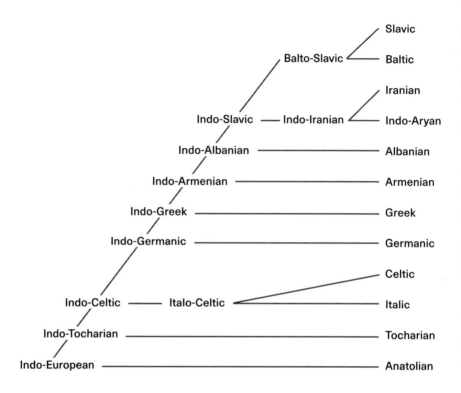

7.2 Thomas Olander's scheme for assessing the antiquity of a reconstruction based on Don Ringe's phylogeny (see 4.12). Olander's 'Indo-Tocharian' equates with my use of Core-Indo-European.

examine the phylogeny of Indo-European and has recently made a case for strict adherence to this phylogeny in evaluating a reconstruction so that we would have a sliding scale of demonstrable antiquity [**7.2**]. It would begin when one recovers a cognate set between Anatolian and any other Indo-European language (Indo-Anatolian, the earliest level of reconstructions).[20] If there was no cognate in Anatolian the reconstruction might then be relegated to the next phase (Indo-Tocharian, under the presumption that Tocharian was the next branch to differentiate and leave the nest). Failing a Tocharian cognate we would move to the next phase Indo-Celtic and so forth.

While Olander's proposal certainly has the advantage of clarity, there are (at least) two issues of concern in employing this approach. The first one is not confined to Indo-European because Uralic also faces the same problem: both language families split early into two branches (Anatolian and Core-Indo-European; Samoyedic and Finno-Ugric), one of which in terms of cognates does not pull its weight. Anatolian only contributes to about 25 per cent of our Proto-Indo-European reconstructions and Tocharian to about a third. Neither of these branches (Hittite attests about 1,900 'words' of which 46 per cent are dismissed as non-Indo-European loans)[21] provide a comparable amount of data to the classical languages (Sanskrit, Greek and Latin) or the abundant later textual evidence of Germanic, Celtic and Slavic; in effect they have a veto on the majority of our cognate sets.[22] On the other hand, as we have already seen, the split between Anatolian and the rest of Indo-European does play a critical part in the current solutions to the homeland problem, so the distinction seems justified here, and we have to live with the Anatolian veto if we want to take a cognate set back to the earliest stage of the protolanguage, Proto-Indo-Anatolian.

Second, moving to Olander's second tier of Indo-Tocharian (Core-Indo-European) as the next stage has a lot of (although not the entire) support of linguists and if, as we will later see, there is considerable endorsement of the idea that the ancestors of the Tocharians migrated well away from all other Indo-Europeans at a very early date, one could live with that. But subsequently we encounter serious debate about the ordering of the splits as Olander himself admits and, I suspect, to go any further takes us into multiple constituency problems. For example, according to Olander's procedure a Celtic and Germanic cognate should secure an earlier stage (Indo-Celtic tier of reconstruction) whose ancestor should be earlier than one that involved a Germanic and a Sanskrit cognate (Indo-Germanic). I think many linguists would feel far more secure with the latter comparison between two languages whose ancestors should have been well separated in space (Germanic and Indic) than the ancestors of two branches (Celtic and Germanic) that could hardly have avoided rubbing shoulders with one another in prehistory and that are grouped closer together in a number of other current phylogenies. We will return to this issue later.

CHAPTER 7

Cautionary tales

Throughout his publications the Austrian-born (and fled) Italicist Ernst Pulgram (1915–2005) warned that linguistic palaeontology could only 'result in illusory findings', as the reconstructed proto-culture is 'not actually placeable in time and place'.[23] In one of his most influential and entertaining books on the origins of the languages of Italy, he dismissed linguistic palaeontology with a cautionary tale of how a future linguist, attempting to reconstruct the culture of the homeland of the Romance languages, could reconstruct common words for 'café', 'beer', 'tobacco' and 'bishop' and thereby summon up images of ancient Rome populated by beer-swilling bishops, sitting in cafés, puffing on their cigars.[24] A great put-down, and often cited as evidence against the use of linguistic palaeontology, but as irritating as hell to any linguist (as Pulgram probably knew very well) since the anachronistic vocabulary would never have been reconstructed to the same time frame as the rest of Common Latin because their phonetic shape clearly marked them out as later loanwords across the various Romance languages.[25] This, however, does not address all the reasons one might be sceptical of linguistic palaeontology and, fortunately, Harold Bender, in his excellent 1922 study of Indo-European origins, listed the commonest objections to the validity of the practice. Let's look at these briefly and tack on some more that occur in the literature, before we begin a closer examination of the evidence.

1. *The absence of a reconstructed word does not mean that it did not exist in the proto-language.* In Rudolf von Ihering's cornucopia of unusual solutions to the homeland problem, he dismisses a northern homeland because words for 'stable', 'hay' and 'straw' (requisites for stabling livestock in a cold environment) 'are wanting to the Aryan mother-tongue, which is positive proof that the things themselves did not exist'.[26] Or we might recall Benfey's exclusion of a homeland in Asia because a common word for 'lion', 'tiger' or 'camel' could not be reconstructed. The lack of words for sea, saltwater fish, tidal movements or nautical transport beyond the most basic has been often employed to exclude a homeland bordering on any sea coast,

be it the Mediterranean or, more consequently, the Baltic or North seas.[27] And despite protests to the contrary by Herman Hirt,[28] the minimal attestation for words associated with fishing developed into a trope among those utilizing negative evidence to exclude homelands both in northern Europe and the Pontic-Caspian.[29]

Against this, one can always counter that a reconstruction describing a localized environment could easily be lost by the daughter languages if they moved away from the region in which the word was localized. The homeland may actually have been overrun with camel-devouring lions, but once the Indo-Europeans had dispersed to lands without such entertaining diversions, they could easily lose the relevant vocabulary.[30]

By and large, arguments *ex silentio* ('from silence') when applied to single items have been dismissed as being at all probative, since there are numerous examples of concepts that were probably once covered by inherited words being replaced by foreign loanwords. On the other hand, some argue that when entire semantic fields appear to be absent or are minimally represented – what Paul Thieme (1905–2001), the great Sanskrit scholar and ardent proponent of employing linguistic palaeontology in pursuit of the Urheimat, called *negative kumulative Evidenz*[31] – this is significant. Conversely, Wolfgang Dressler has argued that 'cumulative *argumenta ex silentio* are hardly more plausible than individual ones'.[32] We are clearly again in a constituency issue where the argument depends more on the tone of one's voice as a sacred dictum is issued than either evidence or logic. While the nature of the archaeological record can routinely admit arguments based on the absence of evidence,[33] the degradation of evidence across a language family is probably not so epistemologically forgiving, and there is good reason to adhere to a higher standard of argument and avoid negative evidence when the field is already contentious enough. On the other hand, I can't help but ask the rhetorical question: how many swallows *do* you need to make a summer?

2. *Insufficient attestation*. This, of course, is the major problem that we have just discussed and will have to return to again.

3. *Uncertain semantic reconstruction.* Not all cognate sets point to an easily identifiable proto-meaning. For example, in contrast to the rather unambiguous reconstruction of a word for 'sheep', we have the cognate set shown in **7.3** that indicates some form of implement, but it is anyone's guess what that might have been.

Lithuanian	*kirvis*	'axe'
Russian	*červ*	'sickel'
Sanskrit	*kr̥vi-*	'weaving instrument'
PIE	**kʷr̥wi-'*	'a multi-tool?'

7.3 An example of a semantically ambiguous Proto-Indo-European (PIE) reconstruction.

Not much hangs on this comparison since any cognate set that does not yield a relatively secure meaning is not going to be accepted as diagnostic for establishing the homeland. Alas, as we will soon see, this is easier said than done. Here, however, we should probably address the objections of those critics that contrast the comparative method, which provides us with the basic evidence for the *reconstructed form* of the word involving the application of regular sound laws, with the recovery of the *meaning* of the word, for which there is no appeal to either the logical procedures of inductive or deductive reasoning – the precise meaning of the word itself cannot be 'reconstructed' in any logical sense but is a product of debatable guesswork.[34] Defenders of the method, however, can freely admit that semantic reconstructions are indeed not generated by any rules of inductive or deductive reasoning but rather the application of *abductive* reasoning, the attempt to provide the 'best explanation of why cognates possess the contents they do', which are routinely assessed in terms of 'simplicity, generality, and coherence'.[35] We'll return to this below.

4. *Migration leads to reapplication of words to new species or objects.* Bender, who was the lead etymologist on the 1934 edition of *Webster's New International Dictionary*, illustrated this by relating how the word 'gopher' was applied to a 'squirrel' in Wisconsin, a

'rat' in Missouri, a 'snake' in Georgia and a 'turtle' in Florida. We have good examples of this in Indo-European, especially among bird names. For example, a PIE *teter-* normally returns meanings that suggest it was a large gamebird, but we can't specify which because it is a 'capercaillie' (Germanic, Baltic, Russian and Greek), a 'pheasant' (Old Church Slavonic and Iranian), a 'partridge' (Sanskrit) or a 'hooded crow' (Middle Irish). So, yes, some words were obviously reapplied to different things, but this is normally indicated in the variety of the reconstructed meanings. Sometimes we can probably narrow the meaning somewhat – for example, *tauros* generally carries a male bovine meaning 'bull', 'bullock', 'bison' or 'aurochs' (the wild cattle of Eurasia), but it may also mean 'mountain goat' in Khotanese Saka, an Iranian language recorded in Xinjiang, western China. We will later see among the arboreal terms a notorious example of this problem and how it has been handled.

5. *A word may be widespread and have the same meaning but not belong to the proto-language.* Here, of course, we are dealing with loanwords and this is a problem that linguists routinely confront in comparative linguistics. We have already reviewed some of the evidence for loanwords in Proto-Indo-European and, where they can be reconstructed to Proto-Indo-European, they can be treated as native as the inherited vocabulary. We have just examined *tauros*, which is commonly assumed to be a loanword either from Semitic or into both Indo-European and Semitic from a third source. In other cases, we can recover loanwords between Indo-European languages – for example, as the Latin word for 'cow' (*bōs*) is not the expected outcome of PIE *$g^w\bar{o}us$* in Latin (it should have been Latin *us* or *vos*) it is presumed to be a loanword and, fortunately, we can identify the probable source because we also have the written records of the closely related Osco-Umbrian language where the 'cow' word does begin with a *b* (*bum*). While linguists are alert to the possibility of loanwords, their phonetic shape and the time depth of their borrowing can at times render them exceedingly difficult if not impossible to identify. Linguists

are well aware of the problem and can employ a variety of techniques to ferret out words that simply don't belong.[36]

6. *Vocabulary transcends experience.* It is possible for a population to preserve words for either something no longer in their environment or an item that only existed in their imagination. An example of the former is Old Irish *nathir* 'snake' from Proto-Celtic **natrik-* 'snake', where the one animal whose absence from the island is almost emblematic. But given the fact that the northeast of Ireland is situated only 20 km (12 miles) from adder-infested Scotland (apologies), the preservation of the word in Irish is hardly miraculous. Austrian Hittite scholar Heinz Kronasser (1913–1968), a sceptic of the use of linguistic palaeontology, directly applied this criticism to the homeland problem when he observed that, as the Slavic languages allow us to reconstruct a Proto-Slavic **slonъ* 'elephant', must we presume that the Proto-Slavic homeland hosted 'elephants', and whether this was any different from the reconstruction of a word for 'horse' in Proto-Indo-European?[37] But here we are dealing with one of the most recent branches of Indo-European whose census date for what qualifies as Proto-Slavic runs into the early Middle Ages when elephants had begun to appear in European literature and folklore.

Although Bender could list these various criticisms of linguistic palaeontology, he found them unconvincing when it was a matter of common sense and concluded:

> If a number of Indo-European languages had a word derived in each case from the same stem, and if the literature of each language indicated that the word in that language signified, for example, the same, or approximately the same animal as in the other languages, and if the animal were familiar enough to make borrowing unlikely, then it would be absurd to deny the probability that the ancient Indo-Europeans knew that animal.[38]

In short, Bender cautioned against throwing out the baby with the bathwater and argued that we should engage with every reconstruction on its own merits or lack of merit. There is, nevertheless, another objection that needs to be addressed.

Although Pulgram's cautionary tale is linguistically flawed, the underlying thesis does pose a serious question regarding the chronology of our reconstructions. Indo-Europeanist James Clackson employs the metaphor of a constellation of stars that we perceive as a single shape (plough, scorpion or whatever) but that in fact consists of stars at varying distances from one another to convey his conclusion that 'the starred forms of reconstruction, although presented as of uniform time depths, may in fact amalgamate material of completely different times unrealistically, and the patterns that emerge from the data need not reflect the actual prehistoric situation'.[39]

This was not a new critique and has been around since at least the late 19th century. In 1872 Johannes Schmidt dismissed a reconstructed language as 'a scientific fiction', likening a reconstructed sentence to a translation of a line from a gospel where one word was derived from the 9th-century Tatian, the next from the 4th-century Ulfilas, and the next from 16th-century Martin Luther.[40] The customarily incisive German linguist Paul Kretschmer (1866–1956) argued that while the reconstructions of the proto-language might be dated in a relative fashion to the sound changes involved, they could not be provided with absolute dates nor be assigned to a single period.[41] The Scottish Celticist John Fraser (1882–1945) not only argued much the same case in 1926, but employed the image of a 'composite photograph which is not a faithful picture of any one stage of development' and even offered the cautionary comment that 'when the Indo-Europeans knew the horse they might not at all have been in the same place as that where they knew the birch'.[42]

There are genuine issues here and ones that are perhaps not so critical. To begin with Fraser's warning, let us assume that we have solid reconstructions for both 'horse' and 'birch' (we do and the 'birch' test for locating the homeland has been around since Julius Klaproth in 1830[43]). Now also let's assume that the Proto-Indo-Europeans originally lived in a horse-less homeland where one couldn't see the sky for the birch trees, but after a couple of centuries they moved to a treeless steppe covered with grass-gorging horses for another five hundred years before the language dissolved into its different branches, which should approximate Fraser's worse-case scenario. But then we can ask, why did generations of Indo-Europeans preserve the name of the birch and associate the name consistently with the same species (except the Latins) when they hadn't seen one for five centuries? In Fraser's scenario, one would have expected that we could reconstruct a word for 'horse' but find insufficient evidence for 'birch'. If we can reconstruct both words, that suggests the second premise was wrong and that wherever the Indo-Europeans *last* lived, it was in a place where both horses and birch trees lived in peace. The vocabulary of any language is going to be cumulative, continually adding (as well as shedding) words, and so the 'birch' word could have entered the language before or after the 'horse' word. Reconstruction takes us back to the last linguistic ancestor when the language possessed both the 'horse' and 'birch' words. In fact, some linguists engaged in homeland hunting have not only recognized that the reconstructed vocabulary had been assembled over time, but also attempted to employ aspects of this recognition to locate the homeland and fine-tune the dispersal of the languages.

Indo-European cultural time depth

There have been two major approaches to analysing the relative chronological differences of our reconstruction: one is internal, where one attempts to assess the cultural layers of Proto-Indo-European largely through a grammatical analysis of the vocabulary, and the second involves a more nuanced analysis of the semantic fields of the inherited vocabulary according to the phylogeny of Indo-European.

The first of these can be illustrated with reference to English. Today, plurals are routinely created by simply adding -*s* to a word – one dog: two dogs, one pig: two pigs – and any new word would be automatically treated the same – one gruffalo: two gruffaloes – which shows that the plural formation in -*s* is still active and is not merely a relic of an earlier system. However, in Old English there were other ways to form plurals and we find occasional relics in modern English. For example, we say one mouse: two mice and one louse: two lice, but these are relic systems and we do not apply the same rule to all similar-sounding words – an estate agent does not attempt to show you one house but two 'hice', nor are a group of people from Liverpool known as 'Scicer' (Scouser). In some cases, an extremely rare relic might survive, such as with one ox: two oxen. It might surprise some that plurals in -*n* were extremely common in Old English – for example, [1] *dogga*: [2] *doggan* 'dogs', [1] *hara*: [2] *haran* 'hares', [1] *tunge*: [2] *tungan* 'tongues' – and this is still the commonest way of making plurals in our close linguistic neighbour, Dutch. Needless to say, this option is no longer open in English.[44]

Similarly, we find in Proto-Indo-European grammatical structures that appear to be relics, which ceased to be operational in the daughter languages but where the forms still leave traces scattered across the Indo-European branches. The main source of discussion is the noun, which was structured with a root followed by a stem and then a grammatical ending (like the -*s* plural in English). It has been usually assumed that the oldest forms of nouns are what are known as heteroclitics, where the stem itself changes from the form found in the subject case to a different form for the other cases. This often involved the change from an -*r*- to an -*n*- in the stem – for example, PIE **wód-r* 'water' does not become the expected ***wéd-r-s* 'of water' but rather **wéd-n-s* – but this system is only preserved in Anatolian (i.e. Hittite *wátar*: *wetenas*). The system survives only as a relic in all the other Indo-European branches, where the language settles on one or the other sound – for example, in **wésr̥* 'spring', Lithuanian runs only with an -*r* (*vāsara*) but Sanskrit went with the -*n* (*vasantá-*). If the *r/n* heteroclitics seem to be the oldest grammatically formed nouns, the -*o* and -*a* stems (e.g. **wl̥kʷ-o-s* 'wolf') continued to be produced even after the breakdown of Proto-Indo-European, which suggested to some linguists that they were the most recent formations; all of the other stems are built on consonants (where *i* and *u* are regarded as the consonants *y* and *w*).

Now, the heteroclitics often appear to comprise some of the most basic elements of vocabulary, such as 'fire' (**péh₂ur*), 'blood' (**h₁ésh₂r̥*) and 'liver' (**yekʷr̥(t)*).[45] Matching the relative age of the nouns against their meanings encouraged linguists to employ the grammatical evidence to trace the cultural evolution of the Indo-Europeans through time. For example, in 1937 German linguist Alfons Nehring (1890–1967) noted that, while many basic concepts were formed employing heteroclitics (nature, parts of the body), no plants were treated in this way and so the heteroclitics were formed in a pre-agricultural period of Indo-European (unaware that the word for 'plough' is a heteroclitic)[46] – a notion that American linguist Winfred Lehmann (1916–2007) would 'rediscover' fifty-two years later when he argued that Pre-Indo-European, the time of the heteroclitics, knew neither terms for hunting, nor agriculture, nor pottery – a time that he set to c. 8000–5000 BCE.[47] Unfortunately, this approach seldom if ever led to conclusive results and a cultural reconstruction of a society predating hunting might possibly fit some descriptions of early hominin scavengers but not any population relevant to *Homo sapiens*, much less the Indo-Europeans. Moreover, there is something troublesome about an analysis that implies the Indo-Europeans or their immediate ancestors only came to the realization that they had fire, blood, livers or names for the lights in the sky in the millennia immediately preceding their expansion. The origin of language and the recognition that there was a sun in the sky or people had livers must surely predate Proto-Indo-European not by a few thousand years, but by tens of thousands of years. In short, presumably there was a time when the heteroclitic nouns were replacing still earlier ones, but that would take us down a different (though interesting) path.

The second approach to correlating the lexical and cultural evolution of Indo-European has been the semantic analysis of common Indo-European words. Nehring and, especially, the Austrian linguist (and Atlantis hunter) Wilhelm Brandenstein[48] (1898–1967) argued that although we can reconstruct common Proto-Indo-European words in both the Indo-Iranian and European languages, semantic analysis of the words indicates that while the European languages yield meanings consistent with a settled arable agricultural economy, the Indo-Iranian languages attest an earlier semantic level for the same words. For example, while PIE *$h_2eǵros$ routinely denotes an agricultural field in the European languages (the Latin loanword in English *agriculture* is derived from this root), it only indicates a 'plain' in Indo-Iranian; while PIE *$h_2melĝ$- yields 'milk' in the European cognates, its meaning in Indo-Aryan is merely 'wipe, rub off'. Brandenstein prepared a mini-dictionary of such contrasting meanings, which was employed to suggest that the Indo-Iranians had practised an economy that did not include arable agriculture, and so either the Indo-European homeland was large enough to embrace both a western (European) arable component and an eastern (Indo-Iranian) pastoral society, or the homeland itself was situated on the open steppe before the Indo-Europeans moved westwards and adopted agriculture and shifted the semantics of earlier words to accommodate the European environment and economy (including some nasty diseases acquired when they entered a far damper climate). A similar approach, perhaps less controversial, are the claims that we also see Proto-Indo-Anatolian roots rendered with more primitive meanings in Hittite (our main representative of the Anatolian branch) than the other Indo-European languages – for example, *h_2erh_3- 'plough' is the usual PIE reconstruction but in Hittite it renders just 'to grind, to crush', hence, it is argued, Anatolian agriculture may have been pre-plough.[49]

Many of Brandenstein's semantic arguments were dismantled by Franz Specht (1888–1949) – for example, *$h_2eĝros$ 'field' derives from the verbal root *$h_2eĝ$- 'drive cattle', so it must originally have been associated with a field for domestic livestock.[50] There are several problems with Brandenstein's approaches, the leading one being the questionable validity of what Brandenstein called the irreversible *Bedeutungswandel* ('semantic shift'). Semantic change can be notoriously unpredictable and is not easily confined by laws, and so one's assessment of a change such as 'open field' > 'ploughed field' or 'crush' > 'plough' is more an assertion based on a degree of plausibility enhanced by the elegance of the argument rather than hard science. After all, one can 'plough an exam', meaning to be crushed or buried by it, fail. Moreover, the attempts to render the Indo-Iranians as the bearers of the earliest Indo-European economy (pastoralism without agriculture) run up against their frequent position in the Indo-Anatolian phylogeny that would often (although not always) have them depart late from the Indo-European continuum, rather than see the rest of the Indo-Europeans depart after them (see **7.2**).

CHAPTER 7

The constellation problem

Now we must return to the argument that the reconstructed vocabulary does not provide a consistent image of Proto-Indo-European at a specific time but, as the metaphor of the constellation suggests, is only our mental construct of words (stars) from different periods (light years from Earth).

What we are dealing with here is whether the time frame of our Proto-Indo-Anatolian reconstructions is so large as to be effectively meaningless. The practical issue is how do we know whether a reconstructed word that is spatially or temporally diagnostic for the homeland problem was actually a part of the language in the homeland rather than a word that circulated after Indo-European dispersals? It seems best to start with what we (think we) know and then see how far we can extend our leash.

We can begin by employing the written record to determine the earliest date for the different languages. By *c.* 1500–1300 BCE we already have several centuries of Hittite evidence (as well as Anatolian personal names going back to at least 1900 BCE if not a few centuries earlier)[51] in addition to our earliest evidence of Greek (Linear B tablets) and Indo-Aryan (personal names and some loanwords in Hurrian and Hittite sources). So by *c.* 1500 BCE we have three distinct branches and we know one of these (Anatolian) could be pushed back to at least *c.* 2000 BCE. Beyond this we can only engage in extrapolation. Since Indo-Aryan is one member of an earlier Indo-Iranian mega-branch and this involves a number of really marked differences from Proto-Indo-European we can feel fairly safe in rolling the terminal date back to *c.* 2000 BCE for the split dates when these two branches (Indo-Aryan and Iranian) separated from the rest of the Indo-European languages. The differences between Proto-Greek (which is not Linear B and so must be earlier) and Proto-Indo-Iranian would also encourage us to assume that they had been separated earlier than *c.* 2000 BCE. These are only rough intuitive estimates but we are in good company. American linguist Warren Cowgill (1929–1985), for example, estimated that the differences between Anatolian, Greek and Indo-Iranian at *c.* 1500 BCE required a separation time of at least a thousand years but probably less than two thousand years.⁵² Outside of some computational estimates, *c.* 2500 BCE tends to be a generally accepted ballpark figure, although some prefer a somewhat earlier date. Recently, for example, Alwin Kloekhorst, a specialist on the Anatolian languages, has suggested that the various languages (Hittite, Luvian, Palaic) were already so different when we first encounter them that they should have emerged from Proto-Anatolian *c.* 3000 BCE and that Anatolian itself split from Core-Indo-European (or Olander's Indo-Tocharian) *c.* 4200–4000 BCE.⁵³ Kloekhorst then dates the Tocharian split, widely agreed to be the second branch to emerge, to *c.* 3400 BCE.

For those who prefer their dates generated computationally (see **4.13** for the different chronological estimates), we find some of the more recent published studies offer similar figures for the Anatolian split, ranging from 4500 to 3700 BCE.⁵⁴ Kloekhorst's estimate for the Tocharian split is also in rough accord with the more statistically based methods (Moscow and Berkeley *c.* 3500 BCE), although in their most recent paper the Auckland group has given a median split date for both Anatolian and Tocharian of *c.* 5000 BCE (within a range of *c.* 6600–3400 BCE).⁵⁵ To drag us back to the problem of linguistic palaeontology, the dates suggest that the differences between the ancestors of Anatolian, Greek and Indo-Iranian by *c.* 2500 BCE were such that it is highly unlikely that undetected loanwords were passing among them.

It is after the Tocharian split that consensus on phylogenies breaks down, and the distance between the progressive disintegration of the proto-language (or the coalescence of a chain of languages) and the emergence of the already differentiated branches disappears into a black box which is phylogenetically and chronologically opaque – so much so that 'the majority of Indo-Europeanists prefer not to discuss Inner IE branchings [= everything except Anatolian and Tocharian] at all'.⁵⁶ Take the three western Indo-European branches: Celtic, Italic and Germanic. The computer-generated split dates for these languages find both the Berkeley and Moscow schools in general agreement, with a date *c.* 2000 BCE, perhaps a bit earlier for Germanic, while, as usual, the Auckland group suggest a significantly earlier median date of *c.* 4465 BCE (5900–3000 BCE) for the same group of languages.

Setting aside for the moment the accuracy of these dates, let us examine to what extent the different branch proto-languages differed from one another and whether they are sufficiently different to prevent a loanword passing among them and being misidentified as a word inherited from Proto-Indo-European. A glance at some of the reconstructed forms naming the human anatomy from these three branches provides an impression of the differences between Proto-Indo-European and some of its western daughter branches, as well as between the branches and some of their early historically attested daughter languages [**7.4**].

The first thing noticeable is that other than a few exceptions, the proto-languages of each branch are significantly different from one another. For example, if either the proto-form or a descendant of a Celtic word was carried into Italy it would likely be recognized as having followed a different set of sound laws and be exposed as a loanword. There are, of course, some exceptions where the original shape of the word in Proto-Indo-European is built from such stable sounds that they are closely replicated in some branches and even the daughter languages – for example, *$\acute{g}enu$- ('jaw'). In such instances a word might indeed be borrowed from one branch to another without detection if it were at a suitably early date, and this is something that a linguist routinely must take into consideration.

If the proto-languages of the branches provide a rough terminal date for identifying most loans, do they provide any information that we can use to estimate how much time there was between Proto-Indo-Anatolian and the formation of the different branches? The historical arguments reviewed here have suggested that we expect some proto-branches by 2500–2000 BCE and still earlier for Proto-Anatolian. Can this be extended across the Indo-European world? Logically, it might be possible because the alternative would suggest a situation where Anatolian, Greek and Indo-Iranian had all emerged as separate branches while the rest of Indo-European world had remained static (as if the occupants of Italy had retained Latin as their common language up to the 8th century CE while the rest of the former Roman Empire had evolved into the Romance languages). So it is certainly plausible to assume that by 2500–2000 BCE the rest of the Indo-European world had ceased to speak Proto-Indo-European. In no way, however, does it necessarily mean that

GEOGRAPHICAL CLUES IN THE INDO-EUROPEAN VOCABULARY

English meaning	Celtic	Italic	Germanic	PIE
nail	*ang{ʷ}īnā ingen	*ongu(-i)- unguis	*naȝla- nægel	*h₃nogh(w)-
mouth	*ās- á	*ōs- ōs	*ōsa- ON oss	*h₁⁄₄óh₁(e)s-
tear	*dakro- dér-	*dakru- d/lacruma	*taxru- tæhher	*(d)h₂eḱru-
tooth	*danto- dét-	*dent- dēns	*tunþu- tōđ	*h₁dónt-
jaw	*genu- gin	*genu- gena	*kennu- cinn	*ǵenu-
knee	*glūnos- glún	*genu genū	*knewa- cnēo(w)	*ǵonu-
thigh	*klowni- clúain	*lou-ni- clūnis	*xlauni- ON hlaun	*ḱlounis
hollow of joint	*koxsā cos	*koksā- coxa	*xaxsō- OHG hahsa	*koḱs-o/eh₂-
heart	*kridyo- cride	*kord- cor	*xertō- heorte	*ḱērd
body	*krif- crí	*korp-os- corpus	*refa- hrif	*kreps
elbow	*olīnā uilen	*olenā- ulna	*alinō eln	*h₃elVn-
tongue	*tangʷāt- tengae	*dnχ(u)wā- lingua	*tunȝō- tunge	*dn̥ǵhuh₂-

7.4 A comparison between selected anatomical words in Proto-Indo-European (PIE) and the reconstructed branches of Celtic, Italic and Germanic (in **bold**) and forms in at least one of the early attested daughter languages (in *italics*): Celtic and Old or Middle Irish; Italic and Latin; and Germanic and Old English or Old Norse (ON)/Old High German (OHG).

the rest of Europe had divided into its historically known branches rather than evolved into a chain of different late Indo-European dialects. It has long appeared (to me at least)[57] that linguists have routinely treated the development of the languages of the rest of Europe as somewhat shallower than Greek, Indo-Iranian or Anatolian. In a recent study of the prehistoric relations between Celtic and Germanic, American linguist

173

John Koch has suggested that in this very period, *c.* 2500–2000 BCE, it is still possible that Indo-European 'speakers from widely separated communities in Europe could probably have understood one another using their native languages'.[58]

A key problem here then is reconciling the split dates suggested by the various Indo-European phylogenies, especially those that have been computed on the basis of word lists, with the reconstructed proto-branches. As Koch reminds us, we are actually dealing with two linguistic stages: the pre- and the proto-. The proto-stage is the 'latest reconstructable stage of the common ancestor' of the attested languages of a particular branch. Recall our earlier exercise in determining the homeland of Proto-Romance that resulted in an answer that ran from the Atlantic to the Black Sea. Now recall that the probable linguistic period of Proto-Romance was dated *c.* 200 BCE to 200 CE (with the last common stage probably closer to 200 CE). At the beginning of that period the Romans had just managed to defeat Hannibal and hold on to most of Italy but by 200 CE the Roman Empire (and the area in which Proto-Romance arose) had extended from the Atlantic to the Black Sea and Anatolia, so an enormous Proto-Romance homeland would be the expected outcome. The reconstruction of a proto-language is determined largely by the phonetic and grammatical changes that distinguish a branch from its previous proto-language. For example, one can list the major phonetic changes from Proto-Indo-European that evolved to define the Proto-Celtic branch [7.5]:

1. syllabic $*\mathring{r}$ and $*\mathring{l}$ > $*ri$ and $*li$ after any consonant and before a stop consonant;
2. $*g^w$ > $*b$;
3. $*bh$ $*dh$ $*gh$ $*g^wh$ > $*b$ $*d$ $*g$ $*g^w$;
4. $*p$ > $*\varphi$ (then disappearing altogether in most positions);
5. long $*\bar{o}$ > long $*\bar{u}$ in final syllables;
6. long $*\bar{o}$ > long $*\bar{a}$ in all other syllables;
7. syllabic $*\mathring{m}$ and $*\mathring{n}$ > $*am$ and $*an$;
8. long $*\bar{e}$ > long $*\bar{\imath}$.

7.5 Major sound changes of Proto-Indo-European to Proto-Celtic.[59]

We could compare some of these changes with those that define Proto-Germanic. For example, while Celtic sees PIE *r̥ and *l̥ > *ri and *li, Proto-Germanic changes *r̥, *l̥ > *ur, *ul. Because of these changes, once the proto-branches have formed, a linguist has some evidence whether a word has been borrowed or whether it has been inherited into both branches at an earlier time.

The other stage is the pre-stage, where the changes that are found completed in the proto-stage have only begun to appear and set a group of dialects or a language on the path to becoming a branch distinct from other branches. To what extent the pre- and proto-stages are identical is unknown, and this issue is at the heart of our constellation problem [7.6]. For example, it is widely acknowledged that the date of Proto-Germanic, the last common ancestor of the Germanic languages, is c. 500 BCE, and usually if there is a challenge to this, it tends to reduce the date towards 100 BCE rather than push it earlier.[60] We can contrast this with the estimates for the date of Proto-Celtic, which falls c. 1200–900 BCE, illustrating the differing horizons assigned to the various European proto-branches. Now compare these dates with the split dates or pre-stages. Koch estimates Pre-Germanic at c. 1900–500/400 BCE and Pre-Celtic at c. 1800/1500–1200 BCE. The corresponding three computational results that we have seen so far are 2350–1900 BCE (Berkeley, Moscow) and

	Koch 2020	Berkeley 2015	Moscow 2021	Auckland 2023
Pre-Celtic	1800–1200 BCE	1900 BCE	2100 BCE	2900 BCE [4200–1700 BCE]
Proto-Celtic	1200–900 BCE	2350–2150 BCE	2100 BCE	1200 BCE [2000–500 BCE]
Pre-Germanic	1900–400 BCE	500–1 BCE	500–300 BCE	2900 BCE [4200–1700 BCE]
Proto-Germanic	500–100 BCE			300 BCE [900 BCE–100 BCE]

7.6 Rough approximations of pre-branch/split date stages and estimates of the date of the Celtic and Germanic proto-languages illustrate the problem of distinguishing between the dates assigned to the separation of the branches and the estimated dates of their actual proto-languages (note: the Auckland 2023 dates are the median of the bracketed dates).

earlier (2889 BCE, Auckland 2023, with a 4193–1718 BCE range). There are several things about these discrepancies that are interesting, the first being merely incidental while the second is absolutely critical.

The computational results for the pre-stages are close to the informed estimates, yet they are based on an entirely different dataset – the presence or absence of a very limited shared lexicon from a word list. A quick thought experiment: a time-traveller returns to the 5th century CE and convinces Saint Patrick that the Irish cognates on the computational word list are the devil's own, and so the good saint has them removed from the Irish language and replaced by their Latin equivalents. Perusing the list the linguist recognizes that his entire word list is made up of Latin loanwords that have undergone some pretty ferocious Irish sound changes – for example, Latin *apostulus* 'apostle' becomes Irish *apstal*. If this happened, our computational linguist would not be able to demonstrate that Irish was an Indo-European language much less belonged to the Celtic branch. It would occupy the same position as Chinese or Mayan. However, any competent historical linguist would still be able to determine that Irish was indeed a member of the Celtic branch of Indo-European. This would be demonstrated by its phonetics and morphology on all the language outside of the test word list that had been removed. In short, word lists are essentially serving as (somewhat precarious) proxies for the evidence of phonetics and grammar.

The most significant issue to come out of the distinction between the pre-stage and the proto-stage is their potential durations. For Germanic the gap between the pre-stage and the proto-stage is anywhere from *c.* 1,500 years to *c.* 2,500 years (Auckland) and, as Koch reminds us, it is not clear whether the changes that resulted in Proto-Germanic were spread evenly through time or 'bunched together within a shorter span'.[61] If they were bunched together at the beginning, it could be argued that Germanic underwent 1,500–2,500 years without any major phonetic changes, meaning there was no difference between the pre- and proto-stages of Germanic evolution. If you bunch the changes at the end, you have a similar period in which you may not be able to distinguish between Pre-Germanic and other Indo-European branches. The black box that separates Pre-Celtic from Proto-Celtic is not quite so large because, although its proto-language is a bit earlier, the range is about c. 300–1,700 years depending on the accepted start date for Celtic separation. We could play similar games with the other European branches such as Italic, Baltic and Slavic, while in a recent paper on the dissolution of Proto-Uralic, Finnish linguist Jaakko Häkkinen[62] estimates the interval in Uralic at somewhere from five hundred years but less than a thousand. In short, we have a series of proto-branches that are usually set to c. 1500–500 BCE and a series of very rough estimates that suggest that they had arrived at that state after about a thousand or (following Auckland) more years. It's time to take what we know and don't know to a critical example.

The wheel

The wheel and wheeled vehicles (two-wheeled carts and four-wheeled wagons) present the most diagnostic markers for the terminal date of reconstructed Proto-Indo-European culture, because their origins in the archaeological record were essentially a 4th-millennium BCE phenomenon. Wheels began c. 4000 BCE with simple discs (which may or may not have been applied to toys, as was the case with New World vehicles), but by c. 3500–3000 BCE the evidence clearly indicates the presence of wheeled vehicles, which, of course, have continued to this very day.[63] The linguistic status of the vocabulary of wheeled vehicles, on the other hand, is extremely contentious.[64] If one can safely ascribe wheeled vehicles to Proto-Indo-European, then the proto-language should not have divided earlier than the 4th millennium BCE, otherwise we would not be able to reconstruct a common vocabulary of wheeled vehicles from the different branches. A number of the most prominent homeland solutions set the Urheimat earlier than the 4th millennium and argue that we cannot safely reconstruct wheeled vehicles to Proto-Indo-European employing linguistic palaeontology.

The linguistic evidence comprises at least five reasonably strong items: *$k^w ék^w lo$- 'wheel', *$Hrotós$ 'wheel', *$h_2 iHs\text{-}eh_2$- 'thill', *$h_2 ek̂s$- 'axle' and *$weĝh$- 'transports by vehicle', plus a number of more contentious words (e.g. *$h_{2/3} wr̥gi$- 'wheel' and *$dhroghós$ 'wheel'); this would, on first glance, seem like a pretty convincing semantic field. Yet the ascription of the wheel and wheeled vehicles to Indo-European has been challenged and so we need to examine the issues involved.

First, it has been argued that the very multiplicity of different words for 'wheel' suggests that we are encountering the wheel terminology *after* the differentiation of the proto-language. This argument was suggested by Robert Coleman (1929–2001), the New Zealand-born Professor of Comparative Philology at Cambridge, in his comments on Colin Renfrew's Anatolian Farmer model.[65] As his paragraph-long critique has often been ignored by supporters of the reconstructions but cited by critics, I quote it in full because it derives from a highly respected scholar and raises some interesting issues of logic (and also because of the fond memories I have of his hospitality).

> Thus, while *$w̥lk^wo$-* 'wolf' and *$g^we{}_3w$-* 'cow', for instance, are widely enough attested to justify their places in the proto-lexicon, many other roots are more problematic. Thus four different roots are used for 'wheel': (1) *$dhregh$-* 'to run' in Greek *trokhós*; (2) *reth-* 'to run, roll' in Latin *rota*, Lithuanian *rãtas*; (3) *k^wel-* 'to rotate, turn' in Old Church Slavonic *kolo*; and (4) its reduplicated form *k^wek^wlo-* in Old English *hwēol*, Vedic *cakráh*, Tocharian *kukäl*. Some languages attest more than one, as Old Irish *droch* and *roth* 'wheel', *cul* 'cart' and Avestan *čaxrō* 'wheel', *raθō* 'chariot'. From all this it looks as if 'wheel' was not in the proto-lexicon and the various words for it were created independently after the dispersal, in some areas no doubt by loan-translation from adjacent Indo-European dialects/languages.[66]

This critique was branded by Paul Heggarty and Colin Renfrew as a 'default principle in linguistic palaeontology', which asserts that 'not one but two roots for the same meaning, variably attested in different languages across a family, are in fact standardly to be interpreted as indicating that the single ancestor language had already begun to diverge before that meaning arose (to explain how they could independently choose different terms for it)'.[67] This rule has been occasionally employed in the past – for example, by Sigmund Feist regarding the fact that we have a variety of names for 'goat' spread across various Indo-European languages, indicating that there was no common term[68] and, therefore, there was no evidence that the Proto-Indo-Europeans knew the goat. Nehring counted nine roots for 'goat', all *o-* or *a-* stems, suggesting to him that it was domesticated very late.[69] On the other hand, Hirt took the same evidence to argue that Proto-Indo-European had a full complement of words for 'goat' but that they were only regionally preserved.[70] Most interesting was Thieme's argument that as the domestic goat was unknown before *c.* 3000 BCE (which we know now is wrong), the fact that it could be reconstructed to Proto-Indo-European provided a terminus for Proto-Indo-European. As for the multiple names, he explained them as having been generated by the peculiar beliefs surrounding male goats or the introduction of different breeds of goats from different sources.[71]

Let's begin our evaluation with *$k^w\acute{e}k^wlo$-* 'wheel'. The word is unattested in Anatolian but does meet Olander's requirements of Indo-Tocharian (Core-Indo-European), with cognates in Tocharian (*kokale* 'wagon') in the east, Indo-Iranian (Sanskrit *cakra-* 'wheel'; Avestan *čaxra-* 'wheel') in South Asia, perhaps Greece (*kúklos*, where it usually just means something 'circular' but is also applied to 'wheel' in Homer), and Germanic (English *wheel*). It is a noun derived from the verbal root *k^wel-*, usually translated as 'turn' (although Alexander Lubotsky has recently argued that the verb in fact means 'roam').[72]

Critics of accepting this word as Proto-Indo-European in date have suggested that we simply have the independent creation of a new word in various already independent branches to form a noun meaning 'something that turns'. Ringe, however, argues that if this were so, why did the various branches all choose the same verbal root when there were three other verbs that also meant 'turn'. Moreover, the word *$k^w\acute{e}k^wlo$-* was constructed in an extremely unusual way, involving the reduplication of the initial sound (*k^wel-* > *k^we-k^w-*) and the reduction of the root vowel (*el-* > *$\mathring{l}$*); therefore, any argument that this was undertaken multiple times from Germany to Turkestan 'is practically impossible'.[73] In short, what we seem to have here is a lexical item (we will worry about its precise meaning in a moment) that would meet the requirements of both spread and the type of idiosyncratic formation that supports its creation in the proto-language and not in the individual branches.

We are now in the truly weird position that if *$k^w ék^w lo$- were the only word for 'wheel' we could find and reconstruct, we would feel confident that the Core-Indo-Europeans (but admittedly not the Proto-Anatolians since we do not find the word in Anatolian) knew the 'wheel'. Yet because of the dreaded 'default principle', which is triggered by the presence of other words for 'wheel', our evidence somehow evaporates! In the opening of Coleman's paragraph he admits *$g^w ōus$ 'cow' to Proto-Indo-European but we also have *$h_1 eǵh$- 'cow' and *$wokéh_2$- 'cow', with no clear idea how the meanings of these words might be distinguished so, I suppose, the 'default principle' must again be invoked: finding three words for 'cow', we have a matter: antimatter situation where the non-*$g^w ōus$ words destroy the *$g^w ōus$ word from the Indo-European lexicon. This principle seems awfully close to assuming that every concept in a language is permitted only one word and one word only; the *Roget's Thesaurus* of Proto-Indo-European must be an incredibly thin volume! The fact is that our reconstructed meanings are always going to involve general semantics, and we often miss the original nuance or the specificity of meaning or much of the more nuanced technical vocabulary. In any stock-raising society we might expect an abundant number of words and distinctions pertaining to each species such as 'cow', 'bull', 'heifer', 'milch cow', 'dry cow', 'bullock' and 'ox'. Early Irish, for example, boasts sixty-two different words for bovines filling out nine such semantic categories and yet no more than six of these words survived from Proto-Celtic.[74] We only get the chance leavings of a proto-language that certainly had much more extended lexicons and semantic distinctions than we will ever be able to recover.

As for the multiple terms for wheels and wagons, American linguist Martin Huld has argued that they should be understood as words reflecting different stages of the evolution of vehicles within Proto-Indo-European itself. Thus a *$dhrogós$ initially referred to the runner on a sledge and was extended to refer to the earliest wheel, followed by the *$Hrotós$, the typical tripartite block wheel employed on the four-wheeled wagon, and then the *$k^w ék^w lo$-, the wheel applied to the two-wheeled cart.[75]

The critical issue here is the distribution of the cognates, which does not appear to support the notion that they were regional creations with some borrowing. For example, we have *$kŕsos$ 'wagon' but it is limited to two presumably adjacent branches, Celtic and Italic, while *$tengh$-s- 'pole' is found only in Italic and Germanic. These could plausibly be dismissed as the type of regional innovations that were passing among Indo-European populations either before they had achieved their pre-stage or even during the pre-stage if sufficient phonetic differences for detection had not yet emerged. On the other hand, the five main terms being advanced as Proto-Indo-European all have an Indo-Iranian cognate, which implies a terminal date of c. 2500 BCE irrespective of the proto-language dates of its European cognates.

A second line of critique is that we cannot be absolutely certain of the accuracy of our reconstructed meanings. Here we are usually talking about the variety of meanings found in the various cognate sets. For example, the words derived from *h_2iHs-eh_2- refer to the 'pole of a vehicle' in Anatolian, Slavic and Indo-Iranian, but it appears as a nautical term in Greek (*oiēïon*), referring to the tiller or helm of a boat. I suppose we could play it safe and say the original meaning was simply a 'pole' without reference to its use, but what are the odds then of a relatively modern language (Slovenian) having independently developed the same specific reference to a wheeled vehicle found both in Hittite and Sanskrit if it originally designated nothing more than a 'pole'? Indeed, as Stefan Höfler recently argued, the Anatolian and Indo-Aryan forms appear to be derivations of the form underlying the Slavic cognate, which he derives from a verb *h_2yeh_2 'move (a vehicle, on a vehicle)'. And as for the nautical meaning in the Greek derivative, Höfler reminds us: 'the (typically stern-mounted) steering oar of a boat resembles the pole of a cart in form and (at least figuratively) in function, a metaphorical transfer of an old word for the latter to designate the former is quite conceivable'.[76]

A number of the terms relating to vehicles are identical to anatomical words – for example, *h_2eks- 'shoulder span: axle', *h_2nobh- 'navel: nave' and (arguably) *k^wek^wlo- 'shoulder joint: wheel' – so each can be challenged on the grounds that the 'original' meaning was a body part. But again, if one disputes that during the period of the proto-language the

Indo-Europeans employed an anatomical analogy to name various parts of a vehicle (compare English where we find clothing terms: the British 'bonnet' = American 'hood'), why the identical formation again over so many different groups?

In an attempt to demonstrate that *k^wek^wlo-* could predate wheeled transport, Heggarty and Renfrew cite the reconstructed poetic phrase *sh_2uens $k^wék^wlos$* 'sun's wheel' as an example of how we might have a word for 'wheel' that had nothing to do with transport but refers metaphorically to cyclic phenomena and 'could very plausibly predate wheeled transport. To make *prima facie* assumptions as to which specific concrete referents might originally have been referred to by given reconstructed roots is an inherently dubious enterprise.'[77] Setting aside the fact that the mythology concerning the solar wheel involves well-known Indo-European solar deities either rolling a wheel along or, more often, having it pulled along by a vehicle,[78] the real problem here is the assumption that we are actually even attempting to recover what was 'originally' meant in a word when we are actually seeking the 'Last Semantic Ancestor' and not what it might have been derived from. Also, the odds are surely in favour of assuming a semantic development 'wheel' > 'something circular or disc-like' than suggesting that one derived the word for 'wheel' from an abstract notion of circularity. All of these arguments involve abductive reasoning that seeks the simplest and clearest explanation for the cognate set that would certainly not appear to involve distant loanwords or independent creations and generally return a meaning that we would logically associate with wheeled vehicles.

In his extensive exploration of the problems involved with linguistic palaeontology, the late French linguist Xavier Tremblay (1971–2011) laid out five criteria of assessment: that the reconstruction is not merely of the root morpheme but requires its entire formation; that the reconstruction excludes borrowing; that it is widely attested across branches separated by numerous isoglosses; that the reconstruction is not trivial; and that the meaning is precise and stable. In his list of words that pass these tests he numbers *$k^wék^wlo$-*.[79]

For the homeland hunter, the question of wheeled vehicles in Core-Indo-European (but not necessarily Proto-Indo-Anatolian) has been sniped at by critics, but until there is a fully developed critical analysis that proves otherwise, I find it difficult to omit wheeled vehicles from the reconstructed Indo-European cultural vocabulary. To reject all of the assembled evidence requires one to come up with a series of convincing alternative explanations for dismissing each item as too recent when, as we will see, a 4th-millennium date for Core-Indo-European, although not necessarily Proto-Indo-Anatolian, does not hinge solely on the reconstruction of wheeled vehicles alone.

We have laboured with the metaphor of the proto-language as a constellation implying that our starred forms could come from almost any period. I am willing to live with the metaphor, but I would also like to choose the constellation. Although contested, there is at least some evidence that the Proto-Indo-Europeans recognized at least one, because both Indo-Aryan and Greek shared the designation Bear (or Bears) for Ursa Major (the Plough, the Big Dipper).[80] It consists of seven major stars, five of which are between 80 and 83 light years distant, and two outliers at 104 and 123 light years (in a galaxy *c*. 87,000 light years across). Reconstructed Core-Indo-European could live with that metaphor: most of the reconstructed vocabulary probably derives from *c*. 3500–2500 BCE, although Proto-Indo-Anatolian might need to be placed earlier. While there will always be a constituency that will never accept any of the evidence for linguistic palaeontology, I think the fairest approach is to treat and test each item individually. We can now take a look at the core evidence that tends to be generally accepted and then those items that have at one time or another been regarded as critical evidence relating to the specific location of the homeland.

Time depth

The lexical evidence is reasonably secure in supporting the hypothesis that the Indo-European languages only began to differentiate from one another after their speakers had begun to devise words for the semantic fields of livestock raising and some form of cereal-based agriculture. In terms of animals, we find a distinction between *$*pek̑u$*-* 'movable wealth; domestic livestock' and *$*g̑^{wb}wer$*-* 'wild animal', and among the animals consistently identified in terms of their domestic variety we have *$g^w\bar{o}us$ 'cow', *$h_1e\hat{g}h$- 'cow', *$uk^{(w)}s\bar{e}n$- 'ox, bull'; *$h_2\acute{o}wis$ (or *$h_3\acute{o}wis$) 'sheep', *$w\rho h_1\acute{e}n$ 'lamb'; *$bhu\hat{g}os$ 'he-goat', *$h_2ei\hat{g}s$ 'goat', *dig- 'goat', *$kapros$ 'goat', *$suHs$ 'pig' and *$p\acute{o}r\hat{k}os$ 'piglet', and *$\hat{k}(u)w\bar{o}n$ 'dog'. That these words refer to domestic animals rather than wild is reinforced by the existence of *$tauros$ 'bull, aurochs' (a possible Caucasian loanword into Proto-Indo-European) where it could have referred to the aurochs, the (now extinct) wild cattle of Eurasia, or bison, in Balto-Slavic, the territory of its last European refuge. As neither the sheep nor the goat had wild forms in Europe before the Neolithic it is not surprising that we lack words for the undomesticated species. There is a word limited to the northwest (Italic, Germanic and Slavic), *$h_1eperos$, which may give us our 'wild boar', while the predecessor of the domestic dog was, naturally, the *w_olk^wos 'wolf'. There are more early words, but their geographical distribution is more confined.

In addition to the names of the domestic animals we also have words for products, among which *$w_olh_2neh_2$- 'wool' is temporally diagnostic (although contested), because the earliest archaeological appearance of wool emerges c. 4000–3000 BCE when domestic sheep were bred to yield a woolly rather than a coarse hairy coat and textiles made from plant fibres were beginning to be replaced by wool. We have seen that the age of the reconstructed word for 'wool' is problematic because of phonological issues relating the proposed Hittite form with the other Indo-European cognates (and it may be a Northeast Caucasian or Hurrian loanword) so in terms of chronology, therefore, the minimalist position would be to date the word for 'wool' after the departure of both Anatolian and Tocharian; I suspect, however, that many would still regard it as good Indo-Anatolian.

The vocabulary associated with cereal agriculture is more modest and in a recent article, after a thorough winnowing of my own list of potential Proto-Indo-European agricultural terms,[81] the authors concluded that 'the lexical evidence for cereal use is relatively modest, but not zero',[82] and they list a number of words reconstructable to Proto-Indo-Anatolian (PIA) *$(H)ieu(H)$- 'cereal' and *$\hat{g}hr\acute{e}sdh$-i- 'cereal', and to Core-Indo-European (where some of the cognate sets are not used in a clearly agricultural context) they admit *h_2erh_3- 'plough',

H₂erh₃-ur/n- '(arable) field', **peis-* 'grind (grain)', **se-sh₁-io-* 'a cereal', **h₂ed-o(s)-* 'a (parched?) cereal', **dhoH-neh₂-* '(cereal) seed' and **pelH-u-* 'chaff'. While one might snipe at the assumption that the words applied to domestic cereals and not simply wild cereals, the word for 'plough' helps tip the balance in favour of domestic.

In terms of chronologically sensitive technology, knowledge of metallurgy has always been an obvious semantic field. In the two most recent attempts to sift through the lexical evidence, both conclude that we have **h₂eyes-* 'copper; bronze', **h₂eusom* 'gold' and **h₂r̥ǵn̥to-* 'silver'. They are, however, all only reconstructable to Olander's 'Proto-Indo-Celtic' stage, there being no certain evidence for cognates in Anatolian or Tocharian.[83] Copper objects are known from sites in Anatolia as early as 8200–7500 BCE onwards,[84] so this does not provide a particularly useful chronological marker. On the other hand, gold and silver appear in Anatolia and neighbouring regions from Iran north through the Caucasus and southern steppe by the 4th millennium BCE, where the Maykop culture displays the conspicuous consumption of gold and silver in the period *c.* 3800–3300 BCE. This again would fit the same technological horizon that sees the earliest wheeled vehicles and, if you insist, wool. Moreover, both studies also examine technologically later evidence for metallurgy from the Bronze (bronze, tin, lead) and Iron (iron) ages, which reveal only regionally attested acquaintance with such items. This helps to support the notion that linguists are identifying a reasonably coherent Proto-Indo-European 4th-millennium BCE technological horizon and can distinguish it from later (post-separation) developments.

Finally, as we have seen, it is more than likely that the Proto-Indo-Europeans knew wheeled vehicles and had developed a largely if not entirely local terminology to deal with them. We cannot positively attribute wheeled vehicles to Anatolian, and so it is customary not to assign carts and wagons to the Anatolian branch until it was introduced to vehicles from the outside. The development of wheeled vehicles, however, would hardly be a surprise since we do have evidence of animal traction from Proto-Indo-Anatolian onwards. Besides the word for 'pole' (**h₂iHs-eh₂-*), Anatolian also preserved two words associated with the 'yoke' (**yugóm* and **dhwerh_x-*). More controversially, we have a verb *weǵh-* 'ride in a vehicle', which is the basis for a series of nouns indicating a 'wagon' found from Ireland to India (e.g. English *wain* but not 'wagon', which is a Dutch loanword), and we have a putative Proto-Indo-Celtic cognate set indicating *$h_2ensiyo/eh_2$-* 'reins'. As we have seen, the earliest wheeled vehicles emerge from the steppe region to Mesopotamia and are no earlier than *c.* 4000 BCE. So we have what is approximately a 4th-millennium BCE horizon in which we can assign the appearance of wheeled vehicles, gold, silver and wool; there are no words solidly reconstructable to Proto-Indo-European whose referents must be more recent.

Depths of time

The Indo-European time depth suggested above has been dismissed by supporters of the Palaeolithic Continuity model of Italian linguist Mario Alinei (1926–2018) and Belgian archaeologist Marcel Otte, who proposed on archaeological grounds that there has been no major discontinuity in European prehistory since the entrance of physically modern humans from southwest Asia *c.* 40,000 years ago during the spread of the Aurignacian culture (see Chapter 9). This is sustained by Alinei's linguistic arguments, the evidence of which fills over nine hundred pages.[85] It argues that the lexicon of a language directly reflects datable cultural events, so that we can date both the words and, in this case, inventions fairly precisely, e.g. *telegraph* (1805), *telephone* (1878). So far so good, but then things become more problematic when we consider the reconstructed vocabulary of Indo-European, most of which designates nature, parts of the body, animals and cultural practices that would have been known to our earliest human ancestors. This implies that ever since humans developed language they would not only have possessed names for the 'sun', 'moon', 'head', 'tongue', 'mother', 'bear' and so on, but these words continued from their initial creation to the present in the Indo-European languages. Alinei takes a concept such as 'to die' (PIE **mer-*) that could go back even before biologically modern humans although it continues in the Indo-European lexicon. But he notes that, since there are no common words for 'bury' or 'grave' – practices that we already allegedly witness among the Neanderthals – this proves that the Indo-European languages must have already separated by the Middle or Upper Palaeolithic. This reliance on negative evidence is also employed to keep the division of the Indo-European languages to the Upper Palaeolithic by the assertion that there was no common word for 'fish' (because by then we begin to see fishing included in the economies of Europe), nor a common word for 'bow and arrow' when we find evidence for this weapon.

This reliance on negative evidence can be reduced to absurdity since the Indo-Europeans apparently couldn't have utilized the bow as we have no reconstructed words for 'fingers' or 'thumb', consequently the Indo-Europeans had not yet grown appendages with which they could pull the bow string. When it comes to diagnostic evidence such as wheeled vehicles, Alinei dismisses *$Hrot(h_2)$- as Proto-Indo-European, because the verb upon which it is built only survives in Celtic, which indicates (to him) that it must have originated among the Celts and been spread by them to all the other languages c. 2500 BCE. This contradicts all of our archaeological evidence for the dispersal of wheeled vehicles. I am afraid that Alinei's monumental work remains monumentally unconvincing.

Locating the homeland

The primary application of linguistic palaeontology to the homeland problem is the homeland's location in space; similar evidence has been employed by linguists tracing the origins of other language families throughout the world. Regarding the Indo-Europeans there have emerged a series of star concepts, largely trees and animals, that have been employed to delimit or, more often, exclude from consideration a territory occupied by the Indo-Europeans before their dispersal. Each of these will be briefly considered.

Bear

PIE *$h_2\underset{\circ}{r}tkos$ 'bear' is solidly reconstructed with cognates, all meaning 'bear', in Celtic, Italic, Albanian, Greek, Armenian and Indo-Iranian, to which is usually added Hittite *ḫartakka-*, referring to a large predatory animal and kind of priest (bear-priest?), which would give it Proto-Indo-

Anatolian status. The reconstruction of a PIE 'bear' has been used to exclude the steppe region where it is claimed that the bear was absent, an old claim that has been very recently renewed.[86] Nevertheless, bear remains have been identified from Serednii Stih settlements (see Chapter 9) as well as other steppe burials (bear-tooth pendants are found), which denies this word any diagnostic significance for locating the homeland.[87]

Beaver

PIE *bhébhrus 'beaver' is attested in Celtic, Italic, Germanic, Baltic, Slavic and Iranian (in Indo-Aryan its meaning has been shifted to 'mongoose'). Beavers tend to fall outside of the Mediterranean, and areas south of the northern Caspian and Aral seas, but it is also known from prehistoric sites in both Anatolia (e.g. a single bone from Pınarbaşı, Turkey) and the Caucasus. Its distribution has been primarily employed to exclude homelands located in Central Asia/Bactria and India (unless you assume that it originally meant 'mongoose' and all the other Indo-Europeans shifted its meaning).

Bee

Words for 'bee' are found in several regional groups. In the northwest we have *bhi-kó- 'bee', which is limited to Celtic, Italic, Germanic, Baltic and Slavic with some formal differences in Italic and Baltic; in the central region we have *melítih₂- 'honey bee', found only in Albanian and Greek, and the word itself derives from the word for 'honey'. This can easily be dismissed as a late regional word; an isogloss comprising cognates found both in the northwest and central region is *dhren- and *km̥Hp-h₂-, both 'drone', which are found in Germanic and Greek. The strongest claims to antiquity are assigned to PIA *mélit 'honey', as it is found in Celtic, Italic, Germanic, Albanian, Greek, Armenian, Anatolian and Iranian, and Core-Indo-European *médhu 'mead', found in Celtic, Germanic, Baltic, Slavic, Greek, Iranian, Indic and Tocharian.

Although the words for 'bee' tend to only be attested in either regional groups or by Germanic-Greek isoglosses, the antiquity of the bee in Indo-European culture extends back to Proto-Indo-Anatolian as indicated by reconstructions for the product of the bee, i.e. 'honey' and 'mead' are reconstructed at least to Core-Indo-European. The absence of honey bees has been traditionally employed to exclude Siberia but little else from the homeland area.

Beech

A northwest-central *bheh₂ǵós 'beech?' is attested in Celtic, Germanic, Italic, Slavic Albanian and Greek and has been one of the primary linguistic arguments employed in determining the homeland, as the beech is traditionally distributed to the west of a line running from Kaliningrad in Russia to Odessa in Ukraine (the so-called 'beech line'). For this reason, it emerged as one of the several major objections to the Steppe solution to the homeland problem (or any other solution that sought the homeland further east). The 'beech argument', however, has a number of critical weaknesses. First, since it lacks lexical attestation east of Greece (claims for a cognate in Ossetic, the Iranian language of Iron Age steppe refugees in the Caucasus, have been rejected), the 'beech' word could be dismissed as a local European word that circulated after Indo-European dispersals. Secondly, the reconstructed meaning 'beech' rests entirely on the cognate sets of Italic and Germanic. The only Celtic representative occurs in Gaulish place names, and it is uncertain whether the word refers to the beech or the oak. In all the Slavic languages the word returns the meaning 'elder', while in both Albanian and Greek the cognates mean 'oak'. This is obviously one of those classic cases of an original meaning shifting, probably because the speakers have moved into new environments and reapplied the name of a tree in their former homeland to a comparable tree in their new one.

As for the shift of name from 'beech' to 'oak' in Greek, Thieme argued that this was easily explained by the fact that the Indo-Europeans entering Greece found no beech trees with their consumable nuts so, finding a comparable food source in a species of 'oak' with edible acorns, they reapplied the beech name to this new tree.[88] This argument does not extend to the shift from an original 'beech' to 'oak' meaning in Albanian and northern Greece, as the beech is native to Albania and at least northern Greece. Indeed, it was in southern and central Europe that the beech first appeared and only began dispersing northwards about 4000 BCE.

American anthropologist, linguist and poet Paul Friedrich (1927–2016) took the evidence of semantic shift further when he noted that Greek (*oksúa*) had also shifted the meaning of the word for 'ash' (PIE *$h_2es(k)$-* 'ash') to indicate the 'beech' and that the 'yew' word (PIE *taksos* 'yew') had changed to 'bow' and the yew had been renamed (*smílaks*) – all suggesting that the Indo-Europeans had immigrated into Greece (which would exclude Greece from the homeland area).[89] Furthermore, even if a word 'beech' was wholly accepted as Proto-Indo-European, other similar species of the beech are known from Crimea, the Caucasus and northern Anatolia, so it would have little if any impact on the major competing theories of the present time.

Birch

PIE *bherHǵos* 'birch' is attested in Italic, Germanic, Baltic, Slavic, Iranian and Indic, invariably under the meaning of 'birch' except for Latin where it shifted the meaning to 'ash' (which, ironically, means that the Linnean identification of the 'ash tree' (*Fraxinus*) perpetuates the misapplication of the name in Latin). As the birch tree is not generally found south of the Alps, the shift in its application in Italic is understandable. Although the birch was occasionally thought to exclude Anatolia as a homeland, birch pollen has been recovered from lake sediments there, so other than some marginal areas not in any case suspected as part of the homeland (e.g. peninsular Italy), the birch has no bearing on the homeland. It might be emphasized that cognates for tree names cluster in north and central Europe and are far more weakly attested in the south and east. Consequently, like domesticated plants, they are employed by some to indicate that the homeland must be in north-central Europe[90] or that the Indo-Europeans gained these words only as they moved into the more forested regions of Europe from a homeland further to the east or south.

Eel

A northwest-central *HVnghel-* 'eel' is attested in Italic, Baltic, Slavic and Greek, giving this word regional status. The eel fails to meet the requirements of being Proto-Indo-European and so is of no certain utility, but for those who have accepted it as Proto-Indo-European, despite no Asian or Anatolian cognates, it has been employed to exclude the North Pontic region under the presumption that the eel did not frequent its rivers. Although I can't cite any archaeological evidence for eel remains in this region, the eel's current distribution does include the rivers of the Pontic as far east as the Kuban.

Horse

The horse (PIA *$h_1éḱwos$ 'horse') is solidly attested with cognates from Celtic, Italic, Germanic, Baltic, Greek, Iranian, Indic, Tocharian and Anatolian, and probably Armenian, where it has shifted its meaning to 'donkey'.[91] The 'horse' word became a point of contention between those who argued that it was only lately brought into the world of the Indo-Europeans (as a domestic animal) and, therefore, was given a relatively late productive declensional suffix (-*o*), and those who thought it was more ancient and known before domestication. In order to support his theory of a homeland in northern Europe, where wild horse remains had been found in Mesolithic layers, Specht argued that *$h_1éḱwos$ was originally a *u*-stem and was only later changed to an -*o*-stem.[92] On the basis of the Anatolian cognates, it can be argued that Specht may have been right and that the word was originally a *u*-stem (*$h_1éḱu$-) retained by Anatolian after it split from the proto-language, where it was then shifted to the far more productive (popular) *o*-stem formation by the rest of the Indo-Europeans.[93] This highlights one of the key issues regarding the horse: did the Proto-Indo-Europeans know only the wild horse or were they also acquainted with the domestic horse?

There are some, admittedly weak, linguistic arguments to support identifying 'horse' as domestic. First, we also have some attestation for a common word for 'mare' (*$h_1éḱweh_2$), which is seen in Italic, Baltic, Iranian and Indic. This is a regular formation for a feminine noun, so it might be dismissed as a banal formation, but some have argued (on the slenderest of grounds) that if we compare this with the names of a clearly wild animal, such as *$wĺk^wos$ 'wolf' versus *$wĺk^wih_2$- 'she-wolf', we should expect *$h_1éḱwih_2$- if the mare were wild. Another line of evidence is the derivative form *$h_1eḱwót$ that underlies the Latin and Greek words for 'horse-rider'. We also have evidence from both Baltic and Indo-Aryan of *$wólos$, where both refer to the 'tail of a horse', which would at least signal its importance in early Indo-European society. There are also additional regional words for 'horse' with *márkos* 'horse' in the west (a Celtic-Germanic isogloss) and *ghéyos* 'horse' (an Armenian-Indo-Aryan isogloss). The *márkos* word in Germanic shares the same ending as the 'she-wolf', i.e. *markih₂-* (which underlies the English word 'mare'), and has led to the suggestion that this might indicate that it is being applied to native wild horses in northern Europe. There is also a widely dispersed *polH-*, apparently derived from a verb indicating 'give birth' that is employed for young animals where Germanic, Greek and Albanian all render 'foal' (but Armenian 'kid'). Finally, we have parallels in the poetic language of the Greeks, Iranians and Indo-Aryans that exhibit the formula 'swift horses'. None of these arguments would be regarded as conclusive, but cumulatively they do show a lexical preoccupation with the horse commensurate with that shown to cattle and sheep, which are rather securely assumed to have been domesticated. To this there is an abundance of horse-associated mythology and ritual that is recoverable from the traditions of the earliest Indo-Europeans, although back projecting these into a common past has always been debatable.

If we adopt the least objectionable approach – that the horse was known as far back as Proto-Indo-Anatolian and we are agnostic as to whether it was wild or domesticated – how does this bear on the location of the homeland? Although the horse was nearly ubiquitous across Eurasia during the Ice Age and both frequently hunted and depicted on cave paintings, after the end of the Ice Age and certainly by the Neolithic, it appears to have survived only in certain regions. It was altogether absent from Ireland, the peninsular part of Italy, Greece, western Anatolia, the Near East and India and had to be introduced to those regions at a later time – in the case of Italy and Greece, in the Bronze Age. These areas are therefore usually excluded from the homeland area. They also render an association of Indo-European spreading across the Mediterranean with the spread of agriculture rather 'challenging' (why would putative Indo-European farmers who had settled in Greece or Italy retain a word for 'horse' when they had not seen one for many centuries?). In other areas of Europe there is some evidence for hunting the horse in Iberia, Britain and western and central Europe. As for Anatolia, wild horse has been found across the central plateau from the Neolithic, and by the 4th millennium BCE there is a case for assuming the domestic horse in the same region, such as the site of Çadır Höyük in Turkey; the possibility of a local centre of domestication has even been suggested.[94] Finally, there is evidence for intensive horse hunting in the steppelands ranging from Ukraine to across Kazakhstan.

Regarding domestication, the earliest widely accepted evidence for horse domestication derives from the site of Botai in Kazakhstan, a site that yielded more than 100,000 horse bones and, most importantly for the question of domestication, evidence of corralled horses, including their faeces and evidence that they had been milked (chemical evidence of horse milk fat in ceramics).[95] There is also some evidence from the dentition of the horses that some had worn a bit. This would date domestication to *c.* 3500 BCE. Recent genetic evidence indicates that Botai did not provide the source of the domestic horses that eventually spread across Eurasia and south into the Anatolia, the Middle East and towards India. The relevant genetic lineage (Dom2) appears to have emerged in the Lower Volga-Don region, becoming dominant over the course of the 6th millennium BCE until *c.* 2200–2000 BCE when Dom2 horses began to rapidly disperse. This process runs parallel with the increased exploitation of the horse in the Pontic-Caspian steppe and the earliest expansion of steppe populations westwards, where they have been associated with the Yamnaya culture (of the Pontic-Caspian steppe).[96] Recently, contrary to earlier evidence, the characteristic Dom2 ancestry has also been recovered from some horses associated with the Corded Ware culture that ranged from the Atlantic to the Urals.[97] That the horses were initially associated with horse riding is now supported by the examination of Yamnaya horse remains from sites in eastern Europe dating to *c.* 3000–2500 BCE, which revealed osteological evidence for 'horsemanship syndrome' indicative that they had been ridden[98] as well as genetic changes associated with reducing back pathologies that one might argue are more consistent with horse riding than the pulling of chariots.[99] However, the genetic evidence suggests that horses were not initially ridden across the rest of Europe. Although horse riding does appear to predate the full development of the Dom2-type, the major expansion of the domestic horse is tied to the time in which horses, incapable of pulling the heavier wagons that were drawn by oxen, were finally harnessed to a new weapon of war, the chariot, c. 2000 BCE.

The whole question of horse domestication is still in that period of discovery and contradiction where it rages in the blogosphere. Thus, for the homeland hunter, the safest conclusion is that the homeland should have had horses (wild or domestic) and that horses could be found north, through and south of the Caucasus. Nevertheless, there is growing evidence that the earliest domestication of the horse in terms of relevance to the homeland problem appears (so far) to be associated with the Pontic-Caspian steppe. If the horse is regarded as domesticated, we are dealing with an expansion of domestic horses from the steppe region outwards from c. 3000 BCE onwards, although an earlier origin in Anatolia is perhaps possible.

Mountain

In seeking to locate the Indo-European homeland, Gamkrelidze and Ivanov led with: 'The first thing that can be claimed about the homeland with any reasonable certainty is that it was a region with a mountainous topography',[100] while the presence of a number of words for 'mountain' in Proto-Indo-European induced Russian linguist Anna Dybo to assert that 'the steppe must be excluded from the regions potentially inhabited by Proto-Indo-Europeans'.[101] We can see from cognate lists that there was a PIE *bherǵh- 'hill; height; mountain' attested in Celtic, Germanic, Slavic, Armenian and Iranian. There is also *g^worH- 'mountain' with cognates in Baltic, Slavic, Albanian, Iranian and Indic. A possibly lower feature may have been *kolHōn 'hill', seen in Celtic, Germanic (e.g. English *hill*), Baltic and Greek. Gamkrelidze and Ivanov also accept *men- 'mountain', seen in Celtic, Italic and Iranian, although these could be claimed to be independent derivations from a root meaning 'to project'. The words only convey the concept of 'mountain' (which is a relative term) but Gamkrelidze and Ivanov adduce mythological evidence to suggest that we should be envisaging extremely high mountains reaching to the sky, forming clouds that bring both rain and swiftly flowing rivers. They conclude that the entire semantic field associated with mountains indicates that it could only have been created in a high mountainous region, so we get a homeland within the Caucasus mountains, which supports their Greater Armenian model.

This entire approach induces a terrible bout of déjà vu when one recalls that nearly a century earlier Pictet, after coming up with no fewer than fourteen (mostly spurious) Indo-European words for mountains[102] and sifting through similar evidence, concluded that the lexical evidence indicated that the homeland could only have been located in a country of mountains and valleys (*montagnes et de vallées*) watered by numerous rivers – a situation that perfectly suited a homeland not in the Caucasus but in Bactria where our tall mountains would be the Hindu Kush, west of the Himalayas.[103] Such arguments are hardly persuasive, since mountains are relative to landscapes and generically described as high, cloud covered and a source of rivers without respect to their altitude. There is hardly a homeland solution that is situated in a region where its population would not be aware of the phenomenon of the mountain, so words for 'mountain' cannot be regarded as seriously diagnostic for its location (and are just as supportive of Osgood's Antarctic homeland as they are for Bactria or Armenia). Incidentally, one of the frequent geo-linguistic tropes is that people who live in mountainous regions represent refugees who have fled into such regions; they are the losers, not the victors in language dispersals.[104]

Salmon

PIE *$l\acute{o}ks$* 'salmon; salmon-trout' is attested in Germanic, Baltic, Slavic, Armenian, Iranian and Tocharian. This is a reconstruction where everything hangs on the precise meaning in the proto-language. In Germanic, Baltic and Slavic it designates the Atlantic salmon (*Salmo salar*), a fish confined to the Atlantic and Baltic and the rivers draining into them. Within the more plausible homeland solutions, if this were reconstructed as the original meaning, it would confine the homeland to northern Europe and one of the northern homeland solutions (Nordic or Baltic). The meaning among the cognates in Armenian and Iranian, however, designates the 'salmon trout' (*Salmo trutta*), while the Tocharian cognate merely means 'fish'. Obviously, the salmon trout is found over a vastly greater territory than the Atlantic salmon. A classic study of the issue by Richard Diebold has generally been accepted as demonstrating that the original referent was far more likely to have been 'salmon trout', which was later shifted to Atlantic salmon as Indo-Europeans migrated towards northwest Europe[105] – although Peter Kitson insists that the linguistic evidence could still be read either way and that Diebold's argument cannot disprove reconstructing the word as 'salmon' rather than 'salmon trout'.[106] The salmon argument when focused on the distribution of the salmon trout is of little geographical use other than excluding much of Central Asia.

Salt

PIE *$seh_2(e)l$- 'salt' is attested in Celtic, Italic, Germanic, Baltic, Slavic, Albanian, Greek, Armenian, Indo-Aryan and Tocharian. We do not know the Anatolian word as it was expressed with a Sumerogram (MUN), which means that rather than employing their own word, the Hittites often employed the words or symbols from earlier writing systems in the same way we employ the ampersand & to indicate 'and'. The word means 'salt' and also 'sea, salt water' in Italic, Greek and Sanskrit. And with that, you can probably see where this is going: which sea or salty lake? Schrader argued that the most likely source of the word was the salt that could be gained from the northern shores of the Black Sea, which, naturally, supported the Steppe model,[107] while Thieme looked to the massive deposits of northern Germany,[108] thus supporting the Nordic model. The problem with using this word in homeland hunting is that salt sources – seas, lakes or rock salt deposits – are so ubiquitous, and the need for salt in preservation or providing a dietary supplement to primarily cereal agriculturalists so general, that it is difficult to imagine how one could squeeze a diagnostic geographical clue out of it.

Sea

PIE *$móri$ 'sea; lake' is reconstructed from Celtic, Italic, Germanic, Baltic, Slavic and Iranian. Celtic, Italic and Slavic indicate exclusively 'sea', while Germanic and Iranian (Ossetic) can also reference an inland body of water, a lake. A possible *$h_3réuno$-* 'sea' has also been suggested on the basis of Anatolian and Indic.¹⁰⁹ The key topographical issue here is whether the word indicated exclusively a sea or an inland body of water. Some cited the evidence for the adoption of other words for the sea in groups that neighboured seas (e.g. Germanic, Greek and Indic) as evidence that they did not arrive in their historical seats with a word for 'sea', which would suggest that the word originally meant 'lake' (and the homeland was far from a coastal area). Once this card has been played, the question is which body of water was being referenced? Pictet creatively included both the Caspian Sea and the intermediary desert (with its wave-like sand dunes) as the original 'sea' of his Bactrian homeland.¹¹⁰ Hirt went for either the North Sea or the Baltic Sea, but was honest enough to recognize that the game had more to do with where you thought the homeland was in advance.¹¹¹ So also Schrader, who thought the location of the sea was homeland-dependent (for him, the Black Sea), but the existence of the concept of the sea told little about its location unless one wanted to embrace negative evidence that lacking words for tides suggested an inland body of water (or the Black Sea).¹¹²

On the other hand, Alexander Jóhannesson in his quest to tie the sound of words to geography noted that of 330 Indo-European words beginning with the letter *s*, 93 indicated running water so presumably the early Indo-Europeans lived by the sea, creating their vocabulary while listening to the lapping waves (*ssss*) and generating words beginning with velars (*$*k$*, *$*g$*, etc.) in imitation of the seagulls.¹¹³ Gamkrelidze and Ivanov reconstructed an assortment of words for 'sea', but did not find any grounds to employ the evidence to anchor the homeland in a particular geographical region – although they did propose an Indo-European etymology for the Aratta river that was mentioned in Sumerian documents and supposedly located near the Caspian, which, they observed, was the approximate area of their proposed homeland.¹¹⁴

Squirrel

PIE *$*werwer$-* 'squirrel' is attested (admittedly with some problems) in Celtic, Italic, Germanic, Baltic, Slavic and Iranian. It generally means 'squirrel' but in Italic it designates the 'ferret' and in Lithuanian it can mean both 'squirrel' and 'polecat'. Old English *ācweorna* 'oak-squirrel' may suggest that *weorna* wasn't enough to distinguish itself as meaning 'squirrel'. The red squirrel enters discussion because Hirt employed it as one of the reasons to exclude a steppe homeland (no trees: no squirrels).[115] Although the red squirrel does not show up on sites of the open steppe, it is known from the neighbouring Cucuteni-Trypillia culture as well as sites in the southern Urals, and has also been recovered from Iron Age sites north of the Black Sea. The same could be said for the other possible referents, such as the polecat, pine or stone marten, in case **werwer* covered a wider range of (so far as we can tell not particularly important food or fur) species of the North Pontic.[116] The Iranian cognate refers to the Persian squirrel since the red squirrel was unknown in Iran.

Tortoise

A Central Indo-European (IE) **ghéluHs* 'tortoise' is supported by cognates from just Slavic and Greek, so its distribution is a regional isogloss even though its formation might suggest far greater antiquity. It was assumed to be of Proto-Indo-European date by Schrader and employed by him to exclude a homeland in the far north of Europe, which lies beyond the limits (and tolerance) of the tortoise. As the tortoise's prehistoric distribution includes sites of the Neolithic Funnel-Beaker culture in northern Europe and Neolithic sites in both Latvia and Estonia, this does very little to limit potential homeland theories. In fact, of all the putatively diagnostic animals, the tortoise has managed to travel the furthest, as two of them circled the moon in a Russian space probe in 1968.

Wine/grapes

PIE **woinom* 'wine' is reconstructed on the basis of cognates in Latin, Greek, Albanian, Hittite and Luvian, which takes us to Proto-Indo-Anatolian. How many other branches contribute to this set is arguable, with some linguists limiting it to the above while others admit some additional branches. For example, Gamkrelidze and Ivanov would expand the cognate sets to the Germanic forms (German *wein*, English *wine*, etc.) and possibly Celtic and Baltic, whereas others would regard these as loanwords from Latin. Most recently Luke Gorton[117] argues that rather than explaining many of the cognates as loanwords from either Latin *vinum* or between each other, there are good reasons to see all these as independent of one another. With or without the additional cognates, 'wine' is regarded as strongly reconstructed to Proto-Indo-European. Moreover, it has a plausible internal etymology in being ultimately derived from the verbal root **wei(H)-* 'twist', which underlies words for 'grape-vine' (the fruit plant that grows by twisting and entwining) and supports the notion that the word arose natively in Indo-European. This is important because we also find Akkadian *īnu-*, Hattic *windu-*, Hebrew *yayin*, Georgian *ywino* and other neighbouring languages that appear as a cluster of loanwords, which suggests that neighbouring cultures, probably far more notable today as wine producers, actually borrowed their words for wine from Indo-European.

This narrative has been given a different spin by Gorton, who focuses on the etymological development that takes us from 'twist' to 'the twisty thing' (i.e. 'grape-vine') to 'the beverage made from the twisty thing' (i.e. 'wine'). The full working of this evolution in terms of the rules of Indo-European word formation is seen only in Anatolian, and here we already see that the end result of the two Anatolian languages (Hittite and Luvian) disagree on the final step. From this Gorton concludes that in reconstructing the meaning of the Proto-Indo-Anatolian word, we can only verify it as far as stage 2 (i.e. 'the twisty thing' or 'grape-vine'), and that the meaning 'wine' only emerged after Anatolian had separated. And, as for the other Indo-European languages, he cites evidence that they can be divided into two groups in terms of how they ultimately derived their word for 'wine': an inner group of Greek, Armenian and Albanian and an outer or peripheral group consisting of Celtic, Italic, Germanic and Balto-Slavic.

The minimal or safest conclusion from all of this is that Proto-Indo-Anatolian exploited the grape (*Vitis vinifera sylvestris*), whose natural range coupled with archaeological evidence for grape pips is primarily distributed from the southern margins of the Caspian Sea throughout the Caucasus and around either side of the Black Sea and on into Greece with localized distributions both along the Danube and in the central and west Mediterranean. How far north one might expect to find occasional traces of grape pips is problematic, or at least, a bit unexpected, as they have been found on Neolithic sites not only in southern Britain but also as far north as Sweden. If we imagine that the referent is not simply the grape-vine but the making of wine, then the area collapses towards the Caucasus, where we encounter our earliest evidence for the making of grape-wine from two Neolithic sites in Georgia (*c.* 6000–5800 BCE)[118] and full wine-making kits by *c.* 4000 BCE.[119]

The use of 'wine/grape' as a diagnostic indicator of the homeland depends much on whether one accepts a reconstruction that only goes as far as the grape or whether one accepts a reconstruction of 'wine'. Given the interrelated nexus of meanings, this is one of the most sensitive indicators and suggests that a homeland in the general vicinity of the Caucasus, either south or north, provides a more plausible homeland than one located more distant.

To sum up this review, while linguistic palaeontology suggests that the last semantic ancestors probably fell between *c.* 4000 and 2500 BCE, by which time wheeled vehicles, copper, gold, silver and possibly wool have been reconstructed to the proto-language, it does not provide positive evidence for any single homeland theory, at least not in the way the reconstruction of a word like 'amber', for example, might support a Baltic homeland. Rather, we are dealing with broadly circumstantial negative evidence to exclude territories as likely homelands or evidence that can be dismissed as not demonstrably of Proto-Indo-European date or uncertain meaning.

CHAPTER 8

Cultural Anthropology: Origin Tales and Culture History

The great Pomeranian-born American linguist Edward Sapir (1884–1939), who brought the comparative method in linguistics to the study of Amerindian languages, encouraged anthropologists not to rule out native testimony when investigating the origins of a people, although he did warn them to be critical.[1] Before the Indo-European family was discovered, the 'native testimony' was the Bible and the quest was the location of the Garden of Eden, Mount Ararat or the Tower of Babel. The nearest comparable source that the study of the early Indo-Europeans could propose derived from the Iranian sacred book of Zarathustra, the Avesta, where there is an account of how the supreme god, Ahura Mazda, created the lands of the Iranians beginning with a place called the *Airiianəm Vaējah*, in a location notable for its ten winter months and only two summer months. As *vaējah* has proven somewhat difficult to interpret, there has been a number of different suggestions, such as 'expanse', 'springs' or 'rapids'; when 'seed' was accepted by some, it was a short leap to the 'seed of the Aryans' (i.e. the place of their origins).

Once this path was taken, the search for the *Airiianəm Vaējah* became the search for the Indo-European homeland, with J. G. Rhode the first off the mark to find it south of the Aral Sea between the Oxus and Jakartes in 1820.[2] Charles-Alexandre Piétrement (1826–1906), a French army veterinarian who wrote extensively on the origin of the domestic horse, had no doubt that it was in the *Airiianəm Vaējah* that the Indo-Europeans 'perfected their language' and expanded to civilize the rest of the world.[3] Piétrement placed the homeland southeast of Lake Balkhash[4] and Hermann Brunnhofer in Armenia (see page 116),[5] while Karl Penka, one of the founders of a racial approach to Indo-European origins, located it in Scandinavia (see Chapter 10).[6] For those who believe that the homeland has been correctly determined, it has often been placed in Chorasmia (modern Khwarazm), the territory along the Amu Darya river just south of the (now almost entirely desiccated) Aral Sea. Others have set it further to the southeast near the Pamirs, while Indologist Michael Witzel makes good arguments for situating it in the highlands of central Afghanistan, which at least meets the climatic requirements.[7] This entire exercise, at least in so far as the *Airiianəm Vaējah* was identified with the Indo-European homeland, was already discredited by 1880 when the Belgian priest and scholar Charles de Harlez (1832–1899), who had translated the Avesta, pointed out that there was absolutely no evidence that the *Airiianəm Vaējah* was ever regarded as the homeland of the Indians (who also ticked the 'Aryan' box) much less the Indo-Europeans as a whole.[8]

The sacred books of India have also been pressed into service to locate the Indo-European homeland and have been one of the main components supporting the Out of India model. Here the game rests on demonstrating that Indic culture and traditions are absolutely local to India and denying that there is evidence of Indo-Europeans coming to India from elsewhere, which leads to the conclusion that India must be the homeland. So arguments ran as follows: that because the Himalayas are known as the northern mountains, this indicates that the Indo-Aryans must have originally lived south of the Himalayas, or when one of the Indian poets refers to the major Indic rivers as 'my Ganges' or 'my Sarasvati', that is not the language expected of a foreign immigrant.[9] Yet if the homeland were in India, how does one deal with, say, the Roman writer Tacitus's comment at the beginning of his treatise on the ancient Germans: 'The people of Germany appear to me indigenous and free from intermixture with foreigners, either as settlers or casual visitors'.[10] Now, if the Indians claim to be indigenous and the Germans also claim to be indigenous and ... I think you can see where this is going.

The dragon gambit

Another approach adopted by homeland hunters elsewhere in the world is assessing the environmental fit of cultural practices and beliefs to determine whether they were local or whether we should presume immigration. For example, the Keres people who occupy seven pueblos (villages) in New Mexico speak a language totally unrelated to any of their neighbours and their origins have been frequently disputed. The anthropologist Edward Dozier (1916–1971) observed that the Keresans were greatly preoccupied with rainfall ceremonies, far more than their Pueblo neighbours (and he ought to have known as he was born and raised in the Tewa Pueblo and the first Native American to acquire a PhD in Anthropology). He argued that this was incongruent with the fact that throughout their region people practised irrigation agriculture and, therefore, it was likely that the Keresans had migrated from a rainfall-deficient region to the north.[11] Does early Indo-European culture offer anything comparable?

In his mammoth study of Indo-European poetics, *How to Kill a Dragon*, American linguist Calvert Watkins (1933–2013) assembled evidence to reconstruct the formula $*h_2n\rlap{\,}r$-$g^whént\ h_1óg^whim$ 'the man slew the serpent'. Watkins notes that 'This formula shapes the narration of "heroic" killing or overcoming of adversaries over the Indo-European world for millennia. The formula is the vehicle for the central theme of a proto-text, a central part of the symbolic culture of the speakers of Proto-Indo-European itself.'[12] The one topic that escaped his notice (or interest, and his bibliography) are the attempts to utilize this central motif of the Indo-European hero myth to locate where the dragon itself lived!

If one needed an expert on dragons, Baron Hans Paul von Wolzogen was probably your man, because he served as the editor of Richard Wagner's own newspaper, which published on all things Wagnerian, and also as the biographer of the composer. Wolzogen believed that the earliest attested dragon-slaying myth as found in the Indian Rig Veda was also the most environmentally grounded, since here the dragon, Vṛtra, was known for holding back the waters and therefore symbolized heat and drought until the god Indra slew the dragon and released the waters. But as one drifted to the west, this confrontation was distorted. For example, in Greece what in India was the symbol of heat-death frolicked in the water rather than held them back until it was killed by Perseus. Ultimately, the dragon myth appears in Norse legend, where the greatest threat before global warming was hardly the summer heat but the cold of winter. So here we get a fire-breathing dragon that, for Wolzogen, was certainly 'no real mythic image for the winter'. In short, Wagner's Siegfried is basically portrayed as shutting off the central heating. All of this indicates that the environmental home of the Indo-European dragon lay in a hot climate in Asia and not in Europe.[13] The irony of this argument is that Wolzogen's weekly paper easily morphed into a Nazi propaganda outlet that espoused the Northern homeland model, the very model that he was criticizing.

Another dragon-focused foray into the homeland problem was made by Fritz Graebner (1877–1934), one of the founders of the *Kulturkreis* school of anthropology (see below). Having time on his hands after being first invited to work in Australia and then interned there during the First World War, he began his massive study of mythology ranging from Indo-European to Polynesian. He found (for him) striking parallels in the heroes of the dragon-slaying myths in Indo-European and Polynesian tradition (where the hero Maui dispatches a giant eel with an axe). To these he added a random collection of evidence such as similar stone axes, ponchos and springtime swinging games. Graebner set the Urheimat in Central Asia, about as close as he could get to the Bay of Bengal, which he believed to be the home of the Polynesians.[14]

Needless to say, the Nordic school was not going to yield to such arguments. They found their champion in the German biologist Ernst Krause (1839–1903), a prolific writer whose works included books on both Erasmus and Charles Darwin and, more intriguing, a natural history of ghosts. But he also waded into the field of Indo-European myth and homeland with his monograph titled (translated here) *The Land of Tuisko: Homeland of the Aryan Tribes and Gods* (1891).[15] Krause argued that there were two types of myths: homeless ones that were universal and those that were created in a distinct climate and environment. The latter essentially referenced battles between summer and winter – for example, in killing the sea-monster, the Greek Perseus is killing the disease- and death-dealing winter sun. And where are the seasons most strongly felt? It was obvious then that the dragon-slaying myth must be set to northern Europe and not in Asia. Additional evidence came from reckoning years in terms of winters, which Krause claimed made good sense in northern Europe but had little relevance in India. As for dragon-hunting solutions to the homeland problem, I happily defer to the early American linguist and champion of animal rights E. P. Evans (1831–1917), who had enough of the squabbling and in 1886 observed that: 'All these theories are possible. Indeed, there is nothing dire that the dragon may not symbolize, nothing dreadful to encounter that has not been called by this name, from a Megalosaurus to a mother-in-law.'[16]

Weather north and south continually cropped up in homeland debates. Penka, one of the founders of the Nordic model, argued that an Indo-European flood myth referenced the flooding of Scandinavia.[17] Such imagery could also be reversed, as Wilhelm Brandenstein remarked regarding the myth of an Indo-European sky-god fertilizing a mother earth with rain: such a concept would seem to have been a bit redundant in a wet northern or central Europe but would make far better sense in an arid environment, like the Asiatic steppe.[18]

Kulturkreise

In the early 20th century a school of anthropology emerged in Germany and Austria that believed that extensive similarities between diverse peoples could be best explained not as stages of a worldwide evolutionary trajectory but rather by way of diffusion from *Kulturkreise* ('culture circles'). Members of this school worked on a global scale, attempting to identify major cultural regions in Polynesia, Africa and the New World, and they also tackled the Indo-European homeland problem as we have seen with reference to Graebner. But the really serious work applying the *Kulturkreislehre* approach to the Indo-Europeans was undertaken by two Catholic priests of a missionary order, Wilhelm Schmidt (1869–1954) and Wilhelm Koppers (1886–1961).[19] The two isolated out from both linguistic and cultural evidence what they regarded as the major attributes of the Indo-Europeans, who were depicted as essentially pastoralists, patriarchal and patrilineal. Their religion comprised worship of a sky-god who could also be expressed in terms of a series of seven gods (Schmidt had written a twelve-volume study explaining how an original monotheism eventually evolved into polytheism), divine twins, a fire cult and an elaborate horse sacrifice. The latter involved a spring sacrifice of a young and unridden horse, light in colour, ritually washed before the sacrifice, dedicated to the highest god, with the breaking of any of its bones prohibited, dispatched by strangulation and a ritual that also involved a sacred drink. As they could find parallels to all of these traits in Central Asia among Altaic steppe peoples, this suggested that the entire complex should be derived from the Asiatic steppe. The fact that the Central Asian horse sacrifice was less complex than the Indo-European, Koppers argued, indicated that it was more primitive and hence more original.

Once such a trait list was devised, a number of homeland hunters employed it to exclude potential homeland models. For example, the emphasis on patrilineal descent and patriarchy was sometimes marshalled to discredit any theory that placed the homeland in either western or northern Europe, because there were early historical traits suggesting the occasional presence of matrilineal succession or women in positions of power among the early Celts and Germans.[20] Hermann Güntert (1886–1948), the editor of the German journal devoted to linguistic palaeontology *Wörter und Sachen*, excluded the possibility of a Nordic homeland because its economy was too agricultural, too focused on fishing and its religion was too much concerned with soil fertility rather than the type of male-dominated pantheon usually reconstructed for the Indo-Europeans.[21]

One of the problems with the *Kulturkreis* approach is that the game can be played by others. The co-author of the earliest encyclopaedia of Indo-European culture, Alfons Nehring, argued that in addition to patriarchy the early Indo-Europeans also exhibited a higher role for women (he reconstructed a PIE word for 'queen' and noted that there was both mythological and linguistic support for 'mother earth'), which was, for him at least, evidence of an east Mediterranean or Caucasus influence.[22]

The main opponents of the Central Asiatic model, however, came from adherents of the Nordic school, who attempted to systematically rebut the items cited by Koppers and his supporters. For example, one of Koppers's former students, the Austrian ethnologist Fritz Flor (1905–1939), rejected the ideas of his PhD supervisor and argued that almost every comparison that Koppers had made between the Indo-Europeans and Altaic peoples of Central Asia – such as fire cults and sky-gods – could be better made with the Uralic people. He argued that the role of the horse in Central Asia was entirely different from that reconstructed to Proto-Indo-European.[23] For Flor and others, the Central Asiatic nomads were exclusively horse-riders while the Indo-Europeans were wagon-drivers. In fact, there is no evidence for associating the Proto-Indo-Europeans with horse-drawn vehicles and the concept of wheeled vehicles and horses should be kept separate. As we have seen in the previous chapter, the earliest vehicles were drawn by oxen since they were far too heavy to have been pulled by the earliest domestic horses. Horse-drawn vehicles emerge with the invention of the chariot around 2000 BCE, a date by which we estimate that Indo-European linguistic unity was well over. Setting this aside, the most serious issue with the *Kulturkreis* approach is that it assumed a unique historical origin for every cultural trait when so often it was dealing with generic traits that could be found on any continent. Moreover, it was making assumptions regarding the origins of pastoral nomadism based solely on a particular intertwining of historical and anthropological evidence, thus privileging the Altaic peoples of Central Asia as if they were the earliest.

In summary

The homeland hunter should probably not be too fearful of dragons or claims of people being indigenous. Origin myths are just that: myths constructed to explain where people came from, and while there might always be a grain of truth, sifting it out from everything else tends to be impractical. We are able to reconstruct a potential Indo-European cosmogonic myth from the common elements found in a number of Indo-European branches. Fundamentally, the creation of the universe and humans appears to have involved the sacrifice and dismemberment of either a giant or a cow, and human (here Indo-European) society is initiated with the sacrifice of one twin brother by another.[24] Alternatively, humans spring from a tree, possibly an ash tree. So if one wants to follow the mythic trail to the Indo-European homeland our checklist comprises a giant, a cow, an ash tree and twins (good luck!).

The application of anthropological models is a more serious approach, not so much because the technique itself has great credibility but because its results are often taken into consideration along with the evidence of linguistic palaeontology, and so are employed in an attempt to reinforce the conclusions posed by a different approach. Much of the image of the Indo-Europeans as a mobile, pastoral and patriarchal population who utilized the domestic horse and engaged in aggressive behaviour is built from linguistic clues filtered through some pretty simplistic anthropological assessments of the type of cultural behaviour one might infer from the linguistic evidence. On the other hand, the concept of centres of cultural diffusion such as the *Kulturkreise* does not have much valence, and any assessment must rely on archaeological rather than ethnological evidence.

CHAPTER 9

Archaeology: Evaluating Archaeological Cultures as Linguistic Models

Next to linguistics, archaeology has generally been regarded as the second major player in locating the homeland, although there have been linguists enough who wished that those who work with trowels and spades would keep their noses out of what they regard as a purely linguistic issue. The engagement of archaeology in the Indo-European homeland problem largely began at the end of the 19th century when archaeological evidence was being assembled into a cultural-historical framework. This saw a shift from viewing archaeological remains as primarily temporal stations in the evolution of human society – that is, from some form of barbarism to increasingly complex societies – to an approach where sites could be grouped into regional cultures that might expand their territories or evolve into more recent (and differently labelled) cultures. Cultural maps or charts were devised to display the relationship between the different cultures through time and, with reference to locating the homeland, the cultures would be followed in time to the emergence of the different Indo-European branches in the historical period. In short, prehistoric cultural history could be cast within the same framework as historical successions. For example, in France we could recite a sequence beginning with the Franks, then back to the Romans, then the Gauls, and now continue into what were seen as comparable archaeological entities: La Tène culture, Hallstatt, Urnfield and so on back to the Neolithic (Linear Ware or Cardial Ware) or even Palaeolithic.

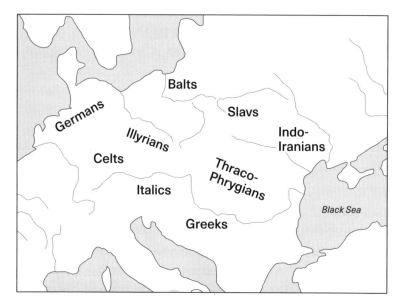

9.1 Georg Wilke's archaeological map of the areas of origin of the various Indo-European branches, which, he argued, coincided with their position in Johannes Schmidt's wave model (see **4.16**).

German archaeologist Georg Wilke (1859–1938) regarded the solution most easily determined by employing inductive reasoning: he began with the historical location of each Indo-European branch (Celtic, Germanic and Italic, etc.; [**9.1**]) and then worked back to their respective homelands through the archaeological record, ultimately to a common homeland focused around central Europe before they had dispersed.[1]

Indeed, this retrospective technique became a particularly popular approach to research into 'ethnogenesis' in Soviet-era Russian publications. And just as historical cultures could be given linguistic identifications, many archaeologists could not resist the temptation to extend the concept of a linguistic entity to the prehistoric cultures. So it is hardly surprising that this cultural-historical model was most closely associated with Gustav Kossinna, who was both a linguist and an archaeologist. Kossinna concentrated on elucidating the origins of the Germanic people and also the Indo-Europeans as a whole, and was a dominant force in European archaeology in the early 20th century.[2]

Notwithstanding the fact that archaeologists continually remind themselves that their archaeological cultures are their own creations and not ancient constructs, and that pots don't equate with a people or language, most archaeological discussion of Indo-European origins still involves some form of narrative cast in terms of cultural history, where material culture and the evidence for prehistoric behaviour serve as proxy evidence for some form of social or ethnic construct. Although discussion concerning the various cultures generally reaches into matters of fine detail regarding ceramic decoration, stone technology or burial ritual, much of the really meaningful discussion has tended to treat the cultures as gaming pieces of various value that might be moved over a Eurasian chessboard. In this chapter, I intend to present what I regard as the classic archaeological models organized according to the date they assign to Indo-European origins.

The Palaeolithic game

One of the reasons for the collapse of the Asian homeland model was the realization that Europe had a past much before the early civilizations of the Near East, seen most spectacularly in the excavations into the French Palaeolithic (that the Near East might have also had an equally if not older Palaeolithic was often ignored). But throughout the late 19th and most of the 20th century a Palaeolithic solution was rarely suggested and when proposed, it appeared more as an act of desperation than a well-thought-out hypothesis. For some, a Palaeolithic solution was driven by those who asked whether there was a single archaeological culture that correlated with the distribution of all the Indo-European languages. Only one culture seemed to come remotely close to the elusive 'Culture X' and that was the Aurignacian, which plays a central part of the Palaeolithic Continuity model. The Aurignacian is the cultural horizon that saw the introduction of fully modern humans who replaced the

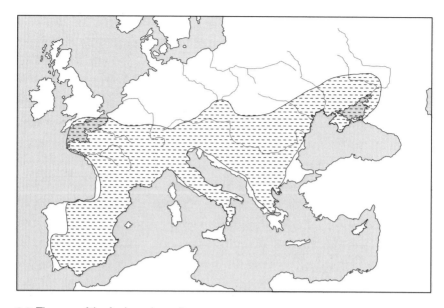

9.2 The area of the Aurignacian culture.

Neanderthals and spread across Europe with a technology that exploited flint blades, bone and antler tools. It was also associated with cave art and figurines [**9.2**]. The archaeological fighter cover for this theory, primarily sustained linguistically by Mario Alinei as we saw in Chapter 7, is Marcel Otte, the Professor of Prehistory at the University of Liège, Belgium. Otte argued that there has been no discontinuity observed in European populations since 40,000 years ago.[3] Such a claim can only be sustained with a straight face if one wishes to employ the Monty Python-like rebuttal: other than complete changes in economy, settlement patterns, architecture, technology, burial ritual, religion and the genetic composition of the population, what evidence for discontinuity after 40,000 years can you propose?

There are some who have resolved the multiple culture homeland problem by reducing the number of cultures and, instead of retreating into the Palaeolithic, moving the start period into the subsequent

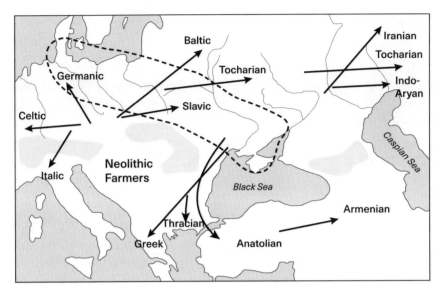

9.3 The hypothesized formation of the Indo-European homeland (dotted line) during the Mesolithic (after L. Zaliznyak, 2016). The lighter shading represents the mountains.

Mesolithic and thereby devising an Urheimat that stretched from the Baltic to the Black or Caspian Sea.[4] The most recent version of this model has been advanced by the Ukrainian archaeologist Leonid Zaliznyak, who associated the origins and spread of the Indo-European languages with migrations from the west Baltic region beginning in the Mesolithic that underlay the later Funnel-Beaker, Globular Amphora and, as we will see, the western components of the steppe cultures.[5] These were viewed as part of an almost continuous migration stream that began *c.* 12,000 BCE and continued into historical times with the Goths [**9.3**].

Despairing of finding a single culture that spanned the earliest known distribution of the Indo-European languages, some scholars shifted attention to the next best thing: a culture large enough to serve as a homeland for a great language family and whose borders either showed signs of expansion during its own existence or, at least, in what were presumed to be its later descendants. Such cultures were only being defined in the early 20th century and the time depth at which they were being searched for was the Neolithic-Eneolithic (Copper-Stone Age; I will employ 'Eneolithic' throughout the text to also cover the terms Chalcolithic or Copper Age), since it was presumed that any later cultures (Bronze-Iron Ages) were so recent that they must be associated with individual branches of the Indo-European family. As to what type of culture, Kossinna made it very clear that he was looking for something pretty aggressive. He believed that the Indo-European expansion was the result of a powerful, warlike minority who conquered larger but weaker populations who were thereby reduced to slavery and occupied a lower caste forced to adopt the language of their conquerors.[6] Although there were cultures that matched Kossinna's requirements, these would come later during one of the greatest periods of transformation in Eurasian culture – the Neolithic.

Anatolian farmers

Ever since the 19th century it has been argued that it was the Indo-Europeans who introduced agriculture to Europe from their Asian homeland, usually set between the Caspian Sea and the Hindu Kush mountains. And when archaeological evidence for early agriculture began to emerge early in the 20th century, it was Central Asia that provided the main focus. In 1908 the American geologist Raphael Pumpelly (1837–1923) presented the results of his excavation at Anau in southern Turkmenistan. These provided (what he regarded as) evidence for his hypothesis that the domestication of plants and animals was initiated by climate change whereby aridity drove human and animal populations together into oases in Central Asia, such close proximity between humans, beast and plant encouraging domestication. Once begun, agriculture and farming populations dispersed in all directions. Pumpelly was well aware of the significance of this hypothesis for locating the Indo-European homeland and that such migrations 'might have brought to Europe the Aryan peoples, Aryan culture, and Aryan languages'. In fact, he confessed to have written an entire chapter on the Aryan migrations that he excluded from his excavation report as he did not feel entirely qualified to deal with such matters, although he believed that his report could serve 'for both use and controversy in this connection'.[7]

By the 1960s the deserts of Turkmenistan were being replaced by the evidence of early farming sites in the hilly flanks of the Zagros mountains, Palestine and eastern Anatolia. Such evidence indicated that by c. 8000 BCE local foragers in central Anatolia had begun to incorporate some domestic plants (wheat, barley, lentils and peas) into their economy and also began the herding of sheep.[8] Over a period of centuries, reliance on domesticates grew to fully mixed farming sites by c. 7000 BCE, including the world-renowned site of Çatalhöyük in Turkey. This economy reached the northwest corner of Anatolia by c. 6500 BCE and crossed into Greece and the Balkans.[9] By 1973[10] Colin Renfrew started to float his hypothesis that associated the expansion of the Indo-Europeans with Neolithic dispersals, which he followed in 1987 with a full monograph on the Anatolian Farmer model entitled *Archaeology and Language*.[11] The model has been frequently updated from its initial framework. Rather than (as too often done) reprinting a version of the original map or attempting to recount all the subsequent changes to the model in detail,[12] I will make an attempt to streamline my description with an eye to presenting it in what I would regard as a reasonably robust form before 2015, which, we will see, marks a watershed year in the Indo-European homeland saga [9.4].

The Urheimat is set to Anatolia, usually the central and western part, where it is associated with the earliest farming communities in this region, c. 7000 BCE. From here Indo-European farmers migrated westwards to both Greece and through the Balkans, establishing villages and incrementally spreading through the rest of Europe along two major routes. One of these passed along the coastal margins of the Mediterranean where the colonists were primarily associated with the Cardial or Impressed Ware horizon, carrying agriculture as far west as the Atlantic. The other route went through the Balkans into the Danubian drainage basin and moved westwards as far as the Netherlands and northern France. From here it was uncertain whether the vector for the spread of agriculture was primarily the movement of people or the acculturation of neighbouring hunter-gatherer populations on the Atlantic periphery.[13] Whichever was

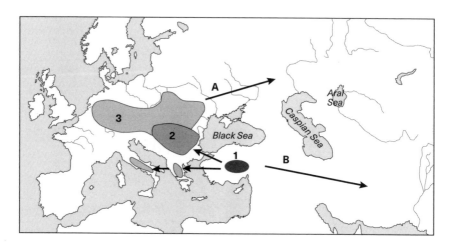

9.4 The Anatolian Farmer model of Indo-European origins. The homeland (and the Anatolian branch) is located in Anatolia (**1**) whose farmers migrate both into the Balkans and along the Mediterranean coast towards the Atlantic. In 1999 the Balkans was proposed as a secondary homeland (**2**) where 'Archaic Indo-European' evolved those features not found in the Anatolian branch. The further expansion northwestwards (**3**) carried the ancestors of Italic, Celtic and Germanic, while the rest of Indo-European (with Greek possibly connected) emerged or spread out of the Balkans. In 1999 the Tocharians as well as the Indo-Iranians were seen as being derived from an expansion eastwards into the steppe (arrow **A** denotes the Steppe model, which is co-opted into the Anatolian Farmer model); by 2014, however, the Anatolian model favoured an association between the spread of agriculture from eastern Anatolia (arrow **B**) towards the Indus to explain Indo-Iranian.

the case, by c. 4000 BCE farming had been carried as far west as Ireland and as far north as southern Scandinavia. Northeast of the Danube, related farming communities expanded as far east as the Dnipro river (the Cucuteni-Trypillia culture). All of these expansions resulted in the distribution of the Indo-European languages of Europe.

By 1999, Renfrew had recognized the need for a secondary homeland in the Balkans (the linguist Aron Dolgopolsky had been asserting this since 1988)[14] for his 'Archaic Proto-Indo-European', which would date to c. 6500–5000 BCE and provide a common area for the non-Anatolian branches of Indo-European to develop together (thereby transforming Marija Gimbutas's very non-Indo-European 'Old Europe' – for which, see below) into the secondary homeland of Core-Indo-European. This then could see a further spread to the northwest of the more 'archaic' Celtic, Germanic and Italic, while the rest of the European languages, as well as Tocharian and Indo-Iranian, might emerge from the Balkans. The ancestors of the Tocharians and Indo-Iranians were thus explained by absorbing the Steppe model into the Anatolian Farmer model. This meant that the original model, which explained each branch as an in situ result of the initial expansion of Anatolian farmers, might remain on the table, but there was also now always a plan B that allowed for later migrations to explain the emergence of various European branches (although they were ultimately rooted in the Anatolian Neolithic). As for Indo-Iranian, there were always several explanatory options from the beginning of the model. The absorption of the Steppe model was one (arrow **A** in **9.4**) but it was also suggested – and by the 2014 version apparently settled upon – that as India itself gained agriculture from the west somewhat later than Anatolia, it could be argued that the expansion of agriculture and Indo-European languages was not only to the west but also to the east (arrow **B**), across eastern Anatolia and the Zagros through Iran and eventually to northern India.

The major attraction of this model was that it tied the spread of language to an economic and demographic vector that explained how the Indo-European languages both spread so quickly and replaced the native languages of Europe. With an agricultural economy placed at the centre, the Indo-Europeans would have experienced continuous population growth in excess of any neighbouring hunter-gatherer population; this then drove the need to expand into new territories and also provided the means of out-competing, indeed swallowing, any non-Indo-European languages in the way. The Anatolian Farmer model not only consumed most of the hunter-gatherers in its way, but it also tended to devour a number of other models. For example, some have supported a Balkan homeland (e.g. the renowned linguist and historian of the Near East, Igor Diakonov[15]). Admittedly, this region has not received much support, especially as it constituted the core area of Gimbutas's non-Indo-European 'Old Europe'.[16]

A reduced version of a Balkan homeland would be an attempt to confine the homeland to the territory of the Cucuteni-Trypillia culture (5500–2750 BCE; [**9.5**]), which extended from Romania across Moldova through western Ukraine.[17] This culture is primarily known for its settlements, which includes a cluster of the largest Neolithic communities in Europe. Some have argued that it was here that the pastoralism underlying the steppe cultures (and Steppe model) was initiated by an expansion of Cucuteni-Trypillia farmers onto the steppe.[18] This was built on the assumption that the mobile stock-breeding economy that characterized the steppe could only have been created by a population that were previously settled agriculturalists, a segment of whom began to move east and develop an increasingly more mobile economy.[19] To this might be added the impact of exchange mechanisms as there was solid evidence that copper metallurgy and possible evidence that domestic livestock had been introduced to the steppelands from the west. Geographically it could be supported because of its pivotal position between the steppelands on the east and the rest of Europe on the west. Such a location would provide an explanation for the pastoral-east–agricultural-west divide that has often governed homeland models where one wanted to explain pastoralism in terms of an expansion from west of the Dnipro. Moreover, some of the cultural items regarded as diagnostic of Indo-European culture, such as wheels, were known from the Cucuteni-Trypillia culture (and for those who get excited about such things, there are images of swastikas on the ceramics).[20] However, any argument that would confine the origins of Indo-European to the Balkans or specifically to the Cucuteni-Trypillia

EVALUATING ARCHAEOLOGICAL CULTURES AS LINGUISTIC MODELS

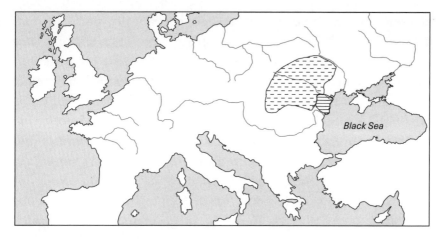

9.5 The Cucuteni-Trypillia culture (5500–2750 BCE), represented by the horizontal hatching, was pivotal in the discussion of the homeland problem because it was located on the border between the agricultural west and the pastoral east, which was highlighted in the dissonance generated by linguistic palaeontology in reconstructing the Proto-Indo-European economy. The smaller area represented by continuous horizontal lines indicates the Usatovo culture, a later culture that combines elements of the Cucuteni-Trypillia with those of the steppe.

culture is usually dismissed because the Neolithic of this region had clearly been imported ultimately from Anatolia. It is extremely difficult to argue that the population of the region was anything other than culturally and linguistically an offshoot of Neolithic Anatolia. In short, it can serve as part of the Anatolian Farmer model but it is difficult to see how it could stand by itself.

More significantly, the Anatolian Farmer model also swallowed the Danubian homeland model, which had enjoyed considerable popularity either as the sole homeland or at least part of a homeland that also comprised the Nordic model. The Linear Ware Neolithic culture saw the spread of the earliest farming communities in the Danube drainage basin *c.* 5500–4500 BCE over an area that extended from Ukraine in the east to the Netherlands and northern France in the west. It occupied the loess (thick windblown and very fertile) soils of central and western Europe and left abundant traces of its villages, consisting of exceedingly long houses as well as cemeteries. It has been occasionally promoted as an Indo-European homeland because it spans an enormous territory, later associated with or proximate to almost all the European branches [9.6]. It also maintained a remarkably similar material culture over the region, a trait that appeared attractive to anyone equating archaeological culture with a common linguistic identity. It was supported by Peter Kitson because it 'correlates notably better than any other single archaeological culture of any period with the core area of Indo-European river-names, which the *kurgan* [=Steppe model] hypothesis fails to account for'.[21]

As with the Balkans, however, it is difficult to disengage the various Neolithic cultures along the Danube from the Anatolian Farmer model, since it is primarily an extension of the same migration that brought farmers from Anatolia to the Balkans. And although it was occasionally promoted, it was also fairly consistently dismissed as a candidate throughout the 20th century. Gordon Childe, probably the most significant archaeologist of European prehistory in the first half of the 20th century, was sceptical that the Danubian culture with its female figurines (mother-goddesses!) was really a good fit for an Indo-European pantheon of dragon slayers.[22] This refrain was vigorously taken up by the Nordic school. Wolfgang Schulz (1881–1936), Austrian philosopher, mythologist and archaeologist (and card-carrying Nazi), dismissed the Danubians as too peaceful, unlike the Funnel-Beaker and Corded Ware cultures, which looked like true *Herrenkulturen* ('dominant cultures').[23] Interestingly enough, the British archaeologist who specialized on the Aegean, Sir John Myres (1869–1954), excluded Anatolia itself as homeland territory because it too was in mother-goddess territory.[24]

Even less plausible as a homeland was the early Neolithic Cardial Ware (Impressed Ware) culture associated with the spread of agriculture from the Adriatic (and western Greece) to Iberia *c.* 6400–5500 BCE, primarily along the Mediterranean coast and islands [9.7]. This has been seen as one of the Achilles heels of the Anatolian Farmer model. On the one hand, it is intrinsically tied to the westward expansions of Anatolian farmers

EVALUATING ARCHAEOLOGICAL CULTURES AS LINGUISTIC MODELS

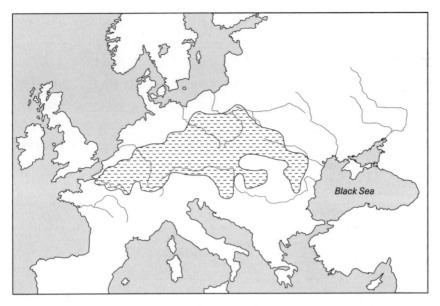

9.6 The Linear Ware culture stretched from the Atlantic to Ukraine and was regarded as a potential homeland not only for the many European branches but also Proto-Indo-European itself.

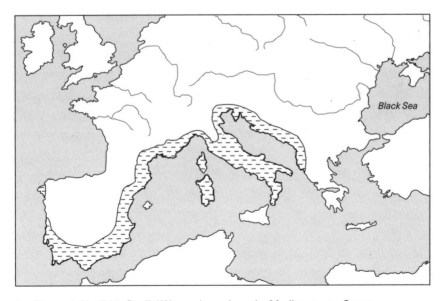

9.7 The early Neolithic Cardial Ware culture along the Mediterranean Coast.

but, on the other, it comprises a territory that tends to be one of the first areas to be excluded on just about every possible category of evidence. For example, as we earlier saw, it is one of the few areas of Europe to present evidence of non-Indo-European languages; its languages seemed to have real trouble maintaining the semantics of Indo-European tree names; and, most importantly, it appeared to require a migration path (Anatolia > Greece > Italy) that contradicted the phylogenetic relationship between these three branches.

The spread of the Neolithic economy northwards towards Scandinavia also has the potential to absorb the Nordic model of Indo-European origins [**9.8**]. While it was realized that the expansion of the Neolithic and the formation of the Funnel-Beaker culture could not be simply explained by a migration of central European farmers, it is still possible to argue that that the acculturation of local hunter-gatherers to farming might have been a vector for the spread of Indo-European languages.

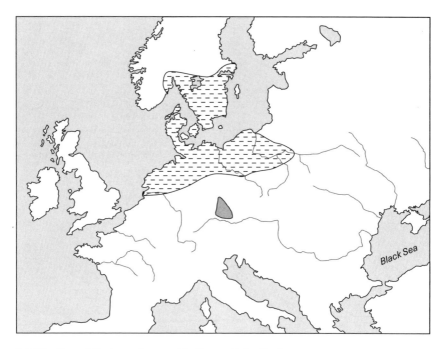

9.8 The Funnel-Beaker culture and (to its south) the Baalberge group.

The archaeological attractions of this model were great enough to render the Anatolian Farmer hypothesis a major player. Nevertheless, it faced hostility from Indo-European linguists because it argued for the dispersion of the Indo-European languages that appeared incongruously early according to the evidence of linguistic palaeontology (whose validity its supporters denied); because of the evidence of Indo-European phylogeny – for example, an archaeological chain that suggested Anatolian > Greek > Italic ignored the linguistic interrelationship of these branches; and because its attempts to swallow other suggested homelands such as the Steppe model were regarded as unpersuasive.[25]

Irrespective of its validity as a solution to the homeland problem, the Anatolian Farmer model must still play a crucial role in our understanding of the linguistic history of Europe. For even if it fails to convince that it was responsible for the dispersal of Indo-European, it is highly probable that it was the major vector for introducing some Neolithic language or languages from Anatolia and spreading it/them across much of Europe. In short, if the Indo-European languages spread from a source other than that of the Anatolian farmers, it is nevertheless highly likely that the European farmers formed a substrate language family, at least in the Balkans, the Danube and the coastal areas of the Mediterranean, over which Indo-European was subsequently superimposed. One way or another, it is difficult to dispense with the notion that at least some of the Indo-European languages of Europe retain vocabulary borrowed from the Anatolian farmers.[26] We will take up this suggestion again.

The Nordic model

Much of the earliest case for a Nordic homeland was fuelled by providing archaeological cover for an explicitly racial argument that the Indo-European languages were spread by a population originating in northern Europe whose descendants still occupied the territory. In fact, for Kossinna – the main exponent of the Nordic model in the early 20th century – the homeland of the Germanic languages (which he had attempted to establish) was virtually the same as the homeland of the Indo-Europeans. The archaeological structure of his argument was largely based on the continuity of culture in northern Europe and south Scandinavia, from its occupation after the retreat of the ice sheets until the historical period. So the ancestors of the Proto-Indo-Europeans were seen in the Mesolithic cultures of the north (the Maglemose and the Kongemose, *c.* 6000–5200 BCE) and the following Ertebølle culture (5300–4000 BCE). The Ertebølle continued an economy based on fishing and hunting but also saw the appearance of ceramic containers and contacts with farmers of the Linear Ware culture to their south (in some of its earliest presentations it was argued that the Linear Ware actually derived from the north, which proved totally unconvincing).

The main floruit of Proto-Indo-European could then be assigned to the following Funnel-Beaker culture, which marked the spread of agricultural communities across northern and northeastern Europe (*c.* 4500–2700 BCE), where they left both settlement sites but also megalithic and large earthen tombs. Its location included northern Germany and southern Scandinavia and, therefore, was the core element of the Nordic model, but it also extended eastwards across Poland and even to the northwest of Ukraine so could be employed to support a Baltic homeland. Yet within the Nordic model, the major expansion of the Indo-Europeans to the south and east is to be associated with the Corded Ware culture (see below), which is believed to have been a local phenomenon that evolved out of the Funnel-Beaker culture.

The Steppe cultures

The Steppe model was originally proposed on geographical or linguistic grounds that were not anchored to a specific archaeological culture, or encompassed areas that subsumed what we would today regard as totally unrelated archaeological cultures. As knowledge of the archaeology of the Ukrainian and south Russian steppe increased, it became clear that there was not a single steppe culture but a series of spatially, chronologically and economically diverse cultures. The main distinction is between the settled farming populations and those who practised economies based primarily on hunting-gathering-fishing, or the limited exploitation of some domestic animals. The settled agriculturalists were primarily members of the Cucuteni-Trypillia culture (see **9.5**), whose sites spanned the fertile soils running from the Carpathians (in Romania) to just beyond the Dnipro in the vicinity of Kiev (Ukraine) during the period *c*. 5500–2750 BCE. As we have just discussed, the culture is seen as an offshoot of the spread of the Neolithic from Anatolia and offers an abundance of environmental and economic evidence congruent with either reconstructed Proto-Indo-European or, at least, the evidence ancestral to the European branches. In solutions that conceptualized an eastern (Indo-Iranian) pastoral economy and a western (European) economy, the Cucuteni-Trypillia culture was seen to underlie the European branches or, in some instances, could be proposed as the Proto-Indo-European homeland.[27]

Moving east beyond the Cucuteni-Trypillia are a group of cultures that are regionally and temporally defined, those on the west generally centred on the Dnipro-Don region and those on the east between the Volga and the Urals. There seems to be a gradual transition from the Mesolithic to the Neolithic, marked by the introduction of ceramics and domestic livestock, although regionally both hunting and fishing appears to have played a significant role, the latter especially along the Dnipro where the Dnipro-Donets culture emerges. For ease of presentation, I will outline the sequence of cultures using the largest blocks that enter into discussion of the Steppe model, even if it requires some gross oversimplification.

In the western region the Dnipro-Donets culture (*c*. 5200–4200 BCE) is primarily known from more than thirty often large cemeteries (over one hundred burials; [**9.9**]). The cemeteries comprised burials in communal pits or trenches (in a linear arrangement), with frequent evidence of exposure before burial or only partial burial – for example, of skulls. The economy was a mixture of hunting-gathering-fishing with some domesticated animals and (not always reliable) evidence for some domestic plants. There was an abundance of grave gifts or dress ornaments, including objects of copper, stone maces and plaques made of boars' tusks. This culture usually occupies the position of a substrate population in the Steppe model. In some of its material culture – for example, the use of boar-tusk pendants and stone maces – it is paralleled by the Samara

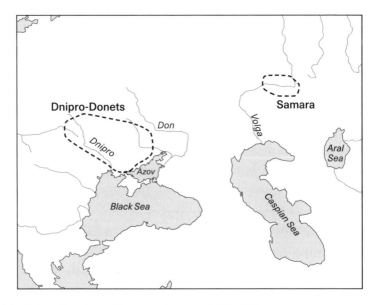

9.9 The Dnipro-Donets and Samara cultures, *c.* 5200–4200 BCE.

culture of about the same time, known from the Middle Volga region, where we find some similarities in economy and burial, including the cultic burial of horse remains. In short, there appears to have been something of an interaction sphere extending from the Dnipro on the west to the Volga on the east with most of the evidence, settlement or burial, largely confined to the river valleys.

Superimposed over the Dnipro-Donets culture is the Serednii Stih (Russian Srednij Stog) culture that occupied the same general area of the earlier Dnipro-Donets and dates to *c.* 4400–3400 BCE [**9.10**]. It indicates a new culture with a very different ceramic style, pointed-based, shell-tempered ware, and a new burial rite – the body was laid on its back with knees flexed upward – which was to become a major behavioural pattern in the following culture. There is also an increase in horse remains; sometimes horse is the dominant mammal consumed and there has long been a suspicion (initially driven unfortunately by the

EVALUATING ARCHAEOLOGICAL CULTURES AS LINGUISTIC MODELS

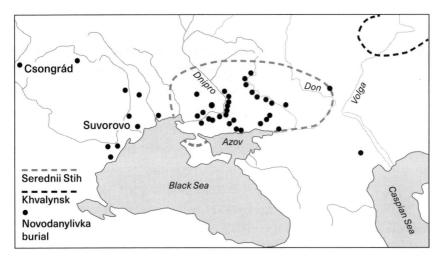

9.10 The major Eneolithic steppe cultures before the Yamnaya, showing the Serednii Stih (with the Novodanylivka) culture in the Dnipro-Don region and the Khvalynsk culture in the Middle Volga region.

misdating of an intrusive domesticated Iron Age horse on a Serednii Stih site) that by now the horse had been domesticated.

Within the same general region are found burials of the Suvorovo-Novodanylivka type, burials that appear to derive from the Serednii Stih culture but the graves are more elaborate (they may be stone-lined) and much richer, with long flint blades, copper ornaments and stone maces, which have been interpreted as symbols of power. The graves are primarily concentrated north of the Sea of Azov but also extend as far west as Suvorovo in Bulgaria, where we find burials both in flat graves and now also under tumuli (kurgans) that contained timber or stone chambers. Funerary rituals here followed those we find in the Serednii Stih culture, including a horse-headed stone mace similar to those found further to the east. Within the Steppe model, this expansion of a steppe culture into the Danube region usually marks the initial expansion of the Indo-Europeans.

CHAPTER 9

The shift from the Dnipro-Donets to the Serednii Stih culture has been variously treated as a local evolution or the product of influences (migration?) from the east, specifically from the Middle Volga region where the local successor of the Samara culture is the Khvalynsk culture (4700–3800 BCE), primarily known from the Khvalynsk cemetery of over two hundred burials [**9.10**].[28] This cemetery (actually two cemeteries) attests to a society with domestic animals (although no evidence for domestic cereals), the ritual sacrifice of the horse along with other livestock, over 370 copper objects and burial that usually involved laying the body on its back but strongly flexing the knees, similar to the rite seen in the west in Serednii Stih cemeteries and like them, also powdered with ochre.

Subsequently, most of the Pontic-Caspian steppe was occupied by the Yamnaya (or Pit-grave) culture (3300–2500 BCE), which spanned the region from the Danube east just beyond the Urals [**9.11**]. Again, we are dealing with a culture primarily known from its burials but including some settlement sites, even some fortified settlements. The burials continue the earlier way of laying out the deceased found in the Serednii Stih and Khvalynsk cultures (the so-called 'Yamnaya position'; see also Chapter 15) but the graves are now routinely placed under barrows (kurgans) or have been secondarily inserted into earlier kurgans (these mounds would be reused and extended from the Yamnaya period up to the Middle Ages, when pastoral Turkic-speaking tribes occupied the steppe).

By *c.* 3300 BCE a portion of the eastern border of the Yamnaya culture migrated eastwards several thousand kilometres and settled in the Minusinsk Basin between the Yenisei river and the Altai mountains where it formed the Afanasievo culture [**9.12**]. The Yamnaya also expanded westwards into the Balkans (about five hundred kurgans have been identified so far), where Yamnaya kurgans can be found along the Danube valley at least as far as the Tisza river in Hungary. Within the Steppe model these movements initiate the dispersal of the Indo-European languages, with a possible earlier incursion associated with the Suvorovo-Novodanylivka-type burials.

This more narrow (and more easily validated) narrative of Suvorovo-Novodanylivka, Serednii Stih, Yamnaya and Afanasievo expansions was extended into a much vaster interpretive framework by Marija

EVALUATING ARCHAEOLOGICAL CULTURES AS LINGUISTIC MODELS

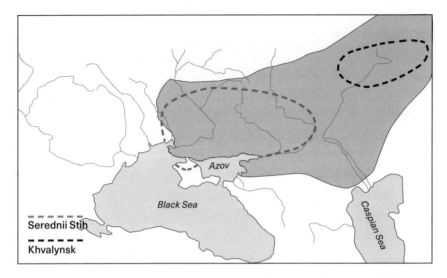

9.11 The Yamnaya culture (shaded area) with the earlier areas of the Serednii Stih and Khvalynsk cultures indicated. The latter two have both been proposed as the ancestral cultures to the Yamnaya.

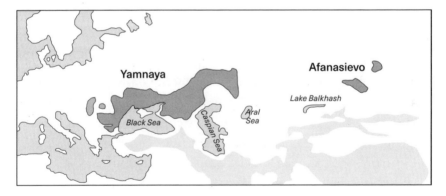

9.12 The Yamnaya culture and the related Afanasievo culture reflect an expansion from the steppe as far west as Hungary and as far east as the Altai region and the Minusinsk Basin.

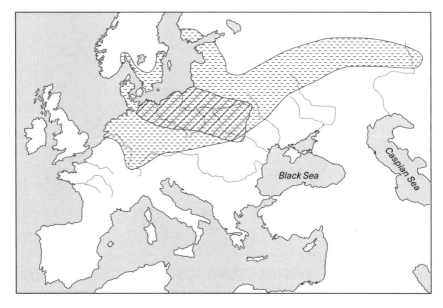

9.13 The Corded Ware (horizontal hatching) and Globular Amphora (diagonal hatching) cultures.

Gimbutas.[29] She took the more generic evidence from the steppe cultures (for example, individual burial, use of barrow/kurgan, cord decoration, use of ochre) to extend the case for steppe dispersals to a series of neighbouring European archaeological cultures such as the Baalberge in Germany (see **9.8**), the Globular Amphora culture of central Europe [**9.13**] and especially the Corded Ware [**9.13**]. She defined these as 'Kurganized' cultures – hybrid cultures that had been culturally and linguistically absorbed by the expansion of steppe cultures. In this way much of Europe could be drawn into the orbit of the Steppe hypothesis. The most important of these so-called 'Kurganized' cultures was the Corded Ware.

The Corded Ware gambit

The Corded Ware culture of 3200–2300 BCE replaced the earlier Funnel-Beaker culture and some of the Danubian cultures [**9.13**] and covered an enormous expanse to the west and east. It extended from the Netherlands across Europe and, via a series of variants, reached as far east as the Urals, marking it out as a prospective homeland candidate with a continental territorial expansion. For the homeland hunters of the 20th century, the Corded Ware culture with its expansion over earlier cultures, especially to the east (potential Indo-Iranians?), was just what one might have expected of the earliest Indo-Europeans.[30] And also labelling it the 'Battle-axe culture' marketed it as the aggressive macho presence that the more bloodthirsty homeland hunters were looking for.

Out of a wealth of archaeological debate, a consensus emerged over the course of the 20th century that the Corded Ware culture was a key player in any solution to the homeland problem. Largely a mortuary culture with very few settlements, it satisfied the major constituency that regarded the Proto-Indo-Europeans as pastoralists rather than settled farmers (unlike the case for the Linear Ware culture or any of the other Neolithic cultures of Europe). And from the burials, where gender roles were clearly marked by what side the deceased was placed, coupled with the evidence that men were often buried with stone battle-axes or other weapons and the presence of horse remains (and later wheeled vehicles), the Corded Ware culture appeared to tick many of the major Indo-European boxes. It was either the equivalent of the homeland or at least a part of the expansion, as its territory coincided with a significant portion of the earliest Indo-Europeans of Europe. It also provided plausible staging areas for the evolution of Germanic, Baltic and Slavic and possible homeland areas for Italic and Celtic [**9.14**], especially if one could associate the expansions of the somewhat later Beaker culture (2800–1800 BCE) with the Corded Ware culture. And, according to many archaeologists, certainly the Nordic school, the Corded Ware culture had evolved locally.[31]

As the Corded Ware region ran on a west-to-east axis, the major issue regarding its origins was which side was the earliest? The Polish

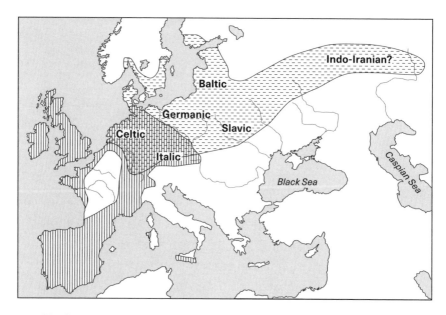

9.14 The Corded Ware (horizontal dashes) and Beaker (vertical lines) cultures and putative associations with various Indo-European language branches. The origin of the Beaker culture was long disputed between two camps: one that sought it in Iberia and another who believed it had been connected with the slightly earlier Corded Ware horizon.

archaeologist Włodzimierz Antoniewicz (1893–1973) argued for a 'western' and hence local origin in 1936, which, naturally, suited the Nordic model. By contrast, three years earlier another Polish (and later British) archaeologist Tadeusz Sulimirski (1898–1983) not only concluded that the earliest Corded Ware remains were in the east, but regarded the culture as the result of a massive migration of steppe nomads who spread the Indo-European languages from a homeland in Central Asia.[32] Although Sulimirski later came to reject his initial thesis, there were always others such as Miroslav Buchvaldek (1930–2002), a leading authority on the Corded Ware, who looked to the east for its origins.[33] The debate has slogged on to the present and rather than detail the history of the scrimmaging, it is probably far easier to outline the main issues and how they fit within the various solutions to the homeland problem.

Critics argue that the Corded Ware and the Yamnaya (or earlier steppe cultures) are essentially two separate and unrelated roughly contemporaneous cultures, so it is impossible to derive one from the other. In short, whatever similarities linked the two, such as single burial under a mound and the use of cord decoration on pottery, the differences between the two cultures were far greater than the few similarities. Lothar Kilian (1911–2000), an ethnic German born in Lithuania who produced monographs on the origins of both the Balts and Germans as well as the Indo-Europeans, drew up a list of twenty-three characteristic features of both the Corded Ware and Yamnaya cultures and concluded that they only shared four of them,[34] and these four seemed rather generic – for example, barrows are found in archaeological cultures all over the world, corded decoration is hardly unique and otherwise the ceramics were very different. One of the key features of Corded Ware burials is the marking of gender, with males buried on their right side and females on their left; there is no evidence of this in the Yamnaya culture, while such a practice is seen earlier in various local late Neolithic cultures (e.g. the Tiszapolgár, Bodrogkeresztúr and Lengyel cultures) that long preceded Corded Ware.[35] Moreover, while the deposit of weapons, usually stone battle-axes, is often routinely associated with the burial of Corded Ware males, Yamnaya burials contain very little evidence of a male-associated weapon complex[36] (although there are some male status items in the Novodanylivka culture).

All of these points were made numerous times by Alexander Häusler, probably the foremost non-Soviet expert on the steppe and the relationship between the Pontic-Caspian cultures and those of the rest of Europe, particularly within the context of the Indo-European homeland problem. A major part of Häusler's voluminous publication record amounts to a Summa Contra Gimbutas.[37] Thus, conclusive evidence that the Corded Ware was in any way an offshoot of a more easterly (steppe) culture was simply not forthcoming, despite a sense among many archaeologists that there must be some form of relationship. The best that could be done was to credit the Yamnaya culture with providing a cultural or ideological package that may have influenced the evolution of the Corded Ware culture, but the latter was by no means seen as the result of a significant migration of steppe peoples.[38]

So, although we find that the Corded Ware culture is a major archaeological player in any homeland solution, it is not the whole solution. It could never mount a convincing case to explain the origins of most of the peoples of the Balkans, Greece or Anatolia, and – unless one imagines that taking out a Sharpie and drawing a long arrow from central Europe to western China is convincing evidence – it does not actually solve the problem of Tocharian origins. If the archaeologist believes there is sufficient evidence for continuity from earlier periods, be they in central Europe or the far north, then both the Nordic and the Danubian (and Anatolian Farmer) models are all potentially in play. The Steppe model is only in play archaeologically if one believes that the similarities between the Yamnaya (or earlier steppe cultures) and Corded Ware cultures are evidence of a much more thorough process of acculturation. Generally, archaeologists in the former Soviet Union did not regard the steppe as the homeland of the Indo-Europeans but merely that of the Indo-Iranians, and therefore, kurgan burials could be interpreted within the structure of the ancient Indian class system,[39] designs on Cucuteni-Trypillian pottery could be interpreted through the means of Indian religion and one could 'assume that the Rig Veda originated on the banks of the Dnipro'.[40]

Asian homeland models: the archaeological evidence

According to Kossinna, in the early 20th century there was no reputable scholar left who supported an Asian Urheimat other than the great Swedish archaeologist Oscar Montelius (1843–1921). He pioneered the construction of both relative and absolute chronologies of European cultures by synchronizing them with the cultural development of Egypt and the Near East; for Montelius, culture always flowed from the east to west. Yet an Asian origin never totally disappeared, although it has taken on a variety of forms. Here I will try to present briefly how archaeology might bear on Asian homeland models.

India

As one of the earliest homeland models and still being promoted as the Out of India solution to the homeland problem, archaeological support for a South Asian homeland has never been particularly robust. If dispersal from the homeland must have been in motion before 2500 BCE, the only cultural entity that usually comes into question is the early Neolithic site of Mehrgarh (*c.* 7000–2500 BCE) and associated sites, which track the development from an early Neolithic village to the early urbanism underlying the later Indus Valley civilization. There is no convincing evidence that Mehrgarh was instrumental in spreading its economy or its material culture to the north or west, the main area of Indo-European languages. And as for the distinctive Indus Valley civilization (3300–1300 BCE) with its spectacular urban sites, while there were extensive trade relations to both the north (Central Asia) and west (to Mesopotamia), the furthest evidence for actual expansion, the trade centre of Shortugai in northern Afghanistan, dates from *c.* 2000 BCE and is chronologically (and culturally) irrelevant to the expansion of Indo-European languages to the west.

In India a unique and spectacular civilization arose, but there has never been an archaeological case that its culture had managed to spread across the rest of the territory of the Indo-European world. Its attraction (setting aside purely political motives) is that no one has ever been able to mount a truly convincing archaeological argument to support a migration *into* India that would account for the Indo-Aryans; the arguments for migration have been essentially linguistic.[41] Although there is a string of potential intrusive archaeological cultures that have been claimed as the vector of the Indo-Aryan languages, none have been found to be particularly convincing.[42] This has provided the basis of the Indian homeland hypothesis: if you can't prove that Indo-Europeans came to India from outside, they must have been indigenous. But a robust defence does not equate with a successful offence and the Indian homeland model fails to even get off the ground. Nevertheless, I would not dismiss the volume of criticism against the various models for Indo-Aryan invasions into India: the critics may be setting the bar very high, but that is probably how it should be.

Central Asia

The region extending from the eastern shores of the Caspian Sea east to the frontiers of China was another popular region for planting putative homelands in the 19th century. Here again, however, solutions were largely driven by geographical rather than strictly archaeological evidence. Grossly oversimplifying an enormous region of many diverse environments and cultures, I will concentrate on the most obvious bodies of evidence [9.15].

As we have seen, Raphael Pumpelly's excavations at Anau in southern Turkmenistan were tentatively viewed as supporting the concept of a Central Asian Urheimat associated with the origins and spread of agriculture, a forerunner of the Anatolian Farmer model. Agriculture did spread locally across this region and produced a series of urban cultures, largely localized to the oases, climaxing with the Bactria-Margiana Archaeological Complex (BMAC; also known as the Oxus civilization) (2250–1700 BCE). While the various cultures experienced trade relations with the south, there is no convincing evidence that there emerged a local culture in Central Asia that spread to the west.

In addition to the farming track, there were also societies in Central Asia exploiting the more challenging regions engaged primarily in hunting-gathering-fishing although gradually incorporating domestic

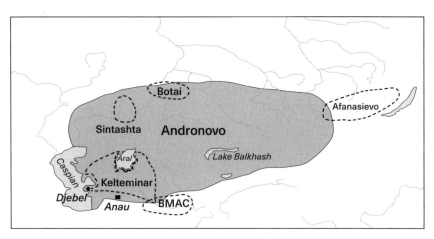

9.15 Cultures of Central Asia. Within the Steppe model, the Sintashta and Andronovo cultures are associated with the Indo-Iranians, while the Afanasievo culture is often proposed as a (distant) ancestor of the Tocharians.

livestock from their neighbours. These included the Kelteminar culture (5500–3500 BCE), which ranged from the Caspian to beyond the (former) Aral Sea. One scholar has recently and (unexpectedly) equated this culture with the Uralic homeland on linguistic-geographical grounds.[43] To the north in Kazakhstan lay the Botai culture (3700–3100 BCE), whose eponymous site yielded, as we saw in Chapter 7, a permanent settlement of more than 160 houses for a population that largely sustained itself on horse (over 100,000 horse bones were recovered), some of which were arguably domesticated (evidence for milking mares).[44] The site was of obvious importance to the issue of whether the Indo-Europeans were associated with the initial spread of the domestic horse, but subsequent genetic evidence indicates that the later domestic horse populations of Eurasia derive predominantly from sources further west.

In short, there is no promising archaeological evidence from Central Asia that might enter into the discussion, although this area must have been crossed by early Indo-Europeans during their dispersal. Moreover, as we have already seen with respect to Yamnaya expansion eastwards, the steppe area of this region was traversed from the west as early as *c.* 3500 BCE (the Afanasievo culture). Much of the area was subsequently occupied, again from the west, by the Sintashta culture (2200–1750 BCE) and soon afterwards the Andronovo culture (in fact, a group of related cultures) *c.* 2000–900 BCE. Even though the historical trajectory of nomadic tribes pouring into Europe from the east was prominent in 19th-century debate (think of the Huns, Avars and Mongols), the archaeological evidence suggests that the flow of people and cultures was in the opposite direction in the 4th and 3rd millennia BCE.

Caspian-Caucasus

The archaeological cultures of Central Asia have never provided a potential fit with an Indo-European homeland, yet there are several sites that became part of the narrative that are situated near the Caspian Sea in Turkmenistan. About 1950 Soviet archaeologists excavated a number of cave sites, such as Djebel Cave, which produced early (although not well-datable) evidence of domestic livestock associated with flint tools and pottery. When it came time to trace the origin of some of the steppe cultures of the Volga region, the Caspian evidence was promoted as a possible source. This was so much so that in the early development of the Steppe model, the original source of the steppe cultures was often not sought in the Middle Volga region but in the southeast Caspian.[45] That a chain of intermediate sites from the early Neolithic Caspian sites and the steppe has not been demonstrated has greatly diminished the plausibility of an east Caspian origin. Nevertheless, the essential problem – the source of the domestic animals of the steppe populations – still remains. If one entertains the idea of a link between the dispersal of the Neolithic economy and the movement of languages, the physical source of the domestic animals with respect to homeland models can hardly be ignored. We have already seen that the domestic economy of the Anatolian Farmer model probably derives from eastern Anatolia, the Fertile Crescent and/or the Levant, and this economy was carried across Europe, providing the economic basis of the other European homeland models. The problem with the Steppe model is that the earliest appearance of domestic animals in the Middle Dnipro, ostensibly derived from the descendants of those belonging to Anatolian farmers to their west, dates to *c.* 5500 BCE or later,[46] while domestic animals on the Volga arrived *c.* 4800–4600 BCE.[47] As the Volga sites are almost exclusively cemeteries boasting rich graves marked by the presence of copper ornaments imported from the west and the sacrifices of domestic animals,[48] this would predispose us to assume that the livestock also derived from the west. This is certainly a defensible hypothesis, but there did exist another route from the Fertile Crescent north through the Caucasus and then northeast up the Volga.

Our evidence for the spread of the Neolithic economy from the Fertile Crescent through the Caucasus begins about 6000 BCE in the area of the confluence of the Kura and Araxes rivers [**9.16**]. Here we find the Aratashen-Shulaveri-Shomutepe culture; about the same time (6000–5750 BCE) a Neolithic economy arrived at sites in the northern Caucasus. From here it crossed the mountains into the piedmont region, forming the Darkveti-Meshoko culture, whose earliest dates so far are *c.* 4600–4500 BCE. While such dates render it technically impossible to account for domestic animals that appeared several hundred years earlier in the

EVALUATING ARCHAEOLOGICAL CULTURES AS LINGUISTIC MODELS

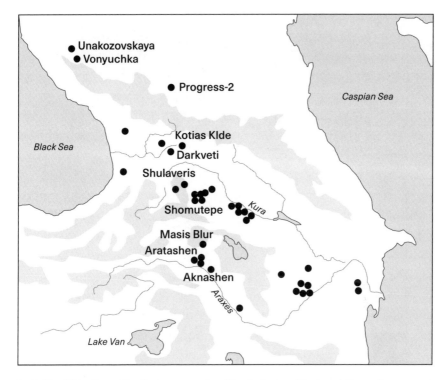

9.16 Neolithic sites of the Caucasus region. The Aratashen-Shulaveri-Shomutepe culture (*c.* 6000–5000 BCE) was primarily confined between the Kura and Araxes rivers. The lighter shaded areas represent the mountains.

Middle Volga region, we know so little about this culture that much earlier dated sites are by no means implausible. So we cannot totally exclude the possibility of a Caucasian source for the domesticated livestock found in the Middle Volga.[49]

If the paragraph above appears as an exercise in special pleading, there is some justification for introducing the potential of a homeland situated south of the Caucasus. In the Greater Armenian model of Gamkrelidze and Ivanov, for example, when pressed for the archaeological culture most likely to be associated with the Indo-European homeland, the authors selected the Neolithic Halaf culture (*c.* 6100–5100 BCE) [**9.17**].

CHAPTER 9

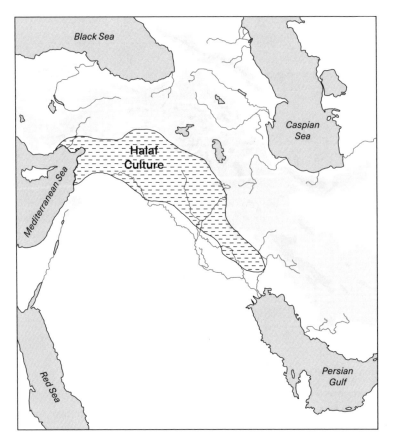

9.17 The Halaf culture (c. 6100–5100 BCE), or at least a portion of it, was identified with the Indo-European homeland in the original version of the Greater Armenian model.

This spanned the region from eastern Anatolia, Syria and northern Iraq (i.e. the upper reaches of the Tigris and Euphrates rivers) and may have been related to the population that carried the Neolithic economy into the Caucasus.

Moreover, towards the end of the Neolithic but still within a time frame that one could associate with the homeland, the Maykop culture arose (c. 3800–3000 BCE; [**9.18**]) in the territory immediately north of the Caucasus that was earlier occupied by the Darkveti-Meshoko. It is currently known from about three hundred barrows (kurgans) and thirty settlements that occupy a territory from the Taman peninsula (where

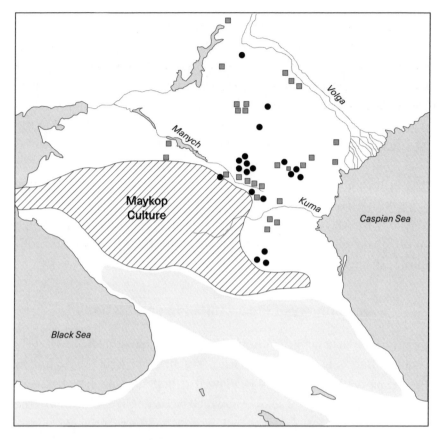

9.18 The Maykop culture (c. 3800–3000 BCE). Eneolithic steppe burials are indicated by open squares and Steppe Maykop burials by filled circles.

Russian author Mikhail Lermontov's *Hero of our Time* found himself enduring the dirtiest village in the Russian Empire) to the borders of Dagestan in the eastern Caucasus. Most burials are poor but there are also enormous barrows associated with an elite that were furnished with a large assortment of precious objects made of bronze, gold and silver, along with ornaments of exotic materials such as lapis lazuli, carnelian and turquoise from Central Asia; other items clearly showed influences from northern Iran and Mesopotamia. In essence, there is all the appearances of an elite who either brought with them artistic traditions from south of the Caucasus or, possibly, simply imported exotic material.

Although the Maykop culture was confined to the piedmont area of the Caucasus, there was an 'offshoot' Steppe Maykop (*c.* 3800–3000 BCE), which combined traditions of the Maykop culture with the pastoral societies of the steppe, ranging from the Caucasus northwards towards the Volga. Essentially, we have a foreign prestigious elite culture with a superior metal technology that moved into the steppelands before the emergence of the Yamnaya culture. This provides another potential homeland whose origins lay in the Caucasus where one might propose that, in introducing a supposedly superior cattle-based pastoral economy along with wheeled vehicles (early wheeled vehicles are associated with Maykop), the Maykop culture underlay the later expansion of the steppe cultures and could have provided a vector for the spread of the Indo-European languages.[50]

A summary of the archaeological solutions

By 2015 the archaeological solutions to the homeland problem had largely resolved into four major hypotheses. The first of these, the Anatolian Farmer model, had essentially swallowed up both the Balkan and the central European homeland solutions, which were merely extensions of the migrations of the earliest farmers. One could argue that the old Nordic homeland could also be absorbed but that would have required an assessment of how much the spread of agriculture to the north was driven by demic diffusion (population movement) and how much by acculturation (cultural borrowing) and, if the latter, whether the second process could have allowed the language of the earlier hunter-gatherers to not only survive but also evolve into Proto-Indo-European. The Anatolian Farmer model could also be employed to consume the Steppe model, yet here the material culture, economy and certainly burial ritual are so markedly different that while one can trace the movement of copper and possibly livestock across the steppe, local evolution still seems to dominate in the region.[51] The model could also assimilate the Corded Ware solution if it could be demonstrated that the latter was a purely local phenomenon that emerged directly from the descendants of the earlier Anatolian farmers.

The obvious attraction of the Anatolian Farmer model pre-2015 was that it provided a plausible vector for the expansion of a language across Europe and so it was probably more convincing to archaeologists. On the other hand, it was heavily criticized by Indo-European linguists since it rejected the application of linguistic palaeontology, which contradicted its cultural fit with Indo-European, it appeared to set Indo-European expansions several millennia earlier than expected, and although attempts were made to synchronize it with the phylogeny of Indo-European, this exercise seldom convinced. It also faced application of the exclusion principle, because it set the homeland either within or near an area where the earliest records suggested the presence of a non-Indo-European language (Hattic in central Anatolia), while 46 per cent of its attested vocabulary of the supposedly local Anatolian Hittites appeared to be borrowed. Dutch linguist Alwin Kloekhorst, the author of one of the etymological dictionaries of Hittite, concluded that:

> almost all the Hittite terms referring to the 'high culture' of the city-states characteristic of Middle/Late Chalcolithic and Early Bronze Age Anatolia are borrowings. This situation is not consistent with a scenario in which Proto-Anatolian (and therefore Hittite) was indigenous to Anatolia: in such a case, we would expect the Hittites to have indigenous words for all aspects of the high culture of Anatolia (and to find some of these words in the other Indo-European languages as well).[52]

Moreover, the Anatolian farmer model was also saddled with the implication of an Indo-European expansion across the Mediterranean where there were traces of non-Indo-European languages.

The archaeological evidence for the second, Nordic model had largely collapsed and was essentially contingent on attempts to suggest substantial cultural and population movement from the Baltic region towards the steppe, involving the Funnel-Beaker or Globular Amphora cultures or convincing those dealing with Corded Ware origins that it began in the north before undergoing major expansion.

CHAPTER 9

The third major contender based on archaeological evidence was the Steppe model because it accorded reasonably well (although not necessarily perfectly) with linguistic palaeontology, showed evidence of major expansions both east and west and presented some mechanisms (mobility provided by the domestic horse, ox-drawn wagons and pastoralism) that might have supported rapid expansion. Although it established itself as the potential source of a major initial expansion, largely confined to adjacent grassland territories to the east and west, beyond the distribution of Yamnaya kurgans (the Tisza river of Hungary) or the northern part of Central Asia, it did not offer much in the way of hard evidence that it had expanded into South Asia (Indo-Aryan) or much of Europe. The hypothesized expansion from the steppe into Europe depended almost entirely on its ability to demonstrate a fundamental relationship with the emergence of the Corded Ware horizon.

Finally, the archaeological evidence for a homeland somewhere between eastern Anatolia and the Caucasus/Caspian was very much a long shot supported by only a few archaeologists with quite divergent theories. One of its principal linguistic attractions is that it provided an explanation for Near Eastern (Semitic, Sumerian) loanwords in Proto-Indo-European. It also provided a local or proximate origin for the Anatolians and resolved the origin of all other Indo-Europeans with a two-homeland model: a primary homeland south of the Caucasus and a secondary homeland, usually in the Steppe or perhaps in the Balkans.

Archaeologists had long had access to additional evidence of prehistoric populations, and it is this aspect we will need to explore in the next chapter.

CHAPTER 10

Hair Colour, Skulls and the Emergence of Modern Genetics

Physical anthropology (or bio-archaeology) has played a major – although often sinister – role in homeland solutions since the latter part of the 19th century. Swedish naturalist Carl von Linné (1707–1778) had already classified humans into four major races (European, Asian, African and American), and with the rise of Darwinism and interest in human evolution in the mid-19th century, it was only a matter of time before scholars added physical anthropology to the toolkit of homeland hunters. For example, Charles Darwin's champion Thomas Huxley waded into the Indo-European problem in 1890 to support a homeland (of blonds) between the Baltic and the Urals. The problem of the physical type of the Proto-Indo-Europeans was fairly obvious: Indo-European speakers ranged from tall blond Scandinavians to much darker Indo-Aryans. Scholars couldn't resist asking which (if any) physical type was 'original'. Before Europe began revealing its prehistoric past, it was generally assumed that it was peopled from Asia, but once archaeological evidence became available from Europe, one could think outside the earlier box. Already in 1826 Heinrich Schulz, in his account of the Germanic people, railed against applying the *ex oriente lux* theory to everything in Europe, which denied a local origin for its *eigne Menschenart* ('own race').[1] And in the same year the French naturalist Antoine Desmoulins[2] (1794/1796–1828) could claim that the Afghans, Medes, Ossetes, Slavs, Germans, Danes, Swedes, Normans and English, with their blue eyes and blond or red hair, constituted the Indo-Germanic race whose type was unchanged from Iceland to the Ganges.

Scholars tackled the problem of tying the Indo-Europeans to a specific physical type by employing two major lines of evidence: pigmentation and craniometry. The amount of literature on this is enormous, politically controversial and often stultifying. While I once felt obliged to swim in this swamp because I did not believe that it could be ignored,[3] there are fortunately more modern treatments of the subject[4] (archaeologist Jean-Paul Demoule has provided a survey into many of the darker alleys of physical anthropology and the search for the Indo-European homeland[5]). Nevertheless, I shall attempt here to briefly navigate a path through the swamp, since it has led to many often conflicting conclusions about the homeland question.

Pigmentation

The most obvious approach to resolving the racial issue for 19th- and early 20th-century investigators was exploring the pigmentation – the skin, hair and eye colour – of the Indo-Europeans. One might be impressed with the differences seen in present-day populations, but a scholar even in 1900 should have been sceptical about reading the modern appearance of people into the past. Assuming a dispersal date of c. 3000 BCE and a generation interval of about twenty-five years, there would still be almost two hundred generations of physical change between our modern sample and our prehistoric target. What was obviously required was evidence from a period much closer to the target, ignoring modern mixed populations and using the earliest literary sources that provide potential descriptions of earlier Indo-Europeans. Even then, however, the distance in time is still great. Employing a generation interval of twenty-five years, John Day, who in 2000 published a major study of the earlier attempts to employ physical anthropology, suggests that the interval between a 3000 BCE homeland and our earlier Anatolian sources would still be 50 generations, with 90 generations to Homeric Greek and 120 generations to our descriptions of the Roman emperors.[6] That is a lot of generations to maintain 'racial purity', but those who have invested energy in examining this evidence have been content to play with the cards they are dealt.

Attempts to recover the earliest appearance of the Indo-Europeans from artistic works have largely been regarded as suspect, since too many Indo-European branches are only depicted in works of art (painting, sculpture) so recent that they are untrustworthy. Even where we do have early artwork – for example, Egyptian portrayals of Hittite soldiers, Classical sculptures from Greece or Rome, or the murals in the Ajanta caves of India – there are abundant reasons to query whether they are accurate portrayals. The frescoes associated with Tocharian cave shrines depicting lighter-haired Europoids are also suspect as they portray them in Sassanian dress. The problem is often being able to distinguish between actual representation and the demands of artistic tradition, besides which there is always the much greater problem of relating them to a much older ancestral population. In general, it is the textual references that have offered most of our evidence for the appearance of early Indo-Europeans.[7]

Although we would eventually get the trope of the Nordic blue-eyed, blond Aryan,[8] there were those who argued that the original Indo-Europeans had primarily brown or black hair. This was driven partly because setting the homeland in Asia prompted such a natural conclusion, but also because of literary evidence, such as prohibitions against dark-haired Aryans from marrying light-haired (actually it was 'red-haired') women in the Indic Law of Manu, or the dark colour attributed to Sītā's hair in the Indic epic *Ramayana*.[9] The anthropologist Daniel Brinton argued in the 1890s that the original Indo-Europeans consisted of both brunettes and blonds but with the former clearly in the majority as is the case with Europeans today. He pointed out that intermarriage between blonds and brunettes results in 10 per cent more brunettes, which would give them a perpetual advantage.[10]

Despite a flurry of arguments concerning the racial composition of the Indo-Europeans involving the blue-eyed, blond Aryan trope filling pages of the *Bulletin de la Société d'Anthropologie de Paris* in the 1860s,[11] the first really impactful case for blond 'Aryans' was made by Theodor Poesche in 1878.[12] He argued for associating the ancient Indo-Europeans with light skin, blond hair and blue eyes and then, confusing albinism with blondness, he set his homeland of blond Indo-Europeans in the

Pripyat Marshes between Belarus and Ukraine. This was soon rebutted by Karl Penka,[13] an Austrian gymnasium teacher who also assembled abundant evidence for identifying the Indo-Europeans as blonds as discussed in Chapter 2, arguing furthermore that they were also socially superior to darker-haired populations. For example, an Icelandic poem (the *Rigsthula*) described the creation of the different social orders by contrasting the founder of the 'lower' orders, Thrall (who was dark), with the socially superior Jarl (who was blond). The pattern, according to Penka, continued into modern society, where ruling families in France and Spain were described as lighter and blonder than their subjects. Penka pressed his case in a series of monographs that attracted popular attention and laid the foundations for the adoption of the superior Nordic blond trope by political racists in the 20th century. Penka, however, had no truck with having his superior race emerge out of Slavic marshlands, asserting instead that the homeland must have lain in southern Scandinavia. The German (and Jewish) philologist and philosopher Lazarus Geiger (1829–1870) similarly argued that as we know of no non-Indo-European people from whom the Indo-Europeans might have gained their light colour, then wherever we find it we are encountering an unmixed Indo-European type.[14] Canon Isaac Taylor, however, could find a non-Indo-European people from whom he could derive the blond Indo-Europeans. These were the Finns and Estonians who were also tall, blue-eyed blonds, and Taylor concluded that the Indo-Europeans were actually 'an improved race of Finns' (apologies all round).[15]

While we could wallow in this debate indefinitely, it seems far more useful to cite but one more supporter of the blond theory who at least took the arguments beyond the merely anecdotal. The historical geographer Wilhelm Sieglin (1855–1935) trawled through all the Classical descriptions of peoples, individual historical personages, gods and mythological figures to assemble a catalogue of the available evidence, which was published in the year of his death [10.1].[16] Of a total list of 747 characters, 586 were described as blond and only 151 were portrayed with dark hair.

There have been many other evaluations of the written record and attempts to de-blond the evidence by an array of alternative explanations

Blonds		Dark Hair	
Greeks	350	Greeks	45 (or 74)
		Night/Seagods	29
Gods	60	Other gods	6
Mythic persons	140	Mythic persons	18
Historical persons	109	Historical persons	13
Fictitious persons	41	Fictitious persons	8
Centaurs	3	Centaurs	4
Italics	111	Italics	22 (or 29)
		Night/Seagods	7
Gods	27	Other gods	2
Mythic persons	10	Mythic persons	0
Historical persons	63	Historical persons	17

10.1 A segment of one of Wilhelm Sieglin's tables describing the hair colour of classical figures.

or caveats. For example, we must distinguish between the descriptions of external and internal observers, where the former are far more likely to focus on one or two unusual descriptions and then apply it to the entire population (not all Texans are giants nor all Scandinavians blond). And regarding internal descriptions of deities we must deal with colour or solar symbolism that might boost the number of brighter-coloured gods or heroes.[17] Nevertheless, after a thorough sifting of all the literary evidence, Day concluded in 2000 that it could be argued from such evidence 'at least in early adulthood, early IE speakers, and therefore their PIE-speaking ancestors, did tend to be fair- or fairish-haired'.[18]

It should be emphasized that while the Nordic school came to co-opt almost every blond under its mantle and regard it as absolutely conclusive that anyone with light pigmentation must have derived from northern Europe, supporters of other theories were still comfortable in tracing the 'blond race' to different homelands. In 1931, for example, R. J. Kellog derived the blond Proto-Indo-Europeans from south Russia,[19] while those supporting a homeland in central Russia could always squeeze in some detachments of blonds.

Attempts to determine the homeland on the basis of the pigmentation of both modern populations and literary descriptions, although popular, have had no staying power in the quest for Indo-European origins other than to suggest that the ancient Indo-Europeans may have included populations that had light skin, hair or eyes, but such characteristics were in no way confined to the Nordic region as some supporters argued.

Craniometry

The problem with pigmentation (until the recent ancient DNA revolution) is that it merely drew what little evidence we have from the writings or artistic depictions of the individual branches long after the Indo-Europeans had dispersed. The only way of retrieving relevant bio-archaeological data was directly from the physical remains of still earlier populations, the ones associated with the geographical or archaeological solutions to the homeland problem. If you believed in a Central Asian homeland in Bactria, then its resident population such as Iranian-speaking Tajiks were as likely to produce a pure specimen of an original Indo-European as one could ask for. The great explorer of this region, Károly Újfalvy (1842–1904), compared the skull of a Tajik he had measured with one recovered from a prehistoric site in France and declared them nearly identical (although given that there are over 20 million Tajiks that wasn't a great sample). They were also both brachycranial, i.e. broad-headed, which no doubt gratified the French that they had descended from the earliest Aryans.[20] Brachycranial (or brachycephalic when measuring a living specimen) is a category of the cranial/cephalic index, which is defined by measuring the maximum width of a skull, multiplying by 100 and then dividing by the maximum length. Humans were divided into three main categories: dolichocephalic (up to 75), mesocephalic (76–80) and brachycephalic (80 or more). From the late 1870s through the first half of the 20th century a sort of cephalic madness gripped almost any discussion of the physical type of the Indo-Europeans and their homeland, pitting dolichocephalic German scholars against brachycephalic French savants, each certain that their own heads would best fit a Proto-Indo-European hat.

In the earliest decades of the debate the Indo-Europeans were perhaps more often identified as brachycranial but the dolichocranial school eventually came to dominate. And as the skulls from south Scandinavia tended to dolichocrany, it was easy to equate the cranial index with pigmentation. So we ultimately find the anthropologist Ludwig Wilser (1850–1923) placing the Urheimat in Scandinavia where, he claimed, through Darwinian natural selection the harsh climate had produced the world-conquering blond *Homo europaeus dolichocephalus flavus*.[21] And, according to Wilser (who helped pave the way for Nazi racial theory), the closer in time and place one is to their source population, the purer their race. As for the brachycranials, the observation that they were predominantly found in the mountain retreats of the Alps, Carpathians and Balkans indicates that they had clearly not been the dominant population that had spread the Indo-European language but pathetic losers that had to seek refuge.[22] What they were doing in their mountain retreats was anyone's guess: Count Georges Vacher de Lapouge (1854–1936), one-time Professor of Anthropology at the University of Montpellier in France and a leading advocate of racism and champion of the blond dolichocranial theory, wrote that 'the ancestors of the Aryans cultivated wheat when those of the brachycephalics were probably still living like monkeys'.[23]

Over-the-top racial ideas were by no means limited to the dolichocranial camp: the British geographer, anthropologist and polar explorer (Thomas) Griffith Taylor (1880–1963) had observed that brachycephaly had been increasing through time and interpreted this as a positive evolutionary trend that marked the rise of increasingly superior populations. He even synchronized the cephalic index against the Indo-European branches [10.2] to reveal their ascendancy from primitive dolichocephaly to more advanced brachycephaly.

The always entertaining and acerbic Canon Taylor preferred an original brachycephalic racial type, and as for the superior Nordic race he countered: 'The pure Teuton is phlegmatic in temperament, and somewhat dull of intellect; but is brave, warlike, and given to field sports and athletic exercises. He is a tall, flaxen-haired, large-limbed giant, fat and stupid...'[24]

Group	Cephalic Index	Language
Centum	76?	(Tocharian)
(Dolichocephalic)	76	Gaelic
	77	Latin
	78?	(Oscan)
	78	Welsh
	78	Teuton
	79	Greek
Satem	80	Persian
	81	Slavonic
	82	Lithuanian
	83?	(Sanskrit)
	84	Galcha
(Brachycephalic)	85	Armenian

10.2 Griffith Taylor's tables correlating the cephalic index with language group. Some of these measurements are beyond conjectural (e.g. Tocharian). The Galcha belong to the Iranian language branch.

Scepticism regarding this whole enterprise derived from several vantage points. First, the model of tall, blond dolichocephalic Nordics versus short, brunette brachycephalics was by no means consistently supported by the cranial evidence. Both Nordics and Balts were blond, but while Germans boasted of their long heads, Lithuanians were broad-headed, thus torching the link between the cephalic index and pigmentation.[25] Moreover, it was the Lithuanians who possessed the more conservative language. But did any of this really matter when one considered that the Finns and Estonians were also blond but spoke a non-Indo-European Uralic language?

Second, the distinct distributions of the different cranial groups had been exaggerated and were very much at odds with many of the conclusions drawn from archaeological evidence. Penka's supposedly overwhelmingly dolichocranial Scandinavians were a combination of dolichocranial plus mesocranial, while brachycranial skulls constituted up to about 20 per cent of the sample;[26] and an analysis of Funnel-Beaker skulls revealed that a quarter were brachycranial.[27] On the other hand, far from the north in the steppelands of the Black Sea, dolichocranial skulls predominated in the Mariupol cemetery.[28]

Third, there was a considerable number of prominent linguists who saw no association between the geographical origin of the various Caucasian subraces and the origin of the Indo-European languages, and regarded it as ridiculous to ask to which of the pristine sub-branches (Nordic, Mediterranean, etc.) did the Indo-Europeans originally belong. Linguists such as Otto Schrader, Sigmund Feist[29] and R. S. Conway and anatomists such as Julius Kollmann (1834–1918) and G. Sergi (1841–1936) and many others regarded the Indo-Europeans as already mixed before their departure and saw little hope for physical anthropology answering the homeland question. As Max Müller famously wrote: 'An ethnologist who speaks of Aryan race, Aryan blood, Aryan eyes and hair, is as great a sinner as a linguist who speaks of a dolichocephalic dictionary or a brachycephalic grammar.'[30] Even the usually self-assured former American president, Theodore Roosevelt, could write in 1910: 'We do not know which of the widely different stocks now speaking Aryan tongues represents in physical characteristics the ancient Aryan type, nor where the type originated, nor how much it imposed its language on other types, nor how much or how little mixture of blood accompanied the change of tongue.'[31]

Finally, already by 1911 the famous German-born American anthropologist Franz Boas (1858–1942)[32] was demonstrating how fluid the cranial index was: it became increasingly clear that it was not simply a direct product of genetic inheritance but was also strongly impacted by the environment and other factors. The human skull was far more malleable or plastic than the skull measurers had imagined.[33] It might be noted that studies into the cranial index took some pretty strange and unsettling turns: experiments on rats indicated that if you starved them early in life it tended to increase brachycephaly but if you cut off their forelegs to make them bipedal this didn't work and some even became more dolichocephalic.[34] Fortunately (at least for the poor rats), the sole use of the cranial index to describe populations gradually disappeared from most homeland discussions and with it went most of the arguments concerning physical anthropology. Many simply did not want to touch such tainted evidence, despite the fact that by the 1970s there were anthropologists such as the Harvard professor W. W. Howells (1908–2005) who were developing new techniques involving more facial measurements and multivariate analysis that were tested in the field to determine which characteristics provided the most robust genetic evidence to divide populations.[35] As for basing one's research simply on the cranial index, I think here a quote from Wikipedia will suffice: 'The index was once used to categorize human beings in the first half of the 20th century, but today it is used to categorize dogs and cats.' It is far too simplistic to serve as a proxy for past population history, especially where it concerned ancient European populations who generally presented mixed populations.

Multivariate analysis

By the 1970s most, although not all, physical anthropologists were expanding their approach with more advanced statistical techniques. There were handbooks of about a hundred potential measurements that might be taken on a human skull and scientists groped their way forward, attempting to isolate which measurements were the most useful for distinguishing between populations on a genetic basis. Rather than comparing one measurement after another, they employed multivariate analysis, which calculated a single result from an array of measurements through either cluster analysis or principal component analysis. The results of cluster analysis were served up as dendrograms, the same type of trees we are familiar with from the phylogeny of the Indo-European branches. Principal component analysis yielded two-dimensional (and also three-dimensional) scattergrams where one could visualize the similarity and differences in spatial terms.

Despite the enhanced computational power of the new techniques, the results were often problematic. Dendrograms were produced that often made a considerable amount of archaeological or geographical sense (they grouped skulls from the same region or archaeological culture), but they all too frequently threw up results that were as problematic as encountering a literary genre dendrogram that put authors Jane Austen and Stephen King in the same branch – for example, the grouping of Corded Ware skulls from Estonia with skulls from Byblos on the Lebanese coast.[36] Since we are specifically interested in what multivariate analysis of cranial material contributed to the homeland question, we will take the different models in turn.

The Anatolian Farmer model would predict that we might be able to recover evidence that there was a discontinuity between the physical type of European Mesolithic populations and those of the Neolithic, and that the European Neolithic population should closely resemble Neolithic populations of central Anatolia (Çatalhöyük). By 2000 the few studies that tackled this issue were frequently flawed in terms of sample size or selection and, as Day concluded: 'no cranialskeletal study could confirm the hypothesis and, upon further analysis, several tended to reject it'.[37] But several years later some confirmation of a Neolithic immigration from a population resembling Çatalhöyük into southeast Europe was confirmed by multivariate analysis, although the passage of the Neolithic through the Mediterranean appeared to also involve considerable input from local Mesolithic populations.[38]

As for a Danubian homeland, the cranial evidence linked the Linear Ware skulls to those found in the Anatolian Farmer model – for example, with Çatalhöyük in Anatolia or Neolithic sites in Greece and the Balkans.[39] This agreed with archaeological models and emphasizes the difficulty of separating a Danubian homeland from an Anatolian one.

As for the Steppe model, the evidence needs to be divided into several different issues: the formation of the Steppe populations from the Mesolithic into the Bronze Age and the evidence, if any, for dispersals of the Steppe populations both east and west. The Mesolithic population was characterized as a combination of two biological groups, a more robust Proto-European type and a more gracile Mediterranean one with links to the Caucasus and Near East. The Neolithic Cucuteni-Trypillia culture was grouped with other southeast European farming cultures, while the Dnipro-Donets culture saw the total disappearance of the more gracile Mediterranean-type population and its replacement by a uniquely robust proto-European type also known from the Mesolithic occupants of the Baltic region; this has been interpreted as the result of a migration from north to south. There is some continuity in the following Novodanylivka culture, but otherwise there is evidence of another ingression of a more gracile Mediterranean type, seen in the Kemi Oba culture of Crimea and mixed with the earlier robust Proto-European type in the Serednii Stih culture.[40]

The origins of the Yamnaya culture have proved to be more complicated. Because of its vast area, its origins might be dispersed regionally, so much so that anthropologist A. V. Shevchenko (1937–2004) suggested that the crania could be divided into five or six morphological types, each with a different origin. Shevchenko traced all of the putatively Indo-European cultures (as enumerated by Marija Gimbutas) primarily to the Funnel-Beaker culture.[41] Although it differs from the earlier Serednii Stih type, the earlier physical type is regarded as having played a part in the appearance of Yamnaya populations within the territory of Ukraine.[42]

As for Yamnaya expansions to the east, one of the most recurrent results of many of the analyses is the grouping of the Yamnaya and Afanasievo together, thereby linking the European steppe populations with those who came to occupy the Altai-Yenisei region in the Eneolithic.[43] This reinforces observations long before made by Soviet anthropologists and has been supported by more recent craniometric exercises.[44]

As for western expansions, studies of the Yamnaya graves in Romania revealed that the males were very similar to those from the same culture in Ukraine; however, the female population did differ somewhat from their Ukrainian counterparts and were more gracile, resembling more the earlier Neolithic population,[45] which would be consistent with a migration/invasion primarily consisting of males. Comparisons of Yamnaya skulls by Ilse Schwidetzky (1907–1997), the influential Professor of Physical Anthropology at Mainz University, with a number of what Marija Gimbutas regarded as 'Kurganized' populations, such as the Baalberge culture of central Germany (regarded as steppe-derived because of its use of barrow burials), were discounted because the Baalberge more closely resembled local Neolithic populations than those of the steppe.[46] Another 'Kurganized' population, the Baden culture, was explained as a possible hybrid of local Neolithic cultures and steppe cultures.[47] More importantly, the examination of the admittedly small sample of Globular Amphora remains indicated that there was a cline (gradation), with eastern burials more similar to the steppe population but the more western resembling those of the Funnel-Beaker culture.[48]

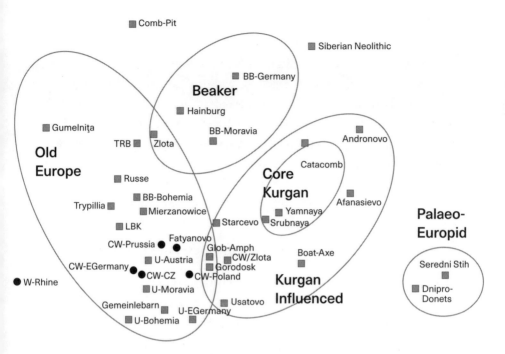

10.3 Roland Menk's scattergram of cranial measurements from the steppe and the rest of Europe. Corded Ware (CW) samples are marked with black dots. Other cultures shown are Bell-Beaker (BB), Funnel-Beaker (TRB), Linear Ware (LBK) and Únetice (U), the Early Bronze Age culture that followed the Corded Ware horizon.

Most importantly, the Swiss anthropologist Roland Menk (1945–1985) examined a sample of over 1,800 skulls employing 28 cranial measurements [**10.3**] from which he concluded:

> Indo-Europeanization of northern Europe (i.e. of the Corded Ware culture...) cannot have taken place by a direct invasion of whatever extent of South Eurasian Kurgan people [= Yamnaya or related steppe population] ... there are virtually no individuals within the whole sample of German Corded Ware people that would fit, statistically, into the South-Ukrainian Kurgan populations.[49]

Other than an expansion to the east, multivariate analysis was providing little support to the Steppe model.

The application of multivariate analysis to cranial measurements helped support the thesis that there was a major population incursion in Europe associated with the expansion of agriculture from Anatolia, thus providing some support to the Anatolian Farmer model. It also indicated that there had been an expansion from the European steppe eastwards as far as the Yenisei river and Altai mountains, but the evidence did not support a link between the main culture of the European steppe (the Yamnaya) and the formation of the Corded Ware culture.

Modern genetics

Although there had long been attempts to tie putative migrations to the evidence of, for example, blood types, it was not until the end of the 1980s that – as was the case with craniometry – we find the application of principal component analysis to a set of genetic markers. Early studies revealed that there was some correlation between genetic boundaries and linguistic boundaries[50] [**10.4**], but as the studies became more sophisticated it also became apparent that the main determining factor was 'geography, rather than language, in the shaping of Y-chromosomal genetic diversity within Europe'.[51]

While such studies illustrated how obvious natural geographical barriers (such as a sea or mountain range) may have created language borders, there were also some correlations between genetics and languages that did not require physical borders, although they were often problematic. For example, there was a genetic border between German and Dutch, but not one between Flemish (a Germanic language) and Walloon (Romance). Perhaps even more problematic was that one could not control for the possible time depth of the differences between the genetic border and whatever linguistic border was being proposed. Most of central and much of southern Europe has undergone language shift over the past two thousand years and so it is difficult to tell whether a genetic-linguistic border was established by an earlier population or a later one. What should be kept in mind here is the underlying reason

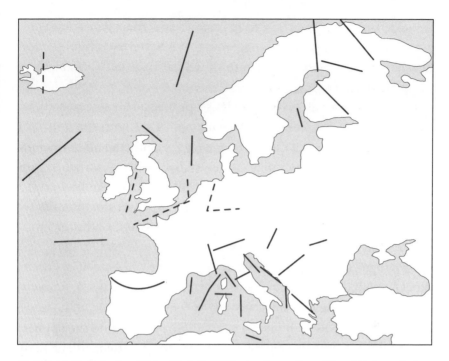

10.4 Guido Barbujani and Robert Sokal's 1990 map of genetic and linguistic boundaries (simplified). The lines indicate boundaries assessed by examining the allele frequencies of thirty-three genes. For example, the line through Iceland reflects a boundary between east and west Iceland, while the boundary marked in the North Atlantic indicates one between Iceland and Norway.

that language and genetic borders might be correlated. As we are dealing with genes and language, a significant variable will obviously be the marriage network and how it articulates with the language of a community. Where it is open and there is free intermarriage, the language border may correlate poorly with genetics. In extreme cases such as Hungarian it would appear that the original Magyar population who introduced their language to Hungary about the 10th century have so freely intermarried with their neighbours that they are now for the most part genetically indistinguishable from them.[52] Similarly, modern Turkish populations in Turkey have been genetically integrated into the earlier Anatolian population. On the other hand, where a language border is not porous it may discourage cross-language marriage and a genetic border may then coincide with a language border. In some cases, archaeologists have projected this into the past and suggested that long-term cultural borders may have been expressions of both closed marriage networks and language borders.[53]

Despite such problems the geneticists pushed on for several decades. By 1994 we were presented with the mammoth *The History and Geography of Human Genes* by Luca Cavalli-Sforza (1922–2018) and his colleagues, which employed the mapping of ninety-five genetic markers across Europe assessed with principal component analysis. The first principal component, which accounted for about 28 per cent of the variance [**10.5 A**], appeared to reveal a trajectory from the Near East through Anatolia and on across Europe; it was interpreted as evidence for the spread of farming.[54] This was embraced as support for the Anatolian Farmer model, although once again it encountered the chronological problem, with some arguing that the trajectory was not that of the first farmers but of the first modern humans, while others looked to later east–west expansions ranging anywhere from 'eastern' populations in the Roman Empire to the incursion of the Ottomans.[55]

Confidence that such an approach was on the right track was diminished by the perplexing map of the second principal component [**10.5 B**], which accounts for about 20 per cent of the variance. Ascribing the clines moving from the north (Sápmi) to the south as caused by a migration of Mongoloid Uralic-speakers to Finland just sounded a little like grasping at straws (as also the idea that it represented the Moors from North Africa overshooting Spain).[56] A natural north–south gradient governed by environmental factors was also suggested and, given the fact that a cline will logically form whenever people tend to marry their neighbours, it may have nothing to do with migrations. Indeed, thirty years later it was shown how such clines could form by processes that had nothing to do with migrations.[57]

The third principal component [**10.5 C**] was focused on the territory north of the Black Sea, with concentric circles emanating out from this area; it accounted for a little less than 9 per cent of the variance so was markedly less important than the earlier (putative) spread of farming. In Cavalli-Sforza's volume it was admitted that the third map might

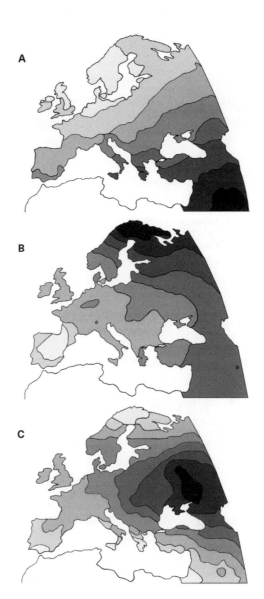

10.5 The first three principal components in Luca Cavalli-Sforza *et al.* (1994).
A was interpreted as supporting the Anatolian Farmer model;
B was ambiguous;
C was regarded as possibly offering some small support to the Steppe model.

support the Steppe model but that given the entire sequence of later migrations from east to west (Cimmerians, Scythians, Sarmatians, Huns, Avars and Hungarians) this was uncertain, although it 'should be given very serious consideration'.[58]

In the following year (1995), Cavalli-Sforza and his collaborators attacked the Indo-European homeland problem head on. In reviewing the evidence for the third principal component, they found stronger support for the Steppe model; they admitted, however, that 'the Neolithic farmers' migration is the most important factor in determining the genetic geography of Europe'. They also found that both models were mutually compatible, apparently suggesting that the Anatolian Farmers introduced some of the Indo-European languages, while the Steppe intruders may have been associated with others. They also acknowledged the central problem of their maps: 'unfortunately synthetic genetic maps are inherently undated'.[59] To this could be added the fact that totally different demographic processes might yield similar clinal patterns. Nevertheless, in another major study by different scholars, published in the same year but employing a different approach (running thousands of simulations against five different homeland models), the Anatolian Farmer model (actually two iterations of the model) was deemed the clear favourite and 'the current patterns of allele frequencies among Indo-Europeans can be explained without resorting to the migrations of Kurgan people'; the study could not demonstrate that such an event did not happen, but if it did, it 'did not leave a significant mark on the allele frequencies of current populations'.[60] The Anatolian Farmer theory was in and the Steppe model was out.

Employing principal component analysis on the distribution of modern genes had led to somewhat ambiguous results. There was debatable support for some form of migration from east to west, which was probably but not conclusively thought to be associated with the spread of farming. This was seen sufficient enough by some to link it to the spread of Indo-European languages (although note that these models did not address Indo-Iranian and Tocharian). Evidence for the Steppe model was either non-existent or inferior – at least in terms of accounting for the distribution of genes across Europe – to a farming model. One of the ironies of these studies is that they began emerging at a time when 'Western' archaeologists were still mired in a period of 'immobilism', a mind-set that had overreacted to the earlier penchant to pin every cultural change on a migration by denying almost any evidence for migration. But by this time the American archaeologist David Anthony had tried to squeeze the concept of prehistoric migrations back into the fold and there was beginning to be an awareness that people might have moved in prehistory, for which archaeologists might be able to gather convincing evidence.[61]

Besides Cavalli-Sforza, the renowned Austrian-born American statistician Robert Sokal (1926–2012) had also turned his attention to investigating the relationship between geography, genes and language. Still mouldering on my computer files is his database of 3,406 cases of alleged migrations in European prehistory and history (which as of 1993 his team had spent eight years compiling), which provided the basis of an enormous pile of offprints that he kindly sent me decades ago. At the end of the article on a computer simulation of the genetic history of Europe, Sokal and his co-authors wrote that the way forward was not likely to come from increasing the numbers of alleles in their study but rather 'the collection and analysis of mtDNA may offer a new perspective on human evolution in Europe'.[62] This was not a novel idea as several years earlier Osbjorn Pearson, then a graduate student in physical anthropology, sent me a letter laying out in detail a research programme involving mitochondrial DNA (mtDNA) that 'could easily have a tremendous impact upon the field of Indo-European studies and greatly add to our understanding ... of how the Indo-European languages were spread'.[63] And that is exactly what happened.

Modern mtDNA

The attraction of employing mtDNA to determine genetic relationships was fairly high. The DNA that forms in the mitochondria (rather than the nucleus) of a cell is directly transmitted from mother to child and so can be followed (where there is no break in the transmission) back thousands of years through the female line. It undergoes mutations through time, resulting in a number of different haplogroups – genetic population groups who share a common ancestor through the male or female line whose ancestry can be clearly followed and therefore yield a family tree structure. Mutations in mtDNA occur more rapidly than in nuclear DNA, so it is easier to use it as a chronological gauge of genetic evolution. Nevertheless, it was hardly a cure-all in that it only follows a single lineage and there is no easy way of determining where the splits along the evolutionary line have occurred. Still, mtDNA was hailed as 'the most informative genetic marker system for studying European prehistory'.[64] When early studies attempted to employ it as a marker for population movements in European prehistory, however, they revealed that the time frame was generally too large to provide much evidence that might be pertinent to a homeland hunter.

According to the evidence, most of the major haplogroups had entered Europe before the Neolithic (U5, U8, Vm, H1, H3, H5, etc.) and that left only haplogroups J (J1a and J1b) and T, which were believed to have entered Europe from southwest Asia about 10,000 years ago and are usually presumed to correlate with the expansion of the first farmers.[65] But while it might be pegged to early farmers, it did not resolve the debate as to whether the expansion of the Neolithic economy was the result of a handful of farmers who acculturated the native population of Europe or the type of demic expansion (waves of immigrants and their offspring) championed by the Anatolian Farmer hypothesis. For example, those who opposed the demic diffusion model argued that about 80 per cent of the mtDNA of European populations had been established over the course of the Palaeolithic and only about 20 per cent could be attributed to immigrant Anatolian farmers.[66] Entering the 21st century, supporters of both theories were still at it and whether one elected for population replacement or cultural transmission, at least both sides were agreed that there had been some immigration associated with the spread of agriculture. As there was no significant appearance of exotic haplogroups after the Neolithic, such evidence might be seen as supporting the Anatolian Farmer hypothesis.

Y-chromosome

Research on the male Y-chromosome faced many of the same problems as mtDNA, in that geneticists attempted to employ the modern genetic profile of Indo-European speakers as a proxy for past population histories. This again required one to anchor the different haplogroups in time and space. The early studies concentrated primarily on haplogroups J and R.

Y-chromosome haplogroup J appeared to be strongest in the southeast and weakest in the west, which suggested an origin in the Near East and (entirely coincidentally) was linked to the spread of farming at the beginning of the Neolithic just like mtDNA J.[67]

The other main haplogroup (R1b) under examination was found to dominate in western Europe and so was thought to reflect the earlier Palaeolithic population that had survived on the western periphery of Europe. It was found highest, for example, in Ireland and because it was also present among the non-Indo-European-speaking Basques, who were often portrayed as speaking a relict Palaeolithic or Mesolithic language, this offered further support to the R1b = Palaeolithic model (along with haplogroup I, which was centred on northwest Europe and was also generally agreed to derive from the Palaeolithic). Within haplogroup R, R1b was the dominant male haplotype of western Europe, while R1a tended to dominate in northeastern Europe but also extended eastwards into the Asiatic territories of the Indo-European languages. Attempts to ascertain the relative proportions of the different male ancestries among modern Europeans tended towards the same answer as female: 80 per cent local Palaeolithic and only about 20 per cent Neolithic immigrants from Anatolia.[68] However, there were those who argued that more recent surveys of male DNA indicated that it (R1b, specifically R-M269) was not Palaeolithic in date but rather had a mean age of about 6,500 years and that it originated in the Near East and entered Europe via Anatolia, all consistent with the demic diffusion model.[69] It was also claimed that the Neolithic spread westwards through the Mediterranean, but here it was conveyed by males with haplogroup E1b1b1b (= E-M81). It was noted that although the Basques carried somewhere between 8 and 20 per cent haplogroup I (from the Palaeolithic), they had 75–87 per cent R1b and so were not essentially a 'relict' population. Problematic was the fact that the mtDNA did not mirror that of the males, and so this explanation required that the earliest farmers were predominantly males who found local wives. This view was by no means conclusive and as recently as 2010 geneticists were at odds regarding Europe's genetic past, especially which modern genetic markers were to be associated with the Neolithic. But a farming incursion – even if limited – was still on the cards.

Haplogroup R (R1a and R1b) had so far been credited with the recolonization of Europe after the last Ice Age and for introducing the Neolithic to Europe. By 2001, however, several papers appeared arguing for a still more recent spread. Geneticist and anthropologist Spencer Wells (and twenty-five other authors) published their survey of the Y-chromosome composition of forty-nine Eurasian populations and concluded that the 'current distribution of the M17 [= R1a] haplotype is likely to represent traces of an ancient population migration originating in southern Russia/Ukraine, where R-M17 is found at high frequency (< 50%)'.[70] The paper specifically regarded this evidence as supportive of the Steppe model and argued that it correlated well with the spread of Indo-Iranian languages towards India. It noted a distinct lack of R1a in western Iran (it was higher in eastern Iran) and suggested that the prior Neolithic population had been too large to be swamped by nomadic tribes. The expanse of R1a into southwest Asia was taken up in the same year in another paper that associated haplogroup J – we have already seen how this was viewed as a widely accepted marker of early Anatolian farmers in Europe – with the spread of agriculture (and the Dravidian languages) east into India, and then followed by an intrusion of pastoral nomads bearing R1a, bringing an Indo-European language into India.[71]

So now at the dawn of the 21st century geneticists were suggesting that Y-haplogroups R1a and R1b were markers of human dispersals during the Palaeolithic (which would support the Palaeolithic Continuity model) and the expansion of farmers from Anatolia across Europe (the Anatolian Farmer model) or pastoral nomads from Ukraine and south Russia (the Steppe model). Thus, modern genetics could be used to support almost any homeland theory.

Coda: ancient DNA

In 2005 archaeologists excavated a series of four group burials comprising thirteen individuals from a Corded Ware cemetery in Eulau, Germany. Clear traces of trauma and violent death on a number of the bodies suggested that several family groups had been killed, 85 per cent of whom were women and children.[72] The excellently preserved skeletons were studied by a range of scientific techniques to determine, among other things, the familial relationship of some of the burials (which had not been done before using molecular techniques), the origin of the deceased (the males and children had been local while most of the women had apparently come from a distance of 60 km/40 miles or more) and their ancient DNA (aDNA). The women exhibited a range of different mtDNA haplogroups (H, I, K, U and X); three males (a father and two sons) were shown to carry Y-haplogroup R1a.

I had missed this article when it originally appeared but thanks to the late Jean Manco (1946–2018) – an architectural historian turned very skilled genetics blogger, who sent me a draft copy of her book *Ancestral Journeys* (when it still bore its original title *Waves of Wanderers*) – I saw that she had regarded this new aDNA evidence within the context of other scholars who had regarded R1a as a late entry to the Eurasian landscape that supported the Steppe model.[73] And, additionally, an important study of aDNA from graves of the Andronovo (*c.* 1800–1200 BCE) and later cultures in the Yenisei region of Russia recovered a series of burials, all of which had the characteristic male haplogroup R1a-M17; the authors evaluated the ancient evidence against the modern distribution of this haplogroup, which, they suggested, supported the Steppe model.[74] But I was still sceptical about any arguments primarily based on reading the past from the modern distribution of DNA haplogroups and made that clear, when at a conference in 2011 in Philadelphia, I found myself agreeing with Colin Renfrew on the dubious efficacy of reconstructing the past with modern DNA. The fact that several Corded Ware skeletons carried R1a was not conclusive in a world where different schools of geneticists were assigning the haplogroup to the Palaeolithic, Neolithic and now Eneolithic/Early Bronze Age.

But the times they were a-changing.

Part 3
The New Way Forward

CHAPTER 11

Game Change

At the beginning of 2015 the search for the Indo-European homeland seemed to be at a stalemate between the two main competitors: the Anatolian Farmer model and the Steppe model. There had been very little to boost the cause of either camp other than approaches that took one into the more rarefied and somewhat suspect area of lexicostatistics or reading the tea leaves of modern distributions of DNA. To recap our earlier discussion in Chapter 4, the greatest support to the Anatolian Farmer hypothesis had been the phylogenetic and chronological work of the Auckland group, which had been published with considerable fanfare in both *Nature* and *Science*.[1] Shortly after, it had been savaged in a series of entertaining blogs by Asya Pereltsvaig and Martin Lewis, who would ultimately devote an entire monograph[2] to pointing out what they regarded as a litany of errors – a hatchet-job that had not really been seen since 1890 when the Indologist Peter von Bradke (1853–1897) devoted an entire book to tediously dismantling the work of Otto Schrader.[3] While some supporters of the Anatolian theory could take comfort in the statistical arguments presented in the papers of the Auckland group, the Steppe camp could cling to the interpretation of similar evidence adumbrated in the work of Andrew Garrett,[4] and then published in full in 2015 by the Berkeley group, who supported the Steppe model,[5] along with others (Jaakko Häkkinen and Hans Holm) who were clearly not fans of the Auckland papers.[6]

As for the reconstructions of the past genetic and linguistic history of the Indo-European world on the basis of modern DNA samples, while some could be tentatively tied to the early evidence for ancient DNA (aDNA), others were spiralling into some entertaining but highly suspect scenarios. For example, in 2013 Anatole Klyosov and Giancarlo Tomezzoli attempted to test the Anatolian Farmer, Steppe and Palaeolithic Continuity models against the genetic evidence. They concluded that Y-chromosome haplogroup R1a carried the genetic ancestor of the Indo-Europeans from the Altai region in Central Asia, where it evolved into Indo-European along the way to Anatolia and then passed into Europe (supporting the Anatolian Farmer model). On the other hand, R1b, which also originated perhaps near the Altai, spread west carrying a series of non-Indo-European languages such as Proto-Turkic, then turned south into Mesopotamia to form Sumerian and continued west again to Iberia to form Basque and spread up the Atlantic coast as the Bell-Beaker culture.[7] The confidence that the authors had in generating their dates, geography and linguistic identifications was impressive, but far exceeded their ability to convince.

January 2015: The Harvard-Jena paper

By 2015, I had been retired for four years, happy to give the homeland problem a rest, and was pleasantly losing myself in the mists of the Irish dreamtime,[8] but early in January, I received a request to review a paper for *Nature*. Generally, I dodge such requests, feigning a total lack of competence, and suggest another specialist, but the title of the article barred my usual evasion tactics. Even though I admitted up front that I was not qualified to assess the statistical aspects of the genetic arguments, I really could not avoid a paper titled 'Massive migration from the steppe is a source for Indo-European languages in Europe'[9] when I had been working on the subject for (by then) forty-two years. When I saw that the paper was based on a dataset of aDNA samples from sixty-nine Europeans who lived between eight thousand and three thousand years ago I gave a sigh of relief: the analysis, which was generated by both the Harvard (Reich) lab, and the laboratory of the Max Planck Institute, Jena in Germany, was not based on back-projecting modern DNA. Finally, we were going to get a look at a sample of the actual players involved in the debate.

The crux of the Harvard-Jena paper was evidence of aDNA derived from a sample of Yamnaya burials from the Middle Volga region in Russia. The genetic signature of the Yamnaya culture appeared to be an admixture of two distinct ancestries. One of these was of the local hunter-gatherer population that had occupied the steppe regions at least since the Mesolithic (named the Eastern Hunter-Gatherer population), and the other was that of a hunting-gathering or agricultural population from the Caucasus or the region immediately south of it (the Caucasus Hunter-Gatherers). It lacked (at the time of the paper but now contradicted by later research) the genetic signature of the earliest farmers from Anatolia (Ancient Anatolian Farmers) who had not only colonized Europe but also penetrated the Caucasus. Although the Harvard-Jena paper had confirmed that there had indeed been migrations from Anatolia that carried farming across Europe, as argued by the Anatolian Farmer model, this was not the genetic signature found in the Yamnaya population, which appeared to refute the argument that the earliest steppe pastoralists were merely the descendants of Anatolian farmers who had spread eastwards and adopted a pastoral economy. This meant that the Neolithic cultures of Anatolia/Europe and the steppe cultures could not be easily fused into a single theory by having the Anatolian Farmer model simply absorb the Steppe model as had been sometimes proposed. Of course, one might still wish to press for some form of acculturation of the steppe cultures from the west, but this was receiving little support from the genetic evidence.

More importantly, the paper went on to demonstrate that the same combination of EHG and CHG, the two major genetic components of the Yamnaya culture, were also found in 80 per cent of a sample of Corded Ware burials from Germany that were analysed [11.1]. These burials dated to *c.* 2500 BCE and represented the earliest evidence for this combination of EHG and CHG outside of the steppe zone. The distance between the two sampled areas was approximately 2,600 km (1,600 miles). In the Neolithic of the region from which the Corded Ware samples had been obtained, the previous population had been a combination of AAF and local European hunter-gatherers (Western Hunter-Gatherers). The paper estimated the ancestry of the Corded

CHAPTER 11

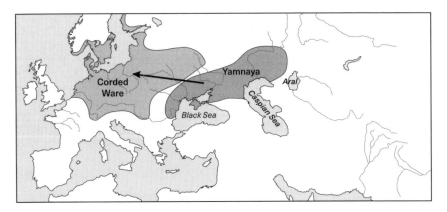

11.1 The results of the genetic studies undertaken at Harvard and Jena indicated that the Corded Ware culture had obtained c. 80 per cent of its genetic signature from the steppe cultures, which had replaced the earlier genetic signature of the Anatolian farmers.

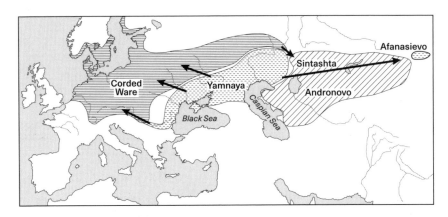

11.2 The Copenhagen paper provided genetic evidence for expansions from the Pontic-Caspian steppe both into the Corded Ware culture and eastwards to the Afanasievo culture. It also indicated that the Andronovo culture, one of the prime suspects in providing the staging area of Indo-Iranian, was more likely to have derived from a variant of the Corded Ware culture rather than directly from the Yamnaya and its local successors.

Ware sample as 79 per cent Yamnaya, 17 per cent Anatolian Farmer and 4 per cent local hunter-gatherers. Moreover, the Yamnaya samples belonged to haplogroup R1b, which is the predominant male haplogroup in western Europe today, suggesting that a steppe population, presumably bearing Indo-European languages, had spread over Europe's earlier Anatolian-derived farming population and largely replaced the earlier genetic lineages with its own. What was particularly noteworthy was that for decades archaeologists had laboured without great success to demonstrate that the Yamnaya culture had somehow kick-started the Corded Ware culture and now the genetic evidence had exceeded all expectation, making a stronger case for a connection than archaeologists would have been comfortable with.[10] It seemed, in fact, too good to be true.

February 2015: The Copenhagen paper

Within a month, another paper from *Nature* arrived in my inbox titled 'Population genomics of Bronze Age Eurasia';[11] I then learned that there had been a race on between the genetics laboratories of Harvard-Jena and the University of Copenhagen. The new paper was more than welcome, since it employed a somewhat different genetic analysis of 101 samples covering the Eurasian Bronze Age. I had wondered whether the conclusions of the Harvard-Jena paper would be replicated and, like others,[12] was also worried that its conclusions were being drawn from extremely small numbers of relevant samples – for example, it only included a handful of Corded Ware samples.

The results of the Copenhagen paper both supported and expanded on the findings of the earlier one [**11.2**]. It supported the concept of a steppe ingression into Europe marked by the presence of an EHG-CHG genetic signature, with the closest affiliation between the Yamnaya and Corded Ware samples, with somewhat less steppe DNA found in the later Beaker samples, a culture that had often been associated with the expansion of Indo-Europeans in Atlantic Europe. The authors had also sampled the Remedello culture of northern Italy, which Marija Gimbutas had proposed to be a 'Kurganized' culture, but it had failed to produce evidence of a steppe signature.

An added dimension of the Copenhagen paper was that it not only supported the case for steppe migrations into central and western Europe, but also explored the impact of the steppe cultures on Asia. It noted, for example, that the Afanasievo culture of the Altai-Minusinsk Basin was 'genetically indistinguishable from Yamnaya, confirming an eastward expansion across the steppe'. This supported the evidence of physical anthropology as well as those archaeologists who had argued that the Afanasievo – an Early Bronze Age culture strongly suspected to be a prehistoric ancestor of the Tocharians (the most elusive branch of the Indo-Europeans) – could be traced to earlier cultures of the Pontic-Caspian steppe.[13] It also produced some surprising results, showing that the Sintashta culture of the southern Urals – a Bronze Age culture presumably ancestral to the Andronovo culture that covered the Asiatic steppe and is often regarded as the staging culture for Indo-Iranian migrations[14] – had not evolved genetically *directly* from the Yamnaya but rather had come by way of the Corded Ware culture (its steppe signature had been admixed with elements from Anatolian Farmers and local west European hunter-gatherers like the Corded Ware samples from Germany).

Game-changers?

The two genetics papers had made remarkably dramatic entries into the world of homeland hunting. Perhaps, more than anything, they had put migration back on the archaeologists' agenda.[15] They had shown that the genetic ancestry of the Yamnaya culture was primarily a combination of local hunter-gatherers (EHG) and a population whose genetic signature was anchored in the Caucasus (CHG), either by interactions with hunter-gatherers or by early farmers of the region. They had also provided evidence of late Neolithic/Eneolithic migrations from the Pontic-Caspian steppe westwards through central Europe, which appeared at least in part to support the Steppe model of Indo-European origins. They also provided evidence of migrations east of the Pontic-Caspian across Kazakhstan to the Altai mountains and Yenisei river, which had been regarded as a possible route of the Tocharian migrations. Moreover, they had shown an association between the groups that had already undergone the amalgamation of steppe and European farmer genes and the Sintashta culture, a sort of 'gateway' culture often implicated in the origins and spread of the Indo-Iranians. Following this aDNA advent, a series of further studies appeared that seemed to largely support and expand on the initial thrust of the two earlier papers.[16] They were indeed game-changers but, as we will see in the next chapters, the game is far from over.

CHAPTER 12

Genetic Landscapes and Homeland Models

Geneticists have presented what seems to be a game-changing new tool in the arsenal of the linguistic homeland hunter but, before examining how far it has brought us, we might very briefly reflect on the past. After all, we have been here before! In the second edition of his *Introduction to the Science of Language* (1880), A. H. Sayce concluded that: 'This Aryan [Indo-European] family of speech was of Asiatic origin. Dr. Latham, indeed, would make it European, and Poesche has lately advocated the same view with great ability; but there are few scholars who have followed them. Their theory rests upon a confusion of language and race.'[1] Three years later, however, he felt the need to revise his view in his introduction to a new edition: 'I must avow my entire conversion to the theory first propounded by Latham, and of late years ably defended on anthropological and linguistic grounds by Poesche and Penka, that the Aryan race had its first seat, not in Asia, but in the Baltic provinces and northern Germany.'[2] Apparently, a confusion of language and race had ceased to be a problem and the physical anthropological arguments of Poesche and Penka had managed to convince Sayce.

We are intercepting the hunt for the Indo-European homeland at a similar inflexion point. In Sayce's time, scholars spent the following decades pouring over pigmentation and cranial indices; now, we enter a new world of genetic admixtures and haplogroups. We should try to walk into this recent explosion of genetic evidence with eyes wide open.

The role of palaeogenomics

There are some obvious differences between the earlier physical anthropological approaches and current geneticists. All too often, the former were a blatant product of racist or nationalistic agendas. While they might have revelled in an Aryan dolichocephalic skull with its blond hair and blue eyes, it is a bit of a struggle imagining your date shrieking with delight 'I just knew you were a Rɪbɪaɪǃ'.[3] Admittedly, and unfortunately, however, whether it is a cranial index or a haplogroup, or an Indo-European dragon that has wandered into the wrong ecosystem, there will always be those who will attempt to employ such evidence to support their own political or ethnic agendas. In 2019, I was one of 117 authors from 19 different countries contributing to a paper on the formation of human populations in South Asia and I doubt that any one of us either imagined or desired that our paper would be employed by some politicians, as it was, to claim that brahmins are not 'true' Indians and should be driven out of India.[4]

While many of the earlier anthropological approaches were merely exercises in confirming an already adopted thesis, modern geneticists have largely designed their approaches to test existing models previously suggested by linguists and archaeologists. And this means that as the evidence evolves or changes, they are perfectly capable of shifting their conclusions. For example, one of the foremost genetics players in the quest for the Indo-European homeland was supporting a Caucasus location in 2022 but has since tilted towards the steppe in 2024[5] (and may very well be somewhere else by the time this book is published).

This somewhat symbiotic relationship between genetics and other disciplines is perfectly understandable. It is not only that the archaeologists have excavated and conserved the human remains that geneticists require to carry out their analyses, but they (along with linguists) are also the ones who have generated the long-standing academic arguments that already have a wide audience. As the goal of major well-funded research projects tends to be articles in the most prestigious scientific journals, collaborative projects between archaeologists, linguists and geneticists attempt to solve high-profile problems of origins and ancestry. Utilizing palaeogenomic evidence to demonstrate that people who used shell-impressed decoration on their pottery were of a different origin from those who drew lines on their pottery might earn a yawn from a reader perusing the appendix of an archaeological journal; uncovering the origin of the largest language family on the planet gets you into *Science* or *Nature* and underwrites your credibility when you apply for your next funding.

But still one question remains: aren't we confusing language with genes? After all, there is absolutely no direct causal relationship between one's genome and what language one speaks.[6] Any human can learn to speak any language and it has absolutely no effect whatsoever on their genome. So why should the spread of a particular genetic fingerprint or a haplogroup such as R1b be regarded as evidence for the spread of a language? If someone's genetic composition is 40 per cent EHG, 40 per cent CHG and 20 per cent WHG, are their nouns and adjectives derived from EHG, their verbs from CHG and their prepositions and conjunctions from WHG? How can you claim that a particular genetic signature was spread by Indo-Europeans when non-Indo-European Estonians, Finns and Hungarians have the same markers? These are the types of 'clever' dismissals that one may hear occasionally from those hostile to any application of palaeogenomics to linguistic problems.

The rejoinder to this is that before literacy, a language could only be learned from someone else (and not a book, tape or website), usually a parent, and the genomic trail of that parent can (at least theoretically) be followed through both space and time – providing some evidence of whether a population was intrusive to an area, whether it had experienced long-term genetic continuity or had admixed with a different intrusive population, and whether it seemed to be engaged in patrilineal or matrilineal descent. Now, I will freely admit, a parent or a child may eventually abandon the language of their parents and pass on the new language to their own children without themselves experiencing any genetic change. As with archaeological evidence, we may find clues regarding the dispersal of a population in both material culture and human behaviour, and we may be able to assemble a fairly convincing case that population A has immigrated into a new territory, that of population B. Palaeogenomics supplies results that can not only corroborate the archaeological evidence but also tip the scales of an argument where that evidence is inconclusive. It can also provide, at both a communal and an individual level, an indication of the genetic relationships of marriage partners and their offspring. Nevertheless, we are still in the early days where geneticists and archaeologists are attempting to work out their mutual relationships. One may well agree (and I will come back to this later) that 'only archaeological contextualization of the palaeogenetic data can establish in what sense and to what degree the palaeogenetic sample represents prehistoric populations and its spatial and temporal distribution is representative of the historical dynamics of the societies to which those populations belonged'.[7]

Fortunately, most papers provide extensive supplementary material that does attempt to contextualize the archaeological source of their samples. And while neither archaeological nor genetic findings can ever tell us directly what happened on the ground linguistically, they can both provide critical circumstantial evidence that helps us evaluate our models.

Palaeogenetic techniques

Geneticists have provided two primary paths to reconstructing past migrations and relationships: uniparental evidence (mitochondrial from the mother, Y-chromosome from the father) and autosomal evidence (derived from both parents).

Uniparental evidence

We have already encountered the use of haplogroups to read past migrations from their distribution in *modern* populations. We first saw how the major male haplogroup R1b was once advanced to demonstrate that it had predominated across western Europe since the Palaeolithic, indicating there had been very little evidence of further significant prehistoric (male) migrations in Europe. According to this interpretation, Europeans were basically descended from their 'cave men' ancestors, which, in homeland terms, either supported a Palaeolithic Continuity model or forced archaeologists to be unusually creative in summoning up the material evidence for language shift and convince their colleagues that migrations did happen in prehistory even if they left no obvious genetic trace. Then, employing different assessments of the date of the haplogroup, it was asserted that we had been wrong and R1b was not a product of the Palaeolithic inheritance, but was in fact associated with the earliest farmers in Europe and attested a massive migration from Anatolia that had swamped the earlier populations with newly arrived R1b males. This provided supposedly conclusive evidence to support the Anatolian Farmer hypothesis. And, finally, we saw R1b proposed as the marker of a still more recent Eneolithic migration across Europe from the Pontic-Caspian steppe where it replaced whatever (non-R1b) was going on genetically during the Palaeolithic and Neolithic.

These interpretations of modern DNA therefore supported three totally opposed models of Indo-European origins and expansions, which left archaeologists like myself feeling that the geneticists had about as much credibility as the earlier skull measurers. We would only be convinced if the evidence were derived from the actual populations whose remains we were excavating, was sufficiently abundant to be representative of those populations, and we had secure geographical and chronological control over the distribution of the genetic evidence. And this is precisely what geneticists have been attempting to do with ancient DNA (aDNA), which initiated a honeymoon period between geneticists and archaeologists where the former were usually good for a free meal as long as the latter were sitting on a store of interesting teeth or petrous bones, the most durable and (for a geneticist) desirable part of a human skull.

While haplogroups provide a very accurate indication of one's ancestry, such evidence is very limited and tells us on its own very little of the genetic universe in which one swims. This narrowness can be appreciated when you consider how your haplogroup, as part of your overall ancestry, diminishes exponentially the further back in time you go. If you are a male, your Y-haplogroup derives from your father, who received his from one of your two grandfathers, who received theirs from one of your four great-grandfathers, who received theirs from just one of your eight great-great-grandfathers (with seven of your other male ancestors now sidelined from your story). I can follow my own line back in time to my direct ancestor (the one who developed the particular mutational flavour of my male haplogroup) in south Scandinavia *c.* 900 CE. Today, I am sitting about 1,100 years and 1,500 km (900 miles) away from him, but the actual route to my home went from Scandinavia to Normandy and then crossed the Channel where my ancestors dwelt for more than five hundred years in England (where my family was once numbered among the 'less evil Protestants of Yorkshire'). My Y-haplogroup forebears then crossed the Atlantic to spend another 350 years farming their way from Virginia to California before returning to Europe about 50 years ago. During that entire journey my mitochondrial DNA (mtDNA) had been sitting in Ireland and passed from mother to daughter for generations, wondering what was taking the rest of my genome so long to catch up. But, according to my (admittedly always to be taken with an enormous grain of salt) DNA ethnicity test, I supposedly have neither Scandinavian nor English ancestry; that has all been swamped by my paternal grandfather's choice of a marriage partner. My Y-chromosome has essentially served as an organic tracking device anchoring me to a single male ancestor about forty generations ago, but without a mountain of more data (DNA samples from all over western Europe and North America capable of following the migration path of these once 'less evil Protestants'), it can't tell how I got from the place of origin to my current location.

If one were simply branded with a haplogroup so deep in time that it was in no way indicative of your more recent migratory history, it would be of very limited use. However, the haplogroups do evolve over time and as each mutation appears it forms a different haplotype within a family tree. Returning to R1b, it is estimated to have formed in the Palaeolithic about 22,800 years ago, but we find a mutated version R-L754 (or R1b1a) splitting off about 20,400 years ago, from which, about 13,300 years ago, emerges R-M269 (or R1b1a1a2), which will explode across Europe in its various subclades. It is the fact that the haplogroups continually split into different haplotypes downstream of their common ancestor that permits us to track discrete population movements across time and space. Since migrations may include full communities or only segments of the community, once the evidence of aDNA increases we will have a better idea of when and where people moved and how the male and female haplogroups tracked across the landscape through time and space, and we will be better able to see the operation of sexual dynamics during migrations, such as the balance between male and female migrants and local populations. It should be emphasized, however, that what we will *not* be able to do with the haplogroup evidence is determine anything about the appearance or ethnicity of the haplogroup bearers, because that is recovered from the autosomal evidence.

Autosomal evidence

Those who make use of the various commercial family search platforms are familiar with their ethnicity service – after submitting a DNA sample the customer receives a percentage breakdown of their ethnicity (English, French, African, Chinese) and also a list of their closest matches to other customers, which can vary from an immediate family member (e.g. mother, daughter) to distant cousins who share a small fraction of their ancestry as far back as about seven generations (about two hundred years ago) or, very rarely, sometimes further. The autosomal chromosomes (i.e. all the chromosomes that are not sex chromosomes) are derived from both of your parents and mixed every generation at approximately 50 per cent from each parent. In theory, you might imagine that if one of your parents was Swedish and the other Turkish, you would inherit about 50 per cent of each parent's ethnicity. In fact, you inherit a random 50 per cent of their DNA and not 50 per cent of those relatively few potential indicators of one's ethnic background, so the results may be skewed, which is why children of the same parents may all have somewhat different ethnicity results. This mixing provides you with all of those genetic physical traits such as hair and eye colour, height and potential to be immune or susceptible to certain diseases. Since it is based on your inheritance from both parents, the autosomal evidence is naturally a result of a modern mating network. Commercial companies employ their assessment of the genetic signatures of modern countries to isolate out relatively narrow (and often unrealistically precise) geographical ethnicities to amuse their clients (results for ethnicities for Europeans can vary so much between different companies that if you shop around long enough you should get the ethnicity you want).

When we view the autosomal patterns of past societies it is apparent that there were population groups that existed during the Palaeolithic of Eurasia that were presumably formed when human populations collapsed into relatively isolated refuge areas during the last Ice Age. These consisted of largely closed mating networks that had been separated from one another for many thousands of years and so have retained the evidence of their much earlier and deeper genetic bottlenecks, which yield very different genetic signatures.

We have already been introduced to some of these major population groups and it is now time to explore how the evidence for autosomal and uniparental DNA impacts on the search for the homeland.[8] Since all too often past discussions have played into a false dichotomy by offering only two choices, here I intend to broaden the discussion so that as many homeland theories as possible are included in our survey.

Setting the genetic landscape[9]

While most homeland solutions are set no earlier than the beginning of the Neolithic, there are still some who propose a rather expansive homeland in an earlier period on several grounds. The first is the observation that hunting-gathering societies could have formed a very large linguistic entity because of low population densities, highly mobile economies and large territorial ranges and the need to maintain distant social relations.[10] This is supported by ethnographic evidence such as the First Nations in Canada, whose language families cover vast regions, and who have been occasionally presented as proxies for the circumstances in Palaeolithic and Mesolithic Eurasia.[11] The second reason is desperation, after failing to identify any single Neolithic or later archaeological culture that might correlate with the area of the earliest Indo-European dispersals. In short, a Late Palaeolithic or Mesolithic solution permits one to draw a circle around two or more regions that have long competed against each other as potential homelands and thereby bring them together under a single roof but set at an earlier time. Moreover, even if these earlier ancestral population groups are eventually swamped by genetically more recent Neolithic or Eneolithic populations, their

CHAPTER 12

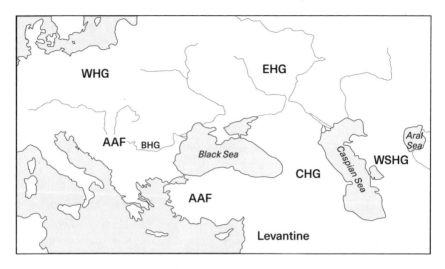

12.1 A map of western Eurasia with the locations of the major ancestral groups indicated in the period c. 15,000–5000 BCE. Within the Western Hunter-Gatherer (WHG) region is recognized a Balkan Hunter-Gatherer (BHG) type centred on the Iron Gates region of the Danube. Before the Neolithic, the WHG group dominated over western, central and parts of eastern Europe but was largely replaced by the spread of Ancient Anatolian Farmers (AAF) over the course of the Neolithic. The other groups shown on the map include Eastern Hunter-Gatherer (EHG), Caucasus Hunter-Gatherer (CHG), West Siberian Hunter-Gatherer (WSHG) and Levantine. The Ancient Ancestral South Indians (AASI) would be located off-map in southern India.

genetic signatures would have seldom been completely erased and so provide significant evidence about the composition of later populations.

Although modern humans were settling Eurasia from c. 60,000–45,000 BCE onwards, they were subjected to a variety of climatological restraints, particularly the Late Glacial Maximum (26,000–19,000 years ago), which confined human populations to refuge areas in southern France and Iberia and other areas south of the ice sheets. After the retreat of the ice, populations expanded again into environments across Europe, and by about 14,000 years ago we encounter what, from a homeland perspective, can be regarded as a relevant area of Eurasia populated by a number of major genetically related population groups. I will briefly summarize what is known about each of them [12.1].

Western Hunter-Gatherers

Emerging out of an earlier (possibly Balkan) refuge was the Western Hunter-Gatherer (WHG) group, which predominated in western and central Europe during the Mesolithic as far east as a rough line that runs from the Baltic Sea to the mouth of the Danube. The WHG cluster housed mtDNA haplogroup U5, which has been around in Europe since at least 30,000 years ago, and its subgroup U5b, which dates from about 20,000 years ago. One of the most prominent of the Palaeolithic Y-chromosome haplogroups was I. For those who do not regard such information as entirely irrelevant, the WHG would appear in fact to have had dark skin but lighter (blue, green) eyes. While a dark skin pigmentation might appear counterintuitive when dealing with a population moving into the north of Europe, some have suggested that because such immigrants were primarily subsisting on a hunting diet, they were not as susceptible to vitamin D deficiency as were later agricultural populations, who required a more efficient way of creating vitamin D (i.e. a lighter skin).[12]

In terms of the homeland problem, the WHG would probably be most closely identified with those who supported the Nordic theory and argued for the evolution of a Nordic physical type in south Scandinavia, and cultural and linguistic continuity in that region from the Mesolithic until the expansion of the Indo-European languages. It might be noted that the WHG appeared to mop up most of the earlier Palaeolithic populations, including those stemming from the Magdalenian culture in western Europe, and so the Palaeolithic Continuity theory seems to have got off to a poor start, in that the 'continuity' of the Aurignacian didn't seem to make it through the last glaciation. Within the broad area of WHG, a Balkan Hunter-Gatherer (BHG) type has been identified in the Iron Gates region of the Danube, which is also found further east among farmers in western Ukraine (Cucuteni-Trypillia culture).[13]

Ancient North Eurasians and Eastern Hunter-Gatherers

The remains of a boy from 24,000 years ago from the site of Mal'ta in central Siberia provides the classic genetic signature of the Ancient North Eurasians (ANE), which was carried by later post-glacial hunter-gatherers of northern Eurasia as well as Native Americans who migrated into the New World. Over time this population appears to have diversified into smaller regional groups, such as the Eastern Hunter-Gatherers (EHG) who lived east of the line from the Baltic to the Black Sea when the WHG dominated in the west. Mixing between the two major clusters occurred around the Baltic Sea (including Scandinavia and Ukraine), where the population was *c*. 70 per cent WHG and 30 per cent EHG, but further east into central Russia it was more exclusively EHG. A recent investigation of the situation after the Late Glacial Maximum treats the division between the WHG and EHG as a 'great divide' that was maintained through the Mesolithic.[14] In the EHG area geneticists have most often recovered mtDNA haplogroups U2, U4 and R1b and Y-haplogroups Q, R and J. And, in an ironic twist of earlier notions, it was the EHG group that bore the genes for lighter skin but, conversely, darker eye colours.

The area occupied by the EHG would have included the Pontic-Caspian steppe and, therefore, would underlie the Steppe model of Indo-European origins. As we have seen in the previous chapter, the genetic evidence for the expansion of a population from the steppe is not associated exclusively with EHG ancestry but requires an admixture with CHG (see below); we will have to examine in detail the relationship between these two populations. The area of the EHG might also be associated with some of the potential locations of the non-Indo-European Uralic homeland.

Anatolian Hunter-Gatherers/Ancient Anatolian Farmers

Continuing to the southeast we have an example of a pre-Neolithic Anatolian population from Pınarbaşı, Turkey, dating to *c*. 13,600–13,000 BCE, which has been labelled Anatolian Hunter-Gatherer (AHG). It is distinct from both the WHG and the Epipalaeolithic/Neolithic Levantine populations to its south, and genetically fits approximately midway between these two and is explained by gene flow between both components in the region of Anatolia. The haplogroups so far known to be associated initially with this group are mtDNA K2b and N1a and Y-chromosomes C1a2 and G2a2.

With the spread of agriculture across Anatolia, the AHG became the Ancient Anatolian Farmer (AAF) group, which predominated in central and western Anatolia and then spread with farming across Europe, where it may also be seen labelled as Early European Farmer (EEF). This group is obviously foundational to the Anatolian Farmer model of homeland origins, or any model seeking a homeland in one of the Neolithic cultures of Europe that were derived from the earliest Anatolian farmers, and from here on I will employ the AAF (rather than EEF) acronym.

Caucasus Hunter-Gatherers

East of the AHG/AAF region, we encounter a very different genetic signature whose earliest representatives were retrieved from two sites in western Georgia – Satsurblia cave, dated to *c.* 11,000 BCE (Upper Palaeolithic), and Kotias Klde, dated to *c.* 8000 BCE (Mesolithic). These represent the Caucasus Hunter-Gatherer (CHG) network, which also embraces populations in the same region during the Neolithic of the Caucasus and south through the Zagros mountains and southeast of the Caspian Sea. The dates for the split between the CHG and AHG are estimated to be in the order of 20,000–30,000 years ago.[15]

The term 'CHG' is also often employed as a genetic cover label for the closely related earliest farmers of the same region (also identified as 'Early Iranian Farmer', see page 304). This network has been associated with a number of non-Indo-European language families as well as the various homelands in or near the Caucasus put forward since the 17th century right up to those suggested by Gamkrelidze and Ivanov's Greater Armenian model or more recent models proposed by both geneticists and some computational linguists.

Levantine (Natufian) group

To the south of the AHG/AAF and southwest of the CHG regions, we find a Levantine population most notably associated with the Natufians (13,000–9,500 BCE), a culture that experienced the transition from hunting-gathering to farming in the Levant region. During the Neolithic, Levantine DNA is seen to increase among ceramic-using Anatolian farmers and also mixes with its CHG neighbours. Linguistically, it tends to be associated with either Proto-Afro-Asiatic or possibly a later descendant (Semitic), so it does not play a significant role in determining the

Indo-European homeland other than providing a possible genetic signature of the source population for a number of loanwords in Indo-European. The commonest Y-haplogroups were E1b, H2 and T1a.

West Siberian Hunter-Gatherers

Further to the east we encounter the West Siberian Hunter-Gatherer (WSHG) group, who are primarily descendants of the earlier ANE/EHG mixed with populations further to the east. The most significant archaeological site associated with the WSHG is Botai in Kazakhstan where, as we saw in earlier chapters, the earliest evidence of horse domestication has been found. In terms of the homeland, the fact that the genetic signature of steppe populations to the east of the Urals (WSHG) differs from that west of the Urals (EHG + CHG) does little to support the notion of a homogeneous pastoral population occupying both the Asiatic and European steppe, nor does it support the idea that the European steppe pastoralists (EHG + CHG) derived from the Asiatic steppe (WSHG) as proposed by the *Kulturkreis* school who promoted the Asiatic Steppe model. Nevertheless, traces of WSHG lineage are found in some populations of the European steppe (see Chapter 15).

Ancient Ancestral South Indians

The hot climate of South Asia does not lend itself to the preservation of aDNA in human remains. Consequently, the genetic picture of the region involves meshing some aDNA material from the outer periphery of the region with reconstructions of the genomic origins of the current population of the area. This has resulted in the identification of the Ancient Ancestral South Indian (AASI)[16] lineage, which is found among all Indian populations but tends to be less diluted in the south, suggesting that it once was the dominant native type that was later admixed with what has been called an Indus Periphery ancestry. AASI is related deeply to the genetic profile of the Andaman Islanders and is found in the Indus Periphery samples admixed with CHG and WSHG. Among the Y-chromosomes recognized is haplogroup H1Id2.[17]

In terms of homelands, we would expect AASI ancestry to play a dominant role in tracking the dispersal of the Indo-Europeans in the Out of

India model. That it appears to play no role in the relevant populations of Anatolia, the Caucasus, the steppe or Europe renders the Indian homeland theory unsupported by genetic evidence.

Genetics and language

The German anthropologist Otto Reche (1879–1966), when not advocating the extermination of the Polish people or authenticating Anna Anderson's claim that she was indeed Princess Anastasia of Russia, argued that 'Race and language have been associated with one another from the very beginning', and that it was 'unthinkable' (*undenkbar*) for two fully different races to produce the same language or for the same race to produce two totally different languages.[18] Despite Reche's certitude, we have already seen that there is no intrinsic relationship between one's genome and one's language: anyone can learn any language and any association between language and genetics is historical and not intrinsically biological. An elite group of warriors sharing the same haplogroup may conquer a neighbouring land and pass their haplogroup down to their male offspring for generations but, if they intermarried with the local women, they could find their children or grandchildren speaking the language of the conquered rather than the elite. And, as for autosomal DNA, we need look no further than the CHG whose territory likely provided the genetic basis for the emergence of Elamite and Hurrian as well as the three major groupings of the Caucasian languages and possibly others [12.2]. In short, each of the major Eurasian ancestral populations that date to the Palaeolithic and Mesolithic could and probably did house multiple language families. On the other hand, given the fact that each of these population groups have roots that are sunk so deep and have been separated for so long, it does seem most unlikely that any single language could have evolved *simultaneously* across two of the groups, such as the AHG and CHG. If you haven't talked with your wife for 10,000 years, you probably have a problem of communication.

In terms of homeland hunting, the inherited (Palaeolithic–Mesolithic) genetic landscape would incline us to dismiss any model that locates the Indo-European homeland across two or more contemporary major

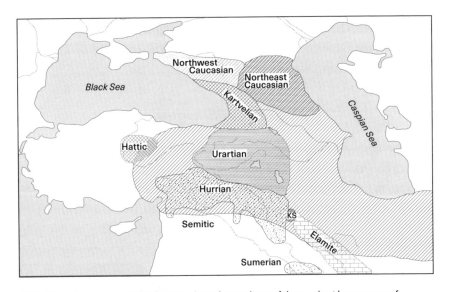

12.2 The primary area of CHG comprises the territory of the ancient languages of Elamite, Kassite (KS), Hurrian, Urartian and at least partially of Hattic, as well as the modern language groups of Kartvelian and both Northwest and Northeast Caucasian.

mating networks. On occasion, for example, we have seen proposed homelands that extend from northern or central Europe (WHG) eastwards across the steppe (EHG) to the Urals, where it is imagined that the whole region evolved into a single Proto-Indo-European language. From a genetic standpoint, such an early proto-homeland would seem difficult to explain.

These large-scale population groups also bear on the plausibility of the linguistic mega-families into which Indo-European has been subsumed, such as Eurasiatic or Nostratic, which by their very nature sinks its origins deeper in Eurasian prehistory. These constructs face a major chronological-genetic problem: their proposed dates (e.g. 15,000 years ago for Eurasiatic coupled with Kartvelian and Dravidian,[19] or Nostratic at a similar date) have to explain how they can claim a common origin for languages spoken within the territory of the Levantine group (Afro-Asiatic), CHG (Elamite, Kartvelian), EHG (Uralic) and East Siberian (Altaic), Dravidian (AASI) and wherever we want to stash

Indo-European. Some of these may be embraced by the more basal ANE, but this would still exclude the language families found from the Caucasus southwards, unless one plunges the origin of such groups into the initial peopling of Eurasia by modern humans.

The probability of an Indo-European homeland emerging out of multiple long-separated genetic regions would seem to be extremely low. Thus, some of the Palaeolithic or Mesolithic solutions that comprise two or more separated population groups such as the WHG and EHG appear to be unlikely. On the other hand, a homeland need not have emerged solely within a single ancestral population, as Reche seemed to suggest, although it obviously could. Because none of the populations occupied an area anywhere approximate to the early distribution of the Indo-European languages, it appears fairly clear that we must look for a population group that expanded its borders into different territories and admixed or replaced the earlier genetic signature. And this is precisely what happens at the beginning of the Neolithic. The genetic landscape of Eurasia bearing on Indo-European origins was massively altered by the expansion of agricultural economies from the Fertile Crescent to the west, north and east (the southern expansion would most likely be associated with Afro-Asiatic languages).

Language shift without genetic shift

While the importance of palaeogenetic arguments in resolving the homeland problem cannot be challenged, such evidence does tempt one to presume that the spread of language must leave a clear genetic trail. However, this reduces evaluations of the various homeland models to purely an assessment of the genetic evidence: is there enough of a genetic trail to demonstrate a migration or intrusion that can support a claim for the spread of a language? While this primarily takes us into the downstream problems of tracing the dispersal of all the Indo-European branches from a homeland, which I shall briefly discuss in Chapter 16, it is probably necessary to at least outline some of the basics of language shift. The models supported by genetic evidence often come down to situations where speakers of the new (the technical term would be 'target') language, here Indo-European, mate with someone who speaks a different language and we conjecture what language their offspring spoke. The type of language shift that we haven't addressed is when an entire population abandons the language of both parents and adopts a new language. How does this look in practice? I once tried to evaluate this question in some detail with respect to Atlantic Europe and many of the same observations can be extended to the rest of Indo-European dispersals.[20]

The fundamental prerequisite for language shift is that the non-Indo-European host population comes into contact with the new language whose bearers may or may not have left a detectable genetic trail. After contact, the host population begins to learn the new language and, therefore, becomes bilingual: a period of societal bilingualism is logically required to bridge the shift from the host language to the target language. The bilingualism may come incrementally as the new language establishes or co-opts various social domains (areas of activity where language is used) in which its language predominates. To give an extreme example, consider the situation of a Mumbai spice merchant. At home he speaks Gujarati but at work he has to shift to Kacchi. If he goes to the market he needs to speak Marathi. If he wants to travel by train, he buys his ticket using Hindi, but if he wants to fly, he shifts to English. A briefer example would be the claim of Charles V, who maintained that he spoke Spanish to God, Italian to women, French to men and German to his horse.[21]

The types of language domains that we might imagine for the relevant periods of prehistory we are dealing with would include the domestic realm (the household of the individuals however defined), the ritual domain, the political domain, the various social domains, which may include warbands, sodalities (special associations or clubs) and special religious groups, and the various domains that might involve the exchange of goods. It is presumed that the speakers of the newly introduced language have established or participate in some forms of activities that are open to the host speakers, but which either require or give an advantage to those able to speak the new language. To take a crude modern example, an obvious domain (akin to the warband) would be the French Foreign Legion, which takes its members from all over the world but where everyone must very rapidly develop some competence in French. Another obvious domain is in the area of exchange: while simple barter may require very few linguistic skills, more complicated transactions demand better linguistic abilities otherwise the linguistically deficient are likely to find themselves cheated. If the speakers of the new language are also introducing a new religion, this could form an important social activity where access to ceremonies could encourage a high degree of competence in the new language.

When it comes to specific Indo-European institutions that may have encouraged language shift, some of the most powerful ones are fosterage,[22] clientage and the warband, along with work alliances with neighbours and feasting. While participation in the warband is probably clear enough, the practice of fosterage – sending children to be placed in the homes of the maternal uncle to be raised – has been suggested for Core-Indo-European and was still a well-known practice among the early Celts. In the late 16th century the poet Edmund Spenser complained that having children fostered in the homes of Gaelic speakers was one of the main reasons that the English elite in Ireland expressed more delight in speaking Irish than their own language.

As the host population becomes more bilingual and employs the new language in more aspects of their lives, this usually leads to the denigration of their mother tongue, which is stigmatized and gradually abandoned until it is only spoken at home and then not at all as the host language experiences language death (or, more aptly put, 'language suicide'). In some cases, the host language might survive as a liturgical language, such as Latin or Avestan.

This model of language shift may be supported by archaeology if we can translate the various social institutions into archaeological expectations. For example, if both archaeology and genetics associate an intrusive population with a new social domain such as a central place where a variety of activities are undertaken (exchange, ritual, boy-meets-girl), this could provide evidence of the type of cultural change accompanying a migration that might encourage language shift.

To conclude, from this review of the techniques and impact of palaeogenomics, we have seen that aDNA (both uniparental and autosomal) can provide evidence of the ancestry of individuals and populations, their movements through time and space, and their marriage networks, all of which may shed light on the movement of languages. The areas relevant to the search for the Indo-European homeland comprise a series of major ancestral populations across western and central Eurasia, each associated with a particular homeland model or models. However, genetically evidenced migrations and interactions are not the only way that languages might expand and there are other models for language dispersal that would leave little to no genetic evidence for the dispersal of a language, especially if language shift is experienced along a chain of genetically diverse populations. Language shift is a process usually preceded by societal bilingualism across a range of socio-linguistic domains in which the competence in the new language provides social advantages. During this process, the new language generally rises in public estimation, while speakers of the language that will be replaced find their own language is progressively stigmatized as socially and practically less attractive until it is abandoned altogether, resulting in language death.

We will return to this topic at the very end of the book, but we need to remember that while the dispersal of a language may necessarily require the movement of at least some people, it need not have left a very obvious genetic trail.

CHAPTER 13

The Anatolian Homeland Model

In the following three chapters I will examine in more detail how the new field of palaeogenomics has impacted the various Indo-European homeland models – in particular, the most convincing solutions identified in the previous chapters, namely the Anatolian, Caucasus and Steppe models. We begin with the evidence associated with the first farmers in Anatolia and Europe and explore the consequences of assuming that the Indo-European homeland was associated with the Ancient Anatolian Farmer (AAF) group.

Ancient Anatolian Farmers

Agriculture developed in the Fertile Crescent and spread westwards, reaching central Anatolia *c.* 8300 BCE. Although its spread has often been expressed in terms of a 'wave of advance', with successful farmers out-competing and out-populating hunter-gatherers, this does not appear to be the case for central Anatolia. This conclusion is supported by both archaeological[1] and genetic evidence. We have already seen how the site of Pınarbaşı offers genetic evidence of Anatolian Hunter-Gatherers (AHG, the ancestor of the AAF). From *c.* 9500 to 7800 BCE, this settlement also presents evidence of village life based as far as can be determined on hunting wild animals (although sheep and/or goats were exploited, these were most likely hunted rather than managed) without any evidence for the exploitation of cereals [**13.1**]. At nearby Boncuklu, which is estimated to overlap the settlement at Pınarbaşı by 300–500 years, there is some evidence for the management of sheep/goats as well as the growing of wheat. Nevertheless, here too farming practices were quite

CHAPTER 13

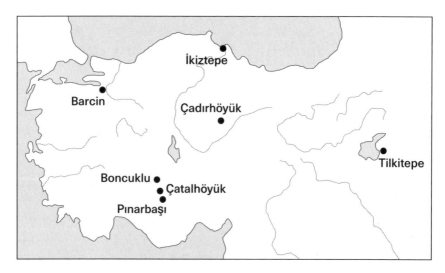

13.1 A map of some Anatolian sites of the Neolithic. The genetic profile of early farmers from the Balkans aligns well with samples from earlier farming communities from Barcin (6600–6000 BCE), which are in turn linked to the still earlier population of Boncuklu.

minimal compared with hunting and the gathering of wild plants, which remains the case throughout Boncuklu's existence (*c.* 8300–7800 BCE). This suggests that a community of hunter-gatherers was probably in contact with farmers further to the east from whom they gained some traces of the domestic economy (wheat). In no way, however, did this induce a sudden shift in their economic strategy, which remained fundamentally hunting and gathering.

The site of Boncuklu produced seven individuals of the aceramic (or no pottery) Neolithic who have been labelled genetically AAF. The site presents mitochondrial haplogroups N1a1a1, K1a and U3, and Y-chromosome haplogroups C and G2a2b2b (G-PF3359). The ancestry of the Boncuklu population was about 90 per cent local AAF and about 10 per cent Caucasus Hunter-Gatherer (CHG), the latter of which would derive from further east and plausibly account for the human vector (intermarriage) that introduced a knowledge of agriculture and some domestic wheat. The amount of CHG increases in Anatolia through time and by *c.* 7100 BCE we see more thoroughly agricultural settlements such as Çatalhöyük East, followed by the major Çatalhöyük settlement itself, which has often been held up as the archaeological exemplar of the Anatolian Farmer model.² Here the predominant Y-haplogroups continued as before to be G2a2 and C1a2. During this transition to full agricultural status (7000–6000 BCE) the amount of CHG in the population increases, but only to *c.* 20 per cent while 80 per cent remained local AHG/AAF.³ So we have a situation where, over the course of more than two millennia from the beginning of the Neolithic, we have increasing evidence for intermarriage with a CHG-bearing population moving or at least mating westwards across Anatolia. But as regards the northwest of Anatolia – which was the staging area for farmers moving into the Balkans⁴ – the amount of CHG there still remained very low until the transition between the Neolithic and the following Eneolithic where it rose to *c.* 30 per cent.⁵

From the perspective of the Anatolian Farmer model, the archaeological and genetic scenarios suggest some consequences that seem more probable than others. To begin with, the lack of a major wave of advance from the Fertile Crescent across Anatolia at the beginning of the Neolithic supports the proposition that, assuming that Proto-Indo-Anatolian spread from early Neolithic central and western Anatolia, then it should be identified with the AHG/AAF inhabitants of Pınarbaşı or Boncuklu rather than CHG populations further to the east – for example, in the Zagros mountains or Mesopotamia – or from populations south in the Levant. Although there are later influences from these zones during the later ceramic Neolithic, to move the homeland any further to the east would result in placing it within a territory whose genetic composition (CHG) would be very much at odds with that of the earliest farmers of central or northwest Anatolia and, more importantly for this homeland model, the earliest farming communities of Europe. This does not mean that you cannot locate the Indo-European homeland in eastern Anatolia, the Caucasus or the Zagros, but if you do so, you are no longer associating the expansion of the Indo-Anatolian languages across Europe with the spread of farming, which is, after all, the fundamental driving force of the Anatolian Farmer model.

CHAPTER 13

The Balkan homeland debate

The Anatolian Farmer model usually accounts for the origin of the Anatolian languages in the most economical way by situating them within Anatolia since at least the Neolithic rather than requiring a later migration. In terms of the linguistic phylogeny of Indo-Anatolian, this would place Proto-Anatolian, the immediate ancestor of the Anatolian languages, either in or near the central homeland where it would remain and eventually enter the written record. All of the rest of the language family – Core-Indo-European – would separate, presumably in its movement into the Balkans where it would undergo all those common linguistic changes that are absent from the Anatolian languages.[6] We have already encountered this suggestion when exploring Colin Renfrew's amended version of his original Anatolian Farmer solution, which was designed to assist the hypothesis in dealing with some of the phylogenetic problems of the initial model.[7] Of course, in treating southeast Europe as the secondary homeland for Proto-Indo-European and the staging area for further Indo-European dispersals, we are planting the homeland in Marija Gimbutas's 'Old Europe', a cluster of Neolithic cultures known for long-term agricultural settlements, a general lack of (obvious) aggression and thousands of female figurines suggestive of a matrifocal society: all traits that Gimbutas argued would not pass a cultural trait list assessment of early Indo-European society. If one does not dismiss all the evidence of linguistic palaeontology, the rebuttal to this would be to suggest that the domestic horse, wheeled vehicles, weapons, aggression and so on were all later phenomena in the spread of Indo-European and so the image summoned up by linguistic palaeontology is irrelevant to the early and middle Neolithic of the Balkans when Core-Indo-European was initially evolving and had not yet dispersed. A Balkan centre also seems to presume that Indo-European-speaking farmers spread eastwards to absorb the Steppe model in order to account for eastward expansions (Tocharian, Indo-Iranian) into Asia. But we have already seen that this appears to run counter to the genetic evidence, which indicates that the primary composition of the steppe people was Eastern Hunter-Gatherer (EHG) and CHG, and that AAF, the genetic signature of Anatolian farmers, was very much a minority element that (as we will see) appears to have entered the region through the Caucasus rather than the Balkans.

That there was a massive influx of farmers into southeast Europe from northwest Anatolia has received firm support from ancient DNA (aDNA) studies – early farmers in the Balkans, for example, derive about 98 per cent of their ancestry from north Anatolian farmers[8] – but this also means that it is difficult to distinguish northwest Anatolian farmers from Balkan farmers, so models of an independent Balkan homeland would appear to be logically subsumed by an overarching Anatolian Farmer model. It is difficult to come up with any reason for isolating out the Balkan Neolithic as genetically different from an Anatolian one, and if the spread of farming is the vehicle for the spread of a language family, it is not clear how one should separate out a Proto-Indo-European segment from the rest of Neolithic expansions. In short, as with the archaeological evidence, genetics renders a Balkan homeland separate from the Anatolian Farmer model extremely unlikely.

The only added genetic 'spice' from the Balkans are the pockets of Neolithic communities that show more evidence for local Western Hunter-Gatherer (WHG) or Balkan Hunter-Gatherer (BHG) ancestry – for example, along the Danube, where in Bulgaria, WHG rises to 15 per cent, and, in general, as one passes from the early to the middle Neolithic the contribution of farmers with WHG rises in the Balkans, central Europe and Iberia. In the latter two regions it is primarily confined to males bearing a WHG signature found within the communities, and they are associated with the appearance of Y-haplogroups I2, R1 and C1. But once these haplogroups have been absorbed into the Neolithic communities, they are eventually assimilated into the genomic signature of the expanding wave of farmers, meaning they cease to become markers of local hunter-gatherers but become fully fledged farmers who simply bear an ancient local hunter-gatherer pedigree. They are no more hunter-gatherers than I am a Viking.

In Chapter 6 we encountered Rasmus Bjørn's interesting proposal of Old Balkanic, an extinct Afro-Asiatic language of the Balkans that was the vector for Afro-Asiatic loanwords into the steppe. Given the fact that the Balkans were introduced to the Neolithic economy by farmers from northwest Anatolia who were overwhelmingly bearers of AAF (rather than Levantine or CHG), I suspect that the only way Old Balkanic can survive as a theory is if AAF was either genetically a relation of Afro-Asiatic or if the vocabulary of its putative loanwords had also been borrowed by northwest Anatolians from an Afro-Asiatic language. While Levantine aDNA does increase through time in Anatolia, the earlier genetic vector that one would associate with the spread of agriculture is still CHG, which has enough language families to spawn as it is without also introducing Afro-Asiatic as well. It will be interesting to see whether anyone can mount creative rebuttals to the archaeological and genetic evidence that suggests that the earliest farmers *did not introduce* an extinct Afro-Asiatic language to Europe.

Another problem is that the genetic evidence not only fails to distinguish between the early farmers of northwest Anatolia and those of the Balkans but also confirms that the migration route associated with Cardial Ware pottery (Anatolia > Balkans > Adriatic > Italy > Iberia) involved essentially the same genetic populations as those who entered the Balkans. It is the Mediterranean that offers some evidence for non-Indo-European languages, especially in the west (Basque, Iberian, Palaeo-Sardo?). It is difficult to argue that Anatolian farmers spread an Indo-European language through southeast Europe while the same farmers brought non-Indo-European languages from the Balkans to Iberia. Of course, one might argue that these languages are relics of the Mesolithic (WHG) populations along the Mediterranean who adopted agriculture but managed to retain their own languages. This is part of an enormous can of worms that I call the 'Peripheral Europe' problem (we will meet this again below and in the final chapter), which in the absence of a clear solution remains a constituency issue. If you believe that the 'wave of advance' of agriculture is so strong that it (almost) guarantees language shift, then we should not expect the native Mesolithic languages of the Mediterranean to have survived. On the other hand, there is always the possibility that one or more Mesolithic communities managed to adopt farming without yielding their language and furthered the expansion of both farming and their own language.

The case for a Danubian homeland

From a genetic standpoint, much of what has been said regarding the Balkan homeland model can be extended to the Danubian model, which ties Indo-European origins to the spread of a strikingly homogenous Linear Ware culture, originating generally in the territory of Hungary and Slovakia *c.* 5500 BCE, and spreading west to the Atlantic and east to Ukraine. The genetic evidence indicates that the Linear Ware population was largely AAF with some admixture with local WHG increasing through time.[9] One recent study placed AAF at approximately 93 per cent and WHG at about 7 per cent.[10] The primary Y-haplogroups were G2a2 and H2, haplogroups that can be traced back to their Anatolian ancestors. Phenotypic analysis revealed (possibly) 33 per cent with brown eye colour and 21 per cent with brown hair colour; the somewhat darker skin colour introduced by the earliest farmers showed no evidence of having become lighter during the course of their spread from Anatolia to the Danube.

The attraction of the Danubian homeland hypothesis has rested on a combination of the sheer size of its territory, coupled with the impression that it was a relatively uniform culture typified by a distinct ceramic and architectural style (the striking Linear Ware long houses known from many excavations were just too tempting for linguists looking for a template for the Proto-Indo-European word for 'house') and certain technological items. All of this encouraged the idea that it represented a stable linguistic entity. While one cannot read the size of the mating group as identical with language groupings, an examination of the amount of in-breeding within the Linear Ware culture suggests that it operated widespread mating networks of about five thousand people, which might be employed to further encourage the notion of a culturally and linguistically uniform area over the period *c.* 5500–4500 BCE. In this it could be contrasted with the early Neolithic of the Balkans, with its proliferation of regional ceramic styles and varying but relatively dense settlement systems, which at least suggested more marked cultural borders that one then could (not necessarily should) read as more diverse language areas (dialects?).[11]

The Danubian area, however, was still clearly part of the same process of Neolithic expansion as the Balkans and genetically tied to northwest Anatolian farmers. As was the case elsewhere, the presence of local WHG ancestry increased with time in the middle and late Neolithic settlements of the region, but we are still dealing with a population that is genetically largely derived from Anatolia. It seems *nearly* impossible to extricate the Danubian homeland model from the fate of the Anatolian Farmer – but we will review this again in the final chapter.

The Nordic homeland

Despite some early delusional attempts to set the origins of European agriculture in northern Europe and render the rest of Europe culturally secondary to a Nordic master race, the expansion of the Neolithic economy from Anatolia through the Balkans and across Danubian Europe is quite clearly supported by the evidence. It may have stalled for nearly a millennium, but it did manage to replace the hunting-gathering societies that had occupied northern Europe. We have seen that the earliest of these Neolithic cultures was the Funnel-Beaker (4500–2700 BCE), which was dispersed over a broad area of northern Europe from the Netherlands in the west to the western fringe of Ukraine. A long dispute as to whether this culture was a product of local hunter-gatherers gradually adopting the new economy and some of the technology of their southern neighbours (which would help support the Nordic homeland model), or whether it resulted from a migration from the south (the Anatolian Farmer model), was settled by geneticists. They uncovered a clear distinction between the Funnel-Beaker culture and their local Mesolithic predecessors as well as members of largely hunting-fishing-gathering societies (the Pitted Ware culture) that lived alongside them in the Baltic region.

The Funnel-Beaker culture contained amounts of local WHG genes (in Denmark from *c.* 10–30 per cent) but was primarily of AAF descent.[12] A number of the mitochondrial haplogroups[13] indicated that Funnel-Beaker women had distant great-grandmothers who had once lived in Anatolia. Coverage of the Y-chromosome indicates a handful of haplogroups derived from the earliest farmers, but is overwhelmingly I2, the signature of earlier hunter-gatherers who had long been absorbed into the earlier farming communities as they spread through southeast and central Europe. The absorption of local males, at least in Denmark, may not have occurred until the late Neolithic,[14] but we are again dealing with the 'Peripheral Europe' effect where farmers trace their genetic origins to earlier local hunter-gatherers. In France, Britain and Ireland, for example, the males of the Neolithic are overwhelmingly the Y-chromosome descendants (I2) of local European hunter-gatherers who have 'gone farmer'.[15] Predicting the linguistic identity of these 'Peripheral Europeans' is admittedly problematic, and the assumption that whatever language was carried from Anatolia was still absorbing the western and northern populations of Europe is just that – an assumption.

Usually included under the Funnel-Beaker umbrella is the Baalberge group of Germany and Bohemia (see **9.8**), which distinguished itself by placing single burials under mounds, a classic marker of the steppe cultures. For this reason, Marija Gimbutas regarded the Baalberge group as a 'Kurganized' culture – that is, a local Funnel-Beaker culture that had been culturally dominated by the first wave of steppe migrants into central Europe.[16] We have already seen that the cranial evidence did not support this theory and we now know that it is also rejected by the aDNA evidence. The mitochondrial haplogroups are largely those that appeared in Europe with the initial Neolithic colonization of the Balkans (e.g. HV, H7, K1, N1, T2, etc.), while the evidence of Y-chromosomes is again our old Palaeolithic relic I2, which we have already seen in Neolithic farmers from the Balkans onwards, and R1b V88, another of the very early haplogroups that had been absorbed by the spread of the first farmers and is particularly prominent in Neolithic Sardinia.[17]

Assessing the admixture of CHG and AAF

Although Anatolian farmers were the initial vector for bringing agriculture into Europe, they do not appear to have initiated the Neolithic Revolution that occurred to their east and south. We have already seen references to the Palaeolithic occupants of eastern Anatolia, the Zagros and the Caucasus as the CHG and this acronym can be extended to the earliest farmers of the region, sometimes also referred to as 'Early Iranian Farmers', since the CHG genetic signature was also present at the early Neolithic site of Ganj Dareh in the middle range of the Zagros mountains dating to *c.* 8000–7000 BCE. It is clear that if Proto-Indo-Anatolian emerged out of the Neolithic Revolution, it involved some cultural input from the CHG population. We have already seen that CHG began to appear in small amounts (*c.* 10 per cent) in central Anatolia among the early aceramic farmers of Boncuklu, and although there is still a major continuity of an AAF population in the region, the percentage of CHG does increase in time (along with Levantine genes from further south).[18] Through an admixture process where Anatolian farmer genes moved east and CHG genes moved west, an AAF-CHG cline stretching from western Anatolia to the southern Caucasus 'started at the beginning of the Late Neolithic (~6500 years BCE)'.[19] And by the Early Bronze Age, the percentage of CHG in Anatolian populations had climbed to approximately 40 per cent, and remained so up through the Middle and Late Bronze Age, where samples derived from what some have presumed to be Hittite speakers are about 60 per cent AAF and 40 per cent CHG.[20] After this period, most studies so far have suggested that there is little evidence for any other early disruptions in what is otherwise described as genetic continuity in Anatolia until the appearance of Turkic (but see below).

Since we are now dealing with AAF and CHG appearing as a 'foreign' element in each other's worlds we should note several things. Although the percentage of CHG does rise in the admixture, it does not become dominant in the areas where we find the various Anatolian languages. This poses an interesting and so far unanswerable problem in trying to read language shift from genetic admixtures. Everything from at least the Neolithic onwards is going to involve admixtures, and there is an understandable temptation to read admixture percentages as linguistic probabilities. When investigating the spread of farming from Anatolia across Europe we have generally been involved in totally unbalanced admixtures with AAF at 90 per cent or more in most cases – suggesting that such a genetic situation *probably* favoured the language of those who were of primarily AAF origin when the admixture formed. But what happens when the admixture is far more balanced, as we find in central and western Anatolia? How much CHG do you need in the admixture to convince that it may be the cause of language shift within Anatolia itself? If the territory to which we ascribe the Anatolian languages experienced an admixture of about 60 per cent AAF and 40 per cent CHG, how do we assess the linguistic implications of such an admixture? Is the 40 per cent CHG sufficient to suggest that it is from this genetic community that the Anatolian languages derived rather than the native AAF? If this were so, then the entire Anatolian Farmer model collapses.

An indication of how problematic the equating of genetic percentages with linguistic probabilities is can be seen in the case of the Sardinian language. Let us accept for a moment (as probably most of the current front-runner theories do) that Italic derives from the Eneolithic expansion of steppe ancestry into central Europe. Although Sardinian is a Romance language, only about 15 per cent of the modern population (and no more than 20 per cent of any sampled ancient population) carries the signature of the steppe migrations that (unlike neighbouring regions) appears quite late in its prehistory.[21] It seems fairly clear that the impact of the Roman absorption of Sardinia into the Italic world was linguistically total yet genetically marginal. One might then argue that even a 15 per cent minority genetic signature is sufficient to support linguistic shift. On the other hand, we are also aware of the mass of Roman social institutions that could encourage language shift and realize that extending this 15 per cent rule to earlier situations would be entirely inappropriate. Or do we also need to build our case with the evidence from haplogroups? And here again we will probably find ourselves unable to evaluate how many intrusive haplogroups (and here also controlling for sex) indicates a linguistically significant change.

In sum, we are presently in no position to translate genetic admixture percentages into probabilities of language shift other than, perhaps, where the percentages are overwhelmingly weighted on one side and are further confirmed by extensive evidence from haplogroups. To this must also be coupled both good control of the chronology of the admixture through time and, as mentioned earlier in a quote, the contextual evidence of the samples indicated by archaeology. This last point cannot be underestimated, because we can only make linguistic sense out of the genetic data if we understand the social context from which our samples derive, and how they might relate to social models for language shift, and whether those models can actually point in which direction the language shift is most likely to occur. And I am painfully aware that I have just made one of those stomach-churning (at least for me) pious aspirational statements that we are far from being able to prove (if ever). Much of this discussion rests on uncritical assumptions about the nature of our data rather than solid science. So far there is no reliable way to translate admixture percentages into the probabilities of language shift, so take any linguistic interpretations I may make with a whopping grain of salt! The situation should improve considerably when we have a much wider application of IBD ('identity by descent', not Irritable Bowel Disease!) assessments of the palaeogenomic evidence, which will permit us to make vastly more fine-scale assessments of population histories.[22] But for now I must continue with the current evidence and admittedly very suspect assumptions.

Finally, AAF diminishes on its west–east axis, where it is found at about 30 per cent in eastern Iran, about 20–25 per cent in the Bactria-Margiana Archaeological Complex (BMAC) and falls to about 7 per cent in eastern Central Asia. The AAF signature is also found penetrating the Caucasus itself, where a site of the earliest major ceramic Neolithic culture of the Caucasus, the Aratashen-Shulaveri-Shomutepe culture dating to *c.* 6000–5000 BCE, revealed three burials modelled as 30 per cent CHG, 15 per cent Levantine and 55 per cent AAF.[23] This indicates that the spread of the ceramic Neolithic through the Caucasus was carried out by a farming population where CHG and AAF genes had already mixed to a substantial degree and been joined by a more southerly Levantine genetic source. In the north Caucasus, AAF has been uncovered from a burial in Unakozovskaya cave that dates to *c.* 4500 BCE, while the later Maykop culture has been modelled with 10 per cent AAF.[24] The admixture of CHG and AAF helps complicate an already complicated problem, and generates a variety of homeland narratives that we will explore in the next two chapters.

CHAPTER 14

The Caucasus Homeland Model

As we have seen, setting an Indo-European homeland in or near the Caucasus has been part of Urheimat solutions at least since Andreas Jäger in the 17th century and we have encountered it from time to time subsequently. In its most developed form, before the advent of ancient DNA (aDNA) evidence, it was promoted in the works of Tamaz Gamkrelidze and Vyacheslav Ivanov, although there set to a period after the earliest agricultural dispersals and, possibly, associated archaeologically with at least a part of the Halaf culture (*c*. 6100–5100 BCE) located in the northern Tigris and Euphrates region (see below and **9.17**). But this is by no means the only way one can posit a homeland associated with the Caucasian Hunter-Gatherer (CHG) genetic signature and here I wish to explore some of the possible options for anchoring the homeland in the territory of this population group. In other words, what are the consequences of assuming that Proto-Indo-Anatolian emerged out of an ancestral CHG population? Before we look at how all of this might work out on the ground, let's consider whether CHG territory is the type of place the proto-language could be established.

CHG and Proto-Anatolian

Assuming that Proto-Indo-Anatolian was part of the CHG population raises the issue of the linguistic neighbourhood of the Caucasus and how attractive it is to locate the Proto-Indo-Anatolian homeland in a CHG region (see **12.2**). The other major Bronze Age languages, ranging from Hattic on the west to Elamite on the east, are all agglutinative (where separate meanings are assigned to a chain of suffixes that are glued to the end of a word; see Chapter 6)[1] while Proto-Indo-Anatolian is, of course, inflexional. Moreover, all the ancient (and modern Caucasian) languages of the region also show a marked tendency to some form of ergativity (a grammatical type marking how the subject of an intransitive verb is indicated).[2] We also find (to a much smaller degree) traces of ergativity in Anatolian and the question here is, did this reflect a genetic areal inheritance (i.e. that Indo-Anatolian was also originally an ergative language[3] like all of its neighbours) or did Anatolian come from elsewhere, settling in Anatolia where it was influenced by local ergative languages? I suspect that most linguists would follow Calvert Watkins, who regarded ergativity to be 'an important common innovation of the Anatolian branch',[4] indicating that ergativity was acquired and not inherited. While controversial attempts have been made to support the notion that some of these neighbouring languages in and around the Caucasus share a deep genetic relationship with Proto-Indo-Anatolian,[5] this is not generally accepted by linguists. In short, we have an unresolved constituency problem as to what extent we can argue that the Caucasus or the region south of the Caucasus associated with CHG genetic ancestry would be a natural linguistic home for the emergence of an inflexional (and not agglutinative) and non-ergative Proto-Indo-Anatolian? This is only a relevant question for those linguists who regard the areal nature of a region a clue to a language family's origins.

Now if we wish to situate Proto-Indo-Anatolian within the CHG expanse, the least-moves argument would favour locating it on the western margins of the early CHG distribution, closest to where we later find the Anatolian languages. To place it further northeast (the Caucasus) or southeast (in the Zagros mountains) would seem to increase the probability that one is either locating the homeland within the historical seats of Hurrian (to the north) or Elamite (to the south) – or somewhere that would require putative Proto-Anatolians to push through the territories of other language families in order to get to Anatolia from a more easterly homeland. I emphasize probability rather than certainty, because we do not know precisely where the various homelands of the non-Indo-European languages of this region were located, but this entire region does seem to be rather thickly occupied by non-Indo-European language families and they must have had a home somewhere. Admittedly, locating Proto-Indo-Anatolian to the immediate east of where we find the Anatolian languages does privilege resolving the problem of Proto-Anatolian origins over a solution that explains all of the subsequent branches, but then, that is the first problem we indeed have to face.

As a thought experiment, let us tentatively locate the Urheimat in eastern Anatolia among a primarily CHG population but with a growing admixture of Ancient Anatolian Farmer (AAF; the AAF-CHG cline) and possible Levantine groups. Although this is a territory that, in the Bronze Age, will be occupied by speakers of the Hurro-Urartian language family, we can brush aside this objection with the 'later immigrants' card because, as we will discuss, this region does seem to experience a major cultural incursion associated with the southern expansion of the Kura-Araxes culture (*c.* 3500–2000 BCE; see below).

Now, what are the requirements of an Urheimat in eastern Anatolia? The first item on the agenda is the split: Proto-Anatolian must separate from the rest of Indo-Anatolian, which will experience common linguistic innovations and evolve into what we reconstruct as Core-Indo-European. We can handle this in one of two ways: either Proto-Anatolian (the immediate ancestor of the Anatolian branch of languages such as Hittite, Luvian, etc.) moves off to avoid the later common innovations assigned to Core-Indo-European or it is Core-Indo-European that moves off, leaving Proto-Anatolian to soldier on, deprived of feminine nouns, various new forms of verbs and a variety of other linguistic innovations. Let us go with the first option, as it seems easier to explain the Anatolian languages if we have them enter their historical seats with the flow of CHG as it moves west along the AAF-CHG cline. So, we now have a CHG Indo-Anatolian homeland in eastern Anatolia and the Proto-Anatolians (again CHG) have moved west into their historical seats in AAF territory.

When did they do that? On the basis of both archaeological and genetic evidence the most likely window is between *c.* 6500 BCE, when the AAF-CHG cline emerges, and *c.* 3500 BCE (when the Kura-Araxes culture closes the door to the west). Such a date for the separation of Proto-Anatolian from what will evolve as Core-Indo-European must therefore be *after* the development of agriculture. We can argue that on both archaeological

Anatolian		PIA
Hittite *karas*	'wheat'	*ǵhrésdh-i-*
Hittite *ewan*	'barley'	*yewo-*
Hittite *u̯eši*	'pasture'	*u̯es-i-*
Hittite *u̯eštara-*	'herd'	*u̯es-tr-*
Hittite *sā(i)-*	'press'	*seh₁-*
Hittite *šēli-*	'grain pile, grain, storage'	*seh₁-li-*
Hittite *hārš-*	'till the land'	*h₂erh₃-*
Hittite *malla-*	'to mill, to grind'	*melh₂-*
Hittite *hāu̯i-*	'sheep'	*h₂⅔ówis*
Hittite **hulana-*	'wool'	*wl̥h₂neh₂-*
Hittite *kiš-*	'to comb, to card'	*kés-ti*
Hittite **kuu̯āu-*, HLuvian *wa/i/*	'cow'	*gʷéh₃-u-s*
Hittite *iūk-*	'yoke'	*yugóm*
Hittite *tūriie/a-*	'to harness'	*dhuh₁r-ye/o-*

14.1 Some Neolithic-associated items of Anatolian vocabulary – Hittite and Hieroglyphic Luvian (HLuvian) – derived from Proto-Indo-Anatolian (PIA).[6] Note that some of the terms related to cereal agriculture have been queried[7] as have words associated with wool and textiles.[8]

and linguistic grounds. First, as we have already seen, the spread of CHG to central Anatolia appears to be contemporaneous with the earliest appearance of agriculture. Despite a recent claim that linguistic palaeontology proves otherwise,[9] Anatolian does appear to retain a series of terms that one would usually associate with an agricultural economy. An admittedly optimistic list of these is presented in **14.1**.

The objection to such cognate lists is whether the semantics of the Anatolian evidence actually returns a direct continuation of an earlier Proto-Indo-Anatolian (PIA) meaning related to agriculture or whether it merely retains a PIA root that originally had a more basic meaning that was preserved in Anatolian and does not support reconstructing agriculture to the proto-language – for example, PIA **seh₁-* 'sow' only returns the meaning 'press' in Hittite *ša(i)-*, while PIA **neik-* 'winnow' returns the meaning 'scatter'.[10] Or do some of the words merely indicate the pre-Neolithic exploitation of wild grasses such as wheat and barley or wild forms of herd animals such as sheep? As I mentioned earlier, a few years ago I published what was effectively a 'hit list' of potential Proto-Indo-Anatolian terms related to cereal agriculture.[11] Some very competent linguists severely reduced my list, concluding that 'it is evident that many agricultural meanings that have habitually been reconstructed for Proto-Indo-European are effectively post-Anatolian'.[12] Nevertheless, they also conceded that 'for the oldest stratum, Indo-Anatolian, the lexical evidence for cereal use is relatively modest, but not zero: we must at least admit the cereal term *$(H)ieu(H)$- and perhaps *$ǵ^b(e)rsd$-'. Consequently, if we wish to set the homeland in a CHG area, it must already have obtained domestic animals and at least some domestic plants.

This is not to say that the words might not have originally evolved among a hunting-gathering population but – by ascribing the language to the CHG at 6500 BCE – the plants and animals were presumably domesticates because that is what we find archaeologically throughout the area of the CHG. That is why one could make a plausible case for associating the westward drift of CHG into Anatolian Hunter-Gatherer (AHG) territory with the movement of Proto-Anatolian from a more easterly homeland from the 7th millennium BCE or later. A later date is often preferred on the basis of linguistic palaeontology, as attempts to date the split between Proto-Anatolian and Core-Indo-European have been made on the basis of several *late* Neolithic or Eneolithic innovations (wool, wheeled vehicles, gold and silver; see Chapter 7) that are found in Anatolian or only appear later in Proto-Indo-European.[13] These have led to estimates of *c.* 4300–3800 BCE[14] or, on the basis of computational approaches, the following: Berkeley *c.* 4400 BCE; Moscow 4150–3450 BCE; and Auckland *c.* 4900 BCE but with a range of 6600–3400 BCE.[15] There are two aspects, one linguistic and one genetic, of all these dates that are worth commenting upon.

First, if you accept any date for the separation of Proto-Anatolian between *c.* 6500 and 3500 BCE and you place the language in central Anatolia at that time, your Proto-Anatolians should have had the full complement of domestic cereals (wheat, barley, lentils, pea, vetch, chickpea and grass pea).[16] Irrespective of our ability to reconstruct such an economy from the linguistic evidence, any model placing the Proto-Anatolians in central Anatolia at this period must presume that they arrived with an arable economy and had names for the variety of domesticated and wild plants that they exploited. Our inability to reconstruct hardly any names for domestic plants from Anatolian sources could be for a variety of reasons. Obviously, we may have potential Indo-Anatolian names in Hittite that simply find no matches with other Indo-European languages (e.g. *šeppitt-* 'a kind of grain'). We also have to deal with a writing system that conspires against us in terms of recovering the native terms from the Bronze Age because of the Hittite practice of writing many words with either Sumerograms or Akkadograms – fixed expressions borrowed into the Hittite writing system from Sumerian or Akkadian. We do something similar today when we mentally mouth the word 'dollar' when we see a $ sign (probably all that is left of the *s* in Spanish pesos) or 'pound' for £ (an L derived from Latin *libra*, meaning 'scales'). The index of plant names recovered from the major Hittite site of Boğazköy, for example, cites 29 Hittite words (including tree names), 53 Sumerograms and 41 Akkadograms, which may conceal potential cognate names, e.g. GÚ.TUR 'lentil', GÚ.GAL 'chickpea' and GÚ.ŠEŠ 'bitter vetch'.[17] Alternatively, the underlying/hidden words may be totally unassociated with Indo-European. Moreover, eighty words for plants and another eighty-nine words for foodstuffs in the Hittite vocabulary are reckoned to be foreign loanwords.[18] Knowing whether Proto-Indo-Anatolian arose within a fully agricultural population (that we cannot recover linguistically) or a population at best marginally engaged in arable agriculture is critical to evaluating various homeland models.

Secondly, by this time the AAF-CHG cline had been in place for several thousand years, so the genetic evidence for an east-to-west migration may well be masked by the fact that the genetic signature of Proto-Anatolians would be nearly indistinguishable from earlier east–west flows of CHG. In fact, an obvious problem is, how can we identify the genetic profile of an Anatolian speaker in the first place? As we have already seen, the territory of the CHG must have housed multiple language families; thus, any determination of which CHG stream might have been associated with Proto-Anatolian is extremely challenging.

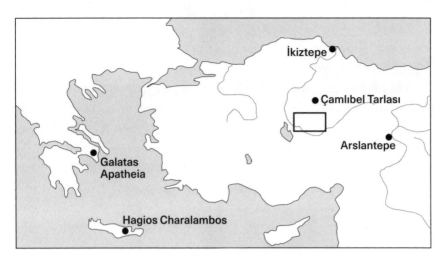

14.2 Sites associated with putative Hittite (box) Y-chromosome haplogroups.

How far we are from accomplishing this can be illustrated by considering one attempt to determine the genetic origins of the Anatolians from samples from several putative Hittite burials in central Anatolia dated to *c.* 1850 BCE.[19] The samples yielded the identification of two Y-haplogroups: G2a2b1 and J2a1. Where else and when are these haplotypes known? G2a2b1 appears at the site of Çamlıbel Tarlası in north-central Anatolia from *c.* 3600 BCE, in a territory we would historically associate with the Hatti, the *non*-Indo-European population who were later absorbed by the Hittites [14.2]. In fact, three of the five putative Hittite samples appear to be from burials that could predate the Hittite conquest of Hatti, while the other two might derive from the conquest period itself when their linguistic identity would be ambiguous.[20] G2a2b1 is also known from İkiztepe (*c.* 3500 BCE) on the north coast, well beyond later Hittite territory (Kaska, and, therefore, perhaps again related to Hattic?), but it is also found in eastern Anatolia *c.* 3400 BCE at Arslantepe (historically Hurrian territory). In short, while it may have derived from a Hittite-speaker, its genetic and linguistic trail may just as easily lead back to a non-Indo-European speaker of Hattic or some other non-Indo-Anatolian language.

As for the other Proto-Anatolian suspect, Y-haplogroup J2a1, its earliest appearance in Anatolia dates to *c*. 3900 BCE and derives from the north coast site of İkiztepe where it continues to *c*. 3300 BCE. It is also found in some abundance at Arslantepe in eastern Anatolia from *c*. 3400 to 2700 BCE. It appears in Bronze Age contexts in Greece at both the Minoan site of Hagios Charalambos cave on Crete (*c*. 2000–1700 BCE) and the Mycenaean site of Galatas Apatheia in the Peloponnese (*c*. 1700–1200 BCE).[21] So far, the putative genetic profile of the Hittites has earlier and later associations with regions that presumably hosted *non*-Indo-Anatolian languages or, in the case of the later Mycenaean site, Greek. Now, I would be the first to admit that building or destroying a case on the basis of incredibly meagre evidence for a few haplogroups should convince no one; I am only playing the hand we are dealt to show how poor it is. But I hope that this provides a sober reminder as to how far we are from having a sufficient amount of evidence – one way or the other – to sort out the problems of migration and language change in Anatolia.

Admittedly, one of the strongest hands played by supporters of the CHG hypothesis is the absence of any evidence for Eastern Hunter-Gatherer (EHG) ancestry or the few characteristic haplogroups associated with it – the expected markers of a steppe origin – at relevant periods in Anatolia, which might indicate the arrival of a population with distant steppe ancestors who introduced Proto-Anatolian.[22] In essence, once AAF and Levantine lineage is excluded, CHG is the only game in town and the burden of proof for anything else clearly rests on the shoulders of Steppe supporters. Against this lack of evidence, the Steppe camp has at least three lines of defence. First, they can maintain that it is still early days and EHG or one of the steppe haplogroups such as R1b may still be found in acceptable quantities and at a suitably early date (see the next chapter). Second, they can note that migrants introducing successful language shifts may still disappear genetically within their host populations. For example, it has been estimated that only 9–22 per cent of modern Turks in Turkey bear genetic evidence of their Central Asian origins.[23] Similarly, comparisons between the actual colonizing horizon of the Magyars (where we do find the type of exotic genetic markers to indicate an origin far to the east)[24] and modern Hungarians only a thousand years later reveal that only 2–4 per cent of the modern population retains evidence of their distant ancestry.²⁵ This emphasizes how important it is to have a sample drawn from the appropriate time (and knowing what that appropriate time period is). And, third, there is some slight evidence for migrations from the steppe region to central Anatolia that has just been published (see Chapter 16). These rebuttals may lie somewhere between informed academic scepticism and clutching at straws, but they do highlight the need for detailed genomic evidence over long periods that can trace the rise and fall of various haplogroups in a population.

Let us move on, assuming for the moment that we will eventually accumulate more convincing genetic support that the Anatolian languages did indeed move into central and western Anatolia from the east. This leaves us with our next problem: how do we deal with the remaining Indo-Anatolians as they evolved into Core-Indo-European? We start with the knowledge that almost all phylogenies and Indo-Europeanists tend to agree that Anatolian separated earliest from the other branches and, equally important, the remaining Core-Indo-Europeans evolved together where, it is claimed, they shared thirty-four innovations.²⁶ This process has been dealt with in two ways. The first is to have the ancestor of the rest of the Indo-Anatolians migrate as a single unit elsewhere, usually to the north where it evolved into Core-Indo-European in a secondary homeland in the Pontic-Caspian steppe, meaning that the Proto-Indo-Anatolian homeland is in eastern Anatolia, while the Core-Indo-European homeland is on the steppe. Alternatively, we can leave them in their primary homeland to evolve into Core-Indo-European and, at some later date, only *some* of the ancestors of the European languages moved northwards while other branches spread both east and west from a homeland south of the Caucasus. This second option is promoted by both Gamkrelidze and Ivanov and those who have updated their earlier Greater Armenian model,²⁷ or reworked the Anatolian Farmer model to associate the spread of the more southerly branches such as Greek and Indo-Iranian with expansions from Anatolia or south of the Caucasus.²⁸

The original Greater Armenian model of Gamkrelidze and Ivanov envisaged a homeland situated in eastern Anatolia, the southern

CHAPTER 14

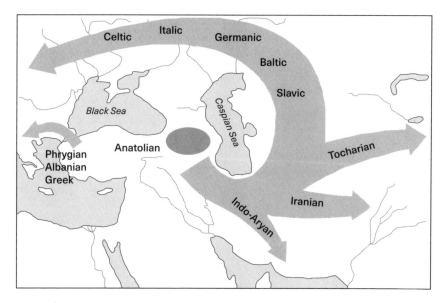

14.3 The Greater Armenian model of Gamkrelidze and Ivanov. Oval indicates approximate area of homeland.

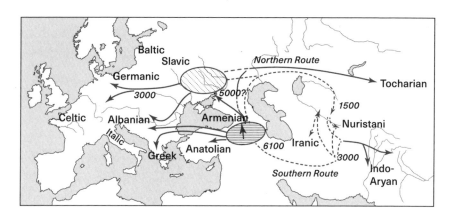

14.4 The 'Hybrid model' of the Auckland team in 2023.

Caucasus and northern Mesopotamia. According to this model, Proto-Anatolian dispersed only a short distance westwards into central Anatolia, followed by a gradual break-up of a common Graeco-Armenian-Indo-Iranian (Southern Indo-European) entity with Greek moving westwards into Greece, and apparently also both Albanian and Phrygian into the Balkans, with the latter returning to Anatolia after the collapse of the Hittites. Also, at a very early period (4th–3rd millennium BCE), the Indo-Iranians began moving eastwards from the north Iranian plain to their historical seats. The (ever-problematic) Tocharians are seen to have departed eastwards across the steppe even before the Indo-Iranians [**14.3**].

As for the 'European' branches, these are believed to have migrated from the original homeland eastwards around the Caspian Sea to the Pontic-Caspian steppe, from which the Steppe model can then explain their dispersal from their secondary homeland. In their most recent version (at least at the time of writing) the Auckland group have proposed a very similar model, rebranded as the 'Hybrid model', utilizing their own phylogeny and a CHG-based homeland apparently situated just south of the Caucasus from whence Anatolian and Tocharian first split, followed by Graeco-Armenian, Albanian and Indo-Iranian. Albanian and Greek (with split dates of 4135 and 3310 BCE respectively) are sent to the west, while Indo-Iranian (with a split date of 4981 BCE) moves east, dividing into its respective branches *c.* 3520 BCE [**14.4**]. We need to take a closer look at how these models might work on the ground.

CHG moves west

So far, we have (at least) two fundamentally different south Caucasian-CHG homeland models. The first places the primary homeland in the south Caucasus and has the Proto-Anatolians move into central Anatolia while *all the rest* of the Indo-European branches move north to evolve into Core-Indo-European in a secondary homeland in the steppe. The second theory does not have the ancestor of all the non-Anatolian branches move off together, but argues that the southern portion of the Indo-European branches expanded west and east, and only a smaller segment moved north to the steppe to spawn some European languages and perhaps Tocharian. This second model faces a hurdle that the first was spared: it must deal with the consequences of an Indo-Anatolian phylogeny that places an earlier Anatolian branch to the west of the homeland (in Anatolia) and then somehow brings Greek and whatever Balkan languages (Albanian, Thracian, Phrygian) it requires even further west.

This problem faced the earlier Gamkrelidze-Ivanov model and continues to confront the most recent attempt at computational phylogeny provided by the Auckland group. If one accepts the median split dates provided in that group's most recent paper (Anatolian 4932 BCE; Greek 3310 BCE), then the Anatolians had about 1,600 years to get comfy in their homes before the Greeks, who must originate to the north or east of the Anatolians, began passing through or around Anatolia to get to their historical seats. The only alternative that I can generate is that the Anatolians got lost somewhere and only managed to find their way into Anatolia *after* the ancestors of the Greeks and Albanians had already passed through on their way to Europe. Their date range provided for Greek is a staggering 2,931 years (4930–1999 BCE), which, for an archaeologist, has one looking for the 'coming of the Greeks' anywhere from the middle Neolithic to the Early Bronze Age. The Auckland team have an even earlier split date for Albanians (4135 BCE, within a range of 5882–2540 BCE), who will have even further to walk.

Since we intercept Hittite moving into north-central Anatolia (the earlier land of the Hatti) and Luvian dominating the west and south, any migration from a Caucasus homeland to the Aegean and Balkans would seem to be confined to the north coast of Anatolia. But it is in the north that we find Palaic, the third and admittedly most poorly known of the Bronze Age Anatolian languages. So we must deal with the migration(s) of Graeco-Balkan Indo-Europeans across a notional distance (from their east Anatolian/south Caucasus homeland) of about 2,000 km (1,200 miles) who left no trace (so far) along any part of their journey. A very long shot would propose that the Phrygians of central Anatolia were actually relics of this migration and not later immigrants from the Balkans but this is most unlikely as the ancient testimony of Herodotus is supported by archaeology.[29]

One scholar who has consistently tried to give the Greater Armenian model archaeological legs is Stanislav Grigoriev,[30] who at least deals with having the Proto-Greeks avoid the obstacle of crossing the earlier territory of the Anatolians by settling the latter in the Balkans (Thrace) and then deriving the Greeks from a migration from northwest Anatolia in Early Helladic II (c. 2450–2200 BCE). This is a well-known and often-suggested solution to the 'coming of the Greeks'. Nevertheless, as Grigoriev himself writes: 'The primordial area of the Greeks should be sought in northeastern Anatolia, from where they moved westward in the second half or the 3rd millennium BC, but a detailed justification of this issue can only be made on Anatolian materials.'[31] And this is what we so far lack. We, therefore, have to wonder about a migration that could yield several Indo-European branches at its end points (Greek, Albanian) but leave no obvious linguistic legacy along the way. In other words, why do we not find the ancestors of the Proto-Greeks or Proto-Albanians all along the southern coast of the Black Sea?

Even more troublesome is the putative path of this migration in northeastern Anatolia, which is also indicated roughly on the map supplied by those supporting the 'Hybrid model' (see **14.4**). The homeland itself is given a date of c. 6100 BCE, while the split date for Greek is around 3300 BCE. Working backwards, we might suppose that the Greeks began their migration from a homeland in eastern Anatolia or immediately to its west at some time after c. 6000 BCE and before 3000 BCE. As mentioned before, this area was occupied by the Kura-Araxes Bronze Age culture in the period c. 3500–2000 BCE,[32] which extended as far north into the Caucasus as Georgia and Dagestan [**14.5**]. By the last centuries of its existence we have evidence that the language of the southern part of the Kura-Araxes included Hurrian; later written testimony from the Caucasus reveals the linguistic identity of that region to be the closely related Urartian language. Hence the Kura-Araxes culture would appear to be associated with the Hurro-Urartian languages. This culture effectively closes the gate at c. 3500 BCE on any expansion westwards from a putative south Caucasus/northern Mesopotamian homeland by placing a (admittedly only 'probable') wall of Hurro-Urartians between a putative Caucasian homeland and Indo-Europeans

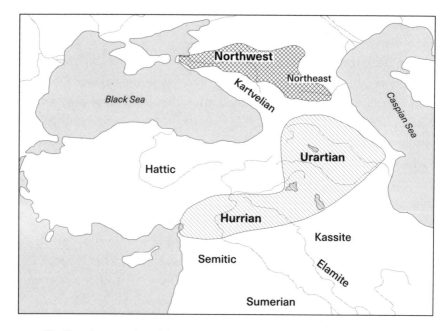

14.5 The Kura-Araxes culture (diagonal hatching) and the Hurro-Urartian languages. In the north we find the area of the Maykop culture (crosshatching), which coincides largely with the area of the Northwest Caucasian languages.

to its west. A Proto-Indo-Anatolian homeland in the south Caucasus/northern Mesopotamia region must therefore date before 3500 BCE.

The period before the Kura-Araxes culture, the Eneolithic, extends from the end of the Neolithic Halaf until the cultural transformation of c. 3500 BCE and – if you are into hidden homelands – eastern Anatolia is probably as good a candidate as you could wish. As archaeologist Giulio Palumbi has remarked: 'eastern Anatolia is still a frontier area as far as research is concerned, with dramatic information gaps; Neolithic developments are little known in the region, and the Chalcolithic is more enigmatic still'.[33] There are few generalizations that can be made, since this period is marked by several different cultural ceramic traditions. One of the main themes, however, appears to be north–south rather than east–west trajectories, apparently driven by the rise in demand for metals and other resources of the Caucasus in the communities of northern

Mesopotamia and adjacent areas of southeast Anatolia.[34] If one wishes to set the homeland in this region at the period between the Halaf and the later Kura-Araxes, there is little evidence that we are talking about a relatively uniform cultural phenomenon covering a broad area, and we have no solid case for it expanding westwards.

The earliest period to offer a possible candidate as a homeland in eastern Anatolia would be the Middle Aceramic period of southeastern Anatolia *c.* 7500–6000 BCE, when we find settled occupation exploiting either wild or domesticated wheat and barley and potentially other domesticable plants as well as ovicaprids (domestic sheep and goats), pigs and, lastly, cattle. The sites are located in a band west of Lake Van in Turkey on the southernmost strip where dry farming was possible.[35] The obvious problem with assigning the origins of a later western expansion from this region is that it is a Neolithic hearth, a centre of domestication, and so both in terms of date and the Indo-European phylogeny, one would assign this far more plausibly to the separation of Proto-Anatolian and presume that the ancestors of Greek and Albanian must have been associated with a still later spread of CHG to the west after the establishment of the AAF-CHG genetic cline by 6500 BCE. In conclusion, the Indo-European phylogeny is not very kind to attempts to derive Greek or the Balkan languages from a homeland *east* of the Anatolians.

CHG moves east

The CHG homeland models (both the Greater Armenian and the so-called 'Hybrid' models) also require a migration eastwards from a south Caucasus homeland that accounts for the Indo-Iranians. The basis of this argument is the predominance of CHG in southern Iran and the presumption that this population probably carried both agriculture and the Indo-Aryan branch into India. The Auckland model suggests a split date of *c.* 4981 BCE (range 6395–3645 BCE) for Indo-Iranian, with the two major branches of Indo-Aryan and Iranian splitting *c.* 3520 BCE (range 4796–2535 BCE). The model does not exclude the possibility of a northern (steppe) entry for the Indo-Iranians (the one proposed by the Steppe model), but reduces its attractiveness by arguing for a separation date for

Indo-Iranian as early as that of all the five European branches associated with the Steppe model. Nor (unlike most phylogenies) does it find any close links between Indo-Iranian and Balto-Slavic, which would favour an Indo-Iranian homeland further north. Earlier, in 2014, Colin Renfrew and Paul Heggarty linked the spread of Indo-Iranian with the spread of agriculture from eastern Anatolia to India via the north Iranian plain.[36] This 'southern route' is cartographically depicted by the Auckland group as a migration from south of the Caucasus along the Zagros mountains and then northeastwards through Iran to Pakistan/northern India (see 14.4). This at least has the advantage of following what little archaeological evidence supports an agricultural trail from the west towards India,[37] but it still faces a mire of problems.

Phylogenetically, we are again into constituency territory, where both the Ringe and Moscow phylogenies place Indo-Iranian alongside Balto-Slavic (thus requiring a geographical solution that gives them a closer common origin) and the computational dates for the Indo-Iranian split are much more recent (Berkeley: *c*. 3000 BCE; Moscow: 2500 BCE). In the most recent assessment of the phylogenetic position of Indo-Iranian, linguist Martin Kümmel concludes that Indo-Iranian does not have a 'clear next relative' and regards it as possible that it departed early. But he also goes on to write:

> There is good evidence for early proximity to Eastern Europe – with different developments shared with either the south (Greek, Albanian, Armenian) or the north (Baltic-Slavic, Germanic), or with the east (satem languages). An original position at the eastern fringe of Europe is corroborated by contacts with both Western and Eastern Uralic.[38]

From a purely linguistic standpoint, placing the origins of the Indo-Iranians south of the Caucasus and having them achieve their historical seats by migrating south along the Zagros or due east around the Caspian appears to be opposed by a considerable majority of linguistic opinion that favours an origin placing the ancestors of Indo-Iranian in contact with eastern European languages. Archaeologically, we have already seen that majority or at least traditional opinion looks to a northern (steppe) origin for Indo-Iranian.

Any attempt to associate the Indo-Aryans with the spread of agriculture from the Zagros eastwards must somehow devise an explanation for why this very area, from *c.* 2250–400 BCE when we have access to their writings, was occupied by the non-Indo-European Elamites. This is not only an issue regarding the fact that the Indo-Iranians or Indo-Aryans would have had to pass through what was clearly a large territory of non-Indo-Europeans, but also raises the question that, if Indo-Iranian had dispersed with agriculture to the east, why do we not find a trail of (proto-?) Indo-Iranian languages occupying the path of their own migration?

There is little doubt that the archaeological origins of those Indo-Europeans who occupied western Iran to form the empires of the Medes and Persians as well as the Indo-Aryans of the northern two-thirds of India are still open questions, devoid of anything remotely resembling a majority opinion or truly solid archaeological evidence. But whether one seeks Indo-Iranian origins south of the Caucasus or derives them from the steppe, both sides have usually tended to agree on one thing: the Sintashta culture (2200–1750 BCE; see **9.15**) of the southern Urals is an important element in any solution to Indo-Iranian origins and is widely accepted as being associated with either Proto-Indo-Iranian or some later downstream period of this branch.[39] As the precursor of the vast Andronovo culture (*c.* 2000–900 BCE), it provides the archaeological basis of the steppe nomads of the later Iron Age, who are the bearers of historically attested eastern Iranian languages ranging from the European steppe (Scythians) to Xinjiang (Khotanese Saka).

So the question of the Sintashta culture's origins is of considerable importance in supporting any homeland solution. The case for a Near Eastern origin has been most extensively advanced by Grigoriev (who is honest enough to admit that 'it is not popular'[40]). As an archaeologist working in the same region as the Sintashta culture, he has assembled a large and detailed comparison between Sintashta and both neighbouring and more distant cultures.[41] Nevertheless, an essentially steppe origin could be regarded as the standard position of most archaeologists involved with the issue.[42] Because of its status as a flashpoint, the Sintashta culture has been well sampled by geneticists (over fifty samples) which, other than a few outliers, clearly supports an origin associated with the Corded Ware horizon and its eastern offshoot, the Fatyanovo culture. This brings the Sintashta well into the archaeological and genetic orbit of those cultures that derive ultimately from the Pontic-Caspian steppe.[43] It might also be noted that attempts to reverse the logic (the argument that the presence of Indo-Iranians in the steppelands indicates how far they had managed to travel from their homeland in India)[44] lacks any archaeological or genetic evidence. We will have to revisit this issue when we come to the Steppe model in the next chapter. Without doubt, however, there are evidently strong archaeological and genetic arguments for seeking the origin of the Iranians – and by extension the Indo-Aryans – in the steppe rather than south of the Caucasus.

CHG moves north

All the different varieties of homelands situated in either the southern Caucasus or northern Mesopotamia propose a secondary homeland to account for at least some if not all the other Indo-European languages (other than Anatolian) in the Pontic-Caspian steppe. To achieve this secondary homeland requires some form of migration from south to north, and requires one to show how CHG ancestry – here for the sake of argument accepted as the genetic vector for Indo-European – spread into the steppelands and ultimately formed the poster-child of steppe dispersals, the Yamnaya culture. In the following section, we will examine this issue in three time periods: the Mesolithic, in case CHG had already established the genetic signature of steppe populations long before the rise of the Yamnaya culture; the Neolithic, which might suggest an association of the spread of CHG with the earliest farmers north of the Caucasus; and the Early Bronze Age of the northern Caucasus, which might explain the spread of CHG northwards as part of the influence of the Early Bronze Age Maykop culture promoting some form of elite dominance over the steppe peoples.

CHG and the Mesolithic

As we saw earlier, most of our evidence for steppe settlement is concentrated in the Dnipro-Donets region in the west and the Middle Volga region in the east (with some archaeological but little genetic evidence from the Lower Volga/Caspian region). Did CHGs enter the steppe during the Mesolithic and admix on a significant scale with the local EHG population and thereby spread Indo-European among local hunter-gatherers? In samples obtained from the Ukrainian Mesolithic, usually localized to the lower Dnipro region, CHG is found at a low *c.* 5 per cent.[45] A 2023 study of samples from both the Mesolithic and the following Neolithic (which largely involved a fish-based economy with a minimum of evidence for domestic livestock) estimated the amount of CHG at about 7 per cent and the authors emphasized the approximately four thousand years of genetic continuity between the Mesolithic and Neolithic (between *c.* 8500 and 4200 BCE).[46] Looking eastwards, the meagre contemporaneous evidence for the Samara region of the Volga also suggests no more than 5 per cent CHG. However, in 2024 the Copenhagen lab published two burials from the Middle Don region (Golubaya Krinitsa; see **15.3**) dating to *c.* 5400 BCE that revealed 18–24 per cent CHG with an estimated admixture date of *c.* 6300 BCE, clearly indicating substantial intermixing between local hunter-gatherers and a population originating in the Caucasus.[47]

As for the uniparental DNA, the Y-chromosome haplogroups from Ukrainian sites were R1a, R1b and I2a, indicating a local origin for the main haplogroups, which we will see continued much later in the Yamnaya culture (this also would include the two early burials with high CHG from the Middle Don region). The evidence for mitochondrial DNA (mtDNA) was mainly variants of haplogroups of U4 and U5, again classic markers of the Yamnaya and its descendants. Haplogroup U4a is found in the Neolithic of the Caucasus but at a later date than in Ukraine, and in the Caucasus it is associated with the Y-haplogroup R1b, which speaks for a slight ingression of a steppe population southwards *into* the Caucasus rather than the reverse. All of this evidence indicates that neither the autosomal evidence (which is far too small to account for the 50:50 ratio with EHG that we find in the later Yamnaya) nor the haplogroups support a model where CHG spread to form the Yamnaya genetic profile during the Mesolithic or earlier, although there does appear to be clear evidence of some gene flow northwards from the Caucasus as early as the Mesolithic.[48]

CHG and the Neolithic

An obvious vector for the spread of Indo-European would be the same as that of the Anatolian Farmer model – that is, the spread of agriculture – so can we mount an argument that after the departure of Proto-Anatolian, early farmers from south of the Caucasus/northern Mesopotamia carried Core-Indo-European northwards through the Caucasus and then introduced their genes, economy and language to the EHG population of the steppelands?

Although the Neolithic economy appears quite early in eastern Anatolia and adjacent regions of the Zagros, it did not penetrate the Caucasus until *c.* 6400 BCE. By far the greatest collection of sites is associated with the Aratashen-Shulaveri-Shomutepe (ASS) culture, which appeared in the Kura-Araxes region *c.* 6000–5000 BCE (see **9.16**). Situated in new locations and bearing a novel architecture (round mud-brick houses), economy (mixed agriculture including emmer wheat, barley, lentils, pea and bitter vetch) and material culture, one can deduce that we are dealing with an intrusive, well-developed Neolithic culture from further south, with about 150 known sites.[49] The precise origins of the ASS are problematic, nor do the ceramics yet appear to provide any clear leads, although bone and antler tools have been compared with implements from eastern Anatolia.[50] There is also evidence of exchange relations with the Halaf culture seen in ceramics, but these are regarded only as evidence of contacts and not of origins, since the northernmost Halaf site is Tilkitepe (see **13.1**) in eastern Anatolia.

Let us recall that before the Neolithic we find the Mesolithic site of Kotias Klde (*c.* 8000–7600 BCE), which is one of the archetypal sites defining the CHG genetic signature. The palaeogenetic evidence indicates a spread of 'southern' populations (AAF/Levantine), seen in our earliest Neolithic samples derived from sites such as Aknashen (*c.* 6000–5800 BCE), a settlement along the Araxes river on the Ararat Plain. Here the local CHG ancestry was retained at about 42 per cent and the rest came from farmers from the south (AAF/Levantine), while the CHG contribution at the nearby site of Masis Blur was reduced to about 14 per cent. The genetic trail northwards from the Kura-Araxes region to the northern Caucasus and on to the steppelands is associated with the 'Aknashen-like' profile and we will have to keep this in mind when we follow the routes of CHG out into the steppe. But we will also have to deal with an alternative flavour of CHG, more closely related to that of the sample taken from the Mesolithic site of Kotias Klde in Georgia, which the Harvard (Reich) lab simply designates 'CHG-related' and was present since before the Neolithic.[51]

One issue with associating the Indo-Europeans with the northwards spread of agriculture is that in the ASS culture we are dealing with an archaeological entity defined according to a series of specific traits (architecture, economy, ceramics and other material culture) that is geographically confined. While the genetic trail leads north there is no material evidence that this culture was fully replicated beyond the southern Caucasus to spread through the steppes. Unlike the Anatolian Farmer model, which involved the spread of one major population group (AAF) over a different population (Western Hunter-Gatherer/WHG), in Europe, the South Caucasus model has the homeland begin in what was once presumably a predominantly CHG territory but by the Neolithic was already heavily admixed with AAF, and then pass through the Caucasus. Only in the steppe does it encounter EHG to form the classic genetic mixture of steppe expansions (EHG + CHG with a smaller amount of AAF). Here we may follow the spread of genetic signatures and possibly domestic livestock northwards, but we are not dealing with the same level of comparable archaeological materiality that we find between Neolithic Anatolia and southeast Europe that was interpreted as a wave of advance.

As the AAF-CHG cline had developed by $c.$ 6500 BCE, it is no surprise that the autosomal DNA associated with the earliest farmers in the Caucasus was already an admixture of CHG and AAF. There are few early Neolithic sites sampled genetically and they all exhibit an admixture. While the earliest samples tend to have more CHG – suggesting the possibility that it was a more CHG-dominant population in the earliest Neolithic – the number of samples is far too small to be confident of such a conclusion.[52] A key issue is that we do not have an adequate picture of the population of the Caucasus on the eve of the Neolithic, and so it is difficult to employ the autosomal evidence to sort out the specific regional origins of the earliest farmers in the Caucasus. This leaves us with the mtDNA and Y-based DNA [**14.6**] and here too there is really very limited evidence, which renders it more difficult to determine the identity of CHG immigrants in the steppe. At best we can note the genetic makeup of the Palaeolithic site of Satsurblia in Georgia (Y: J1b; mt: K3) and the Mesolithic site of Kotias Klde (Y: J2a; mt: H13c) and regard these as 'local' within the CHG world. But without more Mesolithic evidence it is still impossible to be certain whether the earliest, presumably intrusive, farmer population was really distinct from the local hunting-gathering population native to the Kura-Araxes region. We can only note that J2a is also found in early Neolithic Anatolia and Europe as well as several of the earliest Neolithic sites in Armenia, while haplotypes of mtDNA H are also found in the Armenian Neolithic sites. The other site offering Y-chromosome evidence is Areni-1 in Armenia, a cave site noted for its evidence of early winemaking, which dates to c. 4300–4000 BCE and exhibits Y-haplogroup L1a1. Outside of Armenia this haplogroup is most anciently recovered thousands of years later in the Swat Valley in Pakistan, and it is in India and Pakistan that it is highest among modern populations. But, until we are able to fill in the gaps of our knowledge, we will not be able to identify precisely where the earliest farmers in the Caucasus originated nor – assuming that they are the vector also for the origin of Proto-Indo-European – the homeland of all the branches except, perhaps, for Anatolian.

To complicate matters further we should recall that the ASS Neolithic also occupied the heartland of the later Bronze Age Kura-Araxes culture. Most scholars would, I think, regard this culture as far more plausibly ancestral to the Hurro-Urartian language family than Indo-Anatolian. If this is so, then one could construct any number of models to explain the rise of Hurro-Urartian – for example, that it was rooted in the original Mesolithic culture, that it was a product of the earliest farmers bearing

Site	Date (BCE)	Y-chromosome	mtDNA
Satsurblia	11,460–11,225	J1b	K3
Kotias Klde	7940–7599	J2a	H13c
Aknashen	5985–5600	J2a1a1b1a1a	I1(x2)
			H2+152
			H15a1
Masis Blur	5633–5532	J2a1a1a2a	K
Areni-1	4486–3500	L1a1(x3)	H
			H2a1
			K1a8c (x2)
			U4a
			U8b1a1

14.6 Ancient DNA (aDNA) evidence from Neolithic and earlier sites of the Caucasus (x denotes multiples).

an Aknashen-like genetic signature or that it was introduced by farmers later in the Neolithic when still more AAF genes arrived.

As for the northern Caucasus, farming arrived *c.* 6000 BCE. Although it is very poorly known, we might generate a different potential CHG source by proposing that Indo-Anatolian need not have been associated genetically with those farmers who undertook the initial spread of agriculture northwards from the Fertile Crescent. Instead, as we have already seen with regard to the transition from AHG to AAF in central and west Anatolia, we could have a local CHG population of the north Caucasus adopt agriculture from its southern neighbours and have them spread their own genes, economy and language northwards. This way we provide CHG with an economic vector (domestic livestock) that would give their society an advantage as it spread across the hunter-gatherer populations of the Pontic-Caspian but also did not saddle it with the full suite of domestic plants (wheat, barley, peas, lentils and pulses) that linguistic palaeontology has been unable to reconstruct for the proto-language and that are absent from the steppe sites. As the date of domestic livestock in the Middle Volga region falls between *c.* 5000 and 4800 BCE,[53] we might envisage a model whereby CHG populations moved north from the Caucasus and spread their domestic animals and language up the Volga, the introduction of livestock providing a socio-economic stimulus for both their expansion and the spread of language. For example, domesticated animals were found at Ekaterinovka Mys in the Middle Volga, where the human population carried about a quarter of their ancestry from a CHG-related source from the south.[54] As these would not be carriers of Aknashen-type CHG, this might speak for some acculturation of local CHG peoples who preceded those who were descendants of the early farmers of the Kura-Araxes region.

Domestic livestock was found somewhat earlier among peoples along the Dnipro about 5500 BCE.[55] While we could push the argument that the arrival of domestic livestock in the Middle Volga region might have been associated with the spread of CHG, the inception of livestock-keeping in the Dnipro region is more problematic, especially as the earliest evidence (so far) for domesticated animals in the north Caucasus falls between *c.* 4700 and 4300 BCE, about a millennium *later* than the dates from the Dnipro. On the one hand, recent genetic analysis of the lower Dnipro Neolithic populations has claimed that there is no evidence for the genes of European (ultimately Anatolian) farmers,[56] which would leave the most convenient western (Balkan) origin for the earliest domesticates in the Dnipro region strangely unsupported by the evidence of human DNA. On the other hand, the lack of a major injection of CHG into the Dnipro population at such an early date, coupled with the distances involved, convinced Leonid Zaliznyak to dismiss the idea that farmers from the Caucasus brought domestic livestock to the Ukrainian steppe.[57]

The prospect of having two different origins for stock-keeping in the steppe – the Caucasus and the Balkans – poses both archaeological and linguistic problems. If we regard the introduction of domestic livestock to the steppe as a major potential vehicle for the spread of a new language, then knowing from precisely where the economy derived is absolutely critical. And if we entertain the possibility that the steppe derived its domestic economy from two different sources (one western Balkan and one southern Caucasus) this would lead to a pretty devilish linguistic situation. Even if the names of domestic livestock were derived ultimately from a common AAF-CHG homeland in eastern Anatolia, the different routes (Balkans versus Caucasus) and the time of separation would ensure that they were not the same when they arrived in the steppe. Yet both of these (linguistically diverse?) regions have been proposed as the major components of the European steppe 'spread zone' that should have come into existence at least from the initial formation of the Yamnaya cultural area *c.* 3300 BCE – an area where one presumes there was a steppe dominated by a mobile (domestic horse, wheeled vehicle) pastoral population. In short, no matter which homeland solution one embraces, if it involves the Pontic-Caspian steppe as a primary or secondary homeland, we are dealing with problems that are probably a lot more complex than usually imagined.

Setting aside the original source of domestic livestock in the Dnipro region, we do have some evidence that, in the period *c.* 4500–4000 BCE, both domestic livestock and CHG genes had begun to spread north of the Caucasus. In the north Caucasus itself we find the site of Unakozovskaya yielding two burials dating to *c.* 4500 BCE. These fit well within the genetic ambience of the farmers of the region, displaying as much as 80 per cent CHG and boasting the haplogroups one might expect from a population moving from a more southerly region (Y: J2a and mt: R1a), while showing no evidence of the local steppe EHG [**14.7**]. The particular brand of CHG at this site was Aknashen-like, so this could support the notion that whatever the northern limits of the earlier ASS culture (described above), the genetic signature of its population did manage to make it to the north. But further north in the piedmont region of the steppe we encounter two burials from the site of Progress-2 where CHG is at 45 per cent and EHG is 55 per cent, approximating our autosomal targets. Here, however, the flavour of CHG was CHG-related (i.e. more closely tied to the earlier Mesolithic type than that of Aknashen). The haplogroups are Y: R1b and mt: H2 and I3a. I3a is associated with the steppe and steppe-derived cultures, while H2 is found in the Neolithic of the Caucasus and in Neolithic sites in Europe and is suspected to have arrived as part of the spread of a CHG-related population (livestock-keepers?) from the south. Here I have tried to determine the probable origins of the haplogroups – southern (Anatolian-Caucasus)

Period	Site	Date (BCE)	Y-chromosome	mtDNA
Eneolithic Caucasus	Unakozovskaya	4594–4404	J, J2a	R1a (x3)
Eneolithic Steppe	Progress-2	4338–4047	R1b1 (x2)	H2, I3a
	Vonyuchka 1	4332–4238		T2a1b

14.7 Ancient DNA (aDNA) evidence for Eneolithic sites of the north Caucasus and adjacent steppe.

versus northern (steppe) – to clarify the nature of the admixture with respect to uniparental lines and this will be continued throughout the next chapter, although the current state of sampling means that this form of genetic train-spotting is extremely dodgy and often I cannot be confident of assigning any immediate origins to particular haplogroups. A good example comes from another one of our Eneolithic steppe sites, Vonyuchka.

In 14.7 we find that a woman from Vonyuchka 1 carried mtDNA T2a1b. She is the earliest burial I have been able to find with this precise haplogroup; the next instance I can find is about six hundred years later where the same haplogroup is found belonging to a man buried in a megalithic tomb in Spain, about 3,700 km (2,300 miles) away. Then at c. 2200 BCE it turns up again in a Beaker burial in Germany, but two hundred years later we find T2a1b in the burial of a woman in southern Siberia, more than 6,000 km (3,700 miles) to the east. Then, a thousand years later, we find it associated with a male burial in the Swat Valley of Pakistan. The haplogroup then completes its unbridled quest for frequent-flyer miles by appearing in France in the burial of a Gaul dated to c. 100 BCE. If we plotted all these points on a map, connecting the dots in chronological order, we might have a rip-roaring scenario for a television series ('The Marvellous Adventures of T2a1b') but I would hate to have to sell it as a convincing history of human migration. We can, of course, generate explanations for our various dots on a map – for example, finding

T2a1b in south Russia and Spain *before* putative steppe migrations might suggest that it was associated with the spread of the Neolithic from southwest Asia both westwards (to Spain) and northwards (to Russia) and hence have a Near Eastern source.[58] After that, its presence from the Atlantic to the Yenisei river might be attributed to steppe expansions but, given the fact that it was already found in Spain in the Neolithic, why should we have to bring it 'back' to Gaul with the Beakers? It could have been sitting there since the Neolithic or only arrived with the Beaker culture or, perhaps, is evidence of a still later Celtic expansion. Where we have more abundant evidence – for example, Y-haplogroup I2a2b (I2-L38) – we have extensive attempts to plot the course of migrations through time and space[59] but such studies are still relatively rare and in their infancy. The sites of Progress-2 and Vonyuchka 1 also both exhibit traces of West Siberian Hunter-Gatherer (WSHG) ancestry, indicating some gene flow between Central Asia and the European steppe – but hardly enough to support the Asiatic Steppe homeland model.

What we find here then, stemming from the Neolithic of the Caucasus, are two streams of CHG, an earlier CHG-related and a somewhat later Aknashen-like Neolithic, which began penetrating the steppe in the Eneolithic during the 5th millennium BCE. The stream found in the northern Caucasus, with respect to both sex chromosomes, reflects populations derived from the earliest farmers of the Kura-Araxes region. The earliest ones found on the steppe itself, however, appear to derive from an earlier-rooted form of CHG-related and they exhibit Y-chromosomes associated with the steppelands rather than the Caucasus and a mixture of local and Caucasian mtDNA. We will have to follow both of these streams in the next chapter when we trace how they interacted with the native steppe populations and whether they play a critical role in the formation of those more expansive steppe cultures that are traditionally associated with Indo-European origins and dispersals.

CHG and the Maykop culture

The third possible explanation for CHG in the steppe focuses on the Early Bronze Age and the rise of the Maykop culture.[60] After the introduction of agriculture, a pre-Maykop culture arose in the north Caucasus (*c.* 4500–3800 BCE), found at a number of sites with evidence for large stone walls or ditches, economies based on both livestock and hunting, and early copper working. This culture was in contact with the Pontic region, in particular the Cucuteni-Trypillia culture (see **9.5**), seen in parallels in some material culture. From this period the site of Nal'chik emerges, with its cemetery that anticipates later cemeteries on both the steppe and also in central Europe. The 147 burials were placed under small mounds and accompanied by red ochre, two traits typical of the much later Yamnaya culture. But (admittedly somewhat enigmatically) the site also bears similarity to the Corded Ware culture in a way not seen in the Yamnaya: although it lacks the formal burial orientation of the Corded Ware it does employ the same sexual patterning by usually depositing males on their right side and females on their left. At an approximate date of *c.* 5000–4500 BCE, however, it predates both the Yamnaya and Corded Ware cultures by about fifteen hundred years or more.[61] Thus the sexual dimorphism in burial practice where males are routinely laid on their right sides while females are on their left (or the reverse) might arise independently in different regions.

The Maykop culture (*c.* 3800–3000 BCE) occupied the territory stretching from the Sea of Azov across the northern Caucasus almost to the Caspian Sea (see **14.5**). Although about thirty settlements have been discovered these often tend to be slight; the culture is best known from its burials, about three hundred of them under mounds (kurgans). These are generally poorly furnished with grave goods but there are also enormous barrows with extraordinarily rich grave gifts that link the Maykop culture with Central Asia – for example, trade items such as lapis lazuli and turquoise, artistic motifs and fine metalwork (with parallels in Anatolia and Mesopotamia and the cultures north of the Caucasus). The burial ritual was usually flexed on the right side with head oriented to the south, the body sprinkled with red ochre, either inserted into a pit roofed with logs or on the ground surface in a timber-built or stone-built chamber. Exceptional 'royal' burials were incredibly rich, the most famous of which held 2 kg (4½ lb) of gold and 3 kg (6½ lb) of silver objects, along with tools (axes) and weapons (daggers) of copper or bronze. While much of this material finds foreign parallels to the south (although locally manufactured), a uniquely Maykop object is a series of cauldrons fashioned from sheet bronze.

The Maykop culture enters the homeland debate because of its putative impact on the steppe population north of the Caucasus. In the 1980s, Marija Gimbutas's Steppe model viewed this culture as the stimulus of a second wave of Indo-European expansions (*c.* 3400–3200 BCE), but that was not associated with the initial spread nor regarded as a prime vector for the dispersal of Indo-European.[62] Rather, she expanded the definition of the Maykop culture to embrace the entire territory from the Caucasus north of the Black Sea to the mouth of the Danube, incorporating within it a number of early fortified sites in Ukraine, suggesting that the parallels in ceramics, stone and metal artefacts demonstrated 'the probable unification of this region by commercial contacts and perhaps by political power'. There was no question of a 'Maykop solution' to the homeland problem and here it was effectively subsumed into the Steppe model. She also regarded the Maykop phenomenon as a regional break with the earliest centre of dispersal, the Middle Volga area, which was now replaced, at least so far as the rest of Europe was concerned, with the territory between the Danube and the Caucasus.

More recently, however, Danish archaeologist Kristian Kristiansen has argued that the Maykop culture was in fact Proto-Indo-Anatolian, providing the most likely archaeological and genetic source for migrations into both Anatolia and the steppe. In an admittedly conjectural scenario (Kristian is good at that sort of thing), he argues that Maykop was Proto-Anatolian (occupying possibly the same area as Proto-Indo-Anatolian), and that the Proto-Anatolian branch may have crossed by sea to the north coast of Anatolia (İkiztepe near Bafra is a possible route) before descending towards its historical seats in central and southwest Anatolia. As for Core-Indo-European, this was seen as a product of the expansion of Maykop into the neighbouring Volga steppes where it formed the Steppe Maykop, which 'introduced a superior cattle-based pastoral economy and transportation technology to the pre-Yamnaya groups living in the steppe in the mid to late 4th millennium BC'.[63]

The core of a Maykop solution to Indo-European origins essentially rests with not only providing a source of CHG to steppe populations but also (depending on which precise model of their origins you wish to work with[64]) purportedly introducing to the steppe some of its most iconic aspects of mortuary practice such as kurgan burial, wooden chamber and use of ochre, a superior stock-raising economy and a stratified society associated with a prestige (presumably) Indo-European language that would prompt the local EHG population to adopt the language of the CHG elite. Alternatively, it was perhaps a cultural and linguistic vector that, as Alexander Kozintsev has argued, was accompanied by 'little or no gene flow' as it spread late Proto-Indo-European to the steppe.[65]

What is the actual physical evidence of the Maykop population in the steppe? We have already seen that penetration of the steppe by the Maykop culture is attested by the appearance of a Steppe Maykop culture in the Don-Caspian region immediately north of the Caucasus (see 9.18).[66] The number of burials so far recorded is about thirty-two; these are dated to c. 3800–3000 BCE and regarded as early migrations of the Maykop population into the steppe. The accompanying grave goods reveal their source in the Caucasus (ceramics, ornaments, etc.), but it should be emphasized that they are not the first pastoralists in evidence in this area. Earlier, the same region was occupied by a Steppe Eneolithic (c. 4300–3800 BCE), attested by eighteen burials, found in pit graves, displaying a similar posture to the later Yamnaya culture (on their backs but with legs flexed), sprinkled with ochre and with a small kurgan on top. In other words, we have pre-Maykop burials already exhibiting some of the main characteristics of the later Yamnaya culture. The material culture of these graves showed variation as well as similarities, and formed what archaeologist Igor Vasiliev (1948–2004) regarded as a Macro-Eneolithic horizon, an assortment of different populations who were interacting with one another.[67] This was all part of a larger system that linked distant populations from the Dnipro, Don and Middle and Lower Volga during the Neolithic and Eneolithic. The later Steppe Maykop was marked by the introduction of catacomb burials (where the burial chamber was offset from the initial shaft), which would appear far more widely but also later across the steppe region. It might be noted that while the burials assigned to both the Steppe Eneolithic and Steppe Maykop have been found in relatively small numbers, especially given the length of their existence, the following Yamnaya culture, the target of much of our discussion, is known in the same region from 732 burials (3000–2350 BCE). Maykop had an impact on cultures to its north, but the magnitude of its impact on the Caspian steppe appears to be relatively limited.

David Anthony has argued that both the autosomal composition of the Maykop culture and the different suite of Y-haplogroups (Maykop comprises L, J and G2, while Yamnaya is overwhelmingly R1b) make the Maykop culture a poor potential source for Yamnaya origins.[68] This is an opinion shared by others including the influential genetics blogger Davidski.[69] If we wished to imagine that Maykop male elites had moved out onto the steppe and superimposed themselves on local populations, there is no evidence for this in the male genealogies of the Yamnaya population [**14.8**].[70] A further problem with locating a secondary Indo-Anatolian homeland in the Maykop area is obviously the fact that such a homeland has been historically occupied by the North Caucasian languages.

Culture	Site	Date (BCE)	Y-chromosome	mtDNA
Maykop Novosvobodnaya	Klady	3696–3358	G2a2a J2a1 (x2)	R1a T2c1 U1b (x2) X2f
Maykop	Nogir 3	3907–3545	J J2a1	15
	Baksanenok	c. 3700–3000		HV
	Marinskaya 5	3627–3383		U5a1b1
Late Maykop	Sinyukha	3347–3022	L	U4c1 (x3)
	Marinskaya 5	3364–3035	L (x2)	K1a4 T1a2 T2a1
Steppe Maykop	Aygurskiy 2	3630–3372		H2a1 T2e
	Ipatovo 3	3331–2885		X1'2'3
	Sharakhalsun 6	3619–3105	R1 Q1a2	I5b U7b

14.8 Haplogroups of the Maykop and Steppe Maykop cultures.

On balance, of the three possible windows for the spread of CHG to the steppe, a dispersal beginning with the Neolithic tends to appear genetically and chronologically most plausible although there would also be a subsequent impact expected from the later Maykop culture.

CHG and Armenian

One of the greatest hurdles facing a CHG homeland located south of the Caucasus is the linguistic landscape of the Caucasus itself. In assessing the priority of CHG versus EHG in the formation of Indo-European, Armenian occupies a significant position as it is the only Indo-European language that can be placed within the Caucasus itself during the earliest dispersal of the Indo-European branches. There are other Indo-European languages, such as Ossetic and other Iranian languages, whose speakers came to settle in the Caucasus during the Iron Age, but these are downstream of any Iranian homeland and are usually attributed to incursions of steppe nomads such as the Sarmatians or Alans during the Iron Age. On the other hand, Armenian is an independent branch of Indo-European whose origins have long been disputed.[71] A recent paper, however, has shown that an Armenian origin is most plausibly explained genetically by a migration southwards from the steppe that carried the genetic signature of the steppe populations (male haplogroup R1b-M269) into Armenia where it became widespread *after* the Kura-Araxes culture, the archaeological entity most likely associated with the Hurro-Urartian language family. Its arrival date is estimated at *c*. 2500 BCE to account for the level of admixture found in Armenian populations from *c*. 2000 BCE onwards.[72] The date of the genetic evidence coincides very well with the initiation of the Bedeni-Trialeti phase of the Early Kurgan culture,[73] which has long been associated with the southern spread of Indo-Europeans on purely archaeological grounds within the Steppe model.[74]

This evidence has been recently disputed by the Auckland group, who have argued that 'Ancient Armenians carry predominantly a mix of mostly CHG/Iranian-like (40–60 per cent) and Anatolian Neolithic-like ancestry (20–40 per cent) and receive only a late contribution of steppe ancestry during the Late Bronze Age...'[75] One of the reasons for their dismissal is that they regard a date of 2500 BCE as too late for the arrival of Armenians in their historical seat because their computational median split date for it is 3310 BCE. The admixture date is still within the range 4930–1999 BCE, a range that is so broad that it could easily accommodate the evidence for a steppe migration, and it should be noted that their median date is over a millennium earlier than the split dates of *c.* 2000 BCE from the Berkeley and Moscow phylogenies. A controversial computational date for a language split does not trump a convergence of both archaeological and genetic evidence. I think it is far more likely that we should date the arrival of the Armenians in the Middle (not Late) Bronze Age. The only caveat I am aware of is the identification of a somewhat different genetic cluster comprising 50 per cent of the earlier Bronze Age pattern combined with additional steppe ancestry that emerges *c.* 400 BCE–500 CE, which more closely resembles modern Armenians.[76] Either model very much overturns the earlier failed attempts to trace Armenian origins on the basis of modern DNA samples, which concluded that their language (as well as that of the neighbouring Turkic-speaking Azerbaijanis) 'reflect language replacements, which occurred without any detectable genetic contribution of the original Indo-European and Turkic groups'.[77]

The evidence from both archaeology and genetics for the arrival of the Proto-Armenians supports a significant penetration *into* the Caucasus from the steppe to its north. At this point I think it is time to acknowledge the elephant in the room. Any attempt to associate Indo-European dispersals from a region south of the Caucasus, employing either the spread of agriculture or some form of elite dominance, must account for why the Indo-Europeans utterly failed to spread their languages in the Caucasus itself. The South Caucasus model gifts their CHG bearers of Indo-European with the ability to convert the Pontic-Caspian into a secondary homeland that will spawn most if not all the Indo-European languages (perhaps excepting Anatolian), and yet they couldn't leave a linguistic trail along their march northwards. We are either forced to imagine that whatever vector was employed to spread Indo-European through the Caucasus only operated when exiting the Caucasus, or it did leave a linguistic trail of early Indo-European languages but this was entirely swallowed up by the ancestors of the Caucasian languages who were hiding elsewhere (where?). For example, a recent study of the Kartvelian homeland situates its proto-language *c.* 6000 BCE among both early farmers and residual hunter-gatherers in western Georgia,[78] while we have already seen that much of the Kura-Araxes region is more likely to have been associated with the Hurro-Urartian family.

That CHG penetrated the steppe in very significant amounts is incontrovertible, but I find associating Indo-Anatolian or Core-Indo-European origins with its expansion from south of the Caucasus extremely hard to accept, especially if we credit the bearers of CHG with either spreading agriculture or forming elites that would manage to expand their language over almost all of Europe. That is why an expansion of the CHG population initiated from the northern flanks of the Caucasus seems like a far more likely explanation for the presence of CHG ancestry in the steppe cultures. On the other hand, I have just set up another problem that we will have to examine in the next chapter.

Reviewing the Caucasus homeland model

Solutions to the Indo-European homeland problem have included both the Caucasus and the regions immediately to its south since (at least) the 17th century. This is the area where the population group identified as the CHG expanded westwards through Anatolia, forming a cline with AAF *c.* 6500 BCE. It is also acknowledged by most of the major competing models that the Pontic-Caspian steppe served as either the primary or a secondary location of Indo-European origins and expansions and, because the genetic composition associated with the steppe region is an admixture of CHG and EHG, this indicates that CHG is potentially the critical element in the genetic cocktail underlying Indo-European dispersals.

The CHG area itself comprises the historical territories of a series of non-Indo-European languages, including all the modern languages native to the Caucasus as well as a number of ancient languages such as Hurro-Urartian and Elamite, so if the Indo-European homeland lay within it, it could only be a segment of the CHG network. If one sets the homeland south of the Caucasus, from which Proto-Anatolian is the first branch to separate, the logistics of the migration would probably favour a location in or near eastern Anatolia – any further west would situate it within the AAF population; such a location would also require the shortest migration and avoid placing the homeland in a region more probably associated with one of the non-Indo-European languages. The date of a homeland south of the Caucasus would most likely be confined to the period *c.* 6500–3500 BCE for three reasons: Proto-Indo-Anatolian possessed at least some of the vocabulary for domestic plants and animals; during this period there is evidence for a westerly flow of CHG from an earlier agricultural region into the territory historically associated with the Anatolian languages; and by 3500 BCE the Kura-Araxes culture, plausibly associated with the Hurrian language, would effectively close the door to migration westwards.

A homeland set south of the Caucasus, however, does face a few problems. First, it must be explained, for any expansions from the area to the west (e.g. Greek), how a phylogenetically later language achieved its historical location *after* the Anatolian languages had expanded between the putative homeland and Europe. And for expansions to the east (e.g. Indo-Iranian), the question of why there is no trail of Indo-Iranian languages along the route apparently taken by the spread of the Neolithic must be answered. The model must also deal with the genetic evidence indicating that the population forming the Sintashta culture (the most likely predecessor to the Indo-Iranization of the Asian steppe) derives from the steppe and not from a primarily CHG region, and address the major constituency that links Indo-Iranian with Balto-Slavic or early contacts with Uralic, all of which are accommodated far more easily by the Steppe model.

Finally, a Caucasus homeland model requires an explanation of how and when CHG was able to penetrate the steppe and admix in parity with the local EHG to ultimately form the genetic composition of the Yamnaya culture. Of three models discussed, an incursion associated with the northern spread of domestic livestock in the Neolithic is the best supported archaeologically and genetically. In terms of haplogroups, the evidence for the spread of CHG into the steppelands via the Maykop culture reveals little evidence for a major contribution of CHG Y-chromosomes (males) although it may have been an important vector of Aknashen-like CHG. The failure of a putative southern Caucasus homeland to produce any evidence of a trail of Indo-European languages along their migration paths to the north renders this model problematic.

CHAPTER 15

The Steppe Model

For over 120 years, the Pontic-Caspian steppe has been widely regarded as a critical element in explaining the origins and dispersals of the Indo-European languages. At its most optimistic, it has been seen as the primary homeland, while most other solutions have relegated it to the position of one if not the most important of the secondary homelands. In most European homeland models (Nordic, Danubian and Balkan), it has been associated with the staging area of Indo-Iranian origins. In more recent models that look to homelands in Anatolia or the Caucasus and adjacent regions, it is presented as the secondary homeland of a significant number of the Indo-European branches, sometimes all of them except for Anatolian. The critical issue is that the genetic evidence has made it abundantly clear that the steppe populations associated with Indo-European expansions were not simply the result of a purely local evolution but rather required the local Eastern Hunter-Gatherer (EHG) group to have been admixed with Caucasian Hunter-Gatherer (CHG) as well as a portion of Ancient Anatolian Farmer (AAF) and possibly smaller traces of others (Western Hunter-Gatherer/WHG, West Siberian Hunter-Gatherer/WSHG). The most obvious problem, then, is whether Indo-European was a locally evolved language that emerged out of a portion of the EHG population in the Pontic-Caspian region or whether the local EHG population was absorbed linguistically by an intrusive CHG group as the latter spread across the steppe. In a nutshell: in the marriage of CHG and EHG, which partner brought their children up speaking Proto-Indo-Anatolian, the mother of all the Indo-European languages?

CHAPTER 15

Formation of the steppe spread zone

We have seen that since the beginning of the 20th century linguists have debated whether the European steppe was a proper location for a linguistic homeland or merely a thoroughfare through which languages entered at one end and passed to the other as a new language pushed across, swallowing the languages of the previous horizon. When we first encounter the languages of the steppe in the historical record, the area was occupied by speakers of Iranian languages (Cimmerian?, Scythian, Sarmatian, Alan) and then, after a number of centuries, these were largely replaced by Turkic-speaking groups. The Steppe model argues that before the spread of Iranian languages during the Iron Age there was a still earlier Eneolithic/Early Bronze Age linguistic horizon associated with Proto-Indo-Anatolian. It might be noted that very often scholars of the Soviet era suggested that the language horizon that preceded the eastern Iranian steppe nomads was Proto-Indo-Iranian and not an earlier linguistic horizon of Indo-European. In any event, the Pontic-Caspian steppe equates with what linguist Johanna Nichols describes as a linguistic spread zone: 'a region where a single language family spreads out widely, genetic diversity of languages is low, and one language family replaces another over most of the area every few millennia'.[1]

One may feel comfortable in imagining a common language or lingua franca spoken among tribes of mobile pastoralists who occupied this spread zone where we find a common cultural horizon, broadly similar physical type and restricted range of Y-chromosome haplogroups, but the preceding situation before CHG began spreading through the region was likely to have been more complicated. I have always suspected that before the emergence of a pastoral economy with access to superior means of transport (domestic horse, ox-drawn vehicles) the geography of the steppe region may have originally served as an incubator for diverse languages.[2] The reason for this is that here the major rivers tend to run north to south across the entire region and that settlement from the Palaeolithic onwards tended to be confined to the river valleys, especially the major rivers and their tributaries, while the interfluvial regions of open steppe appear to have been very sparsely occupied, if

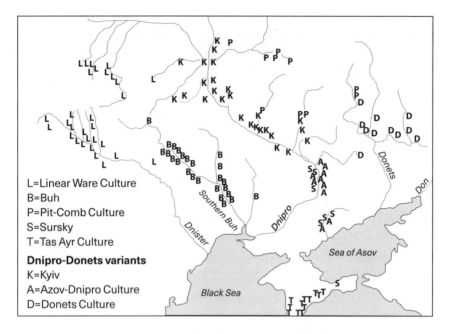

15.1 Neolithic sites of the 7th–5th millennium BCE in Ukraine tend to concentrate on the major rivers and their tributaries, which may have encouraged linguistic isolation and diversification.

at all, serving as possible barriers to communication. A glance at a map of the distribution of Ukrainian Neolithic sites [15.1], for example, suggests a series of different cultures associated with settlement corridors separated by considerable regions of steppe or forest steppe, an environment that may well have encouraged linguistic isolation and diversity across the entire region. Moreover, while the economies may be broadly labelled hunting-gathering, often it may be suspected that the primary activity was fishing, which would encourage more stable settlement in optimal fishing locations. This is supported by a number of substantial Mesolithic and Neolithic cemeteries, especially along the Dnipro river.

Obviously, how much linguistic diversity existed is speculative, but even if we derive all the steppe cultures from an EHG marriage network, their separation in time and space along the different rivers – seen in terms of a variety of different cultural traditions from the Mesolithic onwards[3] – would suggest substantial isolation from one another, all of which could promote linguistic diversity.

Moreover, the evidence of physical anthropology has long suggested that there were various migration streams of populations, some more gracile (skulls whose features are more slender or less pronounced) and others more robust, the latter entering from the northwest into the Dnipro-Donets region associated with WHG groups. The introduction of domestic animals, along with the mobility that the domestication of the horse and the invention of wheeled vehicles permitted are the obvious factors that could have contributed to the emergence of a common language across the region. For this reason, the emergence of the Yamnaya 'cultural-historical horizon' has long made an attractive vector for the expansion of a common language *c.* 3300–2500 BCE. The problem is that the presumably earlier split dates for the Anatolian branch suggest that the Yamnaya culture appears to be too recent to be identified as Proto-Indo-Anatolian and is more likely to be identified with Core-Indo-European. We therefore need to consider what existed before the Yamnaya and to what extent it provides a credible origin for Proto-Indo-Anatolian.

We have seen that attempts to explain the origins of the Yamnaya culture have traditionally involved two geographically separated Eneolithic predecessors – the Khvalynsk culture in the Middle Volga region[4] and the Serednii Stih culture of the Dnipro-Donets region,[5] both with start dates of *c.* 4500–4300 BCE. This situation forces us to take a more granular approach and acknowledge that assembling these two regions into a single Pontic-Caspian cultural zone is problematic. While many supporters of the Steppe model might be content to draw a circle around everything from the Dnipro to the Volga and call it the homeland, the archaeology and the genetics are more complex. We actually have two competing centres of primacy regarding Indo-European origins within the steppe. For example, the argument suggesting the primacy of the

Volga-Don region dates back at least to the 1974 classic study of the Yamnaya culture by Nikolai Merpert (1922–2012), where he argued that the earliest burials were situated in the east.[6] This was accepted in Marija Gimbutas's models and continued in both my earlier (now out-of-date) 1989 account[7] and David Anthony's more recent and detailed 2007 exposition.[8] Anthony emphasizes that it was in the eastern steppe that the arid conditions most strongly promoted a drive towards a mobile economy and where the Khvalynsk culture was the most likely ancestor of the Yamnaya. On the other hand, while acknowledging that the earliest Yamnaya burials were probably in the east, Dmytro Telehin (1919–2011) argued in 1973 that the Yamnaya of the Dnipro-Don region was built on the Serednii Stih culture.[9]

One of the arguments against asserting an independent origin for the Yamnaya in the Dnipro-Donets region is that the Serednii Stih culture reflects not only a cultural change from the previous Neolithic (Dnipro-Donets) culture (genetically EHG + WHG and lacking AAF and possessing very little CHG), but also involved a mixed population comprising a more gracile physical type and a population typically defined as extremely robust proto-Europoids. This suggests that the cultural transformation was not a purely local evolution but included a substantial contribution from big guys from the north. It has been argued that both the gracile examples of Serednii Stih skulls and what little cereal agriculture is attested in Proto-Indo-Anatolian are better explained by contact with the agricultural Cucuteni-Trypillia culture, rather than a more easterly steppe culture that lacks any evidence of domestic cereals.[10]

Here we shall step back and reframe the genetic issues we must resolve. Our objective is to explain the origin of the fully formed Yamnaya culture, which is the main vector of most putative Indo-European expansions in the Steppe model. An analysis of over one hundred samples drawn from Yamnaya burials on the Pontic-Caspian steppe itself and the Afanasievo culture (and not from post-dispersion sources in the Balkans where they may be admixed with local populations) tends to a very roughly 50:50 split between CHG and EHG, with a smaller additional amount of AAF. The Y-chromosome haplogroup is overwhelmingly variants of R1b, followed by moderate amounts of I2a. The evidence for mitochondrial (mtDNA) is far more complex and will be surveyed below (see **15.5**). We know that the EHG population is local to the steppe region and that the CHG population is intrusive from the south. So we need to trace the spread of CHG from the piedmont area north of the Caucasus (see Chapter 16) throughout the Pontic-Caspian region and follow it through the emergence of the Yamnaya culture. In the previous chapter we saw that CHG appeared to have entered the steppe in two genetic flavours: a CHG-related type that retains more of the profile seen in the Mesolithic sample from Kotias Klde in Georgia, and an Aknashen type that is (so far) associated with the earliest Neolithic in the southern Caucasus. We have also seen that the few Y-haplogroups from the Mesolithic of the Caucasus are variants of J2a and L1a1, which continue into the Eneolithic and Early Bronze Age Maykop culture, where we might add G2a. We need to keep an eye out for these three haplogroups as CHG moves north into the steppe. It should be re-emphasized that our evidence from the Caucasus is quite meagre when compared to the size of our samples from the steppe and it is not always easy to determine whether a particular haplogroup appeared earlier on the steppe or in the Caucasus region.

Now we need to develop a picture of what is local to the Pontic-Caspian steppe before its penetration by CHG. The evidence of ancient DNA (aDNA) from Ukrainian Mesolithic males (*c.* 9000–6000 BCE) includes variants of R1a (M459 and YP4141), R1b (V88) and I2a. This indicates that the main (upstream) haplogroups later found in the Yamnaya culture were already present in the Pontic-Caspian at least since the Mesolithic, meaning that the Y-haplogroups that we find in both the Mesolithic and Yamnaya cultures appear to be native to the EHG population [**15.2**].

The Neolithic (5600–4600 BCE) sites of the steppe (and here we are talking largely about ceramic-using hunter-fishers, with the occasional presence of domestic animals) primarily continue the earlier Y-haplogroups of I2a, R1a (M459, YP4141) and R1b (BY17643, PF6287, PF6323 and V88), which naturally supports a model of genetic continuity.

It is with the Eneolithic from *c.* 4500 BCE onwards that we see the major insertion of CHG into the steppelands, and it is best to follow each of the two variations (CHG-related and Aknashen-like) separately into the steppelands.

Period	Date (BCE)	Y-chromosome	mtDNA
Mesolithic	9000–6000	I2a1a1b1	U4b
		R1a-M459	U5a
		R1a-YP4141	U5b
		R1b-V88	
Neolithic	5600–4600	I2, I2a1b (x16)	C
		R1a-M459	H (x7)
		R1a-YP4141	T, T2
		R1b-BY17643(x6)	U2
		R1b-PF6287(x2)	U3
		R1b-PF6323	U4 (x3)
		R1b-V88	U4a (x4) U4b (x8)
			U4d (x4) U5a
			(x15) U5b (x9)

15.2 Ancient DNA (aDNA) from Mesolithic and Neolithic sites in the Pontic-Caspian steppe. Both the Y-chromosome and mtDNA haplogroups appear to be local to the steppe region.

We have already met CHG-related at the site of Progress-2 (c. 4300–4000 BCE) in the north Caucasus steppe (see **14.7**) and it is found along what the Harvard (Reich) lab has termed the Volga cline north at Berezhnovka II (4450–3960 BCE) and then further north still at the critically important cemeteries (Khlopkov Bugor and Khvalynsk I and II) of the Khvalynsk culture (4500–4350 BCE), Ekaterinovka Mys and finally Murzikha II [**15.3**]. The traditional Yamnaya burial posture (the so-called 'Yamnaya position'), supine but with the knees raised, has been found at a number of sites along this cline dating as early as c. 4500 BCE if not before. Moreover, burial mounds have also been recorded at several sites.

The Khvalynsk cemeteries have yielded a surprisingly limited number of male haplogroups: I2a1b, Q1-L472 (x5), R1a-M459, R1b-L754 (x15) [**15.4**]. We have already seen that both R1a and R1b are associated with the steppe, while Q1 has been present in Russia since the Palaeolithic,

CHAPTER 15

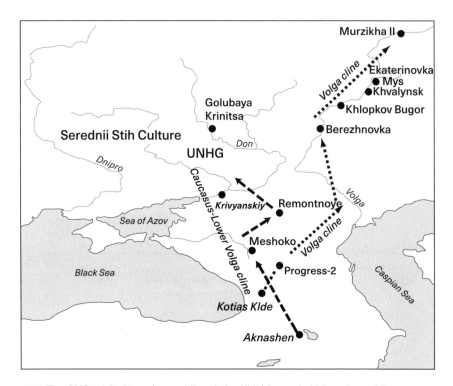

15.3 The CHG-related type (resembling Kotias Klde) formed a Volga cline, while the Aknashen type can be followed along the Caucasus-Lower Volga cline through the pre-Maykop region (Meshoko) northwestwards towards the Dnipro-Donets region where it helped form the Serednii Stih culture (UNHG denotes Ukrainian Neolithic Hunter-Gatherers). The DNA evidence suggests that the Yamnaya genetic signature emerged between the Dnipro and the Don (the area of the Serednii Stih culture) by c. 4200–4000 BCE although it (so far) does not appear to have continued into the Yamnaya but was carried east and appears in the Afanasievo culture. I2a is local from the Mesolithic and is found in the later Yamnaya culture. The mtDNA haplogroups also include some clearly local variants such as I3a and U2e1b, while U5a1 and U5a2d have earlier Mesolithic pedigrees in northern Europe. On the other hand, although H2a1 appears somewhat earlier at Khvalynsk, it is also found in the Neolithic in the Caucasus.

This Volga cline has been interpreted as a genetic network operating along the Volga, where the CHG-related type penetrated from the south and moved up-river, its percentage in the genomic identity of each community diminishing with distance. Notable is the absence of any AAF, which would appear with the spread of the second cline involving Aknashen-like CHG. The Khvalynsk burial posture anticipates that of the later Yamnaya culture and also maintained the tradition of sprinkling red ochre on the burials.

Site	Date (BCE)	Y-chromosome	mtDNA
Progress-2	4300–4200	R1b-V1636 (x2)	I3a, H2
Berezhnovka		R1b-V1636+1?	
Khlopkov Bugor	c. 4500	R1b-L754 (x10)	
		Q1 (x2)	
		I2a1b	
Khvalynsk	4500–4350	R1b-L754 (x15)	H2a1 (x5)
		Q1-L472 (x5)	R1b1 (x2)
		R1a-M459	U2e1b (x4)
		I2a-L699	U4d (x5)
			U5a1 (x11)
			U5a2d (x3)
Murzikha II	c. 4500–4200	Q1a (x9)	R1b
			U2e2a (x4)
			U4a
			U4a1
			U5a1d2 (x2)
			U5a1d2b (x2)
			U5a2b1 (x2)

15.4 Y-chromosome and mtDNA haplogroups along the Volga cline.

The second genetic corridor [15.5] was associated with Aknashen-like CHG, which was believed to have spread northwards from agricultural populations who occupied the northwest Caucasus Meshoko culture (the prelude to the Maykop culture; Aknashen-like ancestry is typical of the CHG found in the Maykop culture), which dates to c. 4600–3800 BCE. It is found in the steppe at several sites near the village of Remontnoye (c. 4200–3600 BCE), where Aknashen-like ancestry accounts for about 45 per cent among burials that also showed some admixture with the Volga cline (a source similar to that found at Berezhnovka). Both the burials at Remontnoye and Berezhnovka were under kurgans, and they also adopted the unusual Yamnaya burial posture of laying out the dead on their back but with their legs flexed, as well as the more widely found sprinkling of red ochre over the deceased.

The Caucasus-Lower Volga cline extended west from Remontnoye towards the Dnipro. As we have seen, this river was a major region of settlement since the Mesolithic. It had developed a distinct genetic profile that a recent report has termed Ukrainian Neolithic Hunter-Gatherer (UNHG) and for our purposes was largely the fairly robust population buried in the Dnipro-Donets cemeteries.[11] This culture lacks evidence for AAF ancestry (which is found at levels of about 10–18 per cent in the Yamnaya culture). It is proposed that the CHG signature, similar to that recovered near Remontnoye, admixed with the local Dnipro-Donets population to produce the Serednii Stih culture, which also used the later Yamnaya burial posture. The recent analysis of Serednii Stih burials indicates that they belong primarily to R1a and I2a1b – the local steppe haplogroups – with one interesting exception. A male Serednii Stih burial from the Don (Krivyanskiy-9) revealed Y-haplogroup J2a (J-M319), which indicated that he had a 'grandfather' from the Caucasus; his problematic mtDNA (T2a1b) has been presumed to be local and his CHG component was apparently CHG-related rather than Aknashen-like. As mentioned above, this culture, together with its contemporary, the Khvalynsk culture in the Middle Volga region, are the two competing sources for generating the Yamnaya culture.

After comparing various genetic models, the Harvard (Reich) lab concluded that the genetic signature of the core of the Yamnaya culture had

Site	Date (BCE)	Y-chromosome	mtDNA
Remontnoye	4152–3637	R-V1636	H2a, R0
Serednii Stih	c. 4500–3500	I-L699 J2a	I4a, K1b2b, T2a1b, U4b, U5a1f1
Yamnaya [Core]	c. 3300–2600	I-L699 (x17), R-M269 [>Z2103] (x49)	C4a2 (x 2), C4a6, H2a1, H2a1e, H2b, H6a1b, H13a1a1, H15b1, K1b2a, N1a, R0a1, R1a1 (x 2), Ia1, T2a1a (x 2), T2c1a2, U1a1a3, U2e1a1, U2e1b, U4 (x 2) U4a1a, U4c1, U5, U5a, U5a1, U5aiai x 2, U5a1d, U5aid1, U5a1d2b, U5a1i, U5a1i1, U5a2b (x 2), U5b2a1a, W3a1, W3a1a (x 2), W6c (x 2)

15.5 Genetic evidence of the Dnipro-Donets Eneolithic, Serednii Stih and Pontic-Caspian Yamnaya cultures.

already been established in the area between the Dnipro and the Don c. 4200–4000 BCE from a population that could be described as about 80 per cent Caucasus-Lower Volga and about 20 per cent UNHG, indicating it basically overlapped with the Serednii Stih culture. These results may be compared with those of a recent publication from the Copenhagen lab, which found that the best evidence for the EHG-CHG admixture underlying the Yamnaya can be found in the Middle Don region, where the cemetery of Golubaya Krinitsa reveals a balance of 65 per cent local hunter-gatherer (EHG) ancestry and 35 per cent CHG.[12] In short, both the Harvard and the Copenhagen labs although employing different models[13] suggest that the genetic origins of the Yamnaya culture originated between the EHG and CHG in the area of the Dnipro-Don, a region that had earlier been advanced in the blogosphere.[14]

In terms of haplogroups we have followed the males so far, but now we should consider the mtDNA evidence from females. We may note the sheer abundance of different mitochondrial haplogroups compared with those of the males [15.5]. When we consider the range of our target culture, the Yamnaya, we find clear evidence of female lines originating both in the Caucasus and others that appear to be local. For example, H13 was known from the Mesolithic in the Caucasus and reappears at Khvalynsk; H15 appears in the Armenian Neolithic and also produced female descendants at Khvalynsk; N1a is found from the Near East through the European Neolithic. On the other hand, variants of U5a, for example, are entirely local to the steppe and predominate in the Khvalynsk and Yamnaya cultures. In terms of the gender balance between males and females, the steppe cultures, particularly the later ones such as Khvalynsk and Yamnaya, indicate a marriage network where a surprisingly narrow genetic range of males mated with a great variety of female lines.

On the basis of current analyses of aDNA we can draw several preliminary conclusions from the evidence:

1. CHG appeared to penetrate the steppe in significant quantities where it is found on sites ranging from *c.* 6400 (Golubaya Krinitsa) to 3800 (Steppe Maykop) BCE, the latter entering a world that had already begun burying the dead under kurgans in the 'Yamnaya position' with red ochre (Steppe Eneolithic).
2. CHG entered the steppe via two channels, one bearing a genetic signature more similar to that obtaining during the Mesolithic and following a trajectory from the Caucasus northwards along the Volga where it admixed with EHG populations. This may have been the result either of a migration northwards from the Caucasus or, alternatively, a movement southwards along the Volga where the local steppe population began a process of intermarriage with populations from the northern Caucasus. This provided the genetic foundation of the Khvalynsk culture in the Middle Volga region.

3. A second channel of CHG resembling that of the early Neolithic population of the Kura-Araxes region (Aknashen-like) also moved through the north Caucasus (Maykop) and then onto the steppe where it formed a Caucasus-Lower Volga cline. This population then moved west and its genetic signature entered into the Dnipro-Don region where it admixed with the local Dnipro-Donets culture and contributed to the formation of the Serednii Stih culture, which was ancestral to the Yamnaya culture.
4. Modelling of the genetic composition of the core Yamnaya culture indicates that it had already formed c. 4200-4000 BCE, a millennium or more before the Yamnaya culture itself emerged, in the Dnipro-Don area. This has been supported by both the Harvard and Copenhagen labs.
5. The evidence from haplogroups reveals an imbalance between the genetic contribution from the Caucasus and that of the steppe. Y-haplogroups associated with CHG are conspicuous by their near total absence among the steppe communities. On the other hand, it is apparent that local males from the steppe intermarried with both local women and women whose maternal ancestors derived from the Caucasus.

Missing males

While one can assemble a list of every trade item recovered from burials across the Pontic-Caspian steppe, it is difficult to transform such evidence into an explanation for a common language. It is all too easy to presume that the dispersal of languages will be obviously recorded when tracing the genetic trails of prehistoric migrations. Unless entire language communities (men, women and children) expand and exterminate all indigenous communities, we will be dealing with some form of language shift where, as we have already seen, it is difficult to generate consistently valid predictive rules. We seem to be facing a situation where males from the steppe communities acquired wives both from their own communities and in a major way from CHG (admixed with AAF) communities. The absence of evidence for CHG Y-haplogroups in the Eneolithic and Early Bronze Age steppe cemeteries is striking. There are at least four potential explanations.

First, are we dealing with absence of evidence or evidence of absence? Our sample of core Yamnaya males now exceeds one hundred, while the Khvalynsk culture adds about thirty-five males, and yet we lack evidence for CHG male lineages (with the exception of the Serednii Stih burial at Krivyanskiy-9) despite the fact that, at least among the Yamnaya, the samples display as much CHG as they do EHG.

A second possible explanation is that CHG male lineages entered the steppe in number but did not employ a kurgan burial rite, thus failing to leave burials that might have yielded Y-haplogroup evidence. While this cannot be completely rejected, we do know that the site of Nal'chik, located in the same general territory from which we might derive at least some of the CHG population, employed burial under low barrows. Therefore, an appeal to a wholly different and not-yet-discovered burial rite seems unlikely, especially when the northern Caucasus cultures contemporaneous with the steppe Eneolithic were the pre-Maykop and Maykop, which were famous for their kurgans. This leads to a further point. It could be argued that the steppe cultures were socially either the offshoots of the more technologically and economically advanced cultures of the Caucasus, or, at least, emulating them by adopting the practice of status burials under a kurgan. If that were indeed the case, then we would expect to find solid evidence of elite CHG male lineages under the steppe kurgans providing someone to emulate. Unfortunately, we have aDNA from only three such burials with males, two of which carry typical steppe lineages (R1a, Q1b), while the third with T-L490 does suggest a southern origin. This is far too small a sample from which to draw conclusions, although it does at least offer some evidence that some males with Y-chromosomes more native to the south penetrated the steppe. To this we could add the Serednii Stih burial from Krivyanskiy-9 whose burial had a Caucasus male pedigree but the burial seems to predate the erection of a kurgan over it.[15] Their absence, however, from the many later Yamnaya burials leaves the model of emulating a CHG elite unsupported by genetic evidence.

A third explanation is that males from the Caucasus were on the steppe but few to none left male lines that survived long enough to enter the archaeological record. This is a difficult one to assess as it requires some assumptions. If we accept (assume) that the main flow of CHG to the steppe began *c.* 4500–4000 BCE from the north Caucasus, one could argue that this coincides with our datasets from both the Dnipro and Volga regions (*c.* 4500–4350 BCE), so there is no major missing interval that we haven't sampled that would allow enough time for putative CHG male lines to have died out in the meantime. On the other hand, this is built on not only an assumption of the date when CHG primarily spread, but also satisfaction that we actually have enough data over this period to draw such a conclusion for the whole region.

The fourth (and most obvious) explanation is that CHG males were largely excluded from the gene pool and it was primarily CHG women who entered the steppe marriage network. We have already encountered the marked imbalances in the diversity of male lineages in the westward expansion of steppe genes that can be seen in both the Corded Ware in continental Europe and the Beaker cultures across Europe, especially Britain and Ireland.[16] In the latter we find an absolute predominance of one specific Y-chromosome lineage (R1b-L21) that out-competed all other male lineages, at least the ones we recover evidence for. For the Corded Ware culture, scholars often invoke the Männerbund, the Indo-European warband, comprising an age-set of younger males who may have served as explorers and raiders, returning not only with booty but also wives/foreign women. The challenge is interpreting what precisely happened on the ground. For example, recently Dutch linguist Tijmen Pronk has referenced the warband as a plausible vector for acquiring wives, stating 'Steppe males mated with local females, while local males apparently became more restricted in their possibilities to father offspring.'[17]

The problem is explaining just how the local CHG brothers appear to be absent from the same marriage network that their sisters were part of, be it in central and western Europe or, also here, on the border between the steppe and the Caucasus. We can generate any number of so far unverified (or unverifiable) explanations, running from the romantic attraction of being carried off by a handsome steppe horseman so you didn't have to marry the local country bumpkin, to the systematic slaughtering of local CHG males by violently aggressive EHG pastoralists. The latter has always been on the archaeological menu for Indo-European expansions and the literature is absolutely awash with descriptions of how various Indo-European groups 'riding on horses, massacred or enslaved indigenous men while taking their women, or they established a ruling elite that passed on more Y chromosomes through sustained polygamy over many centuries'.[18] In Europe we have some evidence of the slaughtering of communities at this time (for example, at Eulau, mentioned in Chapter 10). The selective removal of local CHG men is possible but could hardly be the only explanation and is incredibly difficult to substantiate. If we assume, for example, an interface between steppe populations and the pre-Maykop horizon (*c.* 4500–3800 BCE), we are dealing with a number of sites defended by substantial walls, ditches or natural features such as deep ravines. Whether they were constructed to reduce internecine strife or to protect CHG women from steppe raiders is impossible to know, and archaeologists generally look for an alternative explanation.

We are now very much in the area of speculation, but that is where potentially testable hypotheses are born. For example, from the recent blogosphere, the radical break between the ecology of the Caucasus and the steppelands has been used to argue that there was no CHG migration north into the steppe (farmers had no desire to try their hand at becoming pastoralists), but that steppe (EHG) populations and CHG populations met on the borderlands where they intermarried, the steppe populations then spreading the genes of their admixed descendants back into the steppe.[19] The general concept is possible, but we still need to deal with the apparent differences between the lineages, especially as there is only the slightest trace of a reciprocal spread of EHG among the Early Bronze Age populations of the northern Caucasus. Perhaps linguists have provided a step towards the right solution in presenting evidence from Indo-European kinship terminology that the Indo-Europeans were very much into exogamy, including taking the Eneolithic equivalent of mail-order brides from afar.[20]

The language of the steppe CHG

While we may wrestle with explanations for the imbalance between the contribution of male versus female lineages to the CHG admixture with EHG, there is no doubt that it is emerging as a recurrent pattern, not only in those dispersals associated with the Yamnaya culture but also in the formation of the steppe genetic signature itself. And this takes us to the major issue of this chapter: when EHG males mated with CHG females, which one of the parents spoke Indo-European and whose language did their children speak?

The reconstructed vocabulary of Indo-European marriage and kinship makes it fairly clear that the early Indo-European society was patrilineal – upon marriage the woman was literally **wedh-* 'led, dragged' away to live with her husband's family. Everything about the steppe burials suggests a patrilineal and patrilocal system, especially the way that there is a great variety of females of various genetic lines in cemeteries, whereas the males are almost exclusively members of one or two lines. Had the system been matrilineal we would expect a few female lines in the cemetery and a greater variety of males drawn from different communities. Attempts have been made to investigate how kinship systems (patrilineal versus matrilineal) correlate with language, and in a recent study investigating both matrilineal and patrilineal communities from the Indonesian islands of Sumba and Timor, it was observed that there is a fairly good correlation between kinship and language acquisition. In the patrilineal communities where women may be brought from various different language communities, it will be the husband's language that is transmitted to the children; on the other hand, in matrilineal communities, it will be the wife's language that will be passed on.[21] Obviously, we might hope for more such studies, but the logic is certainly persuasive. In a patrilineal system where women may derive from a variety of different communities, possibly with different native languages, and come to live with husbands who all speak the same language, then the language of the males would be the most practical choice. In the formation of the EHG-CHG admixture then, it is most likely that the language spoken by the EHG member would become the dominant language. And if the Yamnaya culture is indeed a vector for the spread of various Indo-European languages, one could logically assume that Indo-European was inherited through the EHG male side rather than the female CHG side. Unless...?

Here we need to reintroduce the concept of a *Mischsprache* (mixed language), where in Chapter 6 we saw that a number of linguists support the concept that Proto-Indo-Anatolian was the hybrid offspring of Proto-Uralic (or a language resembling Uralic) and a North Caucasian language. This model would argue that there was no Proto-Indo-Anatolian *until* the admixture between EHG and CHG. It seems (to me at least) that the nature of a Proto-Indo-Anatolian mixed language would be regarded as peculiar, even among the very few other truly mixed languages. Michif, a language of a First Nations population in Canada, would come closest to the model proposed for Proto-Indo-Anatolian, since not only does it combine two ethnicities (French and Cree) but these were also aligned by gender, with the French component derived from male trappers and Cree from native women. Evaluating such a proposition is challenging. If, however, we did imagine CHG women from the Caucasus contributing to the Proto-Indo-Anatolian vocabulary, we might expect evidence of it in the fields of domestic plants and livestock.

In Allan Bomhard's list of potential cognates, there are no domestic cereals and few words related to domestic animals.[22] Some are also found in Rasmus Bjørn's list (see **6.11**), which includes 'flax, linen' (PIE **linom*), two words for 'goat' (PIE **dig-* and **h₂eiǵ-*), 'curdled milk' **twer-* and, controversially but significantly, 'wool' (**w̥lh₂neh₂-*).[23] One might have thought that if the Caucasus had been the primary conduit for the introduction of domestic livestock such as cattle it would have been represented here but, according to Bjørn, three words pertaining to cattle are all derived from Afro-Asiatic/Semitic. I suppose we might still argue that they began as Afro-Asiatic words that spread from the south and were then adopted by an Aknashen-related CHG North Caucasian language before being passed on into Proto-Indo-Anatolian. And Ranko Matasović, who has examined the evidence for North Caucasian–Indo-European links and finds some typological grounds associating Indo-European with Caucasian, remarks that 'we were not able to find certain proofs of lexical borrowing between PIE and North Caucasian'.[24] Whatever the attractions of the *Mischsprache* approach, the combination of archaeological and genetic evidence would appear to require the linguistic admixture to have occurred about the time that the Neolithic economy had managed to arrive in the north Caucasus or somewhat later. If the proto-language required the fusion of EHG and CHG, and the latter was associated with the ancestor of one or both of the North Caucasian languages, I would have thought that we should be able to recover far more of the vocabulary that was lent into Proto-Indo-Anatolian in both the Caucasian and Uralic proto-languages.

This is not to deny the obvious – that the proposed CHG-EHG mixing would undoubtedly have led to some linguistic impact from the CHG-bearing members of the initial admixture. Nevertheless, supporters of a *Mischsprache* solution to Indo-European origins still have a lot of work to do if they are going to convince. The patrilineal nature of early Indo-European society and ethnographic evidence suggest that the admixture of EHG and CHG would likely promote the linguistic dominance of the EHG male partners.

CHAPTER 16

Taking Stock: Homeland Solutions and Later Indo-European Expansions

In his 2024 study of the Uralic homeland, Jaakko Häkkinen prefaced his research with the statement: 'Arguments for locating the homeland can be divided into two categories: compelling arguments and suggesting arguments. Compelling arguments are undeniable, and only if they cannot help to locate the homeland must we return to suggesting arguments.'[1] If the reader has learned anything so far, the concept of undeniable 'compelling arguments' with regard to the Indo-European homeland are as rare as albino unicorns. Thus I am well aware that any conclusion given here will be fiercely challenged from some quarter. I find us still very close to E. P. Evans, who in 1886 remarked in his excellent attempt to sort out all the various homeland theories of his own day: 'It must be remembered, however, that in the present state of our knowledge the whole discussion of this subject must be limited to a simple balancing of *pros* and *cons*, and a cautious statement of probabilities. We have to do with mere hypotheses, about which it is interesting to speculate, but absurd to dogmatize.'[2]

Moreover, the resilience of many of the homeland solutions has been truly remarkable. You can shove them into bright sunlight, cut off their heads, drive a stake through their hearts and pump them with endless rounds of silver bullets and yet they have kept coming back. So let's take a final impressionistic look at where the quest for the Indo-European homeland stands in the light of the current state of linguistic, archaeological and genetic evidence in 2024.

The homeland models

Palaeolithic

Unless the Palaeolithic Continuity model can come up with some better arguments, it should wither away. When the geneticists were attempting to read the past purely from modern DNA samples indicating the current distribution of genetic markers, their results appeared to reflect a Europe that had been genetically largely static since the Ice Age. The Palaeolithic Continuity model then had some legs to stand on. Now, however, with the advent of palaeogenomics using ancient DNA (aDNA), it is clear that the genetic history of Eurasia has been anything but stable and has experienced at least three major waves of migration (the post-glacial spread of Western Hunter-Gatherers/WHG, the Neolithic and the Eneolithic), which have erased much of the genetic imprint of Europe's earliest modern human populations. The only way this thesis is going to climb out of its coffin is if it succeeds in convincing us that the Palaeolithic population of Eurasia spoke Proto-Indo-European and managed not only to resist language shift for about 40,000 years but also experienced an inconceivable slow rate of natural language change in the face of major genetic upheavals.

Multi-regional

What about the multi-regional homeland solutions such as the Nordic-Steppe models? Here things are not entirely so hopeless. We have seen that there is a lingering problem with the discordance between the genetic signature of Corded Ware and the now many Yamnaya samples analysed that have indicated a broad autosomal connection – Eastern Hunter-Gatherer (EHG) and Caucasian Hunter-Gatherer (CHG) – but do not reveal a direct-line connection in the Y-chromosome haplogroups: Corded Ware males tend to be R1a while Yamnaya males are variants of R1b. The Russian archaeologist Lev Klejn (1927–2019) employed this discrepancy – along with the physical anthropological evidence indicating the similarity of the robust populations of northern Europe to those of Ukraine – to suggest a common genetic source 'somewhere in the North'. Klejn dated this back into the Mesolithic and was supported by the archaeological evidence of Leonid Zaliznyak.[3] I doubt that such an argument will resuscitate a pre-Neolithic solution, not only because of linguistic palaeontology but also because the genetic autosomal evidence still requires a substantial injection of CHG.

Marija Gimbutas suggested that the earlier Globular Amphora culture of northern and central Europe was the 'Kurganized' vector that carried the steppe culture and language westwards to the Corded Ware culture.[4] Yet the evidence of aDNA finds that its male haplogroups were not those of the Corded Ware but overwhelmingly I2a1 (entirely at home with the early expansion of farmers across Europe) with a few examples of R1b-V88, a rather rare haplogroup that appears in eastern Europe in the Mesolithic and was then absorbed into the genetic profile of farmers spreading across the Mediterranean.[5] Nevertheless, attempts to determine the different components that went into making up the Corded Ware population using identity by descent (IBD) derive about a quarter of the Corded Ware genetic signature from the Globular Amphora culture, which contributes the local *non-steppe* component.[6] As for the missing steppe component, attempts to model the earliest Corded Ware populations in Bohemia reveal that they work best when one includes an injection of ancestry resembling that of middle Neolithic Latvians, hence the missing source of the Y-haplogroups might lie somewhere in poorly sampled northeastern Europe.[7] And if we must include the Dnipro-Donets population in the genetic history of the Serednii Stih, the ancestor of the Yamnaya culture, there may be still some life in a variant of the Baltic-Steppe homeland.

Central Asia

Whether the homeland is thought to have emerged from a mountain fastness in ancient Bactria or among steppe nomads on the Asiatic steppe, such origins are contradicted by the evidence of genetics, which assigns to such populations the West Siberian Hunter-Gatherer (WSHG) marker or genetic signatures of populations from further east (Ancient East Asian). While WSHG does manage to penetrate the easternmost part of Europe, occasionally among some steppe burials of the Volga region, it really does not appear to extend any further west nor does it ever appear outside of its own Central Asian home territory in amounts that would indicate it played a significant role. Moreover, the steppelands of this region were clearly penetrated *from* the west (Yamnaya > Afanasievo), where migrations can be traced both archaeologically and genetically from the Volga east as far as the Yenisei river and Xinjiang. This is followed by both archaeologically and genetically supported west-to-east movements associated with the Sintashta and Andronovo cultures. Only after the expansion of Indo-European populations do we see the tide turn and find major migrations from Asia into Europe. Finally a wreath for Central Asia? One would certainly think so but I doubt I could convince Xavier Rouard, who in 2024 published his 'Ten reasons why Central Asia had to be the PIE original homeland.'[8]

India

Since a probable genetic profile of the population of India has been identified both within the subcontinent and on its periphery, it is abundantly clear that neither its genetic signature nor the archaeology associated with it (for example, the magnificent Indus Valley civilization) extended much further than parts of Central Asia and Mesopotamia. Moreover, at least one-third of the subcontinent is occupied by non-Indo-European speakers. Likewise, a wall of non-Indo-European language families in the Zagros mountains and Mesopotamia sever it from the Indo-Europeans of Europe, and the only other direction of possible Out of India expansion – northwestwards through Central Asia and the steppes – was occupied by cultures that, according to both archaeological and genetic evidence, indicate that they were arriving from the west (Europe) and not from southwest Asia. Nevertheless, the lack of a really solid archaeological case for a migration *into* India, coupled with the fragility of the existing palaeogenetic evidence (a steppe signature associated primarily with females in Swat) means that there is so far no truly convincing case for the Indo-Europeanization of India and much of Iran. Diagnosis: India is not the homeland. We need to acknowledge, however, that despite some promising circumstantial evidence from genetics, the Indo-Aryans are not yet totally explained by any other homeland model.

CHAPTER 16

Anatolian Farmer

From an archaeological and, for a while, genetic perspective, the Anatolian Farmer model provided a viable solution to the Indo-European homeland problem. It has, however, always experienced considerable pushback from linguists, especially for its cavalier treatment of the evidence derived from linguistic palaeontology, phylogeny and chronology. One might argue that it has now been completely supplanted by the Steppe or the Armenian hypotheses, but I suspect we would be engaging in a premature burial, for there are certainly a number of scholars who still support it and even employ aDNA evidence to do so.[9] And while its champion Colin Renfrew acknowledged in his 'Marija Rediviva' lecture to the Institute for the Study of Ancient Cultures that the Steppe hypothesis had been vindicated by the genetic evidence for steppe expansions into Europe, he queried whether the Steppe model could explain the Anatolians, thus leaving the possibility of two dispersals – the first from Neolithic Anatolia and a second one from the steppe.[10] I have tried to imagine how if I were appointed his lordship's defence attorney (I know full well that I would be his last choice), I would run with such a model.

Let us set the homeland in Anatolia and associate it with the Ancient Anatolian Farmer (AAF) genetic signature, which spreads through Europe. It would be presumed that those who remained in Anatolia formed the Anatolian branch, and that some unknown/unattested form of Indo-Anatolian spread through Europe over the period c. 6500–4000 BCE. In order to link this homeland to a later steppe expansion it would be logical to start with the formation of the AAF-CHG cline c. 6500 BCE, which would involve AAF also spreading northeast into the Caucasus where it would be associated with the expansion of the Neolithic economy. The vector for the spread of Indo-European would now be the already admixed AAF-CHG (Aknashen-like) as it moves north from the Caucasus to carry Indo-European ultimately to the Yamnaya (where AAF still appears at c. 15 per cent). We then accept nearly all of the Yamnaya 'events package' that sends Celtic, Italic, Germanic, Baltic and Slavic westwards, and Tocharian and Indo-Iranian east and southeastwards.

How would all this work linguistically, where we have tagged Indo-European expansions to two major overlapping waves: an earlier

Neolithic (Indo-Anatolian-derived) dispersal over most of Europe followed by a later (Core-Indo-European) wave associated with the Yamnaya? The second wave should have encountered a series of different Indo-Anatolian branches running from the Balkans to Ireland that had evolved independently, and no doubt differently, from those that had migrated through the Caucasus and admixed with EHG and created the Yamnaya. These would either be replaced by a new layer of Indo-European associated with the Yamnaya or they will have survived the spread of the Yamnaya leaving us perhaps with a patchwork of Indo-European languages. Some of these languages will have come directly from Indo-Anatolian, while others passed through the Caucasus and evolved on the Pontic-Caspian steppe or even formed as an admixture between the two streams. What we would expect is the linguistic residue of a single language family that essentially divided into two segments (Anatolian and Steppe), each of which experienced about three thousand years of separate existence and then merged over the same territory.

Unfortunately (for my client), we do not discern evidence of two layers of Indo-European languages as we should if they had been spread at the onset of the Neolithic and then millennia later when the steppe languages arrived. A somewhat but not so drastic parallel can be found in England. Both Old Norse and English derive from a common ancestor dated to *c.* 500 BCE, meaning there was about a 1,500-year interval from the collapse of Proto-Germanic to the emergence of Old Norse and Old English. This period for separate evolution is in the order of half that proposed for the two waves (Anatolian-Steppe) model before Old Norse and Old English eventually met up in the Danelaw of England. We can recover clear evidence of a host of Norse loanwords borrowed into English when the Vikings came to settle in the same place as Old English. We would expect the same if not better evidence for multiple layers of Indo-European languages in the two-stage model. (The opposing attorneys would be shouting: where is this evidence for two horizons of Indo-European languages?)

The only language, then, that might be attributed to the Neolithic spread other than the Anatolian branch would perhaps be Greek, where Mycenaean burials exhibit only a weak genetic signal that might be traced back to the steppe. So here one might argue that the original Neolithic language did manage to survive in Greece. But the problem (as has been rehearsed before) is that there is no special downstream relationship between Anatolian and Greek, since the latter must share a common period of development with all the languages that are being explained by the steppe expansion.

We could assemble all the other reasons for rejecting the Anatolian model (its failure to meet the tests of linguistic palaeontology, its very early chronology and its association with a far more extensive cereal economy than can be reconstructed to Proto-Indo-Anatolian), but let us just return to the most obvious. If we wish to associate the AAF with the agricultural and linguistic vector that carried Indo-Anatolian through the Caucasus (admixed with CHG) to the steppelands, why did they not leave any linguistic traces in the Caucasus?

Is the Anatolian Farmer model dead? I would hesitate to pronounce it so and the most recent solution in my Appendix supports it.[11] The Ptolemaic view of an Earth-centred universe survived serious criticism for centuries by patching up any discordant observation with epicycles and equants, so I suspect that others might generate arguments that will keep the Anatolian model out of the morgue. In fact, for the rip-snorting hell of it, I have provided below one perspective that might keep a variety of the Anatolian model on life support (as I warned in an earlier chapter).

Balkan and Danubian

For most, the objections to the Anatolian Farmer model should be enough to snuff out what should be seen as potential homelands downstream of the initial expansion of agriculture through Europe. Yet I think there is a reason for trying to run with one of these downstream homelands, because it exposes a major assumption that often goes unnoticed. I will go for the Danubian homeland model since I think this is the one I can play with most easily.

The initial assumption is that the expansion of agriculture from Anatolia spread a new language (family) across Europe. Until now we have assumed that it was either Indo-Anatolian (the Anatolian Farmer model) or a completely unrelated language (any other model), but there was always a third possibility: the Anatolian Farmers' language was not Indo-Anatolian but an earlier ancestor of Indo-Anatolian that, after several millennia, evolved (or congealed) into a series of different languages, only one of which in the Danube area evolved into Core-Indo-European and after a thousand years of development spread both agriculture and its language northwards towards the Baltic. The incursion of steppe genes and the social organization associated with its population subsequently appeared in central and northern Europe *c.* 3000 BCE, which brought about the emergence of the Corded Ware and northern Beaker cultures. But the language of both the Danubian and Nordic regions did not change to that of the steppe (where, in this model, the steppe intruders spoke any language but an Indo-European one and had about as much impact on the languages of Europe as Scythian, Hunnic or Avar), instead remaining the locally evolved Indo-European despite the major genomic shift. However, they were gifted by the newcomers from the east with the social and technological tools to spread their language. Both David Anthony[12] and I have called attention to Ronald Atkinson's study of language shift associated with the Acholi of Uganda where a minority population, armed with a chiefdom social organization, spread their Luo language over a Nilotic-speaking population in northern Uganda. One of the many interesting aspects of this scenario is the fact that many of the Luo speakers themselves had been similarly swallowed up by the Bantu and it was only a peripheral group of the Luo who managed to adopt the new system, which had absorbed their linguistic relations, and weaponize it to spread their own language. In short, the tools we impute to a culture to give it the edge in spreading its own language are often transferrable and may also be adopted by different languages to spread their own. Agriculture, for example, makes a great vector for spreading a language to hunter-gatherers, but any group of hunter-gatherers who adopt it and still manage to hang on to their own language can also weaponize the new economy or social system to spread their language. This is what I refer to as the 'Peripheral European' issue in Chapter 13.

The time depth of this model removes criticism that the proto-language has been set too early and fails to accord with the evidence of linguistic palaeontology. As we are ascribing a local origin for the Corded

Ware culture, the Asiatic Indo-European languages can all be explained according to the Steppe model since that presumes a genetic source emanating from the spread of Corded Ware to the east. As for the Anatolians, we could either assume that the split between Proto-Anatolian and Proto-Indo-European was very deep and that they arose locally in Anatolia or, as so often before, we locate them among some farmers in the Balkans adjacent to the earliest Danubian communities.

I do not for a moment believe the model I have just propounded, but it illustrates how easy it is, with the application of some Ptolemaic-like fiddle factors, to produce a new variation of the Anatolian Farmer model that keeps it from the grave. I also suspect that if I had not refrained from producing a map with lovely arrows illustrating the migrations of all the Indo-European branches from a homeland on the Danube (back to **4.5**), I could have enjoyed watching it go viral in the blogosphere. I hope this helps to explain why we have been torturing ourselves with this same obstinate issue for several centuries.

Armenia and the Caucasus

We have already discussed the case for a homeland south of the Caucasus or within the Caucasus itself at some depth. One of its strongest attractions is that it places the homeland close enough to the historical seats of the Anatolian branch that a case for Proto-Anatolian origins can be built out of the creation of the AAF-CHG cline from 6500 BCE onwards. Moreover, CHG is obviously a critical genetic component in the construction of the steppe genetic signature, so we get to explain both Proto-Anatolian and Core-Indo-European.

The problems with a CHG homeland have already been rehearsed. Here I will mention only three objections. First, as with AAF, it must somehow explain how CHG spread from either south of the Caucasus or from within the Caucasus itself to the steppe, yet left nothing but a trail of non-Indo-European languages attested from the Bronze Age onwards. Second, its presence in the steppelands appears to lack any significant association with male haplogroups, as one might have expected had it been the primary vector for the spread of a language into what emerges as a clearly patrilineal society. Third, most of the proposed chronologies and dispersal scenarios make less than satisfactory fits with most Indo-European phylogenies.

Pontic-Caspian steppe

Archaeological and genetic evidence supports a fairly convincing case that the Pontic-Caspian steppe must have been at least the secondary homeland for many of the Indo-European languages of Europe, and a proximate staging area for the expansions of the Indo-Europeans into Asia. It also meets the requirements of linguistic palaeontology better than most.[13] Moreover, in its association with a mobile pastoral economy coupled with the possession of both wheeled vehicles and the domestic horse, it possessed an attractive means for the expansion of both its population and its languages. In the contest between it and its other genetic components, its fairly unremitting association with a narrow range of local EHG patrilines makes it a more likely language vector than either of the other elements (CHG or AAF) in the steppe admixture.

Thirty years ago, at a conference in New Delhi, I outlined what I regarded as a five-point checklist of the principles by which any homeland theory should be assessed.[14]

1. *Temporal plausibility*. A satisfactory homeland should meet the requirement of being temporally plausible (its location in time should not be seriously outside of the general consensus of time depth proposed by linguists and the evidence of linguistic palaeontology). The Steppe model appears to satisfy all constituencies except for the Auckland school of computational analysis.
2. *Exclusion principle*. It should not be located in a place that can be shown to have been occupied by non-Indo-Europeans at the relevant time of the homeland. As the Pontic-Caspian is linguistically unknown until the Iron Age, it gets an easy (although hardly earned) pass on this one. However, when it comes to assessing the probability of its closest competitors, such as the Anatolian and Caucasian models, it does have the edge because of the very solid evidence for non-Indo-European

languages throughout the Caucasus and, more anciently, south of the Caucasus during the Bronze Age. The only relevant non-Indo-European entity north of the Caucasus is Uralic, and there are no grounds to situate its own homeland or speakers within the usual borders assigned to the Steppe homeland model.

3. *Relationship principle*. The position of the homeland should accord with the general consensus of the Indo-European phylogeny and the relationship of the various branches. The Steppe model does a fairly good job of providing a likely point of dispersion for the Core-Indo-European languages but does have difficulties explaining Anatolian; also, tracing the relationship between Armenian and Greek within the Steppe model is problematic.

4. *Archaeological plausibility*. The source and dispersal of the Indo-European languages must be supported by archaeological evidence and cannot be based solely (as I wrote many years ago) on a 'proponent's ability to wield a felt-tip pen'. In retrospect, I would now add that it also requires at least plausible palaeogenomic evidence. Again, the Steppe model seems to find support for much of the initial dispersals of the Indo-European branches (excepting again Anatolian, but see below) although, like all other theories, there are problems with following the various branches to their historical seats.

5. *Total distribution principle*. A successful homeland model must be able to explain the origins of all the Indo-European branches and languages. This principle was added to a large extent by my frustration at the many scholars who attempted to make plausible models to explain, say, the European branches, but then simply dealt with Asia by a series of archaeologically unmotivated arrows showing migrations to India and western China; or, dealing with supporters who argued that as no convincing case could be made to derive the origins of Germanic or Indo-Aryan from an external source, this indicated that their pet branch must also be the homeland of all the other Indo-European languages without demonstrating how that would work. To deal with all the branches in any practical detail would require another book (and for this

writer another life). Here it is only my intention to provide a superficial overview as to how the expansions might convincingly have played out employing the Steppe model, and where the most outstanding problems still lie.[15] We will work from east to west.

Language dispersal from the Steppe

Tocharian

The Steppe model usually explains Tocharian origins with an appeal to the remarkable, but archaeologically and genetically supported, evidence for the long-distance migration from the Pontic-Caspian region to the Yenisei river (Minusinsk Basin) and Altai mountains [16.1]. Here we find the Afanasievo culture (3300–2500 BCE), which has been described as genetically identical to that of the Yamnaya and is dominated by Y-haplogroups R1b-Z2103 and some Q-M25 and mitochondrial DNA (mtDNA) haplogroups U4 (x5), U5 (x12), T2 (x4) and J2 (x5) and several others.[16] This gets the descendants as far east as they need to go; in fact, there is evidence that the Afanasievo made it to central Mongolia where they introduced a pastoral (dairy) economy.[17] Unfortunately, while the steppe immigrants made it far enough east, we have not (yet) found them far enough south. But at least we now have some burials from the related Chemurchek group (variously dated 2750/2500–1900/1700 BCE), situated in the Dzungar Basin south of the Altai mountains, which also display a steppe ancestry and where we find the same variant of male haplogroup R1b (R-Z2103) as in the Afanasievo, along with the steppe-derived Q1b1 and comparable mitochondrial evidence (e.g. U5, T2).[18] This still leaves about 230 km (140 miles) to transverse and the Tienshan mountains to cross between one of the southernmost Afanasievo/Chemurchek sites (Nileke) and the main Tocharian centre of Kuqa. Nevertheless, it is not too much to imagine that the ancestors of Tocharian could manage the trip over the next two thousand years.

There are, however, two problems to address.[19] First, we have absolutely no idea what our target looks like genetically. So far no genetically sampled individuals occupying the relevant space and time have been found that might be considered to be certain candidates as Tocharian

CHAPTER 16

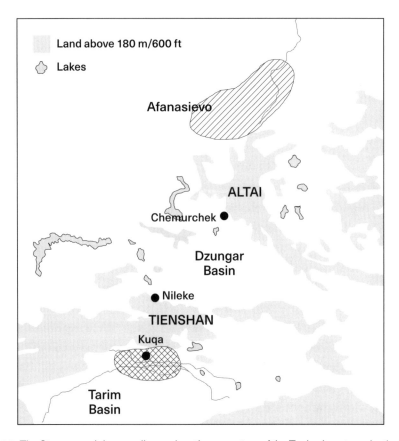

16.1 The Steppe model generally requires the ancestors of the Tocharians to make their way from the Afanasievo culture of the Altai region in the north through the Dzungar Basin (where Afanasievo-related sites of the Chemurchek group retain its genetic profile as far as Nileke) and then further south into the Tarim Basin where the core area of the Tocharians is found around Kuqa (crosshatching).

speakers. The Tocharians were Buddhists and cremated their dead, meaning at present we lack the type of evidence that would abound if we were hunting our early Celtic, Germanic or Greek speakers who left enough skeletal remains for us to analyse. And while it might be tempting to turn to the Europoid mummies found in various regions across the Tarim Basin, none have been retrieved so far from the territories most likely to have been occupied by Tocharian speakers.[20] Second, just to make matters more complicated, we must deal with the issue that Tocharian was not the only Indo-European language to have crossed the steppe to be spoken in the Tarim Basin. In the eastern part of the Tarim we also find Khotanese Saka, an East Iranian language, which probably entered the region as part of the Andronovo expansion of the Middle and Late Bronze Age. We have clear evidence of its presence both north and south of the Tienshan mountains. So the Steppe model gets us as far east, yet still leaves us some way off from establishing a totally convincing solution to Tocharian origins.

Indo-Iranian

A case for a steppe origin for Indo-Iranian certainly exists but, as with Tocharian, it is far from fully supported in terms of delivering a significant portion of the two branches to their historical seats [**16.2**]. The easiest 'win', if you will, is East Iranian, which spanned the steppelands both north of the Black Sea during the Iron Age (Scythians, Sarmatians etc.) and east of the Urals (the Saka). These historically known peoples followed immediately on from the preceding Late Bronze Age Andronovo culture (*c*. 2000–900 BCE) or, as mentioned above, even slightly earlier with the Sintashta culture (2200–1750 BCE). The computational split dates for a common Indo-Iranian tend to fall at 3500 BCE (Moscow) and 3000 BCE (Berkeley), while the division between Indo-Aryan and Iranian tends to fall *c*. 2500 BCE (Moscow) and 2000 BCE (Berkeley). These are figures in the right ballpark of traditional chronologies, all of which are younger than the recent Auckland dates of *c*. 5000 BCE for Indo-Iranian (within an enormous range of 6400–3600 BCE) and *c*. 3520 BCE for the split between Indo-Aryan and Iranian (range 4800–2500 BCE). From a steppe perspective, there is no evidence of a steppe genetic profile moving further south of Central Asia earlier than *c*. 2000 BCE, by which time it begins to appear in the periphery of the Bactria-Margiana Archaeological Complex (BMAC) of Turkmenistan.

The main problem is connecting the steppe with northern India to account for Indo-Aryan and the appearance of Vedic Sanskrit in the former territory of the Indus Valley civilization, as well as an Indo-Aryan presence in former Hurrian territory, where we find traces of such a language c. 1500 BCE in the lands of the Mitanni. Archaeologically, there has always been a roster of cultures regarded as intruders into the Indus region that may have carried Indo-Aryan southwards, but none so far convincing.[21] Recovering aDNA within the climate of India has proved exceptionally difficult, which further complicates our ability to determine the earlier population history of South Asia. The evidence based on modern DNA of the current population, however, does suggest credible models indicating that, while southern India retained its earlier genetic profile with strong links to the genetic profile of Andaman Islanders and represents an Ancient Ancestral Southern Indian (AASI) genetic signature, the northern part of the subcontinent shows evidence of an ingress of genes flowing from the steppelands of the north. The steppe genetic signature penetrated India earlier than the historically attested migrations of Iron Age steppe populations. This resulted in the formation of an Ancestral North Indian (ANI) profile, which is found particularly among brahmins, the caste most closely associated with the preservation of the early Vedic religion.

The evidence is not entirely based on back projection from modern DNA but also involves sampling from a prehistoric population in the Swat Valley of Pakistan, long been regarded as a potential tripwire for any invasion of India. It offers archaeological evidence consistent with at least some of the aspects usually associated with an Indo-European incursion (for example, the side on which someone was buried being determined by gender, horse sacrifice and ritual similarities with steppe-related cultures).[22] A large quantity of samples from the Swat (or Gandhara Grave) culture (c. 1800–400 BCE), mostly centred on the period c. 1200–800 BCE, reveal a population admixed with a steppe-derived component. As was the case with CHG in the Pontic-Caspian region, the steppe DNA largely derived from females rather than males, who admixed with the local population during the period c. 1900–1500 BCE. Nevertheless, there were several males who present the typical steppe Y-haplogroup R1a (R-Z93, Z94; V1180) and the evidence of modern northern Indian populations indicates that the spread of the steppe genetic profile there was largely driven by males.[23]

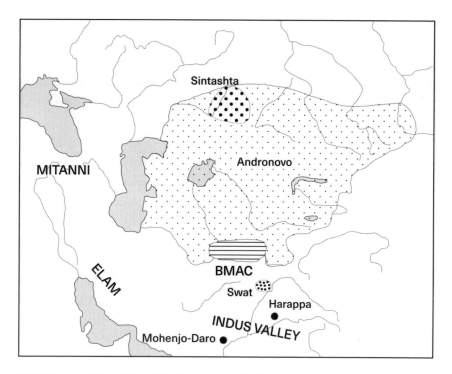

16.2 The test of the validity of the Steppe model in South Asia is to explain the presence of Indo-Iranian languages in the former territory of the Indus Valley civilization, the appearance of Iranian extending into the former territory of Elam, and the presence of Indo-Aryan personal names and chariot-associated vocabulary in the lands of the Mitanni. The genetic evidence can be followed from the Pontic-Caspian steppe through variants of the Corded Ware horizon and then southeastwards through the Sintashta and Andronovo cultures to the Swat Valley, but further expansions into Indo-Iranian territory remain to be archaeologically verified.

The data on steppe Y-haplogroups emphasizes that the earliest steppe expansions eastwards (Afanasievo) and directly south into Armenia were associated with R1b. This contrasts with R1a, which is associated with the putative migration of a steppe population c. 2000–1500 BCE through the Swat Valley and where it still constitutes a 'significant fraction of the Y haplogroups in present-day Iran, Turan and South Asia'.[24] That Indo-Iranian (R1a) tracks differently from the putative ancestor of Tocharian (R1b) is comforting, as these two branches do not seem to share any close phylogenetic relationship linguistically. Tocharian, however, was clearly in contact with an East Iranian language at some point in its history, so the difference between the haplogroups might offer some hope for distinguishing between early Tocharian and early Iranian populations in Xinjiang.

As for a solution to Indo-Iranian origins, the genetic evidence for the Steppe model provides good circumstantial evidence, but it remains to be seen how it might be fitted into a conclusive archaeological model as well. While we perhaps have some form of time frame for steppe intrusions into northern India, we still cannot follow the trail any further than the Swat Valley, which, incidentally, is more likely to be associated with Nuristani (see 1.9), a much smaller branch of Indo-Iranian, rather than Indo-Aryan itself. Similarly, how the genetic evidence should articulate with cultures in Iran south of Andronovo is also still to be established. We appear to be dealing with the soft underbelly of the Steppe model.

Armenian and Greek

We have already surveyed the evidence supporting a steppe incursion into the area of Armenia during the Bronze Age (*c.* 2500–2000 BCE), where the evidence for a steppe genetic signature arrives at approximately the same time as the appearance of the (Armenian) Kurgan culture in the Kura-Araxes region. If we agree with geneticists[25] and assume that the presence of this genetic signature in Armenia during the Bronze Age does indicate the arrival of the Proto-Armenians, it provides persuasive evidence of their origins from the steppe but it also opens up an interesting headache for linguists.

With very few exceptions, almost every phylogeny of Indo-European finds Armenian either sharing a node with Greek (frequently provided with a split date *c.* 2500–2000 BCE[26]), or at least regarded as having a close contact relationship with Greek. We have seen that this has traditionally been accommodated by a model involving a secondary homeland in the Balkans for Greek, the ancient Balkan languages (e.g. Dacian and Thracian), and both Phrygian and Armenian, which were envisaged since the time of Herodotus as migrants from the Balkans to Anatolia and Armenia.

Clearly, if one accepts the proposition that Proto-Armenian arrived in its home by a migration due south from the steppe, it didn't come from a secondary homeland in the Balkans, and the assumption that it had been a close neighbour of Proto-Greek shortly before the latter descended into the Aegean becomes a non-starter.

On the other hand, the concept of viewing the Balkans as a possible secondary homeland derived from the steppe for the creation of Indo-European languages such as Dacian, Thracian and Phrygian has some genetic support. We find both evidence for Yamnaya burials and individuals with 'high steppe ancestry' in the southern Balkans (Croatia, Serbia, Albania and Bulgaria) that attest the typical steppe admixture between EHG and CHG, but here combined with about 23 per cent of the local AAF, which had been introduced from Anatolia during the Neolithic.[27]

We have just excluded Armenian from this region, so how do we deal with its alleged partner, Greek? For many years the Classical historian Robert Drews has associated the arrival of the Greek language with the spread of a chariot-driving aristocracy emanating from the east, specifically the area around Armenia, where he argues that Indo-Iranian, Greek and Armenian are seen to emerge.[28] This would obviously be an attractive solution to our problem if we had anything more than the presence of chariotry appearing in the two regions, but other than this, there is really no convincing archaeological trail that leads from Armenia to Greece. If you can't get the Armenians from the Balkans nor the Greeks from Armenia, what is left to explain the majority of the phylogenies?

An alternative model might situate a common Graeco-Armenian home in the southern steppe and have Proto-Armenian travel south through the Caucasus and the ancestors of the Greeks make their way to the Danube and then journey south through the Balkans and on towards Greece, but while there is enough ink left in my felt-tip pen to draw such arrows my brain still has some control of my fingers. The actual evidence for aDNA in Greece is admittedly poor, especially with regard to the Y-chromosomal evidence. The Neolithic yields, expectedly, G2a, which was well known among Anatolian farmers, and by *c.* 2400 BCE we begin to see the appearance of J2a, which we have already seen working its way westwards from eastern Anatolia. While the early Neolithic in

Greece was probably initiated from Anatolia and there is a close genetic resemblance on both sides of the Aegean, by *c.* 4000 BCE there is a marked flow of CHG across the sea.[29] In the transition from the Neolithic to the Bronze Age, the period in which elsewhere we find evidence for steppe incursions into the Balkans, there is no evidence for the steppe genetic signature from the few Early Bronze Age burials examined from northern Greece. However, by *c.* 2000 BCE, the Middle Bronze Age in Greece, there is evidence for an infusion of the steppe (EHG-CHG) cocktail, which supports 'the hypothesis that populations from the Pontic-Caspian steppe contributed to the ancestry' of Middle Bronze Age Greek populations.[30] Although we lack any characteristically steppe Y-chromosomal evidence, the steppe element is not situated on the X chromosome or with the mtDNA. This suggests that it was probably the product of 'male-biased gene flow from Steppe-like ancestry into the Aegean', which, presumably, we have not yet uncovered. Moreover, a recent study concludes that the pattern of steppe ancestry 'does not support a large-scale population displacement but the north-south gradient indicates the directionality of this migration and population mingling'.[31] In short, we seem to be dealing not so much with the 'coming of the Greeks' as the 'trickling'.

In the Late Bronze Age, we of course know that the Mycenaeans (*c.* 1700–1200 BCE) wrote in (Mycenaean) Greek, and while the steppe signature is present in the small number of Mycenaean samples it only averages about 5 per cent.[32] There is very little evidence for the Y-chromosome (in one case we find J2) but two Mycenaean burials (dated to 1450–1200 BCE) from Pylos (the Palace of Nestor) have yielded R-PF7562, which has been found earlier north of the Caucasus in a kurgan of the Catacomb culture dated to *c.* 2866–2580 BCE.[33] We also find R-Z2106 not only in Armenia but also in the steppelands, as well as in both North Macedonia and Albania, potential staging areas of Proto-Greeks, although how precisely that would work archaeologically has yet to be determined. A recent attempt to determine the precise source of the steppe DNA in Greece concluded 'at the moment it is not possible to more closely identify the region(s) from where the genetic affinity was derived'.[34] It might be noted that the genetic profile of modern Greeks resembles far more the population from the Middle Bronze Age than the Mycenaeans.

The problems with a steppe solution are obviously still challenging in the extreme. By the time the steppe signature begins to emerge in Greece we can reckon that the population was already running with about 17 per cent CHG, which was completely unassociated with the steppe signature (which only amounted to *c.* 4 per cent),[35] and so models of migration from Anatolia in the later Neolithic are still very much on the cards. The genetic evidence for steppe intrusions exists from *c.* 2000 BCE and one of the many more popular archaeological solutions to the 'coming of the Greeks' has looked to the transition between Early Helladic II and III – the period spanning *c.* 2300–2100 BCE. However, we seem a long way from putting the archaeological and genetic evidence together into a coherent narrative that can be traced archaeologically. As long as geneticists conclude that 'the genetic impact of steppe on Aegean populations was quantitatively minor',[36] the Steppe model has its work cut out for it.

North European (Germanic, Baltic and Slavic)

The spatial correspondence between the territory of the Corded Ware culture and the later historical seats of the Germanic, Baltic and Slavic languages has naturally encouraged scholars to associate the northwest Indo-European languages with Corded Ware. And, of course, it was the discovery that about 80 per cent of the autosomal DNA of the Corded Ware genetic signature was derived from the steppelands that thrust aDNA into the middle of all discussion of the homeland. Nevertheless, there remained (as always, at least) two major issues. The first of these was purely concerned with the genetic evidence itself, which currently amounts to about eighty Corded Ware individuals. While the autosomal evidence clearly indicated a major steppe derivation of the sampled Corded Ware burials, there was a major discrepancy between the specific haplogroups. The Yamnaya burials on the steppe, as well as those Yamnaya burials that were intrusive into the Danubian region, were almost exclusively male R1b (overwhelmingly R-Z2103 with some M269 and L23), while the Corded Ware samples were largely R1a (R-M417 and its subclades with a few others), although there was a cluster of Corded Ware burials from Bohemia that were primarily R1b (L151). The overall majority of Corded Ware males lack an R1a ancestor among the

Yamnaya (so far); of those that do possess the more characteristic R1b of the steppe population, most of them tend to belong to a different haplotype (L51) from that of the Yamnaya (Z2103; see **15.5**). It might also be added that the Corded Ware sample showed no evidence of any typical male CHG haplogroups such as G or J.

Generally, all of this is recognized as a major problem that should be solved by greater sampling in the belief that there is a geographically and genetically closer steppe source (a missing link) to the Corded Ware genetic profile. Attention is primarily focused on areas minimally sampled between the steppe world and Corded Ware regions, such as Moldova and Belarus. What has been excluded is any association between the amount of steppe DNA and the date of the burial (the earliest dated burials do not display statistically more steppe DNA than later burials). In short, in one of the more recent attempts to address this entire problem, the authors concluded: 'How exactly the emergence and expansion of the Corded Ware are linked to the emergence and expansion of the Yamnaya horizon remains unclear.'[37]

It should also be emphasized that there is much needed fine-tuning of the genetic evidence with respect to the formation of the various language branches. The specific origin of Germanic, for example, has recently been tackled by the Copenhagen lab, who have uncovered evidence for an (archaeologically unattested) spread of steppe-related populations about eight hundred years after the initial spread of the Corded Ware culture. This later population bears admixture traces with Baltic hunter-gatherers into Scandinavia, which the Copenhagen lab regards as an alternative model for the origins of Germanic (and which would help explain the links found between Germanic and Balto-Slavic).[38] At least, it can be suggested that the association of the Corded Ware (and its genetic signature) with the arrival of the domestic economy in the east Baltic region does provide additional support for the Steppe model.[39]

The second major problem is the lack of a convincing archaeological explanation for the quite massive steppe contribution to the Corded Ware population. The first hint of a solution appeared in the genetic event horizon year of 2015, when I learned that the Copenhagen lab were about to publish evidence of *Yersinia pestis* (bubonic plague) genomes from the teeth of both a Corded Ware skeleton and several burials from the steppe, including one from the Afanasievo culture, the eastern offspring of the Yamnaya.[40] It was difficult to suppress images of disease-carrying steppe pastoralists, who had long become accustomed to the plague, wheezing their way into the rest of Europe (like Europeans introducing smallpox to the Americas) and decimating the native populations as they advanced. As with all good straightforward theories, further evidence introduced some complications, as it appeared that the plague had already spread as far west as Sweden during the Neolithic, well before the arrival of any steppe intruders. The most likely centre of origin was thought to lie in the enormous town-sized settlements of the Cucuteni-Trypillia culture, the original vector being more probably trade networks rather than massive migrations.[41] Still, it could be argued that plague may have reduced Neolithic populations to such an extent that they were far more liable to be replaced by later intrusive pastoralists.

By 2021 the date for the appearance of *Y. pestis* was pushed back still further to a skeleton in Latvia dating to *c.* 5300–5000 BCE, which raised questions about how widespread the disease was (especially if the vector was largely a product of rodent bites; the genetic environment that would promote spread by fleas did not appear until after 2000 BCE), nor could we be certain how deadly it proved.[42] To this might be added, that unless one can demonstrate that the population from the steppe had already developed a certain degree of immunity to the plague, it would be difficult to see how plague bacteria would have given an advantage to their dispersal. Although we have an interesting possible model to explain a widely recognized apparent drop in population towards the end of the Neolithic, we still do not know with any degree of certainty the causes of this or how it might be employed to explain the major genomic shift experienced across central and northern Europe as it entered the Early Bronze Age.

As mentioned, the one obvious observation regarding Corded Ware marriage patterns emphasizes that it involved female exogamy: Corded Ware males selected their wives from both women with steppe ancestry but also frequently from the local population.

Celtic and Italic

A year after the genetic revolution of 2015, new aDNA evidence found itself in support of a century-old hypothesis that associated the Celtic languages with the spread of the Beaker culture (2800–1800 BCE). This was an Eneolithic horizon marked by a particular ceramic beaker and an assortment of recurring grave gifts involving archers' equipment coupled with the early exploitation of copper and gold. Three Early Bronze Age burials, belonging to a culture slightly later than the early Beakers, discovered behind a pub on Rathlin Island off the coast of County Antrim, Northern Ireland, revealed that they harboured significant evidence of steppe ancestry.[43] And soon afterwards a major study of 226 Beaker burials across Europe found that, with the exception of those recovered from Iberia, 84 of the 90 males sampled possessed the characteristic R1b-M269 steppe haplogroup.[44] The coincidence in the distribution of the Beaker culture and the early attestations of the Celtic languages had long been made, and so the Beaker horizon might well be identified with the dispersal of the Celtic languages.[45]

This is the easy and direct explanation, but it is complicated phylogenetically by the fact that the Beaker horizon dates to *c.* 2800–1800 BCE, which generally predates (although not by an enormous amount) the usual split date attributed to the Celtic language. For example, it places Celtic in Ireland *c.* 2400 BCE, but then has to explain why the earliest recorded evidence of Irish (4th–7th century CE) is so similar to Gaulish inscriptions of the first centuries BCE. Consequently, there are some who have argued that such an early date is more easily attributed to an earlier Italo-Celtic phase, rather than an independent Celtic branch.[46] The genetic evidence at least does not contradict this. The earliest evidence for a steppe genetic signature in Italy tends to coincide with the appearance of Beakers in this region, both on islands such as Sicily,[47] and in northern Italy, where it initially dates to *c.* 2000 BCE and is then found, increasing over time, in central Italy some four centuries later. The authors of one major study suggest that the steppe ancestry 'could have arrived through Late N[eolithic]/Bell Beaker groups from central Europe'.[48]

As with the emergence of the other branches, Celtic and Italic both encounter serious problems when it comes to considering later periods.

How does one fit the genetic with the archaeological and phylogenetic evidence? For example, did the Celtic languages actually evolve in Britain and Ireland after the arrival of the Beakers, or were they a product of later intrusions from genetically similar populations from the Continent?[49] These questions, however, take us into issues that do not directly impinge upon locating the Indo-European homeland.

Anatolian

There has long been a series of both linguistic and archaeological arguments to bring the Proto-Anatolians into their historical seats either from the Balkans or from the steppe via the Caucasus. None of these has been particularly convincing (including my own[50]). Most recently, Alwin Kloekhorst has listed four reasons for preferring a western (Balkan) entry for the Proto-Anatolians:

1. The Anatolian languages when first attested are situated in the west and south of Anatolia.
2. The Kızılırmak (Halys) river formed a natural barrier between the earliest Anatolians and the non-Indo-European Hatti to the north who were only assimilated from *c.* 1700 BCE onwards (this would not have served as a barrier to an eastern entry).
3. The expansion of the Anatolians – both Hittites and Luvians – in historical times was west to east and not the reverse.
4. Western invasions also explain the presence of the Phrygians, Armenians and Galatians.[51]

Because of Anatolia's position as the first branch to separate in its widely accepted position in the Indo-European phylogeny, any solution would usually require a pre-Yamnaya (*c.* 3300 BCE) archaeological entity under the assumption that the Yamnaya culture was associated with the expansion of the later Core-Indo-European languages. Attempts to eke out a plausible archaeological solution were generally dependent on extrapolating from the small amount of evidence for very early steppe-associated burials in the lower Danube region to a general (though not convincingly attested) penetration of the entire east Balkans by

3300 BCE. From here were postulated subsequent migrations into northwest Anatolia, usually pegged against various early stages of Troy.[52] The actual evidence for an early steppe penetration of the Danube region was linked to several burials belonging to the Novodanylivka culture, such as the Suvorovo kurgan in eastern Bulgaria dated *c.* 4200–3900 BCE,[53] suitably early to identify with the ancestor of the Anatolian branch (see 9.10). That these burials were both early and derived from the steppe is amply verified by the recent comparison of one such burial at Csongrád in Hungary (4300–4000 BCE) with burials in the Lower Volga region.[54] There is also evidence of a gradual penetration of the Northwest Pontic region (Usatovo, Cernavoda I) in the 5th millennium BCE and afterwards (but pre-Yamnaya) by a genetically steppe population.[55]

A key issue here is that neither autosomal nor Y-chromosome evidence for characteristic steppe genetic markers, such as EHG or Y-haplogroup R1b, had been recovered from the areas of Anatolia where we might have predicted Anatolian speakers. And we have already seen earlier that the attempt to discern traces of steppe genes in a small sample of Late Bronze Age Anatolians proved negative.[56] Similarly, in a later study of the region it was stated that although EHG had penetrated southeast Europe, there was no evidence that it had crossed into Anatolia during the Bronze Age.[57] Any migration of steppe populations, even those whose ancestry had been greatly admixed with local Balkan populations, should have carried significant amounts of AAF and local Balkan WHG genes along with them into Anatolia; there is absolutely no evidence for this.[58] On the other hand, it has been recently claimed that there is some evidence for a migration from the east.

Samples drawn from Bronze Age and later samples in central Anatolia have been claimed to possess about 11 per cent steppe ancestry consistent with having derived from the Caucasus-Lower Volga cline.[59] In addition, there is also some evidence of R1b-V1636, a haplogroup known on the steppe before the emergence of the Yamnaya culture (for example, at Berezhnovka, Progress-2 and Remontnoye), which disappeared from the steppe but has been found in Armenia and eastern Anatolia. As it has been found among individuals who lack autosomal evidence from the steppe this may indicate how this signal was diluted as it made its way into Anatolia. The Harvard (Reich) lab proposes that this is evidence for a migration from the Caucasus-Lower Volga cline southwards *c.* 4400 BCE that admixed along the way through the Caucasus with local populations and ultimately reached central Anatolia, providing a plausible explanation of Anatolian origins within the Steppe model. It must be admitted that the haplogroup evidence does not seem to be found any further west than Arslantepe in eastern Anatolia (see **14.2**). As Arslantepe lay in the border country of Isuwa, it was not conquered by the Hittites until *c.* 1350 BCE, so at best it could only have been on the path west to the land of the Anatolians; it does not place them in their early historical seats.

This is the best case that has been made to tie Anatolian origins to an origin in the Pontic-Caspian steppe, but accepting that turnabout is fair play, I can hardly hail a genetic signature of 11 per cent as solid evidence for the migration of the Anatolians after dismissing such low percentages of genetic admixture throughout this paper. As mentioned several times before, we also need a clear idea of the social context of the samples that carry the steppe signature. And, in case you just missed the constituency issue: the palaeogenomic evidence for an eastern entry of Proto-Anatolians was rejected by the linguistic arguments in favour of a western entry. We are left then with some tentative evidence that steppe genes managed to penetrate eastern Anatolia during the Bronze Age, but we are still a long way from deriving the Anatolians from the steppe.

The Indo-European homeland: A rediscovery

I am well aware that Joshua Whatmough's comments have hung over this entire enterprise from the Preface onwards: how does one make a definitive answer to the question where was the homeland of the Indo-Europeans? My conclusion as to its location is, on the one hand, a bit disheartening, because after a half-century of study I am pretty much where I started: I believe the Indo-European homeland lies in the Pontic-Caspian steppe because it is the one that satisfies the greatest number of constituencies and provides the strongest case for explaining the dispersal of the Indo-Europeans. I will not pretend that it doesn't have a number of weaknesses yet of all the potential homelands that have been proposed, it seems to me to be still the least bad.

On the other hand, I can't help but hear the laughter emanating from the generations of homeland hunters over the last few thousand years. It begins with the ancient Jewish scholars who assembled the Table of Nations in Genesis chapter 10, sometime in the 1st millennium BCE, and those who followed after them – such as the historian Josephus – who assigned ethnic identities to the various names of Japheth's offspring. It also rings out from Bishop Isidore of Seville (560–636 CE), whose *Etymologiae*, the Wikipedia of the Middle Ages, explained the origins of the peoples of Europe from Japheth. And when Andreas Jäger turned to the origins of the language of Scythia in 1686 he identified it with 'the language of Japheth', which evolved (just as Latin evolved into the various Romance languages) into Greek, Latin, Celtic, Germanic and Slavic. For over two millennia the Indo-Europeans have been sought either in the Caucasus, the resting place of the Ark, or the vast steppelands to its north from which they dispersed. In conclusion, I have brought you to where tradition has placed the Indo-European homeland for 2,500 years. Well, I did promise a 'rediscovery'.

Glossary

The definitions provided here are designed solely to assist the reader in understanding discussions involving the homeland problem and should not be regarded as full or even standard definitions.

Linguistic symbols
* An asterisk is employed in historical linguistics to indicate a word whose existence is based on reconstruction rather than any direct testimony, e.g. **yeg-* is reconstructed through the comparison of Old Irish *aig*, English *icicle* and Hittite *eka-*, all 'ice'.
> denotes the direction of derivation, e.g. **yeg-* > Hittite *eka-*.

Aceramic
A (Neolithic) farming site or culture that had not yet acquired ceramic technology (clay pots) thus depriving archaeologists of the item of material culture most diagnostic for the separation of cultures or phases of culture. This is most clearly seen in the earliest farming sites in the Near East and Anatolia where archaeologists recognize a distinct aceramic period before the appearance of the ceramic Neolithic.

Agglutinative language
From Latin *agglutinare* 'to glue together'. A language whose grammar is based on the chainlike assemblage of affixes to a root, each of which usually conveys a clear single meaning and does not affect the root itself. In early evolutionary models of language development, agglutinating languages were regarded as a step up from isolating languages like Chinese, where each morpheme (unit of speech) was a separate word, but a step below inflexional languages like Indo-European.

Anatolian Hunter-Gatherer (AHG)
The genetic lineage that occupied central and western Anatolia and had separated from **CHG** about 25,000 years ago. It provided the basis for the later emergence of **AAF**.

Ancient Anatolian Farmer (AAF)
The ancient genetic lineage that evolved from the earlier Anatolian Hunter-Gatherers (**AHG**), which had split from **CHG** about 25,000–14,000 years ago. By *c*. 8000 BCE the population had adopted agriculture in central Anatolia from which it spread westwards into Europe where it is also designated Early European Farmer (EEF). By *c*. 6500 BCE the westward spread of CHG and the eastward spread of AAF had formed a **cline** from Anatolia to Central Asia. AAF is most closely associated with the Anatolian Farmer model of homeland solutions.

Ancient Ancestral South Indians (AASI)
Dated back as early as 40,000 years ago this genetic lineage with distant relations with the Andaman Islanders formed the 'native' population of the subcontinent into which a series of migrations variously introduced agriculture from the west and, arguably, the Indo-Aryan language via the steppe.

Ancient DNA (aDNA)
DNA derived from past populations that can be employed to trace both the migrations and intermixing of human populations. Samples are most commonly obtained from either the petrous bone or the teeth.

Autosomal DNA
DNA associated with the 22 non-sex human chromosomes that one inherits in roughly equal amounts from both

parents. Much of the current discourse on the evidence for migrations and possible homelands rests on autosomal evidence, especially the various admixtures of the major deep genetic ancestries such as **AAF**, **CHG** and **EHG**.

Balkan Hunter-Gatherer (BHG)
Within the area of **WHG** there has been identified a BHG genetic profile that appeared earliest in the Iron Gates region along the Danube and was a subsequent component of the early farmers in the Cucuteni-Trypillia culture.

Caucasian Hunter-Gatherer (CHG)
A major genetic lineage that separated from the **WHG** between 45,000 and 25,000 years ago and was found earliest in the Caucasus and the region south of it. It later expanded during the Neolithic to the west into Anatolia, east towards Central Asia and was also carried northwards of the Caucasus into the steppelands of Ukraine/Russia.

Centum and Satem
The Indo-European languages have been traditionally divided into two major groups based on how they reflect the Indo-European velar sounds ($k, g, \acute{k}, \acute{g}, k^w, g^w$; see **Isogloss**). For example, the centum branches (Anatolian, Tocharian, Celtic, Italic, Germanic, Greek) tend to retain a hard guttural sound of *$\acute{k}mtom$ 'hundred' as seen in Latin *centum*/kentum/'hundred' while the satem languages soften the sound as in Sanskrit *śatám*/shatam.

Cline
A gradient of variation in a single characteristic over space. Here it usually refers to the measurable increase or decrease of a particular genetic signature from one point to another, e.g. the decrease of **CHG** found in populations as one moves north from the Caspian Sea along the Volga towards central Russia.

Cognate
A word in one language may be cognate with a word in another language when they both derive from a common ancestral language, e.g. English *water* and Hittite *wātar* 'water' both come from the same word in Proto-Indo-Anatolian. The identification of cognate words is not based on similarity but whether the words can be derived from a common ancestor by following well-established sound laws. For example, other cognates of English *water* are the far less similar Irish *uisce*, Albanian *ujë* and Armenian *get*.

Core Indo-European
In this book this term designates all of the branches of the Indo-European language family with the exception of Anatolian, see **Proto-Indo-European**. Readers should note that some linguists confine this term to Greek, Armenian, Balto-Slavic and Indo-Iranian (see **4.12**).

Eastern Hunter-Gatherer (EHG)
The genetic lineage that emerged largely out of the Ancient North Eurasian (ANE) group and by the Mesolithic occupied eastern Europe from the Baltic to the Urals. It was the 'native' genetic pool for most of the populations of the Pontic-Caspian region until the appearance of **CHG** north of the Caucasus where EHG and CHG admixed to produce the genetic signature of the Yamnaya culture, one of the main cultural entities associated with Indo-European expansions.

Gracile
In physical anthropology this indicates skeletal, particularly cranial, features that are smaller or more slender in contrast to more robust characteristics such as heavier brow ridges or more massive jaws.

Haplogroup
All humans share a series of ancestors that have been aligned genetically into various haplogroups that trace both

a Y-chromosome male line or a **mtDNA** female line. The haplogroups are labelled alphabetically. In Europe the most frequent male haplogroups are I, J and especially R (R1a and R1b), while major female haplogroups comprise H, J, T and U. There are two systems for representing the distinct clades of the haplogroups. The longer ISOGG (International Society of Genetic Genealogy) version (e.g. R1b1a2a1a2a1a1a1a1) and the shorthand version (e.g. R-M153).

Haplotype
A set of genetic markers that are linked together and inherited from a common ancestor form a haplotype. Groups of similar haplotypes can then be linked together and provide the basis for defining the various **haplogroups**.

Heteroclitic
From Greek *heteros* 'different' and *klino* 'incline', a group of irregularly declined nouns exhibiting a change in the final stem sound (usually *l* or *r*) to *n* in different cases, e.g. Hittite *wātar* 'water' but *wetenaš* 'of water'. Because the system had died out as an active process in all the branches except for Anatolian, heteroclitic nouns were often regarded as the most archaic elements of the Indo-Anatolian reconstructed vocabulary.

Horizon
The term employed to describe a common cultural phenomenon whose area and internal variation generally exceed what archaeologists would regard as an archaeological culture. For example, in Russian archaeology, the Andronovo culture is actually regarded as comprising several different cultures that bear enough similarity with one another that they can be grouped together into a higher taxonomic class as a horizon.

Identity by descent (IBD)
A technique of tracing population histories by comparing the common inheritance of some genomic region between two individuals. IBD expands the number of ancestors being considered by the more traditional use of sex-defined **haplogroups** that track only two ancestral lineages. The technique permits much finer-scale examination of ancestral populations in both time and space.

Isogloss
A boundary defining a dialect feature usually displayed on a geographical map or within a diagram. A major example in Indo-European is the isogloss that distinguishes between centum and satem languages based on the different ways the Indo-European velars (k, g, k^w, g^w) evolved.

Mischsprache
German 'mixed language'. While all languages may display foreign elements in vocabulary, grammar or sounds, some languages appear to have been forged from two or more different languages to an extent that it is difficult to determine a single ancestor. In Indo-European homeland studies from the 1930s onwards a number of linguists proposed that the Indo-European proto-language represented the fusion of two totally unrelated components in terms of vocabulary and grammar.

Mitochondrial DNA (mtDNA)
DNA extracted from the mitochondria, the power stations of cells, which are inherited through the female line. These provide a record of one's maternal line, which is organized into major ancestral lines of mtDNA **haplogroups**.

Morpheme
A morpheme is the smallest linguistic construct conveying a meaning. In this book it is expressed as a root morpheme and used to indicate those instances where we cannot reconstruct an actual word but only a root. One of the major catalogues of **Proto-Indo-European** is filled with morphemes with vague meanings such as 'swell' or 'bright' to

account for a series of words with extremely divergent meanings.

Proto-Indo-Anatolian (PIA)
A term employed by some linguists to indicate what others would simply label **Proto-Indo-European** on the grounds that Anatolian did not descend from the proto-language attested by all of the other Indo-European languages but an earlier proto-language ancestral to both Anatolian and Core-Indo-European.

Proto-Indo-European (PIE)
The common proto-language of the Indo-European family of languages is traditionally regarded as the ancestor of all of the Indo-European languages, including the Anatolian branch. Nevertheless, there are linguists who prefer to regard Anatolian as a sister language of Proto-Indo-European rather than a daughter language and prefer to label the ancestral language as **Proto-Indo-Anatolian**, in which case Proto-Indo-European is sometimes (as in this book) called Core-Indo-European.

Substrate words
Words derived from a native population after they had been absorbed into a later language – e.g. *caribou, chipmunk, hickory, moose* are all words in American English that were introduced by way of Algonquian languages.

Urheimat
The German word for the 'original homeland' composed of the prefix *ur-* 'original, primeval' and *Heimat* 'homeland'. The popularity of the Indo-European homeland in German scholarship has encouraged the spread of this word into international linguistics' discourse.

Western Hunter-Gatherer (WHG)
The major genetic lineage of western and central Europe following the retreat of the last glaciers was the WHG where they presumably expanded from either the Balkans or further east. Although the spread of **AAF** across Europe during the Neolithic saw the latter dominate genetically, populations of WHG ancestry were also absorbed into the Neolithic expansion and constituted a significant percentage (20–30 per cent) of the ancestry of European Neolithic populations.

West Siberian Hunter-Gatherer (WSHG)
Within the Ancient North Eurasian (ANE) region emerged the WSHG lineage, which was analysed as primarily ANE but mixed with 20 per cent **EHG** and about 6 per cent Ancient Northeast Asian. The most significant population related to it was Botai, a site of the earliest evidence for horse domestication. WSHG is also found in some Eneolithic burials west of the Urals in the Volga region that were ancestral components in the formation of the Yamnaya culture.

Notes to the Text

Preface
1. Whatmough 1928, 130–1.
2. Mallory 1973.
3. Spoiler alert: if you get to the end of Jean-Paul Demoule's very substantial examination of the Indo-European problem you will learn that 'The answer is that (as of today) there is no definitive answer.' (Demoule 2023, 449).
4. Mallory 2013a; 2016a.
5. Mallory and Mair 2000; Mallory 2015.

Chapter 1
1. Hegel 1900, 142.
2. Campbell and Poser 2008, 32.
3. Jones, W. 1798, 422–3.
4. Rendall 1889, 7.
5. Parsons 1767, 80.
6. Fournet 2010. In the third discourse he suggested that the Norse god Odin and the Buddha were the same people (Jones, W. 1807, 37) and that the evidence of parallel sun-worship indicated that the Indians and the Incas were peoples by the 'same race' (Jones, W. 1807, 39). Other hits and misses are detailed in Trautmann, T. 1997, 47–50; Campbell and Poser 2008, 37–41.
7. Pedersen 1962, 7. The idea that the Lithuanians were sprung from the Romans began at least as early as the 15th century (Dini 2010).
8. Olender 1992, 1.
9. Olender 1997, 53.
10. In their defence, 17th-century Dutch 'etymologists' also proposed that language affiliation should be based on comparisons of basic vocabulary, sound correspondences and grammatical structure, the cornerstones of modern comparative research (Campbell and Poser 2008, 17).
11. Skinner 1671, *inaniter subtilem & operose ineptum* (quoted in Metcalf 1974, 241).
12. Olender 1997, 53–4.
13. With the obvious exception of Maltese, which is also a Semitic language.
14. Fournet 2010, 5.
15. The first Sanskrit text transmitted to Europe was recorded in a letter by St Francis Xavier who remarked that it was equivalent to Latin in Europe (Amaladass 1992, 212), and Jesuits played a significant role in bringing Sanskrit to the attention of European scholars. The English Jesuit Thomas Stephens (1549–1619) seems (so far) to have been the first to recognize the kinship between Sanskrit, Latin and Greek.
16. The main source for the history of such research is Borst 1957–63.
17. Metcalf 1974, 233. The title of Jäger's work was *De Lingua Vetustissima Europae Scytho-Celtica et Gothica*.
18. In 1779 in a letter to Prince Adam Czartoryski (Jones, W. 1807, 94), Jones wrote: 'How so many European words crept into the Persian language, I know not with certainty.... Many learned investigators of antiquity are fully persuaded, that a very old and almost primeval language was in use among those northern nations, from which not only the Celtic dialects, but even the Greek and Latin, are derived; in fact we find *patèr* and *metèr* in Persian, nor is *thugatèr* so far removed from *dickter*, or even *onoma* and *nomen* from *nam*, as to make it ridiculous to suppose, that they sprang from the same root. We must confess that these researches are very obscure and uncertain.'
19. Aarsleff 1982, 328, ft 44 provides a brief account of its dissemination and reception.

20 Rask 1818.
21 Bopp 1833.
22 Although this is the earliest recorded use of the term, it is unlikely that Malte-Brun actually coined the term himself (Koerner 1971, 164).
22 In 1818, Rasmus Rask even found it objectionable as the cover label for what today we would call the 'Germanic' languages, which he preferred to call 'Gothic' (Rask 2013, 67–9).
23 James Joyce gives us 'Iro-European' in *Finnegans Wake*, 1968 edn, 36.
24 Taylor, I. [1886] 1892 edn; Morris 1888, 33. See Kellens 2005 for detailed discussion of its use as an ethnic label.
25 Metcalf 1974, 233.
26 This was based in fact on a very unhistorical source, a volume of Sufi propaganda (App 2009, 68).
27 Jones rejected the traditional association of Japheth with European languages and Ham with exclusively Hamitic as he followed the writings of Jacob Bryant and Muslim histories (see Trautmann, T. 1997, 43–4, 53–4).
28 Jones was strongly motivated to incorporate the 'Indo-Europeans' within a much larger project of reconciling the new-found traditions of the East within the Mosaic model of creation and human expansions (see Trautmann, T. 1997, 37–61).

Chapter 2
1 *Die Zeiten änderen sich. Die Menschen änderen sich. Aber der Glaube an die asiatische Wiege hat sich nicht geändert*, Wolzogen 1875, 2.
2 Benfey 1869.
3 Poesche 1878.
4 Penka 1883; 1886.
5 Kossinna 1902; 1921.
6 Schrader 1883; the Steppe theory was advanced in the 2nd edn of 1890 and 3rd edn of 1907.
7 Feist 1913. Feist regarded the 'steppe solution' at that time *ziemlich isoliert* ('pretty isolated').

8 Huxley 1890.
9 Bender 1922.
10 Giles 1922.
11 Devoto 1962.
12 Makkay 1987.
13 Childe 1926; Peake and Fleure 1928; Sulimirski 1933, reprinted in Scherer 1968, 117–40.
14 Koppers (ed.) 1936a; Koppers 1936b.
15 Brandenstein 1936.
16 Nehring 1936.
17 Kühn, H. 1932.
18 Gimbutas 1963, 1974, 1994; see especially the collected papers in Gimbutas 1997.
19 For example, Mallory 1989.
20 Anthony 2007.
21 Gamkrelidze and Ivanov 1984.
22 Kitson 1997, 186.
23 *Ibid.*, 196.
24 Sarianidi 1999.
25 Grigoriev 1999; 2002a; 2002b; 2021.
26 Renfrew 1987.
27 Bouckaert *et al.* 2012; Chang *et al.* 2015; Pereltsvaig and Lewis 2015.
28 Latham 1851, 161–3.
29 Latham 1862, 611.
30 Stocking 1987, 58.
31 Heath 1866.
32 Morris 1888.
33 Taylor, I. [1886] 1888 edn, 250.
34 Brinton 1890, 147–9.
35 Tappeiner 1897.
36 Ihering 1897, 2–5.
37 *Ibid.*, 249–300.
38 Tilak 1903.
39 Biedenkapp 1906, 161–4.
40 Taraporewala 1933.
41 Godwin 1993.
42 Strzygowski 1936.
43 Hapgood 1979, 229.
44 Jóhannesson 1943.
45 Maurus 1913.
46 Schwidetzky, G. 1932.
47 Hodge 1981.
48 Taranets and Stupak 2018.
49 Narain 1987; 2000.
50 Ismail 1989, 32.
51 Zschaetzsch 1922.
52 Demoule 2023, 132–40.
53 Goodrick-Clarke 2002, 89–92.
54 Dressler 1965, 27.
55 Wilke 1918, 17.

56 Dyen 1969, 510. See also Crossland 1971, 826.
57 Marchand 1955.
58 Morris 1888, 64–71.
59 Murray 1823.
60 Ihering 1894, 467–86; 1897.
61 Mallory 2018.
62 Peyrot 2018.
63 Bomhard 2012.
64 Müller 1871, 86.
65 Feist 1933.
66 Ehret 1988; Anthony 2001.
67 Gal 1996, 588.
68 Mallory 2016a.

Chapter 3
1 Kroonen *et al.* 2018a.
2 App 2009; Trautmann, T. 1997.
3 Jones, W. 1798, 423–4.
4 Trautmann, T. 1997, 90–91.
5 Amaladass 1992, 218.
6 Taylor, I. [1886] 1892 edn, 8.
7 Kennedy 1828, 218.
8 Taylor, I. [1886] 1889 edn, 8–13, lists many of the more famous adherents to this theory under the mistaken notion that it was dead by the time of his writing.
9 Quoted from *Der Orient und Europa* (1899) in Daniels 1975, 180.
10 Grimm 1848, 162–3.
11 Recognition of the non-Semitic nature of Sumerian only began around the 1850s.
12 Schlegel 1849, 23.
13 Young 1813, 255.
14 Taylor, I. [1886] 1889 edn, 10–12.
15 Ripley 1900, 453.
16 Kahneman 2012, 277.
17 Taylor, I. [1886] 1889 edn, 17.
18 *Ibid.*, 18.
19 There are some who argue for deriving the Indo-Europeans from the Aurignacian, the transition to modern *Homo sapiens* in Europe, such as Marcel Otte (2012, 2017), which will be dealt with later.
20 Adelung 1806.
21 Quoted in Schrader [1883] 1890 edn, 4.
22 Hehn 1885, 34; Hehn, however, argued that the analogy was imprecise as he did not believe that the earliest Indo-Europeans possessed the domestic horse, which greatly facilitated the movements of the Kalmucks.
23 Feist 1913, 518–19.
24 Taylor, I. [1886] 1889 edn, 40.
25 Bender 1922, 46.
26 This title is shamelessly lifted from R. A. Crossland's account of Indo-European origins (Crossland 1971).
27 Boughton 1898; see also Jain 1964.
28 Jain 1964, 87.
29 Tacitus, *Germania*.
30 https://edition.cnn.com/travel/article/worlds-happiest-countries-2022-wellness/index.html
31 Keith 1937, 20.
32 Hirt 1905, vol. 1, 182; see also Krause 1903, 110.
33 Kitson 1997, 203.
34 Heggarty 2018, 110.
35 Binford 1967.
36 Heggarty *et al.* 2023.
37 For example, Hauer's (1939, 13) dismissal of Wilhelm Kopper's case for an Asiatic homeland.

Chapter 4
1 Victor Hehn (1874) cited in Schrader [1883] 1907 edn, 100.
2 Latham 1851; 1862, 611. Incidentally, Britain only has four reptiles to Ireland's one, the common lizard, and the Irish are probably not much fussed that they lack adders.
3 For example, Athabaskan (Sapir 1936, 234); Numic (Lamb 1958, 98); Pomo (Oswalt 1964); Otomangue (Harvey 1964); Proto-Niger-Congo (Greenberg 1964, 7); Salish (Jorgensen 1969, 105); Austronesian (Pereltsvaig and Lewis 2015, 120–1).
4 Schrader [1883] 1890 edn, 426–43; 1907 edn, 483–507.
5 Hirt 1905; in something of a double-whammy against Schrader, Johannes Hoops produced a like-minded volume in the same year (Hoops 1905).
6 Hirt 1905, vol. 1, 181.
7 Childe 1926, 95.
8 Hirt 1905, vol. 1, 183.
9 Devoto 1962.

10 Wichmann *et al.* 2010, 257.
11 Schmid 1972, 17.
12 Schleicher 1853. In 1863, Schleicher changed the order to Slavo-Germanic as the first to exit, then Graeco-Italo-Celtic and lastly Indo-Iranian.
13 Schleicher 1861, 6.
14 Meillet 1908.
15 Kroeber and Chrétien 1937.
16 Kroeber and Chrétien 1939.
17 Kroeber 1960.
18 Förstemann 1852; 1854.
19 Swadesh 1953.
20 Swadesh took the greatest time depth of diversity, which was between Italic and Slavic, rather than the actual distance between Germanic and Slavic (which was 3,300 years) because two languages in mutual contact would have 'acted as a brake on full divergence' (Swadesh 1953, 351).
21 Swadesh 1960.
22 Trager and Smith 1950.
23 Wittmann 1969.
24 Tischler 1973.
25 Starostin 2013.
26 Ringe *et al.* 2002.
27 Gray and Atkinson 2003; Bouckaert *et al.* 2012.
28 Chang *et al.* 2015.
29 Pereltsvaig and Lewis 2015.
30 Kassian *et al.* 2021.
31 Heggarty *et al.* 2023.
32 Kloekhorst and Pronk 2019b.
33 Malzahn 2016.
34 Gamkrelidze and Ivanov 1984, vol. 1, 415.
35 Bouckaert *et al.* 2012; Chang *et al.* 2015; Kassian *et al.* 2021.
36 Kim 2018, 263.
37 Martirosyan 2013.
38 Schmidt, J. 1872.
39 Wilke 1918, 18, fig. 4.
40 Anttila 1989.
41 Adams 2021.
42 Garrett 2006. Garrett was prompted by his analysis of Greek dialects, which led to the conclusion that there was insufficient evidence to reconstruct a Proto-Greek; Tremblay came to the same conclusion regarding a uniform Proto-Iranian a year earlier (Tremblay 2005, 61).
43 Garrett 2006.
44 Heggarty *et al.* 2010.
45 Robb 1993, 758.
46 Neureiter *et al.* 2021.
47 Dyen *et al.* 1992.
48 Dyen 1956.
49 Diebold 1960.
50 Elemendorf 1965.
51 Manning 2006, 128–53.
52 Dyen 1956, 613.
53 Sutton 1991, 306.
54 Dyen 1956, 621.
55 Diebold 1960, 7.
56 Manning 2006, 129.
57 *Ibid.*, 131.
58 Dressler 1965, 33.
59 Jäger 1686, 19.
60 Poesche 1878, 66.
61 Bender 1922, 53.
62 Conway 1900, 75.
63 Sayce 1880, 122.
64 Kennedy 1828.
65 Kalla 1930, 45–54.
66 Poesche 1878, 66.
67 Arntz 1936b.
68 Charpentier 1926, 162.
69 Poljakov 2015, 206.
70 Müller 1888, 93.
71 Feist 1932, 245; 1933, 184; also Keith 1937.
72 Hirt 1905, vol. 1, 196.
73 Forrer 1934, 126.
74 Mansion 1911, 235–6.
75 Kossinna 1925, 239.
76 Fodor 1965.
77 Mańczak 1992; Kosinski 2023, 116.
78 Heggarty 2000.
79 Rendall 1889, 27.
80 Kronasser 1961, 120.
81 Bichlmeier 2020, 75.
82 Kuiper 1967.
83 Witzel 2006.
84 Ivani *et al.* 2020.
85 Feist 1910, 14–15; 1913, 450–1.
86 Pokorny 1929; 1936.
87 Hall 1966, 19.
88 Keith 1937, 17–18.
89 Schmitt 1936, 361–2.
90 Neumann 1971.
91 Bichlmeier 2020.

92 Beekes 2010, xiii.
93 Kroonen 2012; Kroonen *et al.* 2022; Bjørn 2023.

Chapter 5
1 Gelb 1951. There is, in fact, a PIE **morg-* that seems to indicate 'border' (Mallory and Adams 2006, 288).
2 Brunnhofer 1884.
3 Knauer 1912–13.
4 Telegin 1990.
5 Georgiev 1966.
6 *Ibid.*, 192.
7 Krahe 1954; 1964.
8 Krahe 1970, 68.
9 Schmid 1968; 1972.
10 Udolph 2017.
11 Kühn, H. 1967, 7.
12 Lahovary 1961; Vennemann 2003.
13 Blok 1971.
14 Bichlmeier 2012, 15.
15 Bichlmeier 2017, 46.
16 Kühn, H. 1967, 17
17 Blok 1971.
18 Udolph 2017, 237–8.
19 Bichlmeier 2017, 37.
20 Kühn, H. 1967, 6; Scherer 1960; 1961.
21 For example, Kassian *et al.* 2021.
22 Udolph 2017, 242 (*Die Heimat kann nur innerhalb der Alteuropäischen Hydronymie gesucht werden*).
23 Rassokha 2007, 19–46 doesn't do the job.

Chapter 6
1 Hommel 1879; 1885.
2 Möller 1911, xvi.
3 Kallio 2019.
4 Anderson 1879.
5 Koeppen 1886.
6 Grünthal *et al.* 2022.
7 Campbell and Poser 2008, 63.
8 Wagner 1969, 211.
9 Austerlitz 1970.
10 Klimov 1990.
11 Gamkrelidze and Ivanov 1972.
12 Some relevant general sources include: Carpelan *et al.* (eds) 2001; Grünthal and Kallio (eds) 2012; review article and discussion in Kassian *et al.* 2015; Kloekhorst and Pronk (eds) 2019a.
13 See Kloekhorst and Pronk 2019.
14 Kassian *et al.* 2015.
15 Kallio 2019, 82.
16 Janhunen 2001, 207.
17 Kortlandt 2010b.
18 Kassian *et al.* 2015.
19 Nichols 2021, 359.
20 Campbell and Poser 2008, 162.
21 Simon 2020.
22 Campbell and Poser 2008, 217. A fuller discussion of the problem of 'short function words' is found in Kassian *et al.* 2015, 382–6.
23 McGregor 2018.
24 Grünthal *et al.* 2022, 492; 200 on the supposition that Uralic is divided into Samoyedic and Finno-Ugric and that you need a cognate from each group to constitute a Uralic reconstruction; 700 items can be proposed if you do not require a Samoyedic cognate.
25 Collinder 1965.
26 Campbell and Poser 2008, 380.
27 Koivulehto 2001, 235–8.
28 Napol'skikh 1995. This cites over 200 publications on the subject.
29 Häkkinen 2023.
30 Kloekhorst and Pronk 2019, 6–11.
31 Kozintsev 2019.
32 Makkay 2001, 323.
33 Janhunen 2001, 216.
34 Nichols 2021, 361.
35 Horvath 2019a; 2019b.
36 Greenberg 2000.
37 Kozintsev 2020.
38 Brunner 1969; Levin 1971.
39 Hodge 1981.
40 Schmidt, J. 1890, 54.
41 Hirt 1892. Other criticism came from Schrader [1883] 1907 edn, 106–7; Rosenfeld 1956–7.
42 Blažek 1999a.
43 Schott 1936, in Arntz 1936a, vol. 2, 45–95, a volume otherwise bursting with papers far more in tune with the National Socialist agenda.
44 Uesson 1970, 98.
45 Gamkrelidze and Ivanov 1995, 768–73.
46 Diakonov 1985, 122–33.
47 Bjørn 2023.
48 Bjørn 2017, 137.

49 Gamkrelidze and Ivanov 1995, 774–7.
50 Bjørn 2017, 136–7.
51 Colarusso 1997.
52 Matasović 2012.
53 Bomhard 2015.
54 Bomhard 2019 (for discussants papers and author's rebuttal).
55 Brinton 1890, 149.
56 Forrer 1934.
57 Uhlenbeck 1935; 1937.
58 Trubetzkoy 1939.
59 Gornung 1964; 1970.
60 Pisani 1966; 1974.
61 Kortlandt 2002, in Kortlandt 2010a, 391–403.
62 Bomhard 2019 (for discussants' papers and author's rebuttal).
63 Holopainen 2019.
64 Bjørn 2022.
65 Koch 2020.
66 Pronk-Tiethoff 2013.
67 Kallio 2012.
68 Müller 1871, 86.
69 Schuchardt 1884, 5.
70 Kortlandt 2002, in Kortlandt 2010a, 391.

Chapter 7

1 Ninth discourse in Jones, W. 1807, 199.
2 Müller 1881, 360.
3 Published in Müller 1881, 400–16.
4 Rask 1818, 279, item 45.
5 Eichhoff 1836, 158.
6 *Ibid.*, 159.
7 Kuhn, A. 1845.
8 *Ibid.*, 9.
9 *Ibid.*, 18.
10 Pictet 1859–63.
11 Diebold 1987.
12 Feist 1913, 97.
13 Campbell and Mauricio 2007, 106–7.
14 Benfey 1869.
15 Tremblay 2005 provides a rare exception with a detailed discussion of many of the most critical points.
16 Wodtko *et al.* 2008, 335.
17 Schrader [1883] 1907 edn, 174–5.
18 In *Journal Asiatique*, cited in Reinach 2017, 16.
19 Mallory and Adams 1997; 2006, 107–10.
20 Olander 2023; see also Olander (ed.) 2022.
21 Kloekhorst 2023, 46.
22 Mallory 2019.
23 Pulgram 1959.
24 Pulgram 1958.
25 Olander 2017.
26 Ihering 1897, 2.
27 Keith 1937, 25 excluded Baltic because of lack of words for amber, sea and ships.
28 Hirt 1907, vol 2, 667–8.
29 For example, Classen 1918, 3; Charpentier 1926, 162–3; Brandenstein 1936; Keith 1937, 25–6.
30 Wolzogen 1875, 7.
31 Thieme 1954, 10.
32 Dressler 1965, 35
33 Wallach 2019. https://doi.org/10.1057/s41599-019-0307-9
34 Heggarty and Renfrew 2014a; Heggarty 2018.
35 Mallory, F. 2021, 280.
36 Huld 1990.
37 Kronasser 1961, 122.
38 Bender 1922.
39 Clackson 2000, 450.
40 Schmidt, J. 1872, 30–1.
41 Kretschmer 1896, 21–2.
42 Fraser 1926, 267–9.
43 Demoule 2023, 35.
44 Although some do suggest [1] aurochs: [2] aurochsen.
45 Benveniste 1935, 3–22.
46 Nehring 1936, 149.
47 Lehmann 2005, 222–3.
48 Brandenstein 1936.
49 Kloekhorst 2008, 9–10.
50 Specht 1944.
51 Kroonen *et al.* 2018a.
52 Cowgill and Mayrhofer 1975; also Milewski 1968.
53 Kloekhoerst 2023.
54 Chang *et al.* 2015; Kassian *et al.* 2021.
55 Heggarty *et al.* 2023.
56 Kassian *et al.* 2021, 950.
57 Mallory 1996.
58 Koch 2020, 22.
59 *Ibid.*, 45.
60 *Ibid.*, 37.
61 *Ibid.*, 38.
62 Häkkinen 2023.
63 Holm 2019.

64 Observe, for example, the contrasting opinions in two major monographs on the evidence for wheeled vehicles: Raulwing 2000 and Holm 2019.
65 Coleman 1988.
66 *Ibid.*, 450.
67 Heggarty and Renfrew 2014a, 31.
68 Feist 1913, 153–4.
69 Nehring 1936, 110.
70 Hirt 1905, vol. 1, 288; 1907, vol. 2, 657.
71 Thieme 1954, 576–81.
72 Lubotsky 2023.
73 Anthony and Ringe 2015, 205.
74 Mallory 2019.
75 Huld 2000.
76 Höfler 2023, 116.
77 Heggarty and Renfrew 2014a, 32.
78 West 2007, 201–3.
79 Tremblay 2005, 122–3, 134.
80 West 2007, 351–2.
81 Mallory 2018.
82 Kroonen *et al.* 2022, 31.
83 Olander 2023; Thorsø *et al.* 2023.
84 Muhly 2011.
85 Alinei 1996; 2000.
86 Demoule 2023, 303.
87 Mallory 1982.
88 Thieme 1954, 546.
89 Friedrich 1970.
90 Kitson 1997, 189.
91 Matirosyan 2013, 276.
92 Specht 1944, 36.
93 Kloekhorst and Pronk 2019b, 10.
94 Arbuckle 2009, 196–200.
95 Outram *et al.* 2009.
96 Librado *et al.* 2021.
97 Anthony 2023a.
98 Trautmann, M., *et al.* 2023.
99 Outram 2023.
100 Gamkrelidze and Ivanov 1995, 763.
101 Dybo 2013, 87.
102 Pictet 1859–63, vol. 1, 122–8.
103 *Ibid.*, 538.
104 For example, the French anthropologist Clémence Royer, cited in Demoule 2023, 83.
105 Diebold 1976.
106 Kitson 1997, 190–1.
107 Schrader [1883] 1907 edn, 246–7.
108 Thieme 1954, 30.
109 Kloekhorst 2008, 212.
110 Pictet 1859–63, vol. 1, 110–11.
111 Hirt 1905, vol. 1, 186.
112 Schrader and Nehring 1917–28, 535–6.
113 Jóhannesson 1943, 158–9.
114 Gamkrelidze and Ivanov 1995, 786, ft 30.
115 Hirt 1905, vol. 1, 188.
116 Mallory 1982.
117 Gorton 2017.
118 McGovern *et al.* 2017.
119 Sagona 2018, 196.

Chapter 8
1 Sapir 1916.
2 Rhode 1820; Van den Gheyn 1881, 10–28 provides a history of the topic.
3 Piétrement 1879, 117–18.
4 Piétrement 1879.
5 Brunnhofer 1884, 18.
6 Penka 1883, 53–61.
7 Witzel 2000.
8 De Harlez 1880, 280–3.
9 Triveda 1938–9.
10 Tacitus, *Germania*.
11 Dozier 1958, 23–4.
12 Watkins 1995, vii.
13 Wolzogen 1875.
14 Graebner 1919–20, 1116.
15 Krause 1891, 147.
16 Evans 1886, 643.
17 Penka 1905.
18 Brandenstein 1952, 25.
19 Koppers 1928; 1935; Koppers (ed.) 1936a; Schmidt, W. 1949.
20 Feist 1913, 512; Keith 1937, 21.
21 Güntert 1934.
22 Nehring 1936.
23 Flor 1936. See similar arguments from Hauer 1939.
24 Lincoln 1986.

Chapter 9
1 Wilke 1918.
2 See Demoule 2014 for a history of the Indo-European problem from the vantage of archaeology.
3 Otte 2012; 2017. The theory has also been advanced in terms of the much later spread of human populations from southern refuge areas following the last glaciation (Adams and Otte 1999). See also Ebbesen 2009.

4 Häusler 2002.
5 Zaliznyak 2016; 2020.
6 Kossinna 1902, in Scherer 1968, 45–6.
7 Pumpelly 1908, xxv–xxxi.
8 Baird *et al.* 2018.
9 Özdogan 2011.
10 Renfrew 1973.
11 Renfrew 1987.
12 Renfrew 1999 or Renfrew 2003; Heggarty and Renfrew 2014a, b and c.
13 Zvelebil 1995.
14 Dolgopolsky 1988.
15 Diakonov 1985.
16 Gimbutas 1991.
17 Kristinsson 2012.
18 Goodenough 1970.
19 *Ibid.*; Renfrew 1987.
20 Zavalii 2023, 556–61.
21 Kitson 1997, 201.
22 Childe 1926, 143.
23 Schulz, W. 1935.
24 Myres 1935, 241.
25 Mallory 2014.
26 Kroonen *et al.* 2022.
27 Kristinsson 2012; Zavalii 2023.
28 Anthony *et al.* 2022.
29 Gimbutas 1994; 1997.
30 Menghin 1936.
31 Seger 1936.
32 Sulimirski 1933.
33 Buchvaldek 1980.
34 Kilian 2000, 116–17.
35 Häusler 2006, 85.
36 Di Fraia 2020, 175–6.
37 Häusler 1981; 1995; 2003.
38 Harrison and Heyd 2007.
39 Dovzhenko and Rychkov 1988.
40 Zavalii 2023, 555.
41 Bryant 2001.
42 Mallory 1997b; Bryant 2001, 224–37.
43 Kozintsev 2019.
44 Outram *et al.* 2009.
45 Danylenko 1974; Merpert 1974; Matyushin 1982.
46 Budd and Lillie 2020, 286.
47 Anthony *et al.* 2022.
48 *Ibid.*
49 Shnirelman 1992.
50 Kristiansen 2020, 161.
51 Mallory 2014.
52 Kloekhorst 2023, 47.

Chapter 10
1 Schulz, H. 1826, 221.
2 Desmoulins 1826, 343.
3 Mallory 1990.
4 Day 2000.
5 Demoule 2014.
6 Day 2000, 6, ft 1.
7 *Ibid.*, 130–47.
8 Olender 1992.
9 Piétrement 1879, 141.
10 Brinton 1890, 147–8.
11 For example, Liétard *et al.* 1864; D'Omalius d'Halloy *et al.* 1864.
12 Poesche 1878.
13 Penka 1883.
14 Geiger 1878.
15 Taylor, I. 1886, 248.
16 Sieglin 1935.
17 Sergent 1995, 434–41.
18 Day 2000, 125.
19 Kellog 1931, 374.
20 Topinard 1878, 248–9.
21 Wilser 1899.
22 Wolff 1914, 311–12.
23 Lapouge 1899.
24 Taylor, I. [1886] 1890 edn.
25 Kreve-Michkevicius 1926.
26 Bröste et al. 1956.
27 Gerhardt 1969, 146–7.
28 Makarenko 1933, 13.
29 Feist 1933.
30 Müller 1888, 120.
31 Roosevelt 1923–6, vol. 14, 92.
32 Boas 1911.
33 Ferak and Lichardova 1969.
34 Riesenfeld 1967; 1969.
35 Howells 1966, 1972; White and Parsons 1973.
36 Day 2000, 175.
37 *Ibid.*, 234.
38 Pinhasi and Pluciennik 2004.
39 Day 2000, 224.
40 Potekhina 2020.
41 Shevchenko 1984.
42 Kruts 1972.
43 Day 2000, 175, 186, 192, 202.
44 Hemphill and Mallory 2004.
45 Necrasov 1980.
46 Schwidetzky, I. 1980, 347.
47 Day 2000, 208–9.
48 Schwidetzky, I. 1980, 356–7.
49 Menk 1980.
50 Barbujani and Sokal 1990.

51 Rosser et al. 2000, 1537; Novembre et al. 2008.
52 Barnier et al. 2022.
53 Anthony 2007, 104–13.
54 Cavalli-Sforza et al. 1994, 291–2.
55 Day 2000, 241–4.
56 Ibid., 244–5.
57 Novembre and Stephens 2008.
58 Cavalli-Sforza et al. 1994, 293.
59 Piazza et al. 1995.
60 Barbujani et al. 1995, 126.
61 Anthony 1990; Härke 1998; Burmeister 2000.
62 Barbujani et al. 1995, 129.
63 Osbjorn Pearson: letter dated 13 Apr. 1992.
64 Soares et al. 2010.
65 Ibid., R178.
66 Jobling et al. 2002, 314–19.
67 Ibid., 319–23.
68 Semino et al. 2000; Busby et al. 2012 is cautious of anchoring it to the Neolithic or later.
69 Balaresque et al. 2010.
70 Wells et al. 2001. Other papers that linked the modern distribution of R1a to the Steppe model included Zerjal et al. 1999; Semino et al. 2000.
71 Quitana-Murci et al. 2001.
72 Haak et al. 2008.
73 Manco 2013.
74 Keyser et al. 2009.

Chapter 11

1 Gray and Atkinson 2003; Bouckaert et al. 2012.
2 Pereltsvaig and Lewis 2015. Other critics: Häkkinen 2012.
3 Bradke 1890.
4 Garrett 2006.
5 Chang et al. 2015.
6 Häkkinen 2012; Holm 2020.
7 Klyosov and Tomezzoli 2013; see also Klyosov and Rozhanskii 2012.
8 Mallory 2016b.
9 Haak et al. 2015.
10 Mallory 2023; also Furholt 2018, 169.
11 Allentoft et al. 2015.
12 Di Fraia 2020.
13 Mallory and Mair 2000; Mallory 2015.
14 Kuzmina 2002.
15 Heyd 2017.

16 For example, Mathieson et al. 2015; Mathieson et al. 2018; Damgaard et al. 2018; Wang et al. 2019.

Chapter 12

1 Sayce 1880, 121.
2 Sayce 1883, xii.
3 I wrote this long before I encountered Kosinski 2023, who asserts that the Poles and their fellow Slavs are the closest to the Proto-Indo-Europeans because of the high frequency of R1a among them. Groan.
4 https://www.indiatodayne.in/national/story/dna-test-shows-brahmins-belong-to-russia-rjd-leader-yaduvansh-yadav-551766-2023-05-02
5 Lazaridis et al. 2022a; Lazaridis et al. 2024.
6 Campbell 2015.
7 Vicent García and Martínez-Navarrete 2022, 295; see also Vander Linden 2016.
8 Anthony 2023b.
9 Posth et al. 2023.
10 Robb 1993, 750.
11 Mallory 2008.
12 Childebayeva et al. 2022.
13 Nikitin et al. 2024.
14 Allentoft et al. 2024a.
15 Jones, E. R. et al. 2015.
16 Yang 2022.
17 Narasimhan et al. 2019.
18 Reche 1936, 314.
19 Pagerl et al. 2013, 8475.
20 Mallory 2016a.
21 Ibid., 389.
22 Mallory 2016a; Olsen 2023; Stockhammer 2023.

Chapter 13

1 Baird et al. 2018.
2 Renfrew 1987.
3 Mathieson et al. 2015.
4 Gerritsen and Özbal 2019.
5 Lazaridis et al. 2022a.
6 For example, Renfrew 2003.
7 Renfrew 2003.
8 Mathieson et al. 2015.
9 Nikitin et al. 2019.
10 Childebayeva et al. 2022.

NOTES TO THE TEXT

11 See Robb 1993, 751–2; Nettle 1998; 1999, for the impact of the shift to agriculture on increasing language diversity.
12 Malmström *et al.* 2015; Fraser *et al.* 2018; Skoglund *et al.* 2014; Fernandes *et al.* 2018.
13 For example, N1a, T2b, J1c5, J1c8a, J1d5, J2, K1a2b, K1a5, K1e, K2b1a and V.
14 Allentoft *et al.* 2024b.
15 Seguin-Orlando *et al.* 2021.
16 Gimbutas 1994, 45–8.
17 Marcus *et al.* 2020. doi.org/10.1038/s41467-020-14523-6
18 Mathieson *et al.* 2015.
19 Skourtanioti *et al.* 2020, 1166.
20 Damgaard *et al.* 2018.
21 Marcus *et al.* 2020.
22 Saada *et al.* 2020; McColl *et al.* 2024.
23 Guarino-Vignon *et al.* 2023.
24 Wang *et al.* 2019, fig. 2a bar graph.

Chapter 14

1 Michalowski 2004, 22; Stolper 2004, 73; Gernot 2004, 101
2 Michalowski 2004, 22; Stolper 2004, 84; Gernot 2004, 107; Tuite 2004, 971.
3 Bavant 2008; see also Matasović 2012, 15–17.
4 Watkins 2004, 560; see also Fortson 2004, 157.
5 Fournet and Bomhard 2010, 159.
6 From Kloekhorst 2008.
7 Kroonen *et al.* 2022.
8 Pronk 2021.
9 Goedegebuure 2020 denies the Proto-Anatolians 'agriculture' when, properly speaking, it is only the use of the plough that is being rejected.
10 Kroonen *et al.* 2022, 33.
11 Mallory 2018.
12 Kroonen *et al.* 2022.
13 Darden 2001; Pronk 2021.
14 Kloekhorst and Pronk 2019b.
15 Chang *et al.* 2015; Kassian *et al.* 2021; Heggarty *et al.* 2023.
16 Asouti and Fairbairn 2002; Bogaard *et al.* 2017.
17 Ertem 1974.
18 Kloekhorst 2023, 46–7.
19 Damgaard *et al.* 2018.
20 Kloekhorst 2023, 55.
21 Lazaridis *et al.* 2017.
22 Damgaard *et al.* 2018; Lazaridis *et al.* 2022a.
23 Lazaridis *et al.* 2022a.
24 Fóthi *et al.* 2020.
25 Tibor Fehér, pers. comm.
26 Kloekhorst and Pronk 2019b, 3–6.
27 Gamkrelidze and Ivanov 1985a; 1985b; Grigoriev 2002a; 2002b; 2022.
28 Heggarty 2018; Heggarty *et al.* 2023.
29 Roller 2011.
30 Grigoriev 2022; 2021.
31 Grigoriev 2022, 39.
32 Palumbi and Chataigner 2014.
33 Palumbi 2011, 207.
34 Sagona 2011.
35 Rosenberg and Özdogan 2011.
36 Heggarty and Renfrew 2014b.
37 Mallory 2017.
38 Kümmel 2022.
39 Jones-Bley and Zdanovich (eds) 2002; Kuzmina 2002; Grigoriev 2021, 194–8.
40 Grigoriev 2002b, 148.
41 Grigoriev 2002a.
42 Kuzmina 2002; Anthony 2007.
43 Allentoft *et al.* 2015; Narasimhan *et al.* 2019; Allentoft *et al.* 2024a.
44 Misra 1992, 48–53. Far more mainstream evaluations can be found in Sharma 1994 and Kochhar 1997.
45 Mathieson *et al.* 2018, supplementary table 3.
46 Mattila *et al.* 2023.
47 Allentoft *et al.* 2024a.
48 Lazaridis *et al.* 2024.
49 Sagona 2018, 93–125.
50 Sagona 2018.
51 Lazaridis *et al.* 2024.
52 Lazaridis *et al.* 2022a, Supplementary Materials, 270.
53 Anthony *et al.* 2024.
54 Anthony and Vyazov 2024, 20.
55 Budd and Lillie 2020, 286; Anthony and Vyazov 2024, 20.
56 Mattila *et al.* 2023.
57 Zaliznyak 2016, 38–40.
58 Nikitin *et al.* 2024, Supplement, 26.
59 De Beule 2024.
60 Sagona 2018.
61 Häusler 2006, 107.

62 Gimbutas 1980.
63 Kristiansen 2020, 161.
64 Kozintsev 2019, 312–18.
65 *Ibid.*, 353.
66 Shishlina 2008.
67 Vasiliev 1981.
68 Anthony 2019.
69 Kozintsev 2019, 326.
70 Anthony 2019.
71 Petrosyan 2019.
72 Lazaridis *et al.* 2022a.
73 Sagona 2018, 301.
74 Gimbutas 1973.
75 Heggarty *et al.* 2023, 8.
76 Antonio *et al.* 2024.
77 Nasidze *et al.* 2003, 259–60.
76 Gavashelishvili *et al.* 2023.

Chapter 15
1 Nichols 1998, 220–1.
2 Mallory 2008.
3 Telehin 1982; Zaliznyak 2020.
4 Anthony *et al.* 2022.
5 Telehin 1973; Telegin *et al.* 2001.
6 Merpert 1974; Mallory 1976; 1977.
7 Mallory 1989.
8 Anthony 2007, 300–5.
9 Telehin 1973.
10 Kroonen *et al.* 2022, 34.
11 Telegin and Potekhina 1988.
12 Allentoft *et al.* 2024a, 306.
13 Lazaridis *et al.* 2024, Supplement 2, 171.
14 Fehér 2021.
15 Anthony and Vyazov 2024, Supplement, 92–3.
16 Stockhammer 2023.
17 Pronk 2023, 293.
18 Hay 2016.
19 https://eurogenes.blogspot.com, 23 Sept. 2023.
20 Olsen 2023.
21 Lansing *et al.* 2017.
22 Bomhard 2019.
23 Bjørn 2017, 142–5.
24 Matasović 2012, 24.

Chapter 16
1 Häkkinen 2023, 2.
2 Evans 1886, 643.
3 Klejn 2017.
4 Gimbutas 1994, 78–88; Tassi *et al.* 2017.

5 Marcus *et al.* 2020, Sup. 25–7.
6 Lazaridis *et al.* 2024, Supplement 2, 180.
7 Papac *et al.* 2021, 17.
8 Rouard 2024.
9 Horvath 2021; St. Clair 2021.
10 https://www.youtube.com/watch?v=pmv3J55bdZc
11 Yang *et al.* 2024.
12 Anthony 2007, 117–18.
13 Anthony 2023a.
14 Mallory 1997a.
15 Jean-Paul Demoule offers a critique of most of the cases for Indo-European dispersals in Demoule 2023, 318–50.
16 Allentoft *et al.* 2015.
17 Jeong *et al.* 2020.
18 Zang *et al.* 2021.
19 Mallory 2015.
20 Mallory and Mair 2000; Mallory 2015.
21 Bryant 2001.
22 Narasimhan *et al.* 2019.
23 *Ibid.*, 2019.
24 *Ibid.*, 2019, 319–20. Supplementary Materials, science.sciencemag.org/content/365/6457/eaat7487/suppl/DC1
25 Lazaridis *et al.* 2022a.
26 Gamkrelidze and Ivanov 1995; Hamp 1990; Ringe *et al.* 2002; Chang *et al.* 2015; Kassian *et al.* 2021; Heggarty *et al.* 2023 (earlier with a median date of *c.* 3300, range *c.* 4900–2000 BCE).
27 Lazaridis *et al.* 2022a.
28 Drews 1988; 2017.
29 Skourtanioti *et al.* 2023.
30 Clemente *et al.* 2021.
31 Skourtanioti *et al.* 2023.
32 Lazaridis *et al.* 2017.
33 Lazaridis *et al.* 2022a, Supplement, 332–3.
34 Skourtanioti *et al.* 2023.
35 Lazaridis *et al.* 2022b.
36 *Ibid.*.
37 Haak *et al.* 2023, 70–1.
38 McColl *et al.* 2024.
39 Mittnik *et al.* 2018.
40 Rasmussen *et al.* 2015.
41 Rascovan *et al.* 2019.
42 Susat *et al.* 2021.

43 Cassidy *et al.* 2016.
44 Olalde *et al.* 2018.
45 Gallay 2001.
46 Manco 2013.
46 Fernandes *et al.* 2020.
48 Saupe *et al.* 2021. Other studies revealing evidence for the arrival of steppe-related genes: Aneli *et al.* 2021; Antonio *et al.* 2019.
49 Patterson *et al.* 2022; Mallory 2023.
50 Mallory 1989, 28–30.
51 Kloekhorst 2023, 48–51.
52 Mallory 1989, 24–30, 231–43.
53 Anthony 2007, 249–60.
54 Lazaridis *et al.* 2024.
55 Penske *et al.* 2023.
56 Damgaard *et al.* 2018.
57 Lazaridis *et al.* 2022a.
58 Lazaridis *et al.* 2024, Supplement 2, 197.
59 Lazaridis *et al.* 2024.

Bibliography

Abbreviations
AA   *American Anthropologist*
CA   *Current Anthropology*
IF   *Indogermanische Forschungen*
JIES   *Journal of Indo-European Studies*
Nat Commun   *Nature Communications*
PNAS   *Proceedings of the National Academy of Science*

Aarsleff, H., 1982. *From Locke to Saussure.* London.
Adams, D., 2021. 'A note on two Tocharian B nominal case markers', *JIES* 49, 265–78.
Adams, J., and M. Otte, 1999. 'Did Indo-European languages spread before farming?', *CA* 40, 73–7.
Adelung, J., 1806. *Mithradates, oder allgemeine Sprachenkunde mit dem Vater Unser als Sprachprobe*, vol. 1. Berlin.
Alinei, M., 1996. *Origini delle lingue d'Europa*, vol. 1: *La teoria della continuità*. Bologna.
—— 2000. *Origini delle lingue d'Europa*, vol. 2: *Continuità dal Mesolitico all'età del Ferro nelle principali aree etnolinguistiche*. Bologna.
Allentoft, M., *et al.*, 2015. 'Population genomics of Bronze Age Eurasia', *Nature* 522, 167–72.
—— *et al.*, 2024a. 'Population genomics of post-glacial western Eurasia', *Nature* 625, 301–11.
—— *et al.*, 2024b. '100 ancient genomes show repeated population turnovers in Neolithic Denmark', *Nature* 625, 329–37. https://doi.org/10.1038/s41586-023-06862-3
Amaladass, A., 1992. 'Jesuits and Sanskrit studies', in T. De Souza and C. Borges (eds), *Jesuits in India: In Historical Perspective*. Goa. 209–31.
Anderson, N., 1879. *Studien zur Vergleichung der indogermanischen und finnisch-ugrischen Sprachen*. Dorpat [now Tartu].

Aneli, S., *et al.*, 2021. 'Through 40,000 years of human presence in Southern Europe: The Italian case study', *Human Genetics* 140, 1417–31.
Anthony, D., 1990. 'Migration in archaeology: The baby and the bathwater', *AA* 92 (4), 23–42.
—— 2001. 'Persistent identity and Indo-European archaeology in the western steppes', in Carpelan *et al.* (eds) 2001, 11–35.
—— 2007. *The Horse, the Wheel, and Language: How Bronze-Age Riders from the Eurasian Steppes Shaped the Modern World*. Princeton.
—— 2019. 'Archaeology, genetics, and language in the steppes: A comment on Bomhard', *JIES* 47, 175–98.
—— 2023a. 'Ten constraints that limit the Late PIE homeland to the steppes', in D. Goldstein *et al.* (eds), *Proceedings of the 33rd Annual UCLA Indo-European Conference*. Hamburg. 1–25.
—— 2023b. 'Ancient DNA and migrations: New understandings and misunderstandings', *Journal of Anthropological Archaeology* 70. https://doi.org/10.1016/j.jaa.2023.101508
—— and D. Ringe, 2015. 'The Indo-European homeland from linguistic and archaeological perspectives', *Annual Review of Linguistics* 1, 199–219.
—— *et al.* 2022. 'The Eneolithic cemetery at Khvalynsk on the Volga river', *Praehistorische Zeitschrift* 97, 22–67.
—— and L. Vyazov, 2024. 'The genetic origin of the Indo-Europeans: Archaeological Supplement', in Lazaridis *et al.* 2024.
Antonio, M., *et al.*, 2019. 'Ancient Rome: A genetic crossroads of Europe and the Mediterranean', *Science* 366, 708–14.
—— *et al.*, 2024. 'Stable population structure in Europe since the Iron

Age, despite high mobility', *eLife*, https://doi.org/10.7554/eLife.79714

Anttila, R., 1989. *Historical and Comparative Linguistics*. Amsterdam. [originally pub. 1972].

App, W., 2009. *William Jones's Ancient Theology: Sino-Platonic Papers 191*. Philadelphia.

Arbuckle, B., 2009. 'Chalcolithic caprines, dark age dairy, and Byzantine beef', *Anatolica* 35, 179–226.

Arntz, H., 1936a. *Germanen und Indogermanen*, 2 vols. Heidelberg.

—— 1936b. 'Herman Hirt und die Heimat der Indogermanen', in Arntz 1936a, vol. 2, 25–8.

Asouti, E., and A. Fairbairn, 2002. 'Subsistence economy in Central Anatolia during the Neolithic: The archaeological evidence', in L. Thissen and F. Gerard (eds), *The Neolithic of Central Anatolia*. Istanbul. 181–92.

Austerlitz, R., 1970. 'Agglutination in northern Eurasia in perspective', in R. Jakobson and S. Kawamoto (eds), *Studies in General and Oriental Linguistics Presented to Shirô Hattori on the Occasion of his Sixtieth Birthday*. Tokyo. 1–5.

Baird, D., *et al*., 2018. 'Agricultural origins on the Anatolian plateau', *PNAS* 115, E3077–E3086.

Balaresque, P., *et al*., 2010. 'A predominantly Neolithic origin for European paternal lineages', *PLOS Biology* 8. https://doi.org/10.1371/journal.pbio.1000285

Barbujani, G., and R. Sokal, 1990. 'Zones of sharp genetic change in Europe are also linguistic boundaries', *PNAS* 87, 1816–19.

—— *et al*., 1995. 'Indo-European origins: A computer-simulation test of five hypotheses', *American Journal of Physical Anthropology* 96, 109–32.

Barnier, C., *et al*., 2022. 'A global analysis of matches and mismatches between human genetic and linguistic histories', *PNAS* 119 (47), e2112084119.

Bavant, M., 2008. 'Proto-Indo-European ergativity…still to be discussed', *Poznań Studies in Contemporary Linguistics* 44 (4), 433–47.

Beekes, R. S. P., 2010. *Etymological Dictionary of Greek*. Leiden.

Bender, H., 1922. *The Home of the Indo-Europeans*. Princeton.

Benfey, T., 1869. *Geschichte der Sprachwissenschaft und orientalischen Philologie in Deutschland*. Munich.

Benveniste, E., 1935. *Origines de la formation des noms en Indo-Européen*. Paris.

Bichlmeier, H., 2012. 'Einige ausgewählte Probleme der alteuropäischen Hydronymie aus Sicht der modernen Indogermanistik – ein Plädoyer für eine neue Sicht auf die Dinge', *Acta Linguistica Lithuanica* 66, 11–47.

—— 2017. 'Was kann man an lexikalischen und morphologischen Elementen aus dem Namenschatz der sogenanten "alteuropäische Hydronomie" gewinnen?', in B. Hansen *et al*. (eds), *Etymology and the European Lexicon*. Wiesbaden. 37–51.

—— 2020. 'The non-Indo-European substrate in Germanic: Some notes on the history of the topic', in Bichlmeier *et al*. (eds), *Etymologus: Festschrift for Vaclav Blažek*. Hamburg. 73–92.

Biedenkapp, G., 1906. *Der Nordpol als Völkerheimat*. Jena.

Binford, L., 1967. 'Smudge pits and hide smoking: The use of analogy in archaeological reasoning', *American Antiquity* 32, 1–12.

Bjørn, R., 2017. *Foreign Elements in the Proto-Indo-European Vocabulary*. Copenhagen.

—— 2022. 'Indo-European loanwords and exchange in Bronze Age Central and East Asia', *Evolutionary Human Sciences* 4, e23, 1–24.

—— 2023. 'The lexicon of an Old European Afro-Asiatic language: Evidence from early loanwords in Proto-Indo-European', *Historical Linguistics* 135, 3–42.

Blažek, V., 1999a. *Numerals: Comparative Etymological Analyses and Their Implications*. Brno.

—— 1999b. 'Elam: A bridge between Ancient Near East and Dravidian

India?', in R. Blench and M. Spriggs (eds), *Archaeology and Language IV*. London and New York. 48–78.

Blok, D. P., 1971. 'Chronologisches zum alteuropäischen Flussnamensystem', *Namn och Bygd* 59, 149–61.

Boas, F., 1911. 'Changes in bodily form of descendants of immigrants', *Senate Documents* 208, 60–75.

Bogaard, A., *et al.*, 2017. 'Agricultural innovation and resilience in a long-lived early farming community: The 1,500-year sequence at Neolithic to early Chalcolithic Çatalhöyük, central Anatolia', *Anatolian Studies* 67, 1–28.

Bomhard, A., 1996. *Indo-European and the Nostratic Hypothesis*. Charleston.

—— 2012. *Reconstructing Proto-Nostratic*. Charleston.

—— 2015. *The Origins of Proto-Indo-European: The Caucasian Substrate Hypothesis*. Available on academia.edu.

—— 2019. 'The origins of Proto-Indo-European: The Caucasian substrate hypothesis', *JIES* 47, 9–212 [for discussants' papers and author's rebuttal].

Bopp, F., 1833. *Vergleichende Grammatik des Sanskrit, Zend, Griechischen, Lateinische, Litthauischen, Gothischen und Deutschen*. Berlin.

Borst, A., 1957–63. *Der Turnbau von Babel. Geschichte der Meinungen über Ursprung und Vielfalt der Sprachen und Völker*. Stuttgart.

Bouckaert, R., *et al.*, 2012. 'Mapping the origins and expansion of the Indo-European language family', *Science* 337, 957–60.

Boughton, W., 1898. 'The Aryan question', *American Antiquarian and Oriental Journal* 20, 71–3.

Bradke, P. von, 1890. *Über Methode und Ergebnisse der arischen indogermanischen Altertumswissenschaft*. Giessen.

Brandenstein, W., 1936. *Die erste indogermanische Wanderung*. Vienna.

—— 1952. 'Bemerkungen zum Sinnbezirk des Klimas', in Brandenstein (ed.), *Studien zur indogermanischen Grundsprache*. Vienna. 23–5.

Brinton, D., 1890. *Races and Peoples: Lectures on the Science of Ethnology*. New York.

Bröste, K., *et al.*, 1956. *Prehistoric Man in Denmark: A study in Physical Anthropology*, 2 vols. Copenhagen.

Brunner, L., 1969. *Die gemeinsamen Wurzeln des semitischen und indogermanischen Wortschatzes: Versuch einer Etymologie*. Bern and Munich.

Brunnhofer, H., 1884. *Über den Ursitz der Indogermanen*. Basel.

Bryant, E., 2001. *The Quest for the Origins of Vedic Culture*. Oxford.

Buchvaldek, M., 1980. 'Corded Pottery complex in Central Europe', *JIES* 8, 393–406.

Budd, C., and M. Lillie, 2020. 'The prehistoric populations of Ukraine: Stable Isotope studies of fisher-hunter-forager and pastoralist-incipient farmer dietary pathways', in Lillie and Potekhina (eds) 2020b, 283–308.

Burmeister, S., 2000. 'Archaeology and migration', *CA* 41, 539–67.

Busby, G., *et al.*, 2012. 'The peopling of Europe and the cautionary tale of Y chromosome lineage R-M269', *Proceedings of the Royal Society B* 279 (1730), 884–92.

Campbell, L., 2015. 'Do languages and genes correlate?', *Language Dynamics and Change* 5, 202–26.

—— and M. Mauricio, 2007. *A Glossary of Historical Linguistics*. Edinburgh.

—— and W. Poser, 2008. *Language Classification: History and Method*. Cambridge.

Carpelan, C., *et al.* (eds), 2001. *Early Contacts between Uralic and Indo-European: Linguistic and Archaeological Considerations*. Helsinki.

Cassidy, L., *et al.*, 2016. 'Neolithic and Bronze Age migration to Ireland and the establishment of the insular Atlantic genome', *PNAS* 113 (2), 368–73.

Cavalli-Sforza, L., *et al.*, 1994. *The History and Geography of Human Genes*. Princeton.

Chang, W., *et al.*, 2015. 'Ancestry-constrained phylogenetic analysis supports the Indo-European steppe hypothesis', *Language* 91 (1), 194–244.

Charpentier, J., 1926. 'The original home of the Indo-Europeans', *Bulletin of the School of Oriental Studies, London Institution* 4, 147–70.

Childe, V. G., 1926. *The Aryans: A Study of Indo-European Origins*. London.

Childebayeva, A., *et al.*, 2022. 'Population genetics and signatures of selection in early neolithic European farmers', *Molecular Biology and Evolution* 39. https://doi.org/10.1093/molbev/msac108

Clackson, J., 2000. 'Time depth in Indo-European', in C. Renfrew *et al.* (eds), *Time Depth in Historical Linguistics*, vol. 2. Cambridge. 441–54.

Classen, K., 1918. 'Beiträge zum Indogermanenproblem', *Korrespondenzblatt der deutschen Gesellschaft für Anthropologie, Ethnologie und Urgeschichte* 49, 1–7.

Clemente, F., *et al.*, 2021. 'The genomic history of the Aegean palatial civilizations', *Cell* 184, 2565–86.

Colarusso, J., 1997. 'Proto-Pontic: Phyletic links between Proto-Indo-European and Proto-Northwest Caucasian', *JIES* 25, 119–51.

Coleman, R., 1988. 'Comments on Renfrew', *CA* 29, 449–53.

Collinder, B., 1965. *Hat das Uralische Verwandte? Eine sprachvergleichende Untersuchung*. Uppsala.

Conway, R. S., 1900. 'The riddle of the nations', *Current Review* 77, 74–81.

Cowgill, W., and M. Mayrhofer, 1975. *Indogermanische Grammatik, Band 1*. Heidelberg.

Crossland, R., 1971. 'Immigrants from the North', in I. Edwards *et al.* (eds), *Cambridge Ancient History*, vol. 1, pt 2. Cambridge. 824–76.

Damgaard, P., *et al.*, 2018. 'The first horse herders and the impact of Early Bronze Age steppe expansions into Asia', *Science* 360 (1422). DOI: 10.1126/science.aar7711

Daniels, G., 1975. *One Hundred and Fifty Years of Archaeology*. London.

Danylenko, V., 1974. *Eneolit Ukrainy*. Kiev.

Darden, B., 2001. 'On the question of the Anatolian origin of Indo-Hittite', in R. Drews (ed.), *Greater Anatolia and the Indo-Hittite Language Family*. Washington DC. 184–228.

Day, J., 2000. *Indo-European Origins: The Anthropological Evidence*. Washington DC.

De Beule, H., 2024. 'Reconstructing the journey of Y-DNA haplogroup I2-S2555 to I2-L38', https://www.academia.edu/115363574/RECONSTRUCTING_THE_JOURNEY_OF_Y_DNA_HAPLOGROUP_I2_S2555_TO_I2_L38_Tracing_Genetic_Footprints_Across_Time_and_Space [Accessed 12 May 2024]

De Harlez, C., 1880. 'Les Aryas et leur première patrie', *Revue de linguistique* 13, 279–307.

Demoule, J.-P., 2014. *Mais où sont passes les Indo-Européens?* Paris.

—— 2023. *The Indo-Europeans: Archaeology, Language, Race, and the Search for the Origins of the West*. Oxford.

Desmoulins, A., 1826. *Histoire naturelle des races humaines*. Paris.

Devoto, G., 1962. *Origini Indeuropea*. Florence.

Di Fraia, T., 2020. '"Mettere le brache alla storia": una tentazione pericolosa. Il difficile rapport fra genetica e archeologia', *Notizie Archeologiche Bergomensi* 28, 169–86.

Diakonov, I., 1985. 'On the original home of the speakers of Indo-European', *JIES* 13, 92–174.

Diebold, R., 1960. 'Determining the center of dispersal of language groups', *International Journal of American Linguistics* 26, 1–10.

—— 1976. 'Contributions to the Indo-European salmon problem', in W. Christie (ed.), *Current Progress in Historical Linguistics*. Amsterdam. 341–88.

—— 1987. 'Linguistic ways to prehistory', in S. Skomal and E. Polomé (eds), *Proto-Indo-European: The Archaeology of a Linguistic Problem*. Washington DC. 19–71

Dini, P. U., 2010. *ALILETOESCVR: linguistica baltica delle origini*. Livorno.
Dolgopolsky, A., 1988. 'The Indo-European homeland and lexical contacts of Proto-Indo-European with other languages', *Mediterranean Language Review* 3, 7–31.
—— 1993. 'More about the Indo-European homeland problem', *Mediterranean Language Review* 6–7, 230–48.
D'Omalius d'Halloy, J., 1864. 'Sur les origins Indo-européennes', *Bulletin de la Société d'Anthropologie de Paris* 5, 184–204.
Dovzhenko, N., and N. Rychkov, 1988. 'K probleme sotsial'noe stratifikatsii plemen yamnoy kul'turno-istoricheskoy obshchnosti', in O. Shaposhnikova (ed.), *Novye Pamyatniki Yamnoy Kul'tury Stepnoy Zony Ukrainy*. Kiev. 27–40.
Dozier, E., 1958. 'Ethnological clues for the sources of Rio Grande Pueblo population', in R. Thompson (ed.), *Migration in New World Culture History*. Tucson. 21–32.
Dressler, W., 1965. 'Methodische Vorfragen bei der Bestimmung der "Urheimat"', *Die Sprache* 11, 25–60.
Drews, R., 1988. *The Coming of the Greeks*. Princeton.
—— 2017. *Militarism and the Indo-Europeanizing of Europe*. London and New York.
Dybo, A., 2013. 'Language and archeology: Some methodological problems. 1. Indo-European and Altaic landscapes', *Journal of Language Relationship* 9, 69–92.
Dyen, I., 1956. 'Language distribution and migration theory', *Language* 32, 611–26.
—— 1969. 'Reconstruction, the comparative method, and the proto-language uniformity assumption', *Language* 45, 499–518.
—— et al., 1992. *An Indoeuropean Classification: A Lexicostatistical Experiment* (Transactions of the American Philosophical Society), vol. 82, part 5. Philadelphia.
Ebbesen, K., 2009. *The Origin of the Indo-European Languages/De indoeuropæiske sprogs oprindelse*. Copenhagen.
Egorova, M. A., and A. A. Egorov, 2023. 'Indoevropeyskoe proiskhozhdenie: opredelenie mestonakhozhdeniya prarodiny narodov – nositeley praindoevropeyskogo yazyka', *Voprosy Istorii* 6, 4–25.
Ehret, C., 1988. 'Language shift and the material correlates of language and ethnic shift', *Antiquity* 62, 564–74.
Eichhoff, F. G., 1836. *Parallèle des languages de l'Europe et de l'Inde*. Paris.
Elemendorf, W. W., 1965. 'Linguistic and geographic relations in the Northern Plateau area', *Southwestern Journal of Anthropology* 21, 63–78.
Ertem, H., 1974. *Bogazköy metinlerine göre Hititler devri anadolu'sunun Florasi*. Ankara.
Evans, E. P., 1886. 'The Aryan homestead', *Atlantic Monthly* 57, 633–44.
Fehér, T., 2021. 'The Dnieper homeland of Indo-Europeans', https://www.academia.edu/48919777/The_Dnieper_homeland_of_Indo_Europeans
Feist, S., 1910. *Europa im Lichte der Vorgeschichte und die Ergebnisse der vergleichenden indogermanischen Sprachwissenschaft*. Berlin.
—— 1913. *Kultur, ausbreitung und herkunft der Indogermanen*. Berlin.
—— 1932. 'The origin of the Germanic languages and the Indo-Europeanizing of North Europe', *Language* 8, 245–54.
—— 1933. 'Die Ausbreitung des indogermanischen Sprachstammes über Nordeuropa in vorgeschichtlicher Zeit', in *Actes du deuxième Congrès international de linguistes: Genève 25–29 Aout 1931*. Paris. 184–7.
Ferak, V., and Z. Lichardova, 1969. 'Possible role of "luxuriance" and "inbreeding depression" in the secular changes of cephalic index', *Homo* 20, 90–4.
Fernandes, D. M., et al., 2018. 'A genomic Neolithic time transect of

hunter-farmer admixture in central Poland', *Nature Scientific Reports* 8, 14879. https://doi.org/10.1038/s41598-018-33067-w
—— *et al.*, 2020. 'The spread of steppe and Iranian-related ancestry in the islands of the western Mediterranean'. *Nature Ecology & Evolution* 4, 334–45. https://doi.org/10.1038/s41559-020-1102-0
Fleure, H., 1922. *The Peoples of Europe*. London.
Flor, F., 1936. 'Die Indogermanenfrage in der Völkerkunde', in Arntz 1936a, vol. I, 69–129.
Fodor, I., 1965. *The Rate of Linguistic Change: Limits of the Application of Mathematical Models in Linguistics*. *Janua Linguarum*, vol. 43. The Hague.
Forrer, E., 1934. 'Neue Probleme zum Ursprung der indogermanischen Sprachen', *Mannus* 26, 115–27.
Förstemann, E., 1852. 'Sprachlich-naturhistorisches', *Zeitschrift für vergleichende Sprachforschung* 1, 491–506.
—— 1854. 'Sprachlich-naturhistorisches (Zweiter artikel)', *Zeitschrift für vergleichende Sprachforschung* 3, 43–62.
Fortson, B., 2004. *Indo-European Language and Culture*. Oxford.
Fóthi, E., *et al.*, 2020. 'Genetic analysis of male Hungarian conquerors: European and Asian paternal lineages of the conquering Hungarian tribes', *Archaeological and Anthropological Sciences* 12, 31. https://doi.org/10.1007/s12520-019-00996-0
Fournet, A., 2010. 'A cultural and historical sketch of the concept of proto-language', *The Macro-Comparative Journal* 1, 1–10.
—— and A. Bomhard, 2010. *The Indo-European Elements in Hurrian*. Charleston.
Fraser, J., 1926. 'Linguistic evidence and archaeological and ethnological facts', *Proceedings of the British Academy* 12, 257–72.
Fraser, M., *et al.*, 2018. 'New insights on cultural dualism and population structure in the Middle Neolithic Funnel-Beaker culture on the island of Gotland', *Journal of Archaeological Science Reports* 17, 325–34.
Friedrich, P., 1970. *Proto-Indo-European Trees*. Chicago.
Furholt, M., 2018. 'Massive migrations? The impact of recent aDNA studies on our view of Third Millennium Europe', *European Journal of Archaeology* 21, 159–91.
Gal, S., 1996. 'Language shift', in H. Goebl *et al.* (eds), *Kontaktlinguistic/Contact Linguistics/Linguistique de contact*, vol. I. Berlin and New York. 586–93.
Gallay, A., 2001. 'L'énigme campaniforme', in F. Nicolis (ed.), *Bell Beakers Today: Pottery, People, Culture, Symbols in Prehistoric Europe*, vol. 1. Trento. 41–57.
Gamkrelidze, T., and V. Ivanov, 1972. 'Problema opredelenija pervonachal'noj territorii obitanija i putej migratsii nositelej dialekov obshcheindoevropejskogo jazyka', in *Konferencija po sravitel'no-istoricheskoj grammatike indoevropejskich jazykov*. Moscow. 19–23.
—— and —— 1984. *Indoevropeyskiy yazyk i indoevropeytsy*. Tbilisi.
—— and —— 1985a. 'The ancient Near East and the Indo-European question', *JIES* 13, 3–48.
—— and —— 1985b. 'The migrations of tribes speaking Indo-European dialects from their original homeland in the Near East to their historical habitations in Eurasia', *JIES* 13, 49–91.
—— and —— 1995. *Indo-European and the Indo-Europeans*. Berlin and New York.
Garrett, A., 2006. 'Convergence in the formation of Indo-European subgroups: phylogeny and chronology', in P. Forster and C. Renfrew (eds), *Phylogenetic Methods and the Prehistory of Languages*. Cambridge. 139–51.
Gavashelishvili, A., *et al.*, 2023. 'The time and place of origin of South Caucasian languages: Insights into past human societies, ecosystems and human population genetics', *Nature* 13, 21133.

Geiger, L., 1878. *Zur Entwicklungsgeschichte der Menschheit*. Stuttgart.

Gelb, I., 1951. 'A contribution to the Proto-Indo-European question', *Jahrbuch für kleinasiatische Forschung* 2, 23–36.

Georgiev, V., 1966. 'Die europäische Makrohydronymie und die Frage nach der Urheimat der Indoeuropäer', in D. P. Blok (ed.), *Proceedings of the Eighth International Congress of Onomastic Sciences*. The Hague. 188–95.

Gerhardt, K., 1969. 'Der sogenannte Borreby-Typus', *Homo* 20, 141–59.

Gernot, W., 2004. 'Hurrian', in Woodward (ed.) 2004, 95–118.

Gerritsen, F., and R. Özbal, 2019. 'Barcin Höyük, a seventh millennium settlement in the Eastern Marmara region of Turkey', *Documenta Praehistorica* 46, 58–67.

Giles, P., 1922. 'The Aryans', in E. J. Rapson, *The Cambridge History of India*, vol. 1. Cambridge and New York. 65–76.

Gimbutas, M., 1963. 'The Indo-Europeans: Archaeological problems', *AA* 65, 815–36.

—— 1973. 'The beginning of the Bronze Age in Europe and the Indo-Europeans', *JIES* 1, 163–214.

—— 1974. 'An archaeologist's view of PIE in 1975', *JIES* 2, 189–207.

—— 1980. 'The Kurgan Wave #2 c. 3400–3200 B.C. into Europe and the following transformation of culture', *JIES* 8, 273–316.

—— 1991. *The Civilization of the Goddess*. San Francisco.

—— 1994. *Das Ende Alteuropas: Der Einfall von Steppennomaden aus Südrussland und die Indogermanisierung Mitteleuropas*. Budapest.

—— 1997. *The Kurgan Culture and the Indo-Europeanization of Europe*. Washington DC.

Godwin, J., 1993. *Arktos: The Polar Myth in Science, Symbolism, and Nazi Survival*. London.

Goedegebuure, P., 2020. 'Anatolians on the Move: From Kurgans to Kanesh', The Marija Gimbutas Memorial Lecture. University of Chicago.

Goodenough, W., 1970. 'The evolution of pastoralism and Indo-European origins', in G. Cardona *et al.* (eds), *Indo-European and Indo-Europeans*. Philadelphia. 253–66.

Goodrick-Clarke, N., 2002. *Black Sun: Aryan Cults, Esoteric Nazism and the Politics of Identity*. New York.

Gornung, B. V., 1964. *K voprosu ob obrazovanij indoevropejskoy jazykovoj obshchnosti*. Moscow.

—— 1970. 'Considérations sur le problem de la formation de l'unité linguistique indo-européenne', in *Trudy VII Mezhdunarodnogo kongressa antropologicheskikh i etnograficheskikh nauk*, vol 5. Moscow. 638–45.

Gorton, L., 2017. 'Revisiting Indo-European "wine"', *JIES* 45, 1–26.

Graebner, F., 1919–20. 'Thor und Maui', *Anthropos* 14/15, 1099–119.

Gray, R., and Q. Atkinson, 2003. 'Language-tree divergence times support the Anatolian theory of Indo-European origins', *Nature* 426, 435–9.

Greenberg, J., 1964. 'Historical inferences from linguistic research in Sub-Saharan Africa', in J. Butler (ed.), *Boston University Papers in African History*, vol. 1. Boston. 1–15.

—— 2000. *Indo-European and its Closest Relatives: The Eurasiatic Language Family, Volume 1: Grammar*. Stanford.

Grigoriev, S. A., 1999. *Drevnie indoevropeytsy. Opyt istoricheskoy rekonstruktsii*. Chelyabinsk.

—— 2002a. *Ancient Indo-Europeans*. Chelyabinsk.

—— 2002b. 'The Sintashta culture and the Indo-European homeland problem', in Jones-Bley and Zdanovich (eds) 2002, vol. 1, 148–60.

—— 2021. 'Archaeology, genes and language: The Indo-European perspective', *JIES* 49, 187–230.

—— 2022. 'Origins of the Greeks and Greek dialects', *Journal of Ancient History and Archaeology* 9 (1), 5–46.

Grimm, J., 1848. *Geschichte der deutschen Sprache*, vol. 1. Leipzig.

Grünthal, R., *et al.*, 2022. 'Drastic

demographic events triggered the Uralic spread', *Diachronica* 39, 490–524.
—— and P. Kallio (eds), 2012. *A Linguistic Map of Prehistoric Northern Europe*. Helsinki.
Guarino-Vignon, P., *et al.*, 2023. 'Genome-wide analysis of a collective grave from Mentesh Tepe provides insight into the population structure of early neolithic population in the South Caucasus', *Communications Biology* 6, 319. https://doi.org/10.1038/s42003-023-04681-w
Güntert, H., 1934. *Der Ursprung der Germanen*. Heidelberg.
Haak, W., *et al.*, 2008. 'Ancient DNA, strontium isotopes, and osteological analyses shed light on social and kinship organization of the Later Stone Age', *PNAS* 105 (47), 18226–31.
—— *et al.*, 2015. 'Massive migration from the steppe was a source for Indo-European languages in Europe', *Nature* 522, 207–11. https://doi.org/10.1038/nature14317
—— *et al.*, 2023. 'The Corded Ware Complex in Europe in light of current archaeogenetic and environmental evidence', in Kristiansen *et al.* (eds) 2023, 63–80.
Häkkinen, J., 2012. 'Problems in the method and interpretations of the computational phylogenetics based on linguistic data'. https://www.academia.edu/3494029
—— 2023. 'On locating Proto-Uralic', *Finnisch-Ugrische Forschungen* 68, 43–100.
Hall, R., 1966. *Pidgin and Creole Languages*. Ithaca, NY.
Hamp, E., 1990. 'The Pre-Indo-European languages of northern (central) Europe', in T. Markey and J. Greppin (eds), *When Worlds Collide*. Ann Arbor, MI. 302.
Hapgood, C., 1979. *Maps of the Ancient Sea Kings: Evidence of Advanced Civilization in the Ice Age*. New York. [rev. edn from 1966 1st edn]
Härke, H., 1998. 'Archaeologists and migrations: A problem of attitude?', *CA* 19, 19–45.

Harrison, R., and V. Heyd, 2007. 'The transformation of Europe in the third millennium BC: The example of "Le Petit-Chasseur I + II" (Sion, Valais, Switzerland)', *Prähistorische Zeitschrift* 82, 129–214.
Harvey, H. R., 1964. 'Cultural continuity in Central Mexico: A case for Otomangu', in *XXXV Congreso Internacional de Americanistas, Mexico, 1962: Actas y Memorias*, vol. 2, Mexico. 525–32.
Hauer, J. W., 1939. 'Zum gegenwärtigen Stand der Indogermanenfrage', in *Archiv für Religionswissenschaft*, vol. 36. Leipzig and Berlin. 1–63.
Häusler, A., 1981. 'Zu den Beziehungen zwischen dem nordpontischen Gebiet, Südost- und Mitteleuropa im Neolithikum und der frühen Bronzezeit und ihre Bedeutung für das indoeuropäische Problem', *Przegląd Archeologiczny* 29, 101–49.
—— 1995. 'Über Archäologie und Ursprung der Indogermanen', in M. Kuna and N. Venclová (eds), *Whither Archaeology? Papers in Honour of Evžen Neustupný*. Prague. 211–29.
—— 2002. 'Ursprung und Ausbreitung der Indogermanen: Alternative Erklärungsmodelle', *IF* 107, 47–75.
—— 2003. 'Urkultur der Indogermanen und Bestattungsriten', in A. Bammesberger and T. Vennemann (eds), *Languages in Prehistoric Europe*, Heidelberg. 69–119.
—— 2006. 'Polaritäten, geschlechtsdifferenzierte Bestattungssitten und die Entstehung des grammatischen Geschlechts in den indogermanischen Sprachen', *Jahresschrift für mitteldeutsche Vorgeschichte* 90, 71–149.
Hay, M., 2016. 'Genetic history of the British and the Irish', *Eupedia*, updated October 2016.
Heath, D., 1866. 'On the mute origin of European races', *Journal of the Anthropological Society of London* 4, xxxiii–xlviii.
Hegel, G. W. F., 1900. *The Philosophy of History*. New York.

Heggarty, P., 2000. 'Quantifying change over time in phonetics', in C. Renfrew *et al.* (eds), *Time Depth in Historical Linguistics*, vol. 2. Cambridge. 531–62.
—— 2018. 'Why Indo-European? Clarifying cross-disciplinary misconceptions on farming vs pastoralism', in Kroonen *et al.* (eds) 2018b, 69–119.
—— *et al.*, 2010. 'Splits or waves? Trees or webs? How divergence measures and network analysis can unravel language histories', *Philosophical Transactions of the Royal Society B* 365, 3829–43.
—— and C. Renfrew, 2014a. 'Introduction: Languages', in Renfrew and Bahn (eds) 2014, 19–43.
—— and —— 2014b. '3.16 Western and Central Asia: Languages', in Renfrew and Bahn (eds) 2014, 1678–99.
—— and —— 2014c. '3.29 Europe and the Mediterranean: Languages', in Renfrew and Bahn (eds) 2014, 1977–93.
—— *et al.*, 2023. 'Language trees with sampled ancestors support a hybrid model for the origin of Indo-European languages', *Science* 381, eabg0818.
Hehn, V., 1885. *The Wandering of Plants and Animals from their First Home*, trans. James Steven Stallybrass. London.
Hemphill, B., and J. P. Mallory, 2004. 'Horse-mounted invaders from the Russo-Kazakh steppe or agricultural colonists from western Central Asia? A craniometric investigation of the Bronze Age settlement of Xinjiang', *American Journal of Physical Anthropology* 124, 199–222.
Heyd, V., 2017. 'Kossina's smile', *Antiquity* 91 (356), 348–59.
Hirt, H., 1892. 'Die Heimat der indogermanischen Völker und ihre Wanderungen', *IF* 1, 464–85.
—— 1905–7. *Die Indogermanen: Ihre Verbreitung, ihre Urheimat und ihre Kultur*, 2 vols. Strasbourg.
Hodge, C. T., 1981. 'Indo-Europeans in the Near East', *Anthropological Linguistics* 23 (6), 227–44.

Höfler, S., 2023. 'How to pull a wagon in Indo-European', *IF* 128, 83–124.
Holm, H., 2019. *The Earliest Wheel Finds, their Archaeology and Indo-European Terminology in Time and Space, and Early Migrations around the Caucasus*. Budapest.
—— 2020. 'Steppe homeland of Indo-Europeans favored by a Bayesian approach with revised data and processing', *Glottometrics* 37, 54–81.
Holopainen, S., 2019. 'Indo-Iranian Borrowings in Uralic: Critical overview of the sound substitutions and distribution criterion', PhD Dissertation, University of Helsinki.
Hommel, F., 1879. 'Arier und Semiten', *Korrespondenz-Blatt der deutschen Gesellschaft für Anthropologie, Ethnologie und Urgeschichte*, 52–6, 59–61.
—— 1885. 'Neue Werke über die Urheimat der Indogermanen', *Archiv für Anthropologie* 15, 163–8.
Hoops, J., 1905. *Waldbäume und Kulturpflanzen im germanischen Altertum*. Strasbourg.
Horvath, C.-S., 2019a. 'Reconsidering the geographic origins based on the synthesis of archaeological and linguistic evidence and the newest results in genetics – A Finno-Scythian hypothesis', *Asia Pacific Journal of Advanced Business and Social Studies* 5 (2), 41–70.
—— 2019b. 'Redefining Pre-Indo-European language families of Bronze Age Western Europe: A study based on the synthesis of scientific evidence from archaeology, historical linguistics and genetics', *European Scientific Journal* 15 (26), 1–25.
—— 2021. 'How Eurasia was born: A provisional atlas of prehistoric Eurasia based on genetic data supporting the farming-language dispersal model', *International Relations Quarterly* 12, 1–2, 1–72.
Howells, W. W., 1966. 'Population distances: Biological, linguistic, geographical and environmental', *CA* 7, 531–40.
—— 1972. 'Analyses of patterns of

variation in crania of recent man', in R. Tuttle (ed.), *The Function and Evolutionary Biology of Primates*. Chicago and New York. 123–51.

Huld, M., 1990. 'The linguistic typology of the Old European substrate in North Central Europe', *JIES* 18, 289–423.

—— 2000. 'Reinventing the wheel: the technology of transport', in K. Jones-Bley, *et al*. (eds), *Proceedings of the Eleventh Annual UCLA Indo-European Conference*. Washington DC. 95–114.

Hutchinson, R., 1950. 'Battle-axes in the Aegean', *Proceedings of the Prehistoric Society* 16, 52–64.

Huxley, T. H., 1890. 'The Aryan question and prehistoric man', *The Nineteenth Century*, 750–77.

Ihering, R. von, 1894. *Vorgeschichte der Indoeuropäer*. Leipzig.

—— 1897. *The Evolution of the Aryan*. London.

Ismail, T. A., 1989. *Classic Arabic as the Ancestor of Indo-European Languages and Origin of Speech* (*sic*). Koresh.

Ivani, J., *et al*., 2020. 'Indo-Aryan – a house divided? Evidence for the east–west Indo-Aryan divide and its significance for the study of northern South Asia', *Journal of South Asian Languages and Linguistics* 7, 287–326.

Jäger, A., 1686. *De Lingua Vetustissima Europae, Scytho-Celtica et Gothica*. Wittenberg.

Jain, R. C., 1964. *The Most Ancient Arya Society*. Rajasthan.

Janhunen, J., 2001. 'Indo-Uralic and Ural-Altaic: On the diachronic implications of areal typology', in Carpelan *et al*. (eds) 2001, 207–20.

Jeong, C., *et al*., 2020. 'A dynamic 6,000-year genetic history of Eurasia's eastern steppe', *Cell* 183, 1–15. https://doi.org/10.1016/j.cell.2020.10.015

Jobling, M. A., *et al*., 2002. *Human Evolutionary Genetics*. New York and Abingdon.

Jóhannesson, A., 1943. *Um Frumtungu Indógermana og Frumheimkynni*. Reykjavík.

Jones, E. R., *et al*., 2015. 'Upper Palaeolithic genomes reveal deep roots of modern Eurasians', *Nat Commun* 6, 8912. https://doi.org/10.1038/ncomms9912

Jones, W., 1798. 'The third anniversary discourse', in *Asiatick Researches: or, Transactions of the Society Instituted in Bengal for Inquiring into the History and Antiquities, the Arts, Sciences, and Literature, of Asia*, vol. I. London and New York. 415–31. [reprinted 2000]

—— 1807. *The Works of Sir William Jones with the Life of the Author by Lord Teignmouth*. London.

Jones-Bley, K., and D. G. Zdanovich (eds), 2002. *Complex Societies of Central Eurasia from the 3rd to the 1st Millennium BC*, 2 vols (*JIES* Monograph Series 45 and 46). Washington DC.

Jorgensen, J. G., 1969. *Salish Language and Culture: A Statistical Analysis of Internal Relationships, History and Evolution*. The Hague.

Joyce, J., 1968. *Finnegans Wake*. New York.

Kahneman, D., 2012. *Thinking Fast, Thinking Slow*. London.

Kalla, L., 1930. *The Home of the Aryas*. Delhi.

Kallio, P., 2012. 'The prehistoric loanword strata in Finnic', in Grünthal and Kallio (eds) 2012, 225–38.

—— 2019. 'Daniel Europaeus and Indo-Uralic', in Kloekhorst and Pronk (eds) 2019a, 74–87.

Kassian, A. S., *et al*., 2015. 'Proto-Indo-European-Uralic comparison from the probabilistic point of view', *JIES* 43, 301–92.

—— *et al*., 2021. 'Rapid radiation of the inner Indo-European languages: an advanced approach to Indo-European lexicostatistics', *Linguistics* 59 (4), 949–79.

Keith A. B., 1937. 'The home of the Indo-Europeans', *Indian Historical Quarterly* 13, 1–30.

Kellens, J., 2005. 'Les *Airiia* - ne sont plus des Āryas: ce sont déjá des Iraniens', in G. Fussman *et al*. (eds), *Āryas, aryens et Iraniens en Asie Centrale*. Paris. 233–52.

Kellog, R. J., 1931. 'The problem of Indo-European origins', *Journal of the American Oriental Society* 51, 374.

Kennedy, V., 1828. *Researches into the Origin and Affinity of the Principal Languages of Asia and Europe*. London.

Keyser, C., et al., 2009. 'Ancient DNA provides new insights into the history of south Siberian Kurgan people', *Human Genetics* 126, 395–410. https://doi.org/10.1007/s00439-009-0683-0

Kilian, L., 2000. *De l'origine des Indo-Européens*, trans. Felicitas Schuler. Paris. [originally pub. 1983 as *Zum Ursprung der Indogermanen*]

Kim, R., 2018. 'Greco-Armenian: The persistence of a myth', *IF* 123, 247–71.

Kitson, P., 1997. 'Reconstruction, typology, and the "original homeland" of the Indo-Europeans', in J. Fisiak (ed.), *Linguistic Reconstruction and Typology*. Berlin. 183–239.

Klejn, L., 2017. 'The steppe hypothesis of Indo-European origins remains to be proven', *Acta Archaeologia* 88, 193–203.

Klimov, G. A., 1990. 'Some thoughts on Indo-European-Kartvelian relations', *JIES* 19, 323–41.

Kloekhorst, A., 2008. *Etymological Dictionary of the Hittite Inherited Lexicon*. Leiden.

—— 2023. 'The "Anatolian split" and the "Anatolian Trek"', in Kristiansen et al. (eds) 2023, 42–59.

—— and T. Pronk (eds), 2019a. *The Precursors of Indo-European: The Indo-Anatolian and Indo-Uralic Hypotheses*. Leiden.

—— and —— 2019b. 'Introduction: Reconstructing Proto-Indo-Anatolian and Proto-Indo-Uralic', in Kloekhorst and Pronk (eds) 2019a, 1–14.

Klyosov, A., and I. Rozhanskii, 2012. 'Haplogroup R1a as the Proto-Indo-Europeans and the legendary Aryans as witnessed by the DNA of their current descendants', *Advances in Anthropology* 2, 1–13.

—— and G. Tomezzoli, 2013. 'DNA genealogy and linguistics', *Advances in Anthropology* 3, 2, 101–11.

Knauer, F., 1912–13. 'Der russische Nationalname und die indogermanische Urheimat', *IF* 31, 67–88.

Koch, J., 2020. *Celtic-Germanic: Late Prehistory and Post-Proto-Indo-European Vocabulary in the North and West*. Aberystwyth.

Kochhar, R., 1997. *The Vedic People: Their History and Geography*. London.

Koeppen, T., 1886. *Beiträge zur Frage nach der Urheimath und der Urverwandtschaft des indo-europäischen und des finnisch-ugrischen Volksstammes*. St Petersburg.

Koerner, K., 1971. 'Observations on the sources, transmission, and meaning of "Indo-European" and related terms in the development of linguistics', in J. Maher et al. (eds), *Papers from the 3rd International Conference on Historical Linguistics*, Amsterdam. 153–80.

Koivulehto, J., 2001. 'The earliest contacts between Indo-European and Uralic speakers in the light of lexical loans', in Carpelan et al. (eds) 2001, 235–63.

Koppers, W., 1928. 'Die Religion der Indogermanen in ihren kulturhistorischen Beziehungen', *Anthropos* 24, 1073–89.

—— 1935. 'Die Indogermanenfrage im Lichte der historischen Völkerkunde', *Anthropos* 30, 1–31.

—— (ed.), 1936a. *Die Indogermanen- und Germanenfrage: neue Wege zu ihrer Lösung*. Salzburg and Leipzig.

—— 1936b. 'Pferdeopfer und Pferdekult der Indogermanen', in Koppers (ed.) 1936a, 279–411.

Kortlandt, F., 2002. 'The Indo-Uralic verb', in R. Blokland and C. Hasselbatt (eds), *Finno-Ugrians and Indo-Europeans: Linguistics and Literary Contacts*. Maastricht. 217–27. Reprinted in Kortlandt 2010a, 391–403.

—— 2010a. *Studies in Germanic, Indo-European and Indo-Uralic*. Leiden.

—— 2010b. 'Eight Indo-Uralic verbs?', in Kortlandt 2010a, 387–90 [389]. [originally pub. 1989, in *Münchener Studien zur Sprachwissenschaft* 50, 79–85]

Kosinski, T., 2023. 'Archaeogeneticists on the origin of the Indo-Europeans, with particular emphasis on the Pre-Slavs as their oldest ancestors', *Advances in Anthropology* 13, 111–51.
Kossinna, G., 1902. 'Die indogermanische Frage archäologisch beantwortet', *Zeitschrift für Ethnologie* 34, 161–222. Reprinted in Scherer 1968, 25–109.
—— 1921. *Die Indogermanen, I. Teil: Das indogermanische Urvolk*. Leipzig.
—— 1925. 'Nordische oder asiatische Urheimat der Indogermanen', *Mannus* 17, 237–41.
Kozintsev, A., 2019. 'Proto-Indo-Europeans: The prologue', *JIES* 47, 293–380.
—— 2020. 'On the homelands of Indo-European and Eurasiatic: Geographic aspects of a lexicostatistical classification', *JIES* 48, 121–50.
Krahe, H., 1954. *Sprache und Vorzeit: Europäische Vorgeschichte nach dem Zeugnis der Sprache*. Heidelberg.
—— 1964. *Unsere ältesten Flussnamen*. Wiesbaden.
—— 1970. *Einleitung in das vergleichende Sprachstudium*, ed. Wolfgang Meid. Innsbruck.
Krause, E., 1891. *Tuisko-Land, der arischen Stämme und Götter Urheimat: Erläuterungen zum Sagenschatze der Veden, Edda, Ilias und Odysee*. Glogau.
—— 1903. 'Kann Skandinavien das Stammland der Blonden und der Indo-Germanen sein?', *Globus* 83, 109–10.
Kretschmer, P., 1896. *Einleitung in die Geschichte der griechischen Sprache*. Göttingen.
Kreve-Michkevicius, V., 1926. 'Pirmykste indoeuropieciu gimtine', *Taut air Zodis* 4, 108–25.
Kristiansen, K., 2020. 'The archaeology of Proto-Indo-European and Proto-Anatolian: Locating the split', in M. Serangeli and T. Olander (eds), *Linguistic and Archaeological Perspectives on Early Stages of Indo-European*. Leiden. 157–65.
—— et al. (eds), 2023. *The Indo-European Puzzle Revisited: Integrating Archaeology, Genetics, and Linguistics*. Cambridge.

Kristinsson, A., 2012. 'Indo-European expansion cycles', *JIES* 40, 360–433.
Kroeber, A. L., 1960. 'Statistics, Indo-European, and taxonomy', *Language* 36 (1), 1–21.
—— and C. D. Chrétien, 1937. 'Quantitative classification of Indo-European languages', *Language* 13 (2), 83–103.
—— and —— 1939. 'The statistical technique and Hittite', *Language* 15, 69–71.
Kronasser, H., 1961. 'Vorgeschichte und Indogermanistik', in E. Breitiner (ed.), *Theorie und Praxis der Zusammenarbeit der anthropologischen Disziplinen*. Bergen. 117–40.
Kroonen, G., 2012. 'Non-Indo-European root nouns in Germanic: Evidence in support of the Agricultural Substrate Hypothesis', in Grünthal and Kallio (eds) 2012, 239–60.
—— et al., 2018a. 'Early Indo-European languages, Anatolian, Tocharian and Indo-Iranian'. Linguistic supplement to Damgaard et al. 2018.
—— et al. (eds), 2018b. *Talking Neolithic*. Washington DC.
—— et al., 2022. 'Indo-European cereal terminology suggests a Northwest Pontic homeland for the core Indo-European languages', *PLOS One* 17 (10), 1–45: e0275744. https://doi.org/10.1371/journal.pone.027574
Kruts, S. I., 1972. *Naselenie teritorii Ukrainy epokhi medi-bronzy*. Kiev.
Kuhn, A., 1845. *Zur ältesten Geschichte der indogermanischen Völker*. Berlin.
Kühn, H., 1932. 'Herkunft und Heimat der Indogermanen', *Proceedings of the First International Congress of Prehistoric and Protohistoric Sciences*. London. 237–42.
—— 1967. 'Re. Hans Krahe Unsere ältesten Flussnamen', *Anzeiger für deutsches Altertum und deutsche Literatur* 78, 1–22.
Kuiper, F. B. J., 1967. 'The genesis of a linguistic area', *Indo-Iranian Journal* 10, 81–102.
Kümmel, M., 2022. 'Indo-Iranian', in T. Olander (ed.), *The Indo-European Language Family: A Phylogenetic Perspective*. 246–68.

Kuzmina, E., 2002. *The Origin of the Indo-Iranians*. Leiden.
Lahovary, N., 1961. 'Concordances toponymiques et du vocabulaire des régions alpines, pyrénéennes et montagneuses avec l'Inde dravidienne', in *Atti del VII Congresso Internazionale di Scienze Onomastiche II (Firenze)*. Florence. 221–56.
Lamb, S., 1958. 'Linguistic prehistory in the Great Basin', *International Journal of American Linguistics* 24, 95–100.
Lansing, J., *et al.*, 2017. 'Kinship structures create persistent channels for language transmission', *PNAS* 114 (49), 12910–15.
Lapouge, G. Vacher de, 1899. *L'Aryen, son role social*. Paris.
Latham, R. G., 1851. *Germania*. London.
—— 1862. *Elements of Comparative Philology*. London.
Lazaridis, I., *et al.*, 2017. 'Genetic origins of the Minoans and Mycenaeans', *Nature* 548, 214–18.
—— *et al.*, 2022a. 'The genetic history of the Southern Arc: A bridge between West Asia and Europe', *Science* 377, eabm4247.
—— *et al.*, 2022b. 'A genetic probe into the ancient and medieval history of Southern Europe and West Asia', *Science* 377, 940–51.
—— *et al.*, 2024. 'The genetic origin of the Indo-Europeans'. bioRxiv preprint. https://doi.org/10.1101/2024.04.17.589597
Lehmann, W., 2005. *Pre-Indo-European*. Washington DC.
Levin, S., 1971. *The Indo-European and Semitic Languages*. Albany, NY.
Librado, P., *et al.*, 2021. 'The origins and spread of domestic horses from the Western Eurasian steppes', *Nature* 598, 634–9.
Liétard, G., *et al.*, 1864. 'Sur les migrations ariennes', *Bulletin de la Société d'Anthropologie de Paris* 5, 269–320.
Lillie, M., and I. Potekhina, 2020a. 'Radiocarbon dating of sites in the Dnieper Region and western Ukraine', in Lillie and Potekhina (eds) 2020b, 187–234.

—— and —— (eds), 2020b. *Prehistoric Ukraine: From the First Hunters to the First Farmers*. Oxford.
Lincoln, B., 1986. *Myth, Cosmos and Society: Indo-European themes of creation and destruction*. Cambridge, MA.
Lubotsky, A., 2023. 'Indo-European and Indo-Iranian wagon terminology and the date of the Indo-Iranian split', in Kristiansen *et al.* (eds) 2023, 257–62.
Makarenko, M., 1933. *Mariupilskii mohilnik*. Kiev.
Makkay, J., 1987. 'Linear pottery and the early Indo-Europeans', in S. Skomal and E. Polomé (eds), *Proto-Indo-European: The Archaeology of a Linguistic Problem*. Washington DC. 165–84.
—— 2001. 'The earliest Proto-Indo-European-Proto-Uralic contacts: An Upper Palaeolithic model', in Carpelan *et al.* (eds) 2001, 319–44.
Mallory, F., 2021. 'The case against linguistic palaeontology', *Topoi* 40, 273–84.
Mallory, J. P., 1973. 'A short history of the Indo-European homeland problem', *JIES* 1, 21–65.
—— 1976. 'The chronology of the Early Kurgan tradition (part 1)', *JIES* 4, 257–94.
—— 1977. 'The chronology of the Early Kurgan tradition (part 2)', *JIES* 5, 339–68.
—— 1982. 'Indo-European and Kurgan fauna I: Wild mammals', *JIES* 10, 193–222.
—— 1989. *In Search of the Indo-Europeans*. London and New York.
—— 1990. 'Human populations and the Indo-European problem', *Mankind Quarterly* 33, 131–54.
—— 1996. 'The Indo-European homeland problem: A matter of time', in K. Jones-Bley and M. Huld (eds), *The Indo-Europeanization of Northern Europe*. Washington DC.
—— 1997a. 'The homelands of the Indo-Europeans', in R. Blench and M. Spriggs (eds), *Archaeology and Language I*. London and New York. 93–121.

—— 1997b. 'The Indo-European homeland: An Asian perspective', *Bulletin of the Deccan College Post-Graduate and Research Institute (1994–1995)*, 54/55 [Sir William Jones commemorative volume], 237–54.

—— 2008. 'Migrations in prehistoric Eurasia: Problems in the correlation of archaeology and language', *Aramazd* 3 (2), 7–38.

—— 2013a. 'The Indo-Europeanization of Atlantic Europe', in J. T. Koch and B. Cunliffe (eds), *Celtic from the West 2: Rethinking the Bronze Age and the Arrival of Indo-European in Atlantic Europe*. Oxford and Oakville, CT. 17–39.

—— 2013b. *The Origins of the Irish*. London and New York.

—— 2014. 'Indo-European dispersals and the Eurasian steppe', in V. H. Mair and J. Hickman (eds), *Reconfiguring the Silk Road: New Research on East-West Exchange in Antiquity*. Philadelphia. 73–88.

—— 2015. *The Problem of Tocharian Origins*: Sino-Platonic Papers 259. Philadelphia.

—— 2016a. 'Archaeology and language shift in Atlantic Europe', in J. Koch and B. Cunliffe (eds), *Celtic from the West 3*. Oxford. 387–406.

—— 2016b. *In Search of the Irish Dreamtime*. London and New York.

—— 2017. 'Speculations on the Neolithic origins of the language families of Southwest Asia', in B. Hansen *et al.* (eds), *Usque ad Radices: Indo-European Studies in Honour of Birgit Anette Olsen*. Copenhagen. 503–16.

—— 2018. 'The Indo-Europeans and agriculture', in Kroonen *et al.* (eds) 2018b, 196–241.

—— 2019. 'Proto-Indo-European, Proto-Uralic and Nostratic: A brief excursus into the comparative study of proto-language', in B. Olsen *et al.* (eds), *Tracing the Indo-Europeans: New Evidence from Archaeology and Historical Linguistics*. Oxford. 35–58.

—— 2023. 'From the steppe to Ireland: The impact of aDNA research', in Kristiansen *et al.* (eds) 2023, 129–45.

—— and D. Q. Adams, 1997. *Encyclopedia of Indo-European Culture*. London.

—— and —— 2006. *The Oxford Introduction to Proto-Indo-European and the Proto-Indo-European World*. Oxford.

—— and V. H. Mair, 2000. *The Tarim Mummies: The Mystery of the First Westerners in Ancient China*. London.

Malmström, H., *et al.*, 2015. 'Ancient mitochondrial DNA from the northern fringe of the Neolithic farming expansion in Europe sheds light on the dispersion process', *Philosophical Transactions of the Royal Society B* 370. http://dx.doi.org/10.1098/rstb.2013.0373

Malzahn, M., 2016. 'The second one to branch off? The Tocharian lexicon revisited', in B. Hansen *et al.* (eds), *Etymology and the European Lexicon*. Wiesbaden. 281–92.

Manco, J., 2013. *Ancestral Journeys*. London and New York.

Mańczak, W., 1992. *De la préhistoire des peuples indo-européens*. Kraków.

Manning, P., 2006. '*Homo sapiens* populates the Earth: A provisional synthesis privileging linguistic evidence', *Journal of World History* 17 (2), 115–58.

Mansion, J., 1911. 'Le pays d'origines des Indo-Européens', *Revue des Questions Scientifiques* 70, 217–47.

Marchand, J., 1955. 'Was there ever a uniform Proto-Indo-European?', *Orbis* 4 (2), 428–31.

Marcus, J., *et al.*, 2020. 'Genetic history from the Middle Neolithic to present on the Mediterranean island of Sardinia', *Nat Commun* 11, 939. https://doi.org/10.1038/s41467-020-14523-6

Martirosyan, H., 2013. 'The place of Armenian in the Indo-European language family: The relationship with Greek and Indo-Iranian', *Journal of Language Relationship* 10, 85–137.

Matasović, R., 2012. 'Areal typology of Proto-Indo-European: The case for Caucasian connections', *Transactions of the Philological Society* 110, 1–28.

Mathieson, I., *et al.*, 2015. 'Genome-wide patterns of selection in 230 ancient Eurasians', *Nature* 528, 499–503.
—— *et al.*, 2018. 'The genomic history of southeastern Europe', *Nature* 555, 197–203.
Mattila, T., *et al.*, 2023. 'Genetic continuity, isolation, and gene flow in Stone Age Central and Eastern Europe', *Communications Biology* 6, 793. https://doi.org/10.1038/s42003-023-05131-3
Matyushin, G., 1982. *Eneolit Yuzhnogo Urala*. Moscow.
Maurus, H., 1913. *Die 'natürlichen' Grundstämme der Menschen*. Berlin.
McColl, H., *et al.*, 2024. 'Steppe ancestry in western Eurasia and the spread of the Germanic languages'. bioRxiv preprint. https://doi.org/10.1101/2024.03.13.584607
McGovern, P., *et al.*, 2017. 'Early Neolithic wine of Georgia in the South Caucasus', *PNAS* 114 (48), E10309–E10318. https://doi.org/10.1073/pnas.1714728114
McGregor, S., 2018. *First Settler Theory and the Origins of European Languages*. Columbia, SC.
Meillet, A., 1908. *Les dialects indo-européens*. Paris.
Menghin, O., 1936. 'Grundlinien einer Methodik der urgeschichtlichen Stammeskunde', in Arntz 1936a, vol. 1, 41–67.
Menk, R., 1980. 'A synopsis of the physical anthropology of the Corded Ware Complex on the background of the expansion of the Kurgan Culture', *JIES* 8, 361–92.
Merpert, N. J., 1974. *Drevneyshie Skotovody Volzhsko-Uralskogo Mezdurechya*. Moscow.
Metcalf, G., 1974. 'The Indo-European hypothesis in the Sixteenth and Seventeenth centuries', in D. Hymes (ed.), *Studies in the History of Linguistics*. Bloomington, IN. 233–57.
Michalowski, P., 2004. 'Sumerian', in Woodward (ed.) 2004, 19–59.
Milewski, T., 1968. 'Die Differenzierung der indogermanischen Sprachen', *Lingua Posnaniensis* 12–13, 37–54.

Misra, S. S., 1992. *The Aryan Problem: A Linguistic Approach*. New Delhi.
Mittnik, A., *et al.*, 2018. 'The genetic prehistory of the Baltic Sea region', *Nat Commun* 9, 442. https://doi.org/10.1038/s41467-018-02825-9
Möller, H., 1911. *Vergleichendes indogermanisch-semitisches Wörterbuch*, Göttingen.
Morris, C., 1888. *The Aryan Race: Its origins and Its Achievements*. Chicago.
Muhly, J., 2011. 'Metals and metallurgy', in Steadman and McMahon (eds) 2011, 858–76.
Müller, M., 1871. *Lectures on the Science of Language*. New York.
—— 1881. *Chips from a German Workshop*, vol. 4. New York.
—— 1888. *Biographies of Words and the Home of the Aryans*. London.
Murray, A., 1823. *History of European Languages*. Edinburgh.
Myres, J., 1935. 'The ethnology, habitat, linguistic, and common culture of Indo-Europeans up to the time of the migrations', in E. Eyre (ed.), *European Civilization: Its Origins and Development I*. London. 179–244.
Napol'skikh, V., 1995. *Uralic Original Home: History of Studies. A Preliminary View*. Izhevsk.
Narain, A. K., 1987. 'On the "first" Indo-Europeans: The Tokharian-Yuezhi and their Chinese homeland', in Y. Bregel (ed.), *Papers on Inner Asia*, vol. 2. Bloomington, IN. 1–28.
—— 2000. *The Tokharians*. Shillong.
Narasimhan, V., *et al.*, 2019. 'The formation of human populations in South and Central Asia', *Science* 365 (6457). DOI: 10.1126/science.aat7487
Nasidze, I., *et al.*, 2003. 'Testing hypotheses of language replacement in the Caucasus: Evidence from the Y-chromosome', *Human Genetics* 112, 255–61.
Necrasov, O., 1980. 'Physical anthropological characteristics of skeletons from Kurgan graves in Romania', *JIES* 8, 337–43.
Nehring, A., 1936. 'Studien zur indogermanischen Kultur und Urheimat', in Koppers (ed.) 1936a, 7–229.

Nettle, D., 1998. 'Explaining global patterns of language diversity', *Journal of Anthropological Archaeology* 17, 354–74.
—— 1999. 'Is the rate of linguistic change constant?', *Lingua* 108, 119–36.
Neumann, G., 1971. 'Substrate im Germanischen?', in *Nachrichten der Akademie der Wissenschaften in Göttingen, Philologisch-Historische Klasse, No. 4*. Göttingen. 75–99.
Neureiter, N., *et al.*, 2021. 'Can Bayesian phylogeography reconstruct migrations and expansions in linguistic evolution?', *Royal Society Open Science* 8, 201079. https://doi.org/10.1098/rsos.201079
Nichols, J., 1998. 'The Eurasian spread zone and the Indo-European dispersal', in R. Blench and M. Spriggs (eds), *Archaeology and Language II*. London. 220–66.
—— 2021. 'The origin and dispersal of Uralic: Distributional typological view', *Annual Review of Linguistics* 7, 351–69.
Nikitin, A., *et al.*, 2019. 'Interactions between earliest *Linearbandkeramik* farmers and central European hunter gatherers at the dawn of European Neolithization', *Nature Scientific Reports* 9, 19544. https://doi.org/10.1038/s41598-019-56029-2
—— *et al.*, 2024. 'A genomic history of the North Pontic region from the Neolithic to the Bronze Age'. bioRxiv preprint. https://doi.org/10.1101/2024.04.17.589600
Novembre, J., and M. Stephens, 2008. 'Interpreting principal component analyses of spatial population genetic variation', *Nature Genetics* 40, 646–9.
—— *et al.*, 2008. 'Genes mirror geography within Europe', *Nature Letters* 456, 98–101. https://doi.org/10.1038/nature07331
Olalde, I., *et al.*, 2018. 'The Beaker phenomenon and the genomic transformation of Northwest Europe', *Nature* 555, 190–6.
Olander, T., 2017. 'Drinking beer, smoking tobacco and reconstructing prehistory', in B. Hansen *et al.* (eds), *Usque ad Radices: Indo-European Studies in Honour of Birgit Anette Olsen*. Copenhagen. 605–18.
—— (ed.), 2022. *The Indo-European Language Family: A Phylogenetic Perspective*. Cambridge.
—— 2023. 'Linguistic phylogenetics and words for metals in Indo-European', in Kristiansen *et al.* (eds) 2023, 93–104.
Olender, M., 1992. *The Languages of Paradise*. Cambridge, MA.
—— 1997. 'From the language of Adam to the pluralism of Babel', *Mediterranean Historical Review* 12, 51–9.
Olsen, B., 2023. 'Marriage strategies and fosterage among the Indo-Europeans: A linguistic perspective', in Kristiansen *et al.* (eds) 2023, 296–302.
Oswalt, R. L., 1964. 'The internal relationship of the Pomo family of languages', in *XXXV Congreso Internacional de Americanistas, Mexico, 1962: Actas y Memorias*, vol. 2. Mexico. 413–27.
Otte, M., 2012. 'Les Indo-européens sont arrives en Europe avec Cro-Magnon', in D. Le Bris (ed.), *Aires Linguistiques Aires Culturelles*. Brest. 19–51.
—— 2017. 'Indo-Europeans arrived in Europe with modern man', *Philology* 3, 43–56.
Outram, A. K., 2023. 'Horse domestication as a multi-centered, multi-stage process: Botai and the role of specialized Eneolithic horse pastoralism in the development of human-equine relationships', *Frontiers in Environmental Archaeology* 2, 1134068. https://doi.org/10.3389/fearc.2023.1134068
—— *et al.*, 2009. 'The earliest horse harnessing and milking', *Science* 323 (5919), 1332–5.
Özdogan, M., 2011. 'Eastern Thrace: The contact zone between Anatolia and the Balkans', in Steadman and McMahon (eds) 2011, 657–82.
Pagerl, M., *et al.*, 2013. 'Ultraconserved words point to deep language ancestry across Eurasia', *PNAS* 110 (21), 8471–6.
Palumbi, G., 2011. 'The Chalcolithic of eastern Anatolia', in Steadman and McMahon (eds) 2011, 205–26.

—— and C. Chataigner, 2014. 'The Kura-Araxes culture from the Caucasus to Iran, Anatolia and the Levant: Between unity and diversity. A synthesis', *Paléorient* 40 (2), 247–60.

Papac, L., *et al.*, 2021. 'Dynamic changes in genomic and social structures in third millennium BCE central Europe', *Science Advances* 7, eabi6941.

Parsons, J., 1767. *Remains of Japhet being Historical Enquiries into the Affinity and Origin of the European Languages.* London.

Patterson, N., *et al.*, 2022. 'Large-scale migration into Britain during the Middle to Late Bronze Age', *Nature* 601 (7894), 588–94. https://doi.org/10.1038/s41586-021-04287-4

Peake, H., and H. J. Fleure, 1928. *The Steppe and the Sown.* Oxford.

Pedersen, H., 1962. *The Discovery of Language.* Bloomington, IN. [reprint of 1931 edn]

Penka, K. 1883. *Origines Ariacae: Linguistisch-ethnologische Untersuchungen zur ältesten Geschichte der arischen Völker und Sprachen.* Vienna.

—— 1886. *Die Herkunft der Arier: Neue Beiträge zur historischen Anthropologie der europäischen Völker.* Vienna.

—— 1905. 'Die Flutsagen der arischen Völker', *Politisch-anthropologische Revue* 4, 163–71.

Penske, S., *et al.*, 2023. 'Early contact between late farming and pastoralist socities in southeastern Europe', *Nature* 620, 358–65. https://doi.org/10.1038/s41586-023-06334-8

Pereltsvaig, A., and M. Lewis, 2015. *The Indo-European Controversy: Facts and Fallacies in Historical Linguistics.* Cambridge.

Petrosyan, A., 2019. *The Problem of Armenian Origins: Myth, History, Hypotheses.* Washington DC.

Peyrot, M., 2018. 'Tocharian agricultural terminology: Between inheritance and language contact', in Kroonen *et al.* (eds) 2018b, 241–77.

Piazza, A., *et al.*, 1995. 'Genetics and the origin of European languages', *PNAS* 92, 5836–40.

Pictet, A., 1859–63. *Les origins indo-européennes ou les Aryas primitifs,* 2 vols. Paris.

Piétrement, C.-A., 1879. 'Les Aryas et leur première patrie', *Revue de linguistique* 12, 99–147.

Pinhasi, R., and M. Pluciennik, 2004. 'A regional biological approach to the spread of farming in Europe', *CA* 45, 54. https://doi.org/10.1086/422085

Pisani, V., 1966. 'K indoevropejskoj problem', *Voprosy Jazykoznanija* 4, 3–21.

—— 1974. *Indogermanisch und Europa.* Munich.

Poesche, T., 1878. *Die Arier: Ein Beitrag zur historischen Anthropologie.* Jena.

Pokorny, J., 1929. 'Keltische Lehnwörter und die germanische Lautverschiebung', *Wörter und Sachen* 12, 303–15.

—— 1936. 'Substrattheorie und Urheimat der Indogermanen', *Mitteilungen der anthropologischen Gesellschaft in Wien* 66, 69–91.

Poljakov, O., 2015. *The Marvel of Indo-European Cultures and Languages.* Vilnius.

Posth, C., *et al.*, 2023. 'Palaeogenomics of Upper Palaeolithic to Neolithic European hunter-gatherers', *Nature* 615, 117–26.

Potekhina, I., 2020. 'Prehistoric populations of Ukraine: Population dynamics and group composition', in Lillie and Potekhina (eds) 2020b, 155–86.

Pronk, T., 2021. 'Indo-European secondary products terminology and the dating of Proto-Indo-Anatolian', *JIES* 49, 141–70.

—— 2023. 'Indo-European mobility, kinship, and marriage', in Kristiansen *et al.* (eds) 2023, 289–95.

Pronk-Tiethoff, S., 2013. *The Germanic Loanwords in Proto-Slavic.* Amsterdam.

Pulgram, E., 1958. *The Tongues of Italy.* Cambridge, MA.

—— 1959. 'Proto-Indo-European reality and reconstruction', *Language* 35, 421–6.

Pumpelly, R., 1908. *Explorations in Turkestan: Expedition of 1904:*

Prehistoric Civilizations of Anau. Washington DC.

Quitana-Murci, L., *et al.*, 2001. 'Y-chromosome lineages trace diffusion of people and languages in Southwestern Asia', *American Journal of Human Genetics* 68, 537–42.

Rascovan, N., *et al.*, 2019. 'Emergence and spread of basal lineages of *Yersinia pestis* during the Neolithic decline', *Cell* 176, 295–305.

Rask, R., 1818. *Undersøgelse om det gamle Nordiske eller Islandske Sprogs Oprindelse*. Copenhagen.

—— 2013. *Investigation of the Origin of the Old Norse or Icelandic Language*. Amsterdam and Philadelphia.

Rasmussen, S., *et al.*, 2015. 'Early divergent strains of *Yersinia pestis* in Eurasia 5,5000 years ago', *Cell* 163, 571–82.

Rassokha, I. N., 2007. *Ukrainskaya Prarodina Indoevropytsev*. Kharkiv.

Raulwing, P., 2000. *Horses, Chariots and Indo-Europeans*. Budapest.

Reche, O., 1936. 'Enstehung der nordischen Rasse und Indogermanenfrage', in Arntz 1936a, vol. I, 287–316.

Reinach, S., 2017. *L'origine des Indo-Européens*. Paris. [reprint of *L'origine des Aryens: Histoire d'une controverse*, 1892]

Rendall, G., 1889. *The Cradle of the Aryans*. London.

Renfrew, C., 1973. 'Problems in the general correlation of archaeological and linguistic strata in prehistoric Greece: The model of autochthonous origin', in R. A. Crossland and A. Birchall (eds), *Bronze Age Migrations in the Aegean: Archaeological and Linguistic Problems in Greek Prehistory*. New Jersey. 263–76.

—— 1987. *Archaeology and Language: The Puzzle of Indo-European Origins*. London.

—— 1999. 'Time depth, convergence theory, and innovation in Proto-Indo-European', *JIES* 27, 257–93.

—— 2003. 'Time depth, convergence theory, and innovation in Proto-Indo-European: Old Europe as a PIE linguistic area', in A. Bammesberger and T. Vennemann (eds), *Languages in Prehistoric Europe*. Heidelberg. 17–48.

—— and P. Bahn (eds), 2014. *The Cambridge World Prehistory*. Cambridge.

Rhode, J. G., 1820. *Die heilige Sage des Zendvolkes*. Frankfurt.

Riesenfeld, A., 1967. 'Biodynamics of headform and cranio-facial relationships', *Homo* 18, 233–51.

—— 1969. 'Head balance and brachycephalization', *Homo* 20, 81–90.

Ringe, D., *et al.*, 2002. 'Indo-European and computational cladistics', *Transactions of the Philological Society* 100 (1), 59–129.

Ripley, W., 1900. *The Races of Europe*. London.

Robb, J., 1993. 'A social prehistory of European languages', *Antiquity* 67, 747–60.

Roller, L. E., 2011. 'Phrygian and the Phrygians', in Steadman and McMahon (eds) 2011, 560–78.

Roosevelt, T., 1923–6. *The Works of Theodore Roosevelt Memorial Edition*, vol. 14. New York. 65–106.

Rosenberg, M., and A. E. Özdogan, 2011. 'The Neolithic in southeastern Anatolia', in Steadman and McMahon (eds) 2011, 125–249.

Rosenfeld, H.-F., 1956–7. 'Die germanische Zahlen von 70-90 und die Entstehung des Aufbaus der germanischen Zahlwörter', *Wissenschaftliche Zeitschrift der Ernst-Moritz Arndt-Universität Greifswald*, 171–215.

Rosser, Z., *et al.*, 2000. 'Y-chromosomal diversity in Europe is clinal and influenced primarily by geography, rather than by language', *American Journal of Human Genetics* 67, 1526–43.

Rouard, X., 2024. 'Ten reasons why Central Asia had to be the PIE original homeland', https://www.researchgate.net/publication/378846126_Ten_reasons_why_Central_Asia_had_to_be_the_PIE_original_homeland

Saada, J., *et al.*, 2020. 'Identity-by-descent detection across 487,409 British samples reveals fine scale population structure and ultra-rare variant associations', *Nat Commun* 11, 6130. https://doi.org/10.1038/s41467-020-19588-x

Sagona, A., 2011. 'Anatolia and the Transcaucasus: Themes and variations ca. 6400–1500 B.C.E.', in Steadman and McMahon (eds) 2011, 683–703.

—— 2018. *The Archaeology of the Caucasus*. Cambridge.

Sapir, E., 1916. *Time Perspective in Aboriginal American Culture: A Study in Method*. Ottawa.

—— 1936. 'Internal evidence suggestive of the northern origin of the Navaho', *AA* 38, 224–35.

Sarianidi, S., 1999. 'Near Eastern Asians in Central Asia', *JIES* 27, 295–326.

Saupe, T., *et al.*, 2021. 'Ancient genomes reveal structural shifts after the arrival of Steppe-related ancestry in the Italian Peninsula', *Current Biology* 31, 2576–91.

Sayce, A. H., 1880. *Introduction to the Science of Language*. London.

—— 1883. *Introduction to the Science of Language* [2nd edn]. London.

Scherer, A., 1960. 'Britannien und das "alteuropäische" Flussnamen-system', in W. Iser (ed.), *Britannica: Festschrift für Hermann M. Flasdrech*. Heidelberg. 241–50.

—— 1961. 'Der Ursprung der "alteuropäischen" Hydronomie', in *Atti del VII Congresso Internazionale di Scienze Onomastiche*, vol. 2. Florence. 405–17.

—— 1968. *Die Urheimat der Indogermanen*. Darmstadt.

Schlegel, F. von, 1849. *The Aesthetic and Miscellaneous Works of Friedrich von Schlegel*, trans. E. J. Millington. London.

Schleicher, A., 1853. 'Die ersten Spaltungen des indogermanischen Urvolkes', *Allgemeine Monatsschrift für Wissenschaft und Literatur* 3, 786–7.

—— 1861. *Compendium der vergleichenden Grammatik der indogermanischen Sprachen*. Weimar.

—— 1863. 'Der wirthschaftliche Culturstand des indogermanischen Urvolkes', *Jahrbücher für Nationalökonomie und Statistik* 1, 401–11.

Schmid, W. P., 1968. *Alteuropäisch und Indogermanisch*. Wiesbaden.

—— 1972. 'Baltische Gewässernamen und das vorgeschichtliche Europa', *IF* 77, 1–18.

Schmidt, J., 1872. *Die Verwantschaftsverhältnisse der indogermanischen Sprachen*. Weimar.

—— 1890. *Die Urheimat der Indogermanen und das europäische Zahlsystem*. Berlin.

Schmidt, W., 1949. 'Die Herkunft der Indogermanen und ihr erstes Auftreten in Europa', *Kosmos* 45, 116–18, 159–160.

Schmitt, A., 1936. 'Die germanische Lautverschiebung und ihr Wert für die Frage nach der Heimat der Indogermanen', in Arntz 1936a, vol. 2, 343–62.

Schott, A., 1936. 'Indogermanisch-Semitisch-Sumerisch', in Arntz 1936a, vol. 2, 45–95.

Schrader, O., 1883. *Sprachvergleichung und Urgeschichte: Linguistisch-historische Beiträge zur Erforschung des indogermanischen Altertums*. Jena. 2nd edn 1890, 3rd edn 1907.

—— and A. Nehring, 1917–28. *Reallexikon der indogermanischen Altertumskunde*. Berlin.

Schuchardt, H., 1884. *Slavo-deutsches und Slavo-italienisches*. Graz.

Schulz, H., 1826. *Zur Urgeschichte des deutschen Volksstamms*. Hamm.

Schulz, W., 1935. 'Die Indogermanenfrage in der Vorgeschichtforschung. Völkerbewegungen während der jüngeren Steinzeit', *Zeitschrift für vergleichende Sprachforschung* 62, 184–98.

Schwidetzky, G., 1932. *Schimpansisch Urmonolisch Indogermanisch*. Leipzig.

Schwidetzky, I., 1980. 'The influence of the steppe people based on the physical anthropological data in special consideration to the Corded

Ware-Battle Axe culture', *JIES* 8, 345–60.

Seger, H., 1936. 'Vorgeschichtforschung und Indogermanenproblem', in Arntz 1936a, vol. I, 1–40.

Seguin-Orlando, A., *et al.*, 2021. 'Heterogeneous hunter-gatherer and steppe-related ancestries in Late Neolithic and Bell Beaker genomes from present-day France', *Current Biology* 31, 1072–83.

Semino, O., *et al.*, 2000. 'The genetic legacy of Paleolithic *Homo sapiens sapiens* in extant Europeans: A Y chromosome perspective', *Science* 290, 1155–59.

Sergent, B., 1995. *Les Indo-Européens: Histoire, langues, mythes*. Paris.

Sharma, R., 1994. *Looking for the Aryans*. Madras.

Shevchenko, A., 1984. 'Paleoantropologicheskie dannye k probleme proiskhodeniya Indo-Evropeytsev', in I. F. Vardul (ed.), *Lingvisticheskaya Rekonstruktsiya i Drevneyshaya Istoriya Vostoka*. Moscow. 118–20.

Shishlina, N., 2008. *Reconstruction of the Bronze Age of the Caspian Steppes*. Oxford.

Shnirelman, V., 1992. 'The emergence of a food-producing economy in the steppe and forest-steppe zones of Eastern Europe', *JIES* 20, 123–43.

Sieglin, W., 1935. *Die blonden Haare der indogermanischen Völker des Altertums. Eine Sammlung der antiken Zeugnisse als Beitrag zur Indogermanenfrage*. Munich.

Simon, Z., 2020. 'Urindogermanische Lehnwörter in den uralischen und finno-ugrischen Grundsprachen', *IF* 125, 239–65.

Skoglund, P., *et al.*, 2014. 'Genomic diversity and admixture differs for Stone-Age Scandinavian foragers and farmers', *Science* 334, 747–50. DOI: 10.1126/science.1253448

Skourtanioti, E., *et al.*, 2020. 'Genomic history of Neolithic to Bronze Age Anatolia, Northern Levant, and Southern Caucasus', *Cell* 181, 1158–75.

—— *et al.*, 2023. 'Ancient DNA reveals admixture history and endogamy in the prehistoric Aegean', *Nature Ecology & Evolution* 7, 290–303. https://doi.org/10.1038/s41559-022-01952-3

Soares, P., *et al.*, 2010. 'The archaeogenetics of Europe', *Current Biology* 20, R174–R183.

Specht, F., 1944. *Der Ursprung der indogermanischen Deklination*. Göttingen.

Starostin, G., 2013. 'Lexicostatistics as a basis for language classification: Increasing the pros, reducing the cons', in H. Fangerau *et al.* (ed.), *Classification and Evolution in Biology, Linguistics and the History of Science: Concepts – Methods – Visualization*. Stuttgart. 125–46.

St. Clair, M., 2021. *The Prehistory of Language: A Triangulated Y-chromosome-based Perspective*. Published online at https://www.researchgate.net/publication/356580076_The_Prehistory_of_Language_A_Triangulated_Y-Chromosome-Based_Perspective/stats

Steadman, S. R., and G. McMahon (eds), 2011. *The Oxford Handbook of Ancient Anatolia: 10,000–323 B.C.E.* Oxford.

Stockhammer, P., 2023. 'Fostering women and mobile children in Final Neolithic and Early Bronze Age Central Europe', in Kristiansen *et al.* (eds) 2023, 303–7.

Stocking, G., 1987. *Victorian Anthropology*. London.

Stolper, M., 2004. 'Elamite', in Woodward (ed.) 2004, 60–94.

Strzygowski, J., 1936. 'Warum kann für den vergleichenden Kunstforscher nur der hohen Norden Europas als Ausgangspunkt der 'Indogermanen' in Frage kommen?', in Arntz 1936a, vol. I, 155–75.

Sulimirski, T., 1933. 'Die Schnurkeramischen Kulturen und das indoeuropäische Problem', *La Pologne au VIIe Congrès International des Sciences Historiques*, vol. I. Warsaw. 287–308. Reprinted in Scherer 1968, 117–40.

Susat, J., et al., 2021. 'A 5,000-year-old hunter-gatherer already plagued by *Yersina pestis*', *Cell Reports* 35 (13), 109278.

Sutton, M., 1991. 'Approaches to linguistic prehistory', *North American Archaeologist* 12, 303–24.

Swadesh, M., 1953. 'Archeological and linguistic chronology of Indo-European groups', *AA* 55, 349–52.

—— 1960. 'Unas correlaciones de arqueología y lingüística', in Bosch-Gimpera, P., *El problema indoeuropeo*. Mexico. 345–52.

Tacitus, *Germania*. https://www.gutenberg.org/files/7524/7524-h/7524-h.htm

Tappeiner, F., 1897. 'Der europïasche Mensch ist ein in Europa autochthoner Arier', *Correspondenz-Blatt der deutschen Gesellschaft für Anthropologie, Ethnologie und Urgeschichte*: XXVIII Jahrgang 7, July 1897, 49–50.

Taranets, V. and I. Stupak, 2018. *The African Theory of Aryan Origin*. Odessa.

Taraporewala, I., 1933. 'The Indo-European homeland: A restatement of the question', *Proceedings and Transactions of the Sixth All-India Conference, Patna December 1930*. Patna. 635–42.

Tassi, F., et al., 2017. 'Genome diversity in the Neolithic Globular Amphorae culture and the spread of Indo-European languages', *Proceedings of the Royal Society B*. http://dx.doi.org/10.1098/rspb.2017.1540

Taylor, G., 1921. 'The evolution and distribution of race, culture, and language', *Geographical Review* 11, 54–119.

Taylor, I., 1886. *The Origin of the Aryans*. London. Later edns: 1888, 1889, 1890 and 1892.

Telegin, D., 1990. 'Iranian hydronyms and archaeological cultures in the eastern Ukraine', *JIES* 18, 109–29.

—— and I. Potekhina, 1988. *Neolithic Cemeteries and Populations in the Dnieper Basin*. Oxford.

—— et al., 2001. *Srednestogovskaya i Novodanilovskaya Kul'tury Eneolita Azovo-Chernomorskogo Regiona*. Lugansk.

Telehin, D., 1973. *Seredn'o-stohivs'ka Kul'tura Epokhy Midi*. Kiev.

—— 1982. *Mezolitichny pam'yatki Ukraïny*. Kiev.

Thieme, P., 1954. *Die Heimat der indogermanischen Gemeinsprache*. Wiesbaden.

Thorsø, R., et al., 2023. 'Word mining: Metal names and the Indo-European dispersal', in Kristiansen et al. (eds) 2023, 105–26.

Tilak, L. B. G., 1903. *The Arctic Home in the Vedas: Being also a new key to the interpretation of many Vedic texts and legends*. Pune.

Tischler, J., 1973. *Glottochronologie und Lexikostatistik*. Innsbruck.

Topinard, P., 1878. 'Sur un crâne galtchar de Pendjakend (région de Tashkend, Turkestan oriental)', *Bulletins de la Société d'Anthropologie de Paris*, 3rd ser., 2, 247–51.

Tovkailo, M., 2020. 'The Neolithic period in Ukraine', in Lillie and Potekhina (eds) 2020b, 110–53.

Trager, G., and H. Smith Jr, 1950. 'A chronology of Indo-Hittite', *Studies in Linguistics* 8, 61–70.

Trautmann, M., et al., 2023. 'First bioanthropological evidence for Yamnaya horsemanship', *Science Advances* 9, eade2451, 1–13.

Trautmann, T., 1997. *Aryans and British India*. Berkeley, Los Angeles and London.

Tremblay, X., 2005. 'Grammaire compare et grammaire historique: quelle réalité est recontruite par la grammaire compare?', in G. Fussman et al. (eds), *Āryas, aryens et Iraniens en Asie Centrale*. Paris. 21–195.

Triveda, D., 1938–9. 'The original home of the Aryas', *Annals of the Bhandarkar Oriental Research Institute* 20, 49–68.

Trubetzkoy, N., 1939. 'Gedanken über das Indogermanenproblem', *Acta Linguistica* 1, 81–9.

Tuite, K., 2004. 'Early Georgian', in Woodward (ed.) 2004, 967–87.

Udolph, J., 2017. 'Heimat und Ausbreitung indogermanischer Stämme im Lichte der Namenforschung', *Acta Linguistica Lithuanica* 76, 173–249.

Uesson, A.-M., 1970. *On Linguistic Affinity: The Indo-Uralic Problem.* Malmö.

Uhlenbeck, C. C., 1935. 'Oer-indogermaansch en oer-indogermanen', *Mededeelingen der koninklijke Akademie van Wetenschappen Afdeeling Letterkunde* 77, ser. A, no. 4, 125–48.

—— 1937. 'The Indogermanic mother language and mother tribes complex', *AA* 39, 385–93.

Van den Gheyn, J., 1881. *Le Berceau des Aryas.* Brussels.

Vander Linden, M., 2016. 'Population history in third-millennium-BC Europe: Assessing the contribution of genetics', *World Archaeology* 48 (5), 714–28.

Vasiliev, I., 1981. *Eneolit Povolzhya.* Kuybishev.

Vennemann, T., 2003. *Europa Vasconica - Europa Semitica* (Trends in Linguistics: Studies and Monographs, 138). Berlin.

Vicent García, J., and M. I. Martínez-Navarrete, 2022. 'Paleogenomics and archaeology: Recent debates about the spread of steppe ancestry in westernmost Europe', *Arkheologiya Evraziyskikh Stepey* 2, 290–301.

Wagner, H., 1969. 'The origin of the Celts in the light of linguistic geography', *Transactions of the Philological Society*, 203–50.

Wallach, E., 2019. 'Inference from absence: the case of archaeology', *Palgrave Communications* 5, 94.

Wang, C., et al., 2019. 'Ancient human genome-wide data from a 3000-year interval in the Caucasus corresponds with eco-geographic regions', *Nat Commun* 10, 590. https://doi.org/10.1038/s41467-018-08220-8

Watkins, C., 1995. *How to Kill a Dragon.* New York and Oxford.

—— 2004. 'Hittite', in Woodward (ed.) 2004, 551–75.

Wells, S., et al., 2001. 'The Eurasian heartland: A continental perspective on Y-chromosome diversity', *PNAS* 98 (18), 10244–9.

West, M., 2007. *Indo-European Poetry and Myth.* Oxford.

Whatmough, J., 1928. 'Review: *The Aryans: A study of Indo-European origins* by V. Gordon Childe', *Language* 4, 130–5.

White, N., and P. Parsons, 1973. 'Genetic and socio-cultural differentiation in the aborigines of Arnhem Land, Australia', *American Journal of Physical Anthropology* 38, 5–14.

Wichmann, S., et al., 2010. 'Homelands of the world's language families: A quantitative approach', *Diachronica* 27 (2), 247–76.

Wilke, G., 1918. *Archäologie und Indogermanenproblem.* Halle.

Wilser, L., 1899. *Herkunft und Urgeschichte der Arier.* Heidelberg.

Wittmann, H., 1969. 'A lexical-statistic inquiry into the diachrony of Hittite', *Indogermanische Forschung* 74, 1–10.

Witzel, M., 2000. 'The Home of the Aryans', *Münchener Studien zur Sprachwissenschaft*, 283–338.

—— 2006. 'South Asian agricultural vocabulary', in T. Osada (ed.), *Proceedings of the Pre-Symposium of RHIN and 7th ESCA Harvard-Kyoto Round Table.* Kyoto. 96–120.

Wodtko, D. S., et al., 2008. *Nomina im indogermanischen Lexikon.* Heidelberg.

Wolff, K., 1914. 'Die Urheimat der Indogermanen', *Mannus* 6, 309–21.

Wolzogen, H. von, 1875. 'Der Ursitz des Indogermanen', *Zeitschrift für Völkerpschologie und Sprachwissenschaft* 8, 1–14.

Woodward, R. (ed.), 2004. *The Cambridge Encyclopedia of the World's Ancient Languages.* Cambridge.

Yang, M., 2022. 'A genetic history of migration, diversification, and admixture in Asia', *Human Population Genetics and Genomics* 2 (1), 0001. https://doi.org/10.47248/hpgg2202010001

Yang, S., *et al.*, 2024. 'Inferring language dispersal patterns with velocity field estimation', *Nat Commun* 15, 190. https://doi.org/10.1038/s41467-023-44430-5

Young, T., 1813. 'Review of *Mithradates, oder allgemeine Sprachenkunde*', *The Quarterly Review* 10, 250–92.

Zaliznyak, L., 2016. 'Mesolithic origins of the first Indo-European cultures in Europe according to the archaeological data', *Ukrainian Archaeology*, 26–42.

—— 2020. 'Landscape change, human–landscape interactions and societal developments in the Mesolithic period', in Lillie and Potekhina (eds) 2020b, 87–110.

Zang, F., *et al.*, 2021. 'The genomic origins of the Bronze Age Tarim Basin mummies', *Nature* 599, 256–61.

Zavalii, O., 2023. 'Development of Indo-European hypotheses in Europe of the 19th–20th centuries: From Aryan ideas to the Renaissance of the Trypillian Culture', *Open Journal of Philosophy* 13, 544–64.

Zerjal, T., *et al.*, 1999. 'The use of Y-chromosomal DNA variation to investigate population history', in S. Papiha *et al.* (eds), *Genomic Diversity*. Boston. 91–101.

Zschaetzsch, K., 1922. *Atlantis die Urheimat der Arier*. Berlin.

Zvelebil, M., 1995. 'At the interface of archaeology, linguistics and genetics: Indo-European dispersals and the agricultural transition in Europe', *Journal of European Archaeology* 3 (1), 33–70.

Sources of Illustrations

All figures and maps have been redrawn and often simplified, translated or were constructed from multiple sources. Significant primary sources are indicated below.

1.4 Mallory and Adams 2006, 8, map 1.1; **4.5** Devoto 1962, 342, fig. 70; **4.7** Kennedy 1828, 221; **4.8** Schleicher 1853, 787; **4.9** Schleicher 1861, 7; **4.10** Kroeber 1960, 4, fig. 1; **4.11** Förstemann 1854, 61; **4.12** Pereltsvaig and Lewis 2015, fig. 4; **4.13 A:** Chang *et al.* 2015, 200, fig. 2; **B:** Kassian *et al.* 2021, 956, fig. 2; **C:** Heggarty *et al.* 2023, Supplement 57, fig. S6.1; **4.15** Gamkrelidze and Ivanov 1984, 415; **4.16** Wilke 1918, 18, Abb. 4; **4.17** Anttila 1989, 305, fig. 15.2; **4.19** Poljakov 2015, 203; **4.20** Poljakov 2015, 206; **5.1** Schmid 1972, 11; **6.8** Bomhard 1996, 22, chart 1; **7.2** Olander 2023, 97, fig. 7.3; **9.1** Wilke 1918, 18, Abb. 3; **9.3** Zaliznyak 2016, 33, fig. 8; **9.10** Telegin *et al.* 2001, 31, ris. 1 and 78, ris. 30; **9.16** Sagona 2018, 87, fig. 3.1; **9.18** Shishlina 2008, 158, fig. 108A and 160, fig. 109A; **10.1** Sieglin 1935, 136–7; **10.2** Taylor, G. 1921, 107, tab. vii; **10.3** Menk 1980, 373, fig. 2; **10.4** Barbujani and Sokal 1990, fig. 1; **10.5** Cavalli-Sforza *et al.* 1994, 292–3, figs 5.11.1–3; **11.2** Allentoft *et al.* 2015, fig. 1; **12.2** Blažek 1999b, 53; **14.3** Gamkrelidze and Ivanov 1984, 957; **14.4** Heggarty *et al.* 2023, fig. 1D; **15.1** Tovkailo 2020, 113, fig. 4.1; **15.3** Lazaridis *et al.* 2024, Summary Fig.

Appendix

A partial list of Indo-European Homeland solutions and their proponents.

Author	Date	Continent	Homeland
Jäger, A.	1686	Eurasia	Caucasus
Coeurdoux, G.-L.	1768	Eurasia	Caucasus-Tartary
Jones, W.	1789	Asia	Iran
Schlegel, F. von	1805	Asia	NW India
Adelung, J.	1806	Asia	Iran-Tibet
Young, T.	1813	Asia	Kashmir
Rask, R.	1818	Eurasia	Hungary to Asia Minor
Rhode, J. G.	1820	Asia	Bactria
Link, H. F.	1821	Asia	South Caucasus
Klaproth, J.	1830	Asia	Himalayas-Caucasus
Eichhoff, F. G.	1836	Asia	Kashmir
Pott, A. F.	1840	Asia	Himalayas-Caspian Sea
Lassen, C.	1847	Asia	Pamirs
Grimm, J.	1848	Asia	Asia
Latham, R. G.	1851	Europe	Lithuania?
Schleicher, A.	1852	Asia	Caspian to Pamirs
Renan, E.	1859	Asia	Bactria/Pamirs
Pictet, A.	1859	Asia	Bactria
Müller, M.	1861	Asia	Central Asia
Schleicher, A.	1863	Asia	Karakorums to Caspian
Liétard, G.	1864	Asia	Central Asia
D'Omalius d'Halloy, J.	1864	Europe	Germany
Benfey, T.	1869	Europe	North of Black Sea
Baldwin, J.	1869	Asia	Bactria
Fick, A.	1870	Asia	Ural-Altai
Cuno, J.	1871	Europe	Germany
Müller, F. M.	1872	Europe/Asia	Armenia
Pike, A.	1873	Asia	Sogdiana
Mommsen, T.	1874	Asia	Euphrates
Wolzogen, H., von	1875	Asia	Asia
Poesche, T.	1878	Europe	Lithuania
Geiger, L.	1878	Europe	Germany

APPENDIX

Author	Date	Continent	Homeland
Hommel, F.	1879	Asia	Caspian-Bactria
Piétrement, C.	1879	Asia	SE of Lake Balkhash
Sayce, A. H.	1880	Asia	Bactria
Van den Gheyn, J.	1881	Asia	Central Asia
Monier-Williams, M.	1881	Asia	Pamirs
Penka, K.	1883	Europe	Scandinavia
Brunnhofer, H.	1884	Asia	Armenia
Hommel, F.	1885	Europe/Asia	Caucasus-Bactria
Koeppen, T.	1886	Europe	Middle Volga
Morris, C.	1888	Eurasia	Caucasus
Tomaschek, W.	1888	Europe	Danubian
Taylor, I.	1888	Europe	East Baltic
Rendall, G.	1889	Europe	Scandinavia
D'Arbois de Jubainville, H.	1889	Asia	Bactria
Brinton, D.	1890	Europe	Atlantic
Huxley, T.	1890	Europe	Baltic-Urals
Schrader, O.	1890	Europe	South Russia-Ukraine
Sayce, A. H.	1890	Europe	Scandinavia
Schmidt, J.	1890	Asia	Mesopotamia-Pamirs
Krause, E.	1891	Europe	Scandinavia
Hirt, H.	1892	Europe	Baltic
Boughton, W.	1892	Europe	Baltic
Virchow, R.	1893	Europe	Germany
Boughton, W.	1898	Europe	Baltic
Wilser, L.	1899	Europe	Scandinavia
Much, M.	1902	Europe	Baltic
Kossinna, G.	1902	Europe	Scandinavia
Tilak, L. B. G.	1903	Arctic	North Pole
Helm, K.	1905	Eurasia	NW Europe to Central Asia
Hoops, J.	1905	Europe	Germany-Denmark
Biedenkapp, G.	1906	Arctic	North Pole
Paape, O.	1906	Europe	Scandinavia
Fick, A.	1907	Europe/Asia	North Caucasus
Widney, J.	1907	Asia	Central Asia
Pumpelly, R.	1908	Asia	Central Asia
Möller, H.	1911	Asia	Anatolia-Iran

APPENDIX

Author	Date	Continent	Homeland
Knauer, F.	1912	Europe	Russia
Feist, S.	1913	Europe/Asia	Steppe
Wilke, G.	1918	Europe	Central Europe
Classen, K.	1918	Europe	Central-Eastern
Graebner, F.	1919	Asia	Central Asia
Keary, C.	1921	Asia	Bactria
Bender, H.	1922	Europe	Lithuania
Giles, P.	1922	Europe	Pannonian Plain
Zschaetzsch, K.	1922	Atlantic	Atlantis=Azores
Sayce, A. H.	1927	Asia	Anatolia
Lowenthal, J.	1927	Europe	Danube
De Morgan, J.	1927	Asia	Central Asia
Peake, H., and H. Fleure	1928	Eurasia	Pontic-Caspian to Turkestan
Kellog, R. J.	1931	Europe	Pontic-Caspian
Kühn, H.	1932	Europe	Aurignacian
Sulimirski, T.	1933	Asia	Central Asia
Dawson, C.	1933	Europe	Pontic-Caspian
Taraporewala, I.	1933	Arctic	North Pole
Krichevsky, Y.	1933	Europe	Danube
Forrer, E.	1934	Europe	Ukraine
Myres, J.	1935	Europe	Pontic-Caspian
Schulz, W.	1935	Europe	Northern Europe
Flor, F.	1936	Europe	Northern Europe
Pokorny, J.	1936	Europe	NW Germany-NW Ukraine
Koppers, W.	1936	Asia	Central Asia
Strzygowski, J.	1936	Arctic	Greenland?
Brandenstein, W.	1936	Asia	Central Asia
Benveniste, E.	1939	Europe	Steppe
Triveda, D. S.	1939	Asia	India
Dumézil, G.	1941	Europe	Baltic-Hungary
Paret, O.	1942	Eurasia	North Sea to Central Asia
Heberer, G.	1943	Europe	Central and Northern Europe
Jóhannesson, A.	1943	Europe	Baltic
Neckel, G.	1944	Europe	Northern Europe
Schmidt, W.	1946	Asia	Central Asia
Meyer, E.	1948	Europe	North and Central Europe

APPENDIX

Author	Date	Continent	Homeland
Scherer, A.	1950	Europe	North Sea to Urals
Gelb, I.	1951	Asia	North of Fertile Crescent
Nehring, A.	1954	Europe	Caucasus-Caspian
Thieme, P.	1954	Europe	NE Europe
Merlingen, W.	1955	Europe	North-West Pontic
Pritzwald, K.	1955	Europe	Baltic-Black Sea
Marstrander, S.	1957	Asia	Kirghiz steppe
Pulgram, E.	1958	Eurasia	East Europe-West Asiatic steppe?
Bryusov, A.	1958	Europe	Northern Europe
Bosch-Gimpera, P.	1961	Europe	Poland-Pontic
Devoto, G.	1962	Europe	Central Europe [Linear Ware]
Gimbutas, M.	1963	Europe	Pontic-Caspian
Gornung, B.	1963	Europe	Balkans-Lower Danube
Georgiev, V.	1966	Europe	Rhine to the Don
McEvedy, P.	1967	Europe	North-Central to Balkans
Wagner, H.	1969	Europe/Asia	Baltic/Black Sea – Aral Sea
Gamkrelidze, T., and V. Ivanov	1972	Asia	Greater Armenia
Hapgood, C.	1979	Antarctica	Antarctica
Safronov, V. A.	1980	Asia>Europe	Anatolia>Balkans
Hodge, C. T.	1981	Africa	Egypt
Haudry, J.	1981	Arctic	Polar
Martinet, A.	1986	Europe	Pontic-Caspian
Renfrew, C.	1987	Asia	Anatolia
Makkay, J.	1987	Europe	Linear Ware to Yamnaya
Narain, A. K.	1987	Asia	China
Zvelebil, M., and K. Zvelebil	1988	Asia	Anatolia
Sherratt, A. and S. Sherratt	1988	Asia	Anatolia
Dolgopolsky, A.	1988	Asia	Anatolia
Ismail, T. A.	1989	Asia	Arabia
Mallory, J. P.	1989	Europe	Pontic-Caspian
Misra, S.	1992	Asia	India
Mańczak, W.	1992	Europe	Oder-Vistula
Sergent, B.	1995	Europe	Pontic-Caspian
Kitson, P.	1997	Europe	North-central Europe
Colarusso, J.	1997	Europe	Crimea-Caucasus

APPENDIX

Author	Date	Continent	Homeland
Nichols, J.	1998	Asia	Central Asia
Popko, M.	1999	Europe	Eastern Europe?
Kochhar, R.	2000	Europe	Pontic-Caspian
Häusler, A.	2002	Europe	Nordic-Caspian
Grigoriev, S.	2002	Asia	Kurdistan
Kazanas, N.	2002	Asia	India
Anthony, D.	2007	Europe	Pontic-Caspian
Dergachev, V.	2007	Europe	Pontic-Caspian
Parpola, A.	2008	Europe	Trypillia/Pontic-Caspian
Ebbesen, K.	2009	Eurasia	Western Eurasia Palaeolithic
Sverchkov, L.	2012	Asia	Central Asia
Bouckaert, R. *et al.*	2012	Asia	Anatolia
Kalla, L.	2012	Asia	India-Central Asia
Giannopoulos, T.	2012	Asia	Near East Palaeolithic
Kristinsson, A.	2013	Europe	Ukraine
Heggarty, P., and C. Renfrew	2014	Asia	Anatolia
Anthony, D., and D. Ringe	2015	Europe	Pontic-Caspian
Pereltsvaig, A., and M. Lewis	2015	Europe	Pontic-Caspian
Zaliznyak. L.	2016	Europe	Baltic Mesolithic
Koncha, S.	2017	Europe	Rhine-Donets
Drews, R.	2017	Asia	Anatolia
Udolph, J.	2017	Europe	Baltic
Reich, D.	2018	Asia	South of Caucasus
Heggarty, P.	2018	Asia	Anatolia-Armenia
Taranets, V., and I. Stupak	2018	Africa	Africa
Kozintsev, A.	2019	Asia	SE Caspian
Wang, C., *et al.*	2019	Asia	South of Caucasus
Kristiansen, K.	2020	Asia	North Caucasus
Fehér, T.	2021	Europe	Dnipro
St. Clair, M.	2021	Asia	Anatolia
Horvath, C.-S.	2021	Asia	Southern Anatolia
Lazaridis, I., *et al.*	2022	Asia	South of Caucasus
Egorova. M., and A. Egorov	2023	Europe	Pontic-Caspian
Gavashelishvili, A., *et al.*	2023	Asia	E. Anatolia to S. Caspian
Lazaridis, I., *et al.*	2024	Europe	Pontic-Caspian
Yang, S., *et al.*	2024	Asia	Eastern Anatolia

Index

Page references in *italics* refer to figures.

AAF-CHG cline 304, 309, 312, 321, 327, 366, 370
Acholi 369
Adam 18, 19, 61
Adams, Doug 13, 96, 156
Adelung, Johann Christoph 64
Adriatic 220, 300
Afanasievo culture 228–9, *229*, 236–7, *236*, 256, *257*, 272, *272*, 274, 347, 351, 365, 373–4, *374*, 377, 383
Afghanistan 35, 36, 47, 202, 235
Africa 19, 46, 50, 65, 72, 124, 205, 260
African 46, 245, 282
Afro-Asiatic languages 33, 39, 46, 53, *108*, 136–7, *137*, 138–9, 146–7, *148*, 150, 287, 290–1, 299, 360
agglutinative language 42, 127, 143, 307, 308
agricultural substrate 112
agriculture 36, 40, 42, 52, 67, 112, 122, 139, 168–9, 183–4, 192, 203, 206, 214–20, 224, 236, 242, 258, 264, 266, 271, 285, 286, 291, 297, 298, 300, 302, 303, 307, 309, 310–12, 322–3, 326–7, 329, 333, 339–41, 347, 351, 368; *see also* cereals; domestic animals; pastoral economy
Ahura Mazda 201
Airiianəm Vaējah 201
Ajanta caves 247
Akkadian 108, 125, 312
Akkadogram 312
Aknashen *239*, 326, 329–31, *329*, 333, 342, 348, 350–2, *350*, 355, 360, 366
Alan language 344
Alans 64, 67, 338
Albania 189, 379–80
Albanian language 27, 46, 70, *71*, *81*, 82, 88, *89*, 94, 95, 147, 154, 157, *158*, 189, 199, *316*, 317–19, 321–2
Albanian origins *316*, 317
Aleutians 149
Alexander the Great 64
Alfred the Great 51
Alinei, Mario 186–7, 212
Alps 91, 117, 118, 144, 190, 251
Altai 136, 144, 228, 229, 256, 258, 270, 274, 373, 374
Altaic languages 33, 53, 127, 136, *137*, 144, 206–7, 290
Alteuropäisch 118, 120; *see also* Krahe, Hans; Old European hydronymy
Amu Darya 202
Anastasia 289
Anatolia 12, 24, 27, 36, 40, 46, 67, 73, 75, 77–9, 88, 90, 92, 96, 103, 108–9, 112, 115, 119, 122, 126, 174, 185, 188, 190, 192–4, 215–17, 219, 220, 222–3, 225, 234, 238, 240, 243–4, 255, 258, 260, 265–6, 270, 280, 286, 289, 295–304, 308–11, 313–15, 317–22, 326–9, 331, 334–5, 340–1, 343, 366, 368, 370, 378–9, 381, 385–7
Anatolian languages 24, 29, 46, 51, 52, 59, 70, 74–5, 77–9, *77*, 78, 83, 88, *88*, *89*, 90–1, *91*, 92, 93, 97, 104, 113, 118, 121, 147, 157–9, *158*, 167, 169–73, 179–81, 184–5, 191, 196–7, 199, *213*, 216–17, 223, 243, 246, 298, 304–5, 308–15, *316*, 317–19, 321, 324, 326, 328, 331, 335, 339, 341, 343, 346, 366–8, 370, 372, 385–7
Anatolian Farmer model 36, 37, 40–1, 46, 112, 178, 214–20, *216*, 223–4, 236, 238, 242–3, 255, 258, 260–2, 264, 266, 269–72, 280, 287, 297–9, 302, 305, 315, 326–7, 366, 368, 370–1
Anatolian Hunter-Gatherer (AHG) 86–7, 286, 289, 295, 297, 311, 329
Anatolian origins 75, 298, 308–17, *316*, 366, 385–7
Anau 214, 236, *236*
Ancestral Journeys 267
Ancestral North Indian (ANI) 376
Ancient Anatolian Farmer (AAF) 271, 273, 274, 284, *284*, 286–7, 295–8, 300–4, 306, 309, 312, 314, 326–7, 329, 331, 340–1, 343, 347, 351–2, 355, 366, 368, 370, 371, 379, 386
Ancient Ancestral South Indian (AASI) 84, 288–9, 290, 376
Ancient East Asian 364
Ancient North Eurasian (ANE) 285, 288, 291
Andaman Islanders 288, 376
Anderson, Nikolai 126
Andronovo culture 236–7, *236*, *257*, 267, 272, *272*, 274, 323, 365, 375, 377–8, *377*
Anglo-Saxon Chronicle 31
Anglo-Saxon language 31, *80*, 115; *see also* Old English language
Anglo-Saxons 66, 125
Anquetil-Duperron, Abraham Hyacinthe 23
Antarctica 34, 45, 47, 58; *see also* Polar homeland model
Anthony, David 13, 39, 262, 337, 347, 369
Antoniewicz, W. 232
Anttila, Raimo 13, 95–6
Antwerp 18
Arab 15, 30
Arabia 32, 48
Arabic 47, 66, 146
Aral Sea 127, 134, 188, 201–2, 237
Ararat 201, 326
Aratashen *239*
Aratashen-Shulaveri-Shomutepe culture (ASS) 26–8, 238–9, 306, 326, 331
Aratta river 197
Araxes 116, 238–9, 326, 328, 330, 333, 340, 355, 378
Archaeology and Language 40, 215
argument *ex silentio* 161
Armenia 31, 116, 136, 195, 202, 328, 338, 370, 377–80, 386
Armenian language 24, 27, 46, 48, *70*, *71*, 77, 82, *84*, 88, *89*, 92, 93–5, *95*, 108, 113, 116, 131, *131*, 147–5, 155, 157, *158*, 187–8, 191–2, 194–6, 199, *213*, 252, *316*, 317, 322, 338–9, 372, 378–9
Armenian origins 73, *316*, 338–9, 378–81
Armenians 48, 73, 93, 338–9, 378–9, 385
Armorica 78

INDEX

Arslantepe *313*, 313–14, 387
Aryan 23, 33, 43, 47, *81*, 157, 160, 202, 204, 214, 247, 253, 276–7
Aryans 42, 43, 47, 52, 201, 247, 250–1, 323
Aryo-Pelasgian *81*
ash tree 190, 208
Asian Steppe homeland model 36, *37*, 39, 250, 288, 333
Asiatic Hordes 67
Asiatic steppe 145, 205–6, 274, 288, 364
Assamese *28*
Assyrians 32
Atkinson, Quentin 87, 88; *see also* Auckland computational team
Atkinson, Ronald 369
Atlantic 7, 23, 25, 34, 38, 43, 57, 73, 78, 101, 174, 193, 195, 215–16, 221, 259, 270, 273, 281, 292, 301, 333
Atlantis 42, 44, 47, 168
Auckland computational team 87–9, *89*, 91, *91*, 114, 171, 175–7, *175*, 269, 311, 316–18, 321–2, 338, 371, 375
Aurignacian culture 39, 186, 211–12, *212*, 285
aurochs 163, 184
Ausgangsland 49
Austerlitz, Robert 127
Australia 50, 72, 204
Austria 23, 47, 205
autosomal evidence 279, 282–3, 289, 293, 325, 327–8, 331, 337, 363–4, 381, 386
Avars 64, 67, 237, 261
Avesta 23, 44, 201–2
Avestan language 20, 31, 116, 293
axe 148
axle 159, 177, 181
Azerbaijanis 339
Azores 48
Azov (sea of) 227, 334

Baalberge group 222, *222*, 230, 256, 303; *see also* Funnel-beaker culture
Babel, Tower of 18–19, 33, 49, 147, 201
Babylonian language 80
Babylonians 137
Bactria *37*, 51, 64, 103, 126, 136, 153–4, 188, 195, 250, 306, 364
Bactria-Margiana Archaeological Complex (BMAC) 36, 236, *236*, 306, 375, *377*
Bactrian homeland model *37*, 38
Baden culture 256
Bafra 335
Baillie, Mike 13
Baldwin, J. 429
Balkan languages 27, 94, *94*, 102, 301, 318, 321, 378
Balkan homeland model 36, 40, 218, 242, 298, 299, 301, 343
Balkan Hunter-Gatherer (BHG) 284–5, *284*, 299
Balkan refuge 285
Balkans 25, 73, 75, 77, 93, 113, 117, 127, 139, 144, 147, 215–18, 220, 223, 228, 234, 244, 251, 255, 296–303, 317–19, 330, 347, 367, 370, 378–9, 385–6
Baltic 26–7, 46, 70–1, *71*, 73, 77, *81*, 82, 89, 91, *94*, 95, 96, 104–5, 110, 118, 119, 156–7, *158*, 163, 177, 188, 190–1, 194–8, *213*, 231, 366, 381
Baltic homeland model 35, *36*, *37*, 37–8, 40, 45, 65, 104, 106, 200, 224; *see also* Lithuanian homeland model
Baltic origins 74, *210*, 231, 233, *316*, 381–3
Baltic Sea 73, 197, 285–6
Balto-Slavic languages 71, *81*, 82–3, *84*, 88, 89, 91, 92, 93, 96–7, 113, 156, *158*, 322, 341
Balts 51, 65, 73–4, 106, *210*, 233, 252
Baluchi *28*
Baluchistan 115
Bantu 33, 46, 369
Barcin 296
barley 152–3, 215, 310–11, 321, 326, 329
barrow 228, 230, 233, 240, 241, 256, 334, 356; *see also* kurgan, mounds
Basque language 29, 108, *108*, 120, 126, 131, 148, 270, 300
Basques 42, 109, 265
Battle-axe culture 231; *see also* Corded Ware culture
battle-axes 231, 233
BCMS 27, *27*; *see also* Slavic languages
Beaker 231–2, *232*, 257, *257*, 270, 273, 332–3, 357, 369, 384–5
bear 44, 186–8
beaver 188
Becanus, Johannes Goropius 18; *see also* Gorp, Jan Gerartsen van
Bedeni-Trialeti 338; *see also* Early Kurgan culture (Armenia)
bee 188
beech 189
Beekes, Robert 112
Belarus 74, 104, 248, 382
Belarusian language 26, *27*, 99
Belgium 18, 23, 212
Bender, Harold 38, 64, 103, 160, 162, 164–5
Benfey, Theodor 154, 160
Bengal 7, 15, 204
Bengali *28*
Benveniste, E. 431
Beowulf 51
Berbers 43
Berezhnovka 349, *350*, *351*, 386
Berkeley computational team 88–9, *89*, 91, *91*, 171, *175*, *175*, 269, 311, 322, 339, 375
Bhili *28*
Bible 7, 19, 30, 59, 60, 201
Bichlmeier, Harald 111, 120
Biedenkapp, Georg 44
Bihari *28*
bilingualism 56, 113, 292, 293, 294
Binford, Lewis 67
bio-archaeology 245
birch 165, 166, 190
Bjørn, Rasmus 132–3, 139, 140–2, 145, 147–8, 299, 360
Black Sea 19, 38, 46, 49, 66, 73, 78, 101, 143, 174, 196–9, *213*, 252, 260, 286, 319, 335, 375

435

INDEX

Black Sun 47, 49, 76, 145
Blackfoot 144
Blažek, Vaclav 13
Blok, D. P. 120
boar 184, 225
Boas, Franz 253
Boat-Axe culture *257*; *see also* Corded Ware culture
Bodrogkeresztúr culture 233
Boğazköy 312
Bohemia 56, 303, 364, 381
Bomhard, Allan 137, 142, 144, 360
Boncuklu 295–7, *296*, 304
Bopp, Franz 22, 126
Bosch-Gimpera Pedro 86
Bosnian language 26, 27
Botai 193, *236*, 237, 288
Bouckaert, R. 433
Boughton, Willis 65
bow 187, 190
Boxhorn, Marcus van 18, *21*
brachycephaly 250, 251, 252, 253
Bradke, Peter von 269
brahmins 31, 277, 376
Brandenstein, Wilhelm 39, 168–9, 205
Brassey, N. *21*
Breton language 23, *24*
Bretons 78
Brinton, Daniel Garrison 42, 53, 143, 247
Britain 17, 49, 50, 71, 78, 115, 117–18, 125, 136, 193, 200, 303, 357, 385
British 31, 182, 220, 251
Britons 57
bronze 185, 241, 334
Brunnhofer, Hermann 116, 202
Bryusov, A. 432
bubonic plague 382–3
Buchvaldek, Miroslav 232
Buddhists 374
Bulgaria 27, 47, 117, 227, 299, 379, 386
Bulgarian language 26, *27*, 106, 117
Bulgars 57
bull 148, 163, 180, 184
Burgundians 66
Burnett, J. *21*
Byblos 254

Çadır Höyük 193
Cambridge Apostles 42
camel 152, 154, 160
Çamlıbel Tarlasi 313, *313*
Campbell, Lyle 128
Canada 149, 283, 360
Cardial Ware culture 209, 215, 220–1, *221*, 300
carnelian 241
Carpathians 73, 76, 91, 225, 251
Caspian 31, 46, 66, 126, 134, 142, 188, 197, 199, 213–14, 235, 237–8, 244, 287, 317, 322, 325, 334, 336; *see also* Pontic-Caspian steppe
Cassidy, Lara 13
Catacomb culture *257*, 380
Çatalhöyük 215, 255, *296*, 297

cattle 152, 163, 169, 184, 192, 242, 321, 335, 360
Caucasian Hunter-Gatherer (CHG) 271, 273–4, 278, 284, *284*, 286–90, 287, 296–8, 300, 303–9, 311–12, 314, 317, 321, 324, 325, 326, 327, 329, 330, 331, 333, 335, 337, 338, 339, 340, 341, 343, 344, 347–61, 363, 368, 370–1, 376, 379–82
Caucasian languages *108*, 127, 140–4, 184, 289, 308, 320, 337, 340, 360–1
Caucasus 12, 27, 30, 35–6, 39, 42, 49, 108, 117, 119, 122, 126–7, 136–8, 140–2, 144, 147, 149, 185, 188–90, 194–5, 199–200, 206, 237–42, 244, 255, 271, 274, 277, 287, 289, 291, 295, 297, 299, 304, 306–8, 315–36, *332*, 333–42, 343, 348–58, 360–1, 366–8, 370, 372, 379–80, 385–8
Caucasus homeland model 307, 318, 321, 340, 371; *see also* Greater Armenian model
Caucasus-Lower Volga cline 350, *350*, 352, 355, 386–7
cauldrons 335
Cavalli-Sforza, Luca 260–61, 263
Celtic languages 8, 11, 13, 15–16, 20–5, *24*, 31, 51–2, 56, 70, *71*, 73, 75, 77, 78, 80, *81*, 84, *84*, *88*, *89*, 91, 92, 94, *95*, 96–7, 102–3, 108, 110–11, 115, 118, 120–1, 123, 146, 151, 153, 156–7, *158*, 159, 164, 171–7, *173*, *174*, 180–1, 187–9, 191–2, 194, 196–9, 210, *213*, 216–17, 231, *232*, *316*, 333, 366, 374, 384, 388
Celtic origins 73–4, *210*, 231, *316*, 384–5
Celts 51, 65, 70–4, 80, 91, 187, 206, *210*, 293
Central Asia 27, 41, 43, 52, 62, 64, 74, 138, 144, 146, 188, 196, 204, 207, 214, 232, 235–7, 241, 244, 270, 306, 314, 333–4, 364–5, 375
centre of gravity principle 72, 76
centum 70, 70–1, 74, 75, 95, *252*; *see also* satem
cephalic index 250–2, *252*; *see also* brachycephaly; cranial index; dolichocephaly
ceramics 55, 193, 218, 225, 233, 326–7, 335–6
cereals 54, 183–5, 196, 228, 295, 310–11, 347, 360, 368
Cernavoda culture 386
chaff 185
Chapman, Ken 13
chariot 178, 194, 207, 377, 379
Charles V 292
Charpentier, Jarl 104
Chaucer 50
Chemurchek group 373–4, *374*; *see also* Afanasievo culture
chickpea 311
Childe, V. Gordon 8, 9, 39, 75, 220
chimpanzee 46
China 7, 28, 46, 64, 66, 75, 163, 234, 235, 372
Chinese 15, 27, 29, 45, 143, 146, 176, 282
Chorasmia 202
Chrétien, C. D. 83, 96
Chukchi-Kamchatkan 136, *137*
Cimmerian language 344
Cimmerians 261
Clackson, James 165
clientage 293
cluster analysis 254
Coeurdoux, G. L. *21*

436

INDEX

Colarusso, John 141–2
Colebrooke, Henry Thomas 151
Coleman, Robert 178, 180
Collinder, Bjorn 132
Comb-Pit culture 257
Common Latin 50
conservatism 35, 38, 102–4, 106–7, 109, 114
constituency issues 9, 12, 90, 91, 109, 112, 113, 135, 145, 150, 159, 161, 183, 231, 300, 308, 322, 341, 387
contact relationship 128, 133, 137, 140, 146, 150, 378
Conway, Robert Seymour 103, 253
Copenhagen (Willerslev) lab 272–3, 274, 325, 353, 355, 382
copper 185, 200, 214, 218, 225, 227–8, 238, 242, 334, 384
cord decoration 230, 233
Corded Ware culture 193, 220, 224, 230–4, *230*, *232*, *232*, 233, 242–4, 254, 257–8, *257*, 266–7, 271–4, *272*, 324, 334, 357, 363–4, 369–70, 377, 381, 382, 383
Core-Indo-European 29, 88, 90, 157–9, 171, 179, 182–4, 188–9, 217, 293, 298, 309, 311, 315, 317, 326, 335, 340, 346, 367, 369–70, 372, 385
Cornish 24
Cortaillod Pfyn cultures 77
cow 120–1, 139–40, 147–8, 152, 163, 178, 180, 184, 208, 310
Cowgill, Warren 170
cranial index 251, 253–4, 277
craniometry 246, 250, 258
Crete 314
Crimea 142, 190, 256
Crimean Goths 26
Croatia 379
Croatian language 26–7, 142
Csongrád 227, 386
Cucuteni-Trypillia culture 46, 198, 217–19, *219*, 225, 234, 255, 285, 334, 347, 383
Czech language 26, *27*, 57
Czekanowski, Jan 83

Dacian language 27, 378–9
Dagestan 241, 319
Danes 245
Danish language 19, 26, *26*
Danube 35, 51, 54, 74, 117, 199, 217, 219–20, 223, 227–8, 284–5, 299, 301, 335, 369–70, 379, 385
Danubian homeland model 9, 38, 40, 76–7, 219–20, 234, 255, 301–2, 343, 368; *see also* Linear Ware culture
Dardic 28
Darkveti-Meshoko culture 238, *239*, 240; *see also* Maykop culture
Darwinism 245
Davidski 337
Day, John 13, 246, 249, 255
de Harlez, Charles 202
de Morgan, J. 431
de Saussure, Ferdinand 153
de Smet, Bonaventure 20–1
Delhi 62, 371

Deluge 19, 60; *see also* Noah
Demoule, Jean-Paul 246
Denmark 135, 302
Dergachev, V. 433
Desmoulins, Antoine 245
Devoto, Giacomo 38, 76–7
Diakonov, Igor 40, 139, 218
Diebold, Richard 99, 196
Disintegrant Proto-Language 49
Djebel Cave *236*, 237
Dnipro 54, 56, 73–4, 76, 117–18, 217–18, 225–7, 234, 238, 325, 330–1, 336, 345–7, 350, 352–5, 357, 364
Dnipro-Donets culture 225–8, *226*, 255, *257*, *345*, 347, 352, 355, 364
Dnipro-Donets region 325, 346–7, 350, 353
Dnister 56, 117, 147
Dolgopolsky, Aron 217
dolichocephaly 250–3, 277
domestic animals 184, 224, 228, 238, 311, 330, 346, 348, 360; *see also* pastoral economy
Don 51, 54, 56, 117, 193, 227, 325, 336, 347, 350, 352–4
Donets 117
Dorians 65
Dozier, Edward 203
dragon 44, 203–5, 207, 220, 277
Dravidian 28, 53, 109–10, 120, 136–7, 266, 290
Dressler, Wolfgang 48, 102, 161
Drews, Robert 379
Dumézil, Georges 141
Dutch language 16, 18, 20, 26, *26*, 72, 124, 167, 186, 258
Dybo, Anna 194
Dyen, Isidore 48, 98–9, 101
Dzungar Basin 373–4

Early European Farmer 284, 287; *see also* Ancient Anatolian Farmer (AAF)
Early Helladic II 319, 381
Early Iranian Farmer 287, 304; *see also* Caucasian Hunter-Gatherer (CHG)
Early Kurgan culture (Armenia) 338
Eastern Celtic 24
Eastern Hunter-Gatherer (EHG) 271, 273–4, 278, 284, 286, 288, 290–1, 298, 314, 325–7, 331, 336, 338, 340–1, 343, 346–8, 353–4, 356, 358–61, 363, 367, 371, 379–80, 386
eel 190, 204
Egypt 61, 234
Egyptian language 46, 137, 247
Egyptians 30, 32
Eichhoff, Frédéric 152
Ekaterinovka Mys 330, 349, *350*
Elam 377
Elamite language 53, 108, 136, 289–90, *290*, 307–8, *320*, 340
Elamites 323
Elamo-Dravidian *137*
elder (tree) 189
elephant 164
elite dominance 56, 324, 339

437

INDEX

Elmendorf, William 99
Eneolithic 214, 227, 241, 256, 267, 274, 280, 283, 297, 305, 311, 320, 332–33, 344, 346, 348, 353, 354, 356, 358, 363, 384
Eneolithic Steppe group 241, *241*, 332, *332*
England 7, 56, 69, 281, 367
English language 16, 26, *26*, 47, 50, 53, 66, 70–2, 85–6, 117, 124–5, 129–30, 136, 146, 148, 151, *155*, 166–8, 173, 178–9, 182, 186, 192, 194, 198, 245, 292, 293, 367
ergativity 308
Ertebølle culture 224
Esenç, Tevfik 141
Eskimo-Aleut 136, *137*
Estonia 198, 254
Estonian language 29, 126
Estonians 248, 252, 278
Eteo-Cypriot *108*
Etruscan language 25, *25*, 108, *108*
Etruscans 109
Eulau 266, 358
Euphrates 61, 240, 307
Eurasiatic languages 53, 136, 137, *137*, 144, 290; *see also* Nostratic
Eurasiatic origins 290–1
Euroids 46
Europaeus, Daniel 126–7
Evans, E. P. 205, 362
Eve 19, 61
ex oriente lux 61, 63, 67, 245
exclusion principle 119, 243
exogamy 358, 383
eye colour 246, 282, 286, 301; blue eyes 38, 104, 245, 247–8, 277, 285; brown eyes 301

Faliscan language 25, *25*
family tree 29, 45, 51, 79–81, 88, 91–4, 96–7, 99, 101–2, 131, 137, 157, 254, 263, 281; *see also* phylogeny
Fatyanovo culture *257*, 324
Fehér, Tibor 13
Feist, Sigmund 53, 64, 105, 110, 153, 179, 253
Fertile Crescent 116, 238, 291, 295, 297, 329
field 148, 169, 184
Finnish language 29, 42, 126, 133, *135*, 146
Finno-Ugric languages 132, 159
Finns 42, 248, 252, 278
fire cults 207
First Nations 149, 283, 360
fish 131, 160, 187, 195, 325
fishing 134, 161, 187, 206, 224–5, 236, 302, 345
Flemish language 18, 102, 258
Fleure, Herbert 40
flood myth 205; *see also* Deluge
Flor, Fritz 207
foal 192; *see also* horse, mare
Fodor, István 106
Ford, Pat 13
Forrer, Emil 106, 143–4, 149
Förstemann, Ernst 84–6
fosterage 293

France 23, 56, 61, 63, 66, 74, 108, 209, 215, 220, 248, 250, 251, 284, 303, 332
Franks *26*, 56, 66, 209
Fraser, John 165–6
French language 19, 25, 49, 53, 56, 63, *80*, 85, 99, 100, *100*, 101, 125, 146, 149, 211, 250, 282, 292, 360
French Foreign Legion 292
Friedrich, Paul 190
Frisian language *26*, 72
Funnel-Beaker culture 198, 213, 220, 222, *222*, 224, 231, 243, 252, 256–7, 302–3

Gaelic language 23, 252, 293
Gal, Susan 57
Galatas Apatheia *313*, 314
Galatian language *24*
Galatians 385
Galcha language 252, *252*
Gamkrelidze, Tamaz 39, 40, 91, 92, 127, 139, 140, 194, 197, 198, 239, 287, 307, 315, 316, 318
Gandhara Grave culture 376; *see also* Swat Valley culture
Gandhi, Mahatma 44
Ganges 22, 75, 202, 245
Ganj Dareh 304
Gansu 47
Garden of Eden 18, 33, 201
Garrett, Andrew 88, 97, 269; *see also* Berkeley computational team
Gaul 61, 332
Gaulish language 23, *24*, 189, 384
Gauls 56, 209
Gavashelishvili, A. 433
Geiger, Lazarus 248
Gelb, Ignace 115
Genesis (Book of) 7, 17–18, 61–2, 388; *see also* Babel, Tower of; Bible; Deluge; Noah
Genghis Khan 64
Georgia 163, 200, 287, 319, 327–8, 340, 348
Georgian language 39, 126, 140
Georgiev, Vladimir 117
German language 16, 18, 20, 22–3, 26, 33, 64, 66, 111, 124, 130, 137, 153, 173, 198, 253, 258, 292
Germanic languages 16, 20–2, *24*, 25–6, 51–3, 56, 66, 70, *71*, 72, *73*, 75, 76–7, *77*, 80–3, *80*, *81*, *84*, 85–6, *88*, 89, 91, *92*, 94, *95*, 102, 106, 110–12, 118, 121, 123, 124–5, 138, 146, 148, 151, 157, *158*, 159, 163, 171, 173, *173*, 175–6, 179, 181, 184, 188–99, *213*, 216–17, 223, 231, *232*, 252, 258, *316*, 322, 366–7, 372, 374, 381–2
Germanic origins 73–4, 76, *210*, 231, 233, *316*, 381–3
Germano-Albanian 88
Germans 22, 51, 64, 66, 73–4, 110, 130, 136, 202, 206, *210*, 233, 245, 252
Germany 7, 8, 23, 38, 44, 65–6, 74, 108, 139, 154, 179, 196, 202, 205, 224, 230, 256, 266, 270–1, 274, 276, 303, 332
Giles, Peter 39
Gilyak *137*
Gimbutas, Marija 9, 12, 39, 86, 118, 217–18, 230,

438

233, 256, 273, 298, 303, 335, 347, 364; *see also* Pontic-Caspian steppe
Globular Amphora culture 213, 230, *230*, 243, 256, *257*, 364
glottochronology 84–7
goat 139, 148, 152, 163, 179, 184, 295, 321, 360
gold 132, 146, 185–6, 200, 241, 311, 334, 384
Golubaya Krinitsa 325, *350*, 353–4
Gornung, Boris 144
Goropianism 18, 48
Goropius Becanus 102; *see also* Gorp Jan Gerartsen van; Goropianism
Gorp, Jan Gerartsen van 18
Gorton, Luke 198–9
Gothic language 15–16, 20, 26, 31, 70, 110, 152
Gothic origins 31
Goths 31, 65, 213
Graebner, Fritz 204–5
Graeco-Armenian 88, 92, *92*, 317
grain 310; *see also* cereals
grape 199–200; *see also* wine
grass pea 311
Gray, Russell 87; *see also* Auckland computational team
Greater Armenian model 36, *37*, 39–40, 127, 195, 239–40, 287, 315–16, 319, 321
Greece 7, 16, 62, 65, 79, 81, 92, 96, 112, 189, 192, 199, 204, 215, 220, 234, 247, 255, 314, 317, 368, 379–81
Greek language 8, 13, 15–18, 20–1, *21*, 24, 27, 31, 46, 51, 53, 59, 65, *71*, 73, 75, 77, 78–82, 78, 80, 81, 84–5, *84*, 88, 89, 92–3, *92*, 94, 95–7, *95*, 112–13, 116, 118, 121, 128, 147, 151–2, 156–7, *158*, 159, 163, 170–3, 178, 181, 183, 187–92, 194, 196, 198–9, 216, 223, 246, *252*, 314–15, *316*, 317–19, 321–2, 341, 367–8, 372, 374, 378–80, 388
Greek origins *210*, 213, 318–19, *316*, 317–19, 378–81
Greeks 30, 51, 73–4, 81, 93, 192, 249, 318–19, 379–81
Greenberg, Joseph 136
Greenland 45
Grigoriev, Stanislav 40, 319, 323
Grimm, Jacob 7, 62, 110, 111
Grimm's Law 110, *111*
grind (grain) 185
Gujarati 27, *28*, 292
Gumelniţa culture 257
Güntert, Hermann 206

Hagios Charalambos *313*, 314
hair colour 249; black hair 247; blond hair 43, 104, 245, 247–9, 251–2, 277; brown hair 247, 301; brunettes 43, 247; red hair 245
Häkkinen, Jaakko 177, 269, 362
Halaf 239–40, *240*, 307, 320, 326
Hall, Robert 110
Hallstatt culture 209
Halys 385
Ham 19, 32, 60, 124, 151
Hamites 46
Hamitic languages 19, 124
Hapgood, Charles 45

Harappa 377
Harvard (Reich) lab 270–3, 327, 349, 352–3, 355, 387
Hastinapur 62
Hatti 109, 313, 318, 385
Hattic language 108, *108*, 243, 290, *290*, 307, 313, *320*
Häusler, Alexander 13, 233
Heath, Dunbar Isidore 42
Hebrew language 18, 19, 21, 102
Hegel, G. W. F. 15, 21
Heggarty, Paul 66–7, 178, 182, 322; *see also* Auckland computational team
Hehn, Victor 64
Herodotus 56, 318, 378
Hesse, Hermann 48
heteroclitics 118, 167–8
High German 26
hill 194
Hill, Jim 9, 12
Himalayas 47, 49, 154, 195, 202
Hindi language 27, *28*, 292
Hindu 15, 30–1
Hindu Kush 136, 195, 214
Hirt, Herman 66, 74–6, 104–5, 138–9, 146, 161, 179, 197–8
Hispano-Celtic 23, *24*
historical paradigm 30
Hitler, Adolph 48
Hittite language 27, 83, 86–7, 90, *95*, 159, 164, 167, 169–71, 181, 184, 187, 196, 198–9, 243, 304, 309–10, *310*, 312–13, 318
Hittites 7, 196, 243, 313–14, 317, 385, 387
Hodge, Carleton 46, 137
Höfler, Stefan 181
Holm, Hans 269
Hommel, Fritz 125
honey 140, 146, 188
Hoops, J. 430
horse 67, 105, 144, 152, 164–6, 191–4, 201, 206–8, 226–7, 231, 237, 244, 288, 292, 298, 331, 344, 346, 358, 371; *see also* foal; mare; tail (horse)
horse sacrifice 206, 228, 376
horsemanship syndrome 193
horse-rider 191, 207
How to Kill a Dragon 203
Howells W. W., 253
Huld, Martin 13, 180
Hungarian language 29, *100*, 101, 106, 126, 134, 259
Hungarians 64, 133, 261, 278, 314
Hungary 64, 66, 67, 71, 74, 154, 228–9, 244, 259, 301, 386
Hunnish language 66
Huns 61, 64, 67, 237, 261
hunter-fishers 348
hunter-gatherers 147, 218, 222, 242, 273–4, 285, 295–6, 299, 302–3, 325, 340, 369, 382
hunting 134, 168, 192, 224–5, 236, 271, 283, 285, 287, 289, 295, 302, 311, 328, 334, 345
Hurrian language 108, 170, 184, 289–90, *290*, 308, 313, 319, *320*, 341, 376

INDEX

Hurrians 109
Hurro-Urartian languages *108*, 309, 319–20, 328, 338, 340
Huxley, T. 38, 245
hydronymy 117–18, 120, 122–3

Iberia 23, 108, 121, 193, 220, 232, 270, 284, 299–300, 384
Iberian language 56, 108, *108*, 300
Iberians 108
Ice Age 43, 192, 266, 283, 363
Iceland 7, 22, 45, 105, 245, 259
Icelandic language 22, 26, 45, 105, 151, 248
identity by descent (IBD) 306, 364
Ihering, Rudolf von 43, 51, 54, 160
İkiztepe *296*, 313–14, *313*, 335
Illyrian language 24, 26, *94*
Illyrian origins *210*
Impressed Ware culture 215, 220; *see also* Cardial Ware culture
India 7, 15–16, 20–1, 22, 27–8, 31, 34, 35, 43–4, 47, 50, 60, 62, 65–6, 103–4, 109–10, 186, 188, 192–3, 202, 204–5, 217, 234–5, 247, 266, 277, 284, 288–9, 321–4, 328, 365, 372, 375–6, 378
Indian homeland model 36, 38; *see also* Out of India homeland model
Indians 15, 23, 31, 153, 202, 277, 284, 288–9; *see also* Indo-Aryans
Indic languages 21, 23, 47, 60, 75, *81*, *84*, 98, 116, *158*, 159, 202, 247; *see also* Indo-Aryan languages
Indo-Anatolian languages 16, 29, 83–4, 88, 90, 114, 134, 147, 156–9, 169–70, 172, 182–5, 192, 198–9, 297–8, 307, 309, 311–15, 318–19, 328–9, 335, 337, 340–1, 343–4, 346–7, 360–1, 366–9
Indo-Aryan languages *21*, 23, 28, 59, 70–1, 77–9, 96, 103, 110, 118–19, 121, 169–70, 181, 183, 188, 191–2, 196, 235, 244, 321, 372, 375–8; *see also* Indic languages
Indo-Aryan origins 31, 77, 80, *316*, 321–4
Indo-Aryans 24, 27, 51, 65, *71*, 78, *78*, *81*, *84*, 89, 95, *158*, 192, 202, *213*, 245, *316*, 323–4, 365
Indo-Celtic 22, 158–9, *158*, 185
Indo-European homeland 8–10, 12, 30, 33–4, 36, 41, 43–4, 46–7, 50, 57, 59, 61, 65, 67, 69–70, 75–7, 86, 99, 101, 105–7, 115–16, 119–20, 122, 125–7, 133–4, 136–7, 150, 154, 169, 194, 201, 202, 205, 208–9, 213–15, 220, 225, 233, 237, 239–40, 246, 261, 269, 276–7, 288–9, 291, 294–5, 297, 307, 315, 340, 362, 366, 385, 387–8
Indo-Germanic 22–3, *158*, 159, 245
Indo-Hittite 83; *see also* Indo-Anatolian languages
Indo-Iranian languages *21*, 28, 41, 52, 70–2, 77, 82–5, 91–3, 95–6, 98, 104, 113, 116, 118, 133, 139, 145, 147, 153–4, 156–7, 168–9, 170–3, 179, 181, 187, 216–17, 262, 266, 272, 274, 298, 315, 317, 321–3, 341, 343–4, 375, 377–9
Indo-Iranian origins 74, 76, *210*, 317, 321–4, 343, 375–8, *377*
Indo-Iranians 23, 40, *73*, 74, *75*, 76, 77, 80, *88*, 93, *94*, 116, 145, *158*, 169, *210*, 216–17, 231, *232*, 234, 236, 275, 317, 321–4

Indo-Semitic homeland 137
Indo-Tocharian 158–9
Indo-Uralic 53, 126–30, *132*, 133–4, 136, 139, 144–5, 149–50
Indra 203
Indus 74, 118, 216, 377
Indus Periphery 288
Indus Valley Civilization 235, 365, 375, 377, *377*
inflexional language 51, 143, 308
interference 107
Introduction to the Science of Language 276
Iran 7, 16, 20, 27, 30–2, 64, 66, 74, 126–7, 185, 198, 217, 241, 266, 306, 321–3, 365, 377–8
Iranian languages 20–3, 24, 27–8, 31, 52, 56, 70–1, 71, *81*, 83, *84*, 89, *92*, *95*, 96, 98, 108, 116–18, 120–2, 139, 148, 154, 157, *158*, 163, 170, 188–92, 194–98, 201, *213*, 225, 250, 252, *316*, 321, 323–4, 338, 344, 366, 375, 377–8
Iranian origins 201–2, *316*, 321–4
Iranians 23, 31, 40, 76, 80, 145, 192, 201, 216–17, 275, 317, 323
Iraq 126, 240
Ireland 7, 17, 50, 71, 78, 121, 164, 186, 192, 217, 265, 281, 293, 303, 357, 367, 384–5
Irish language 8, 16, *20*, 23, 24, 31, 48, 131, *131*, 147, 163, 173, 176, 180, *252*, 270, 293, 384
Irish origins 31
Iro-European 22
Iron Gates 284–5
Isidore of Seville 388
Ismail, T. A. 48
isolating language 143
Isuwa 387; *see also* Arslantepe
Italian language 19, 25, 49, *80*, 99, 100, *100*, 292
Italic languages 24, 25, 51, *71*, 73, *73*, *75*, 77, 80, *81*, 82, *84*, 86, *88*, *89*, *92*, *94*, *95*, 96, 97, 101, 111, 118, 121, 157, *158*, 171, 173, *173*, 177, 181, 184, 199, 210, *213*, 216, 217, 223, 231, *232*, 305, *316*, 366, 384
Italic origins 73, *210*, 231, *316*, 384–5
Italics 51, 74, 91, *210*, 249
Italo-Celtic *81*, 82–4, *88*, 91–2, *92*, 97–8, 113, *158*, 384
Italy 7, 17, 23, 25, 49–50, 62, 65–6, 73, 92, 96, 101–2, 108–9, 118, 160, 172, 174, 190, 192, 222, 273, 300, 384
Ivanov, Vyacheslav 39–40, 91–2, 127, 139–40, 194, 197–8, 239, 287, 307, 315–16, 318; *see also* Gamkrelidze, Tamaz; Greater Armenian model

Jäger, Andreas *21*, 21–2, 30, 102, 307, 388
Jain, Ram Chandra 65
Jakartes 201
Janhunen, Juha 128, 135
Japanese language 33, 136
Japheth 19, 31, 32, 60, 124, 388
Japhetic 19, 22, 30, 102
Jarl 104, 248
Jeitun 134
Jóhannesson, Alexander 45, 197
Jones, Sir William 15–17, 20–2, 30–2, 60, 110, 128, 151
Jope, Martyn 13

440

INDEX

Josephus 388
Joyce, James 22
Jung, Carl 48
Junggar Basin 64

Kabardian language 141
Kacchi language 292
Kaelas, Lilli 12
Kahneman, Daniel 63
Kaliningrad 189
Kalla, L. 103–4
Kama 134
Kartvelian languages 39, 126–7, 136–7, *137*, 140–2, *141*, 146, 148, *148*, 150, 290, *290*, *320*, 340
Kashmir 62
Kaska language *108*, 313
Kassian, Alexei 128
Kassite 108, 290, *290*, *320*
Kazakhstan 193, 237, 274, 288
Kazanas, N. 433
Keith, Arthur Berriedale 66
Kellog, R. J. 249
Kelteminar culture 134, *236*, 237
Kemi Oba culture 255
Kempe, Andreas 19
Kennedy, Vans 60, 79–80, 103
Keresans 203
Keynes, John Maynard 42
Khlopkov Bugor 349, *350*, *351*
Khotanese Saka language 163, 323, 375
Khvalynsk culture 227–9, *227*, *229*, 346–7, 349, *350*, *351*, 351–2, 354, 356
Khwarazm 202; *see also* Chorasmia
Kirghiz 154
Kitson, Peter 39, 66, 196, 220
Kızılırmak 385
Klaproth, Julius 165
Klejn, Lev 363
Klimov, Georgy 127
Kloekhorst, Alwin 171, 243, 385
Klyosov, Anatole 270
Knauer, Friedrich 116
Koch, John 13, 174–6
Koeppen, Theodor 126
Koivulehto, Jorma 133
Kollmann, Julius 253
Kongemose culture 224
Koppers, Wilhelm 39, 205–7
Korean language 136
Kortlandt, Frederik 128, 144, 149
Kossinna, Gustav 38, 106, 211, 214, 223, 234
Kotias Klde *239*, 287, 326–9, *329*, 348, 350, *350*
Kozintsev, Alexander 336
Krahe, Hans 117–18, 121
Krause, Ernst 204–5
Kretschmer, Paul 165
Krichevsky, Y. 431
Kristiansen, K. 335
Krivyanskiy *350*, 352, 356
Kroeber, Alfred 83–4, 96
Kronasser, Heinz 164

Kuhn, Adalbert 152–3
Kühn, Herbert 40
Kulturkreis 204–8, 288
Kümmel, Martin 322
Kuqa 373–4, *374*
Kura 116, 238–9, 326; *see also* Araxes
Kura-Araxes culture 309, 319–21, *320*, 328, 338, 341
Kura-Araxes rivers 327, 330, 333, 340, 355, 378
Kurdish 28
kurgan 220, 227, 228, 230, 234, 240, 244, 334, 336, 352, 354, 356, *257*, 380, 386; *see also* barrow; mounds

Lahnda 28
La Tène culture 209
lake 196; *see also* sea
Lake Balkhash 136, 201–2
Lake Van 321
lamb 184
language shift 54–6, 67–8, 102, 109, 258, 279, 291–4, 300, 304–6, 355, 363, 369
lapis lazuli 241, 334
Late Glacial Maximum 284, 286
Latham, Robert Gordon 39, 41, 69–72, 76, 100, 102, 104, 276
Latin language 15–18, 20–1, *21*, 25, *25*, 31, 47–50, 54, 70, 77, *80*, 84–5, 92, 101, 103, 125, 128, 133, 147, 151–3, 156–7, 159–60, 163, 166, 168–9, 172–3, 176, 178, 190–1, 198–9, 252, *252*, 293, 312, 388; *see also* Common Latin; Italic languages; Romance languages
Latvia 198, 383
Latvian language 26–7, *27*
Latvians 364
Laws of Manu 31
least moves argument 32, 101, 308
Lehmann, Winfred 168
Leibniz, Gottfried Wilhelm 20–1
Lengyel culture 233
lentils 215, 311, 326, 329
Lepontic language 23, *24*, 25, *25*, 108
Levant 112, 238, 287, 297
Levantine 284, *284*, 286–7, 290, 300, 304, 306, 309, 314, 326–7
Lewis, Martin 67, 88, 269
lexical-cultural reconstruction 153; *see also* linguistic palaeontology; *Wörter und Sachen*
lexicostatistics 85, 98, 269; *see also* glottochronology
Ligurian language 25, *25*
Lillie, Malcolm 13
Linear A *108*
Linear B 79; *see also* Mycenaean language
Linear Ware culture 35, 38, 76, 77, 209, 219, 221, *221*, 224, 231, 255, 257, 301, *345*; *see also* Danubian homeland model
linguistic palaeontology 12, 151, 153–4, 160–1, 164, 171, 177–8, 182–3, 187, 200, 206, 208, 219, 223, 243–4, 298, 310–11, 329, 364, 366, 368–9, 371; *see also Wörter und Sachen*
Linné, Carl von 245

lion 154, 160
Liszt, Franz 153
Lithuania 7, 41, 154
Lithuanian language 17, 26–7, *27*, 35, 38, 45, 70, 104–6, 109, 114, 118, 152, 167, 178, 197, 252, *252*
Lithuanian homeland model 46, 105, 119; *see also* Baltic homeland model
Lithuanian origins 17, 105–6
Lithuanians 17, 65, 105, 252
Littleton, C. Scott 12, 13
Lituanus, Michalo (Michael the Lithuanian) 17
livestock 52, 139, 152, 160, 169, 183, 218, 225, 228, 237–9, 242, 325, 327, 329–331, 334, 341, 360; *see also* domestic animals; pastoral economy
Lombards 26, 66
London 66
Low German *26*
Lubotsky, Alexander 179
Luo language 369
Luvian language 27, 171, 198–9, 309–10, 318
Luvians 385

Macedonian language 26, *27*, 106
maces 225, 227
Madrid 66
Magdalenian culture 285
Maglemose culture 224
Magyars 64, 67, 133, 259, 314; *see also* Hungarians
Mair, Victor 13
Makkay, Janos 38, 134
Mallory, Fintan 13
Mal'ta 285
Malte-Brun, Conrad 22
Maltese language 29, 126
Manning, Patrick 99, 101
Mansion, Joseph 105
Manu 247
Manx *24*
Marathi language *28*, 292
Marchand, James 50
mare 191, 192; *see also* horse; foal
Mariupol 252
marten 198
Martirosyan, Hrach 93
Masis Blur *239*, 327, *329*
Matasović, Ranko 142, 360
matrilineal 206, 278, 359
Maui 204
Maurus, Horst 45
Mayan language 84, 99, 176
Maykop culture 185, 240–2, *241*, 306, 320, *320*, 324, 333–8, *337*, 342, 348, 350, 352, 354–6, 358
Mbugu language 149
mead 140, 148, 188
Medes 245, 323
Media Lengua language 149
Mediterranean 92, 109–10, 112, 116, 148, 161, 188, 192, 199, 206, 215–16, 220–1, 223, 243, 253, 255, 265, 300, 364
Medny Aleut language 149

Mehrgarh 235
Meillet, Antoine 82, 83, 96, 128, 130, 156
Menk, Roland 257
Merpert, Nikolai 13, 347
Meshoko culture 350, *350*, 352; *see also* Darkveti-Meshoko culture
mesocephalic 250; *see also* cephalic index
mesocranial 252
Mesolithic 42, 51, 122, 144, 191, 213, 224–5, 255, 265, 271, 283, 285–7, 289, 291, 300, 302, 324–8, 331, 345–6, 348–9, 351–2, 354, 363–4
Mesopotamia 59–62, 80, 108, 138–9, 186, 235, 241, 270, 297, 317, 319–21, 324, 326, 334, 365
Messapic language 25, *25*, 118
metallurgy 185, 218; *see also* bronze; copper; gold; silver
metals 320; *see also* metallurgy
Michif language 149, 360
Midgard serpent 45
Migration Theory 98–102, 113; *see also* Dyen, Isidore
Minoan 314
Minusinsk Basin 228–9, 274, 373
Mischsprache 43, 52–3, 147, 149–50, 360, 361; *see also* mixed language
Mitanni 28, *28*, 376, 377
Miwok language 129
mixed language 43, 53, 143, 147–8, 360; *see also Mischsprache*
Mohenjo Daro 377
Mohr, Evelyn Venable 13
Moldova 218, 382
Möller, Hermann 126
Mongolia 373
Mongolian language 46, 66, 136, 137
Mongoloid 42, 260
Mongols 237
Montelius, Oscar 61, 234
Montenegrin language 26, 27
Morris, Charles 42, 51, 109
Moscow computational team 88–9, *89*, 91, *91*, 127–8, 171, 175, *175*, 311, 322, 339, 375
mother-goddess 220
mounds 228, 233, 303, 334, 349; *see also* barrow, kurgan
mountain 194–5
mtDNA 263–5, 267, 281, 285–6, 325, 328–9, *329*, 332, *332*, 333, *337*, 348, *349*, 351–4, *351*, *353*, 373, 380
Müller, Max 53, 62, 104, 147, 253
Mulqueeny, Libby 13
multivariate analysis 254–5, 258
Mumbai 50, 292
mummies 374
Munda language 109, 110
Murray, Alexander 52
Murray, Joanne 13
Murzikha 349, *350*, *351*
Muttersprache 144
Mycenaean language 59, 79, 314, 367, 380
Mycenaeans 380
Myres, J. 220

442

INDEX

Nal'chik 334, 356
Narain, A. K. 47
Natufian 287
Nave 159
navel 159
Nazi 23, 46, 47, 204, 220, 251
Neanderthals 186, 211
Near East 50, 63, 78, 115, 139, 192, 211, 218, 234, 255, 260, 265, 354
Near Eastern 40, 46, 63, 244, 323, 333
Nehring, Alfons 39, 168, 179, 206
Neolithic 38, 46, 50–1, 88, 98, 112, 118, 134, 139, 147, 184, 192–3, 198, 200, 209, 213, 214–15, 217–23, 225, 231, 233, 235, 238–40, 255–6, 262, 264–7, 271, 274, 280, 283–4, 286–7, 291, 296–9, 301–4, 306, 310–11, 318, 320–1, 324–31, 333, 336, 338, 341, 345, 347–51, 354–5, 361, 363–4, 366–8, 379–81, 383
Netherlands 29, 127, 215, 220, 231, 302
Neumann, Günther 111
New Archaeology 9, 67, 68, 99
New Zealand 50, 72, 178
Nichols, Johanna 128, 344
Nile 9, 46, 61, 62, 137
Nileke 373–4, *374*
Noah 19, 33, 35, 51, 60; *see also* Deluge; flood myth
Nordic homeland model *36*, 38, 40, 104, 106, 110, 195–6, 204–7, 219–20, 222–4, 232, 234, 242–3, 285, 302, 343; *see also* Nordic-Steppe homeland model
Nordic physical type 38, 43, 247–9, 251–3, 285, 302
Nordic region 38, 44, 369
Nordic-Steppe homeland model *36*, *37*, 38, 363
Normans 245
Norse language 44, 56, 116, 124, 129, 204, 367
North African homeland model 47
North Caucasian languages 142, 148, *148*, 337, 360
Northern Picene language 25
North Pole 34, 54, 122; *see also* Polar homeland model
North Sea 38, 197
Northeast Caucasian languages 141–2, 147–8, *148*, 184, 290, *290*, *320*
Northwest Caucasian languages 141–2, 144, 147–9, 290, *290*, 320, *320*
Norway 7, 259
Norwegian language 26, *26*
Nostratic languages 53, 136–8, *137*, 140, 142, 146, 290
Nostratic origins 290–1
Novodanylivka culture 227–8, *227*, 233, 255, 386; *see also* Suvorovo-Novodanylivka culture
numerals 131, *131*, 139, 144, 151–2, 156
Nuristani language 28, *28*, *316*, 378

oak 189, 198
Ob 134, 145
ochre 228, 230, 334, 336, 351–2, 354
Ochre-grave culture 77; *see also* Yamnaya culture
Oder 106
Odessa 189
Olander, Thomas 157–9, 171, 179, 185

Old Balkanic language 139–40, *140*, 147, 299–300
Old English language 125, 166–7, 367; *see also* Anglo-Saxon language
Old Europe 118, 217–18, *257*; *see also* Gimbutas, Marija
Old European hydronymy 118–20, *119*, 122; *see also* Krahe, Hans
Old Norse language 8, 13, 45, 53, 116, 173, *173*, 367
Old Prussian language 26, 27, *27*
onomastics 115, 119; *see also* hydronymy
Oriya 28
Oscan language 25, *25*, 252, *252*
Osco-Umbrian languages 163
Osgood, Charles 195
Ossetic language 28, 108, 189, 338
Ostrogoths 26
Otte, Marcel 186, 212
Out of India homeland model *37*, 202, 288–9, 365; *see also* India homeland model
ox 167, 180, 184, 194, 207, 244, 344; *see also* bull; cow
Oxus 201
Oxus civilization 236; *see also* Bactria-Margiana Archaeological Complex (BMAC)

Pahari 28
Pakistan 76, 322, 328, 332, 376
Palaeolithic 39, 42, 51, 63, 186–7, 209, 211–12, 264–7, 270, 279–81, 283, 285–7, 289, 291, 303, 328, 344, 349, 363; *see also* Palaeolithic Continuity homeland model
Palaeolithic Continuity homeland model *36*, *36*, 39, 186, 211, 266, 270, 279, 285, 363
Palaeo-Sardo language 300
Palaic language *108*, 171, 318
Palestine 46, 215
Palumbi, Giulio 320
Pamir language 28
Pamirs 136, 138, 202
Panjabi 28
Parsons, James 17, *21*, 103
Pashto 28
pastoral economy 52, 54, 66–7, 152, 154, 169, 206–8, 218–19, 225, 228, 231, 242, 244, 266, 271, 288, 331, 335–6, 344, 358, 371, 373, 383; *see also* domestic animals; livestock
patriarchal 206, 208
patriarchy 206
patrilineal 206, 278, 359, 361, 370
pea 215, 311, 326, 329
Peake, Harold 40
Pearson, Osbjorn 263
Pedersen, Holger 420
Pelasgian language *81*; *see also* Aryo-Pelasgian
Penka, Karl 202, 205, 248, 252, 276
Pereltsvaig, Asya 88, 269
Peripheral Europe problem 300, 369
Perseus 204–5
Persia 16
Persian language 16, 18, 20, *28*, 31, 60, 64, 148, 198, 252
Persians 15, 323

443

INDEX

Phoenicians 30
Phrygian language 27, 82, 93, 94, 113, 157, 317–18, 378–9
Phrygian origins 73, 75, *210*, 318
Phrygians 24, 73, *73*, 75, 93, *316*, 318, 385
phylogeny 51, 79, 80, 82, 87–90, 92, 94, 97, 99, 113, 121, 147, 158–9, 166, 169, 171, 174, 222–3, 243, 254, 269, 298, 315, 317–18, 321–2, 339, 341, 366, 371–2, 378–9, 385; *see* tree (phylogenetic)
physical anthropology 245
Pictet, Adolphe 153, 195, 197
pidgin 110
Piétrement, Charles-Alexandre 201
pig 133, 152, 166, 184, 321
pigmentation 12, 42, 246, 249–52, 276, 285; *see also* eye colour; hair colour
Pisani, Vittore 144
Pınarbaşı 188, 286, 295, *296*, 297
Pit-Comb Ware culture *77, 345*
Plains Cree language 149
Planck, Max 122, 270
plaques 225
plough 153, 165, 168–9, 184–5
Poesche, Theodor 35, 103–4, 247, 276
Pokorny, Julius 110
Poland 74, 224
Polar homeland model 44; *see also* Antarctica; North Pole
pole 181, 185
polecat 198
Polish language 26, *27*, 106, 289
Poljakov, Oleg 105
Polynesian languages 204
Pontic-Caspian steppe 35, *36*, *37*, 40, 42, 73–4, 139, 161, 193–4, 228, 233, 272, 274, 280, 286, 315, 317, 324, 329, 331, 339–40, 343–4, 346–9, 355, 367, 371, 373, 376–7, 380, 387
Portuguese language 25, 49, 99–101, *100*
Poser, William 128
Pott, August Friedrich 62
primary homeland 52, 83, 103, 127, 149, 187, 244, 279, 290, 298, 301, 315, 317, 331, 340, 343, 360, 370; *see also* secondary homeland
principal component analysis 254, 258, 260, *261*, 262
Pripyat Marshes 104, 247
Progress-2 *239*, 331–3, 349, *350, 351*, 386
Pronk, Tijmen 357
pronouns 129–30, 144, 151, 156
Proto-Anatolian 29, 90, 155, 171–2, 180, 243, 298, 307, 309, 311–12, 314, 317, 321, 326, 335, 341, 370
Proto-Anatolians 180, 308–9, 311–12, 317, 385, 387
Proto-Indo-Anatolian (PIA) 16, 29, 84, 88, 114, 134, 147, 156–7, 159, 169–70, 172, 182–5, 188, 191, 192, 198–9, 297, 304, 307–10, 312, 315, 319, 335, 341, 343–4, 346–7, 360–1, 368
Proto-Indo-European 7, 12, 16, 29, 44–5, 49–50, 52–3, 69, 83, *88*, 90, 93, 99, 103–6, 110–11, 113–14, 116, 118, 123–5, 127, 129, 131–6, 140–3, 145–6, 150, 156, 159, 162–4, 166–8, 170, 172–4, 177, 179–81, 184–7, 190, 194, 198–200, 203, 207, 217, 219, 221, 224–5, 242, 244, 250, 290, 298–9, 301, 311, 328, 336, 363, 370
Proto-Indo-Europeans 32, 52, 54, 74, 106, 135–6, 145, 154, 165–6, 179, 183, 185, 191, 194, 207, 224, 231, 245, 249
proto-language 12, 29, 42, 48–50, 52–3, 80, 83, 86, 91, 93, 96, 106, 124, 131–4, 140, 141, 148, 155–7, 159–60, 163, 165, 171–2, 174–5, 177–8, 180–1, 183, 191, 195, 200, 307, 310, 329, 340, 361, 369
Proto-Pontic language 141
Puhvel, Jaan 13
Pulgram, Ernst 160, 165
pulses 329
Pumpelly, Raphael 214, 236
Punjab 110
Pylos 380

Quechua language 129, 149

Raetians 109
Raetic language 25, *25*, 108, *108*
Rajasthani 28
Raphelengius, Franciscus 20; *see also* Ravelingen, Frans van
Rask, Rasmus 22, 151–2
Rathlin Island 384
Ravelingen, Frans van 20; *see also* Raphelengius, Franciscus
raven 46
reaching down 131
Reich, D. 433
reins 186
Remedello culture 273
Remontnoye *350*, 352–3, *353*, 386
Rendall, Gerald Henry 16, 107
Renfrew, Colin 13, 40, 178, 182, 215, 217, 267, 298, 322, 366
Rhine 74, 117
Rhode, J. G. 201
Richard the Lionheart 51
ride in a vehicle 18; *see* wheeled vehicles
Ridler, Colin 13
Rig Veda 7, 110, 203, 234
Rig Veda Americana 43
Rigsthula 248
Ringe, Don 87–8, 91, 157–8, 179, 322
Ripley, William 62
river name 12, 116–22; *see also* hydronymy
Roman 43, 50, 61, 101, 172, 174, 202, 246, 260, 305
Romance languages 20, 25, 48–50, 72, 78, 99–101, 148, 160, 172, 174, 258, 305, 388
Romance origins 99–101
Romania 47, 100, 218, 225, 256
Romanian language 25, 27, 49, 100, *100*
Romans 17, 43, 174, 209
Rome 16, 160, 247
Roosevelt, Theodore 253
Rouard, Xavier 365
Royal Asiatic Society 15, 151
Rozwadowski, Jan 117–18
Russell, Bertrand 42

INDEX

Russia 8, 44, 56, 65, 74, 119, 126, 189, 249, 266–7, 271, 286, 289, 333, 349
Russian language 20, 26, 27, 39–40, 86, 99, 106, 116, 149, 162–3, 210, 226
Russian steppe 224; see also Pontic-Caspian steppe

Saami language 29, 126
Sackett, Jim 9, 13
Saint Augustine 18
Saint Jerome 59
Saka language 28, 28, 375
Salish languages 99
Salmasius, C. 21
salmon 195
salmon trout 195, 196
salt 196
Samara culture 225, 226, 228
Samoyedic languages 132, 135, 159
Sand, Georges 153
Sanskrit 8, 13, 15–16, 20–1, 27, 31, 34–5, 60, 62, 70, 80, 80, 82, 84–5, 97, 103–5, 110, 116, 118, 128, 151, 153–5, 155, 157, 159, 161–3, 167, 179, 181, 196, 252, 252, 375
Sapir, Edward 76, 201
Sarasvati 202
Sardinia 303, 305
Sardinian language 100, 100, 305
Sardinian origins 305
Sarmatian language 344
Sarmatians 64, 261, 338, 375
Sassetti, F. 21
satem 70, 70–2, 74–5, 95, 116, 133, 145, 252, 322
Satsurblia 287, 328–9, 329
Satyavarman 60
Sayce, Archibald 103, 276
Scaliger, Joseph 19–20
Scandinavia 26, 35, 38, 46, 74, 117, 154, 202, 205, 217, 222, 224, 248, 251, 281, 285–6, 382; see also Nordic homeland model
Scandinavian languages 16, 45, 104, 124, 281
Scandinavians 65, 245, 249, 252
Schlegel, Friedrich von 34, 62
Schleicher, August 79–83, 91, 94
Schmid, Wolfgang P., 118–19
Schmidt, Hans-Peter 13
Schmidt, Johannes 94, 96–7, 138–9, 165
Schmidt, Wilhelm 205–6
Schmitt, Alfred 111
Schott, Albert 139
Schrader, Otto 38, 48, 72–4, 76, 156, 196–8, 253, 269
Schrijver, Peter 13
Schuchardt, Hugo 148
Schulz, Heinrich 245
Schulz, Wolfgang 220
Schulze, B. 21
Schwidetzky, Georg 45–6
Schwidetzky, Ilse 46, 256
Scots Gaelic language 23, 24, 131
Scythia 19, 388
Scythian language 19, 21–2, 28, 30, 102, 116, 344, 369
Scythians 19, 20, 28, 31, 64, 67, 261, 323, 375

sea 160, 196–7, 205, 258, 335, 380; see also lake
secondary homeland 51–2, 54, 75, 77, 113, 138, 216–17, 244, 298, 302, 315, 317, 324, 331, 337, 339–40, 343, 371, 378–9; see also primary homeland
Semites 32
Semitic languages 19, 29, 33, 62, 120, 124–7, 138–40, 144, 146–8, 148, 150, 163, 244, 287, 290, 360; see also Afro-Asiatic languages
Serbia 379
Serbian language 26, 27
Serednii Stih culture 188, 226–9, 227, 228, 229, 256, 257, 346–7, 350, 350, 352–3, 353, 355–6, 364; see also Srednij Stog culture
Serrano, Miguel 34, 47, 76
seven 147, 148
shared aberrancy 130
sheep 105, 139–40, 151–2, 154–6, 162, 184, 192, 215, 295, 310–11, 321
Shem 19, 32, 60, 124
Shevchenko A. V., 256
Shinar 60
Shomutepe 239
Shortugai 235
shoulder: joint 159; span 159
Shulaveris 239
Siberia 116, 189, 285, 332
Siberian Neolithic culture 257
Sicel language 25, 25
Siegfried 204
Sieglin, Wilhelm 248–9
silver 185–6, 200, 241, 311, 334, 362
Sindhi 28
single burial 233
Sintashta 236–7, 236, 272, 274–5, 323–4, 341, 365, 375, 377, 377
Siva 48
sky-god 205–7
Slavic languages 20–1, 21, 24, 26–7, 52, 56, 64, 70–2, 71, 73, 75, 76, 77, 80–3, 81, 84, 86, 89, 91, 94, 95, 96, 99–102, 100, 106, 117, 123, 146, 156–7, 158, 159, 164, 177, 181, 184, 188–90, 194–7, 199, 213, 231, 232, 252, 252, 316, 366, 381, 388
Slavic origins 73–4, 76, 99, 210, 231, 316, 381–3
Slavo-Germanic 81
Slavs 51, 73, 74, 76, 116, 210, 245
Slovakia 301
Slovakian language 26, 27
Slovenian language 26, 27, 181
Smith, Henry Lee 86
social domain 293
Sokal, Robert 259, 263
sound shift 110, 111
South Caucasus homeland model 327, 339
South Picene language 25, 25
South Pole 45, 48
sow (plant) 310
Spain 7, 56, 108, 248, 260, 332
Spanish language 19, 25, 49, 66, 80, 86, 99–100, 100, 149, 292, 312
Specht, Franz 169, 191

445

spread zone 331, 344
squirrel 162, 197–8
Srednij Stog culture 226; *see also* Serednii Stih culture
Srubnaya culture 257
St. Clair, M. 433
Starcevo culture 257
Steppe Eneolithic culture 336
Steppe homeland model 38–42, 46, 67, 74, 76, 88, 118, 134–5, 145, 149, 189, 196, 198, 216–20, 223–5, 227–8, 230, 234, 236, 238, 242, 244, 255, 258, 261–2, 266–7, 269–71, 273–4, 277, 286, 295, 298, 317, 321–2, 324, 335, 338, 341, 343–44, 346–7, 366, 370–8, 381–2, 386–7
steppelands 12, 66–7, 117, 122, 193, 218, 242, 252, 324, 326–7, 333, 342, 348, 358, 365, 368, 370, 375–6, 380–1, 388; *see also* Pontic-Caspian steppe; Steppe homeland model
Steppe Maykop culture 241–2, *241*, 335–7
Sterud, Gene 13
Stiernheim, G. *21*
stock-raising 180, 336; *see also* pastoral economy
Stonehenge 51
Strzygowski, Josef 44, 431
Stupak, Inna 47
substrate language 46, 109–13, 223, 225
Sulimirski, Tadeusz 232
Sumba language 359
Sumerian language 108, *108*, 137, *137*, 139, *148*, 197, 244, 270, *290*, 312, *320*
Sumerogram 196, 312
Suvorovo kurgan 227, 386; *see also* Suvorovo-Novodanylivka culture
Suvorovo-Novodanylivka culture 227–8
Swadesh, Morris 84–7
Swat Valley culture 328, 332, 376, 377, *377*, 378
Swedes 245
Swedish language 26, *26*, *80*, 104, 282
Swiss Lake Dwellings 77
Switzerland 23, 108
Syria 46, 78–9, 109, 126, 240
Syroids 45

Tacitus 65, 202
tail (horse) 192; *see also* foal; horse; mare
Tajiks 250
Taman Peninsula 240
Tanzania 149
Tappeiner, Franz 44
Taranets, Valentin 47
Taraporewala, Irach 44
Tarim Basin 28, 75, 374
Tartars 15, 30, 32
Tartessian *108*
Tas Ayr culture 345
Tati *28*
Taylor, Isaac 42, 52, 53, 63–4, 248, 251
Taylor, Thomas Griffith 251–2
Telehin, Dmytro 13, 347
Teuton 252; *see also* Germanic languages
The History and Geography of Human Genes 260

Thieme, Paul 161, 179, 189, 196
thill 177
Thomassin, Louis 18
Thomsen, Christian 61
Thomsen, Vilhelm 126
Thrace 319
Thracian language 19, 22, *24*, 27, *73*, *75*, *80*, 117, 152, *213*, 318, 378–9
Thracian origins 73–4, *210*
Thracians 56, 73–4
Thraco-Phrygians *210*
Thrall 248
Tibet 64
Tienshan 373, 375
tiger 154, 160
Tigris 240, 307
Tilak, Bal Gangadhar 43–4
Tilkitepe *296*, 326
Timor 359
Tischler, Johann 87
Tisza culture 228, 244
Tiszapolgár culture 233
Tobol 134
Tocharian language *24*, 27–8, *28*, 51–2, 70, 74–5, *77*, 78, 88, *88*, *89*, 90–2, *91*, *92*, *95*, 96–7, 113, *155*, 157–9, *158*, 171, 178–9, 184–5, 188, 191, 195–6, *213*, 217, 252, *252*, 262, 298, *316*, 317–18, 366, 373, 375, 378
Tocharian origins 46, 75, *316*, 373–5, *374*
Tocharians 11, 46, 75, 128, 159, 216–17, 234, 236, 247, 274, 317, 373–5
Tomezzoli, Giancarlo 270
tortoise 198
Trager, George 86
transport by vehicle 177
tree (arboreal) 46, 54, 121, 165–6, 187, 189–90, 198, 208, 222, 312
tree (phylogenetic) 29, 51, 79–81, 88, 91–4, 96–7, 101–2, 131, 157, 222, 254, 263
Tremblay, Xavier 182
Troy 386
Trubetzkoy, Nikolai 144
Turkestan 27, 64, 179
Turkey 188, 193, 215, 259, 286, 314, 321
Turkic languages 56, 136–7, 146, 228, 259, 270, 282, 304, 339, 344
Turkmenistan 214–15, 236–7, 375
Turks 32, 67, 314
turquoise 241, 334
Tuscany 25
twin 208

Ubykh 141
Udolph, Jürgen 119, 121–2
Uesson, Ants-Michael 139
Uganda 369
Ugric *135*
Uhlenbeck, C. C. 144
Újfalvy, Károly 250
Ukraine 7, 38, 56, 104, 142, 147, 189, 193, 218–19, 221, 224–5, 248, 256, 266, 285–6, 301–2, 325, 335, 345, 363

INDEX

Ukrainian language 26, *27*, 99, 147
Ukrainian Neolithic Hunter-Gatherer (UNHG) 350, 352–3
Ukrainian steppe 224; *see also* Pontic-Caspian steppe
Umbrian language 25, *25*
Unakozovskaya *239*, 306, 331, 332
Unetice culture *257*
uniparental evidence 279, 283, 293, 325, 332
Upper Palaeolithic 39, 187, 287
Ural 134, 145
Uralic homeland 126, 133–4, *135*, 145, 237, 286, 362
Uralic languages 29, 33, 42, 53, 71, 100, 126–7, 129, 132–7, *137*, 143–8, *148*, 150, 159, 177, 252, 260, 290, 322, 341, 360–1, 372; *see also* Indo-Uralic
Urals 38, 126, 134, 193, 198, 225, 228, 231, 245, 274, 288, 290, 323, 375
Urartian language 290, *290*, 319, *320*
Urheimat 33–4, 36, 39, 48, 53–4, 59, 66, 72, 74, 76, 86, 101, 104, 107, 117, 123, 125, 135, 137–8, 161, 177, 204, 213, 215, 234, 236, 251, 307, 309; *see also* Indo-European homeland
Urnfield culture 209
Usatovo culture 219, *257*, 386
Ussher, James 59–60

Vacher de Lapouge, Georges 251
Van der Mijl, A. *21*
Vandals 66
Vasiliev, Igor 13, 336
Vatersprache 143; *see also Muttersprache*
Vavilov, Nikolaj 76
Vedas 45
Vedic language 8, 103–4, 178, 375
Venetic language 25, 118
Venus 48
ver sacrum 44
vetch 311, 326
Vikings 7, 56, 115, 299, 367
Vishnu 48
Visigoths 26
Vistula 73–4, 106
Volga 74, 116, 126, 133–4, 145, 193, 225–8, 238–9, 242, 271, 325, 329–30, 335–6, 346–7, 350–2, 354, 357, 364–5, 386
Volga cline 349–52, *350*
Volscian language 25, *25*
Vonyuchka *239*, 332
Vṛtra 44, 203
Vulcanis, Bonaventura 20; *see also* de Smet, Bonaventure

Wagner, Heinrich 127
Wagner, Richard 203–4
wagons 177, 179–81, 185–6, 194, 244; *see also* wheeled vehicles
Wales 56, 115
Wanderwörter 146
warband 292–3, 357
Watkins, Calvert 203, 308
wave of advance 295

wave theory 94, 97, 137, 210; *see also Wellentheorie*
Wellentheorie 94, 137; *see also* wave theory
Wells, Spencer 266
Welsh language 16, 23, *24*, *252*
West Siberian Hunter-Gatherer (WSHG) 84, 284, *284*, 288, 333, 343, 364
Western Hunter-Gatherer (WHG) 78, 271, 284–6, *284*, 290–1, 299–302, 327, 343, 346–7, 363, 386
Whatmough, Joshua 8–9, 387
wheat 152, 215, 218, 251, 295–6, 311, 321, 326, 329
wheel 159, 177–82; *see also* wheeled vehicles
wheeled vehicles 177–8, 180–3, 185–7, 200, 207, 231, 242, 298, 311, 331, 344, 346, 371; *see also* wagons, wheel
Wilke, Georg 48, 210
Williams, J. Caerwyn 13
Wilser, Ludwig 251
Wilson, Daniel 61
wine 141, 148, 198–200; *see also* grape
winnow 310
Wittgenstein, Ludwig 42
Wittmann, Henri 86
Witzel, Michael 202
wolf 167, 178, 184, 191–22
Wolzogen, Hans Paul von 203–4
wool 148, 184, 310, 360
Wörter und Sachen 153, 206; *see also* linguistic palaeontology
Wotan 48

Xinjiang 27, 64, 163, 323, 365, 378

Yaghnobi *28*
Yamnaya culture 77, 193, 227–34, *229*, 237, 242, 244, 256–8, *257*, 271–4, *272*, 324–6, 331, 334–7, 341, 346–56, *353*, 359–60, 363–7, 373, 379, 381–3, 385–6
Y-chromosome 264–6, 270, 279, 281, 285–6, 288, 296, 302–3, 313, 325, 328–9, *332*, 332–3, 337, 342, 344, 347, *349*, *351*, *353*, 356, 357, 363, 380, 386
Yellow River 47
Yenisei 134–5, 145–6, 228, 256, 258, 267, 274, 333, 365, 373
Yersinia pestis 382–3
yew 190
yoke 141, 185, 310
Young, Thomas 23, 62
Yugoslavia 26, 48
Yukaghir *137*

Zagros 108, 215, 217, 287, 297, 303–4, 308, 322–3, 326, 365
Zaliznyak, Leonid 38, 213, 330, 364; *see also* Nordic-Steppe homeland model
Zarathustra 7, 23, 201
Zoroastrian 45
Zschaetzsch, K. 431
Zvelebil, M. 432
Zvelebil, K. 432

for Niamh and Áine

Frontispiece and Page 6: Two Harappan stone seals depicting animals from Mohenjo-Daro, *c.* 2300 BCE. Bridgeman Images.

First published in the United Kingdom in 2025 by
Thames & Hudson Ltd, 181A High Holborn, London WC1V 7QX

First published in the United States of America in 2025 by
Thames & Hudson Inc., 500 Fifth Avenue, New York, New York 10110

The Indo-Europeans Rediscovered © 2025 Thames & Hudson Ltd, London

Text © 2025 J. P. Mallory

All Rights Reserved. No part of this publication may be reproduced or transmitted in any form or by any means, electronic or mechanical, including photocopy, recording or any other information storage and retrieval system, without prior permission in writing from the publisher.

British Library Cataloguing-in-Publication Data
A catalogue record for this book is available from the British Library

Library of Congress Control Number 2024947101

ISBN 978-0-500-02863-6

Impression 01

Printed and bound in China by Shenzhen Reliance Printing Co. Ltd

Be the first to know about our new releases,
exclusive content and author events by visiting
thamesandhudson.com
thamesandhudsonusa.com
thamesandhudson.com.au